The
PRODUCTIVITY
MANUAL

Second Edition

More Ways to Increase Productivity from Gulf Publishing Company

The Adult Learner: A Neglected Species, 4th Edition
Malcolm S. Knowles

Designing Training Programs: The Critical Events Model
Leonard and Zeace Nadler

Gain Sharing: The New Path to Productivity and Profits
John Belcher, Jr.

Handbook of Training Evaluation and Measurement Methods, 2nd Edition
Jack J. Phillips

How to Delegate: A Guide to Getting Things Done
Herbert M. Engel

Managing Cultural Differences, 3rd Edition
Philip Harris and Robert T. Moran

NAFTA: Managing the Cultural Differences
Robert T. Moran and Jeffrey Abbott

Total Quality Management for Engineers
Mohamed Zairi

The Winning Trainer: Winning Ways to Involve People in Learning, 2nd Edition
J. E. Eitington

Gulf Publishing Company
Houston, London, Paris, Zurich, Tokyo

The
PRODUCTIVITY
MANUAL

Second Edition

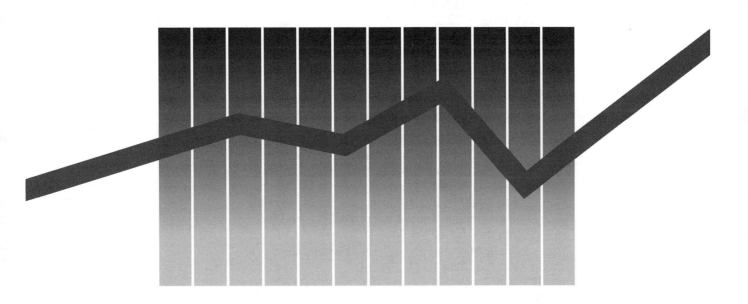

Elizabeth A. Smith

The Productivity Manual

Second Edition

Gulf Publishing Company
Book Division
P.O. Box 2608 □ Houston, Texas 77252-2608

10 9 8 7 6 5 4 3 2 1

Library of Congress Cataloging-in-Publication Data

Smith, Elizabeth A., 1936–
    The productivity manual : methods and activities for involving employees in productivity improvement / Elizabeth A. Smith. — 2nd ed.
        p.   cm. (Building blocks of human potential)
    Includes bibliographical references (p.) and index.
    ISBN 0-88415-652-4
    1. Industrial productivity.   2. Labor productivity.
I. Title.   II. Series.
HD56.S57   1995
658.5—dc20   95-17972
                                                              CIP

Contents

Preface

People having direct and indirect responsibility for assessing, maintaining, and improving productivity can use this manual on the job and in training programs.

Supportive managers who understand and fully use employees' unique abilities, skills, and knowledge can bring about dramatic increases in productivity. Human resources are the most valuable asset any organization possesses.

Applying what is already known about productivity can improve performance at every organizational level. Improved performance means greater job satisfaction, reward, and recognition for the person, and more efficient, cost-effective, and competitive organizations.

Who is really responsible for increasing productivity? We all are. Productivity can be a periodic application of required behavior, or a concerted way of life representing the sum of our experiences and accomplishments. But, the major issue in achieving and maintaining higher levels of productivity still revolves around how well people work together. The growing emphasis on working cooperatively in teams, sharing information and technology, networking, and cross-training, among others, makes working cooperatively and synergistically more important now than ever before.

This second edition contains updated statistics, new reference material, and a new chapter to meet readers' needs for an overview and perspective on quality in service-based and product-based industries. The new Chapter 14 summarizes the current status of quality, provides definitions and numerous examples and tools of quality, and presents guidelines for achieving and maintaining quality.

The expanded Answers and Insights section contains more detailed responses to the questions presented in each chapter. The Suggested Reading section now includes newly published books on leadership, learning, enhancing performance, improving quality, and an array of references on current trends in business.

Elizabeth A. Smith, Ph.D.
Houston, Texas

Acknowledgments

Many people have read this manuscript and provided valuable suggestions. Included are Karen Anne Smith, Julie Smith Martinez, Simone Chapman, Sam McClelland, Sam Bleecker, and John Neuman.

A special thanks goes to Dr. Leonard Nadler, George Washington University, who reviewed the first draft of the manuscript, and provided many helpful suggestions.

Ideas and materials came from my teaching experience in MBA programs at the Air Force Institute of Technology, Strategic Air Command, F. E. Warren Air Force Base, Wyoming, and at Houston Baptist University. Other sources of ideas and materials were from various faculty positions at the University of Texas Health Science Center at Houston, and from industry seminars on motivation and productivity.

Introduction

This manual focuses on the processes of identifying, measuring, and improving productivity. It is unique because the diverse, highly selected content covers a broad range of productivity issues and the solutions-oriented approach helps you understand and evaluate existing information. You can then apply information and methods that best meet your unique needs, and develop and implement realistic, cost-effective ways to assess and improve productivity.

The question-and-answer format used throughout stimulates thinking, samples current knowledge, and encourages you to evaluate your own past and present accomplishments. Answers consolidate ideas, guide, and teach. This straightforward approach enables you to do a better job of evaluating how closely performance matches individual, group, and organizational goals.

In every field of endeavor, learning "the basics" is important. The basics of productivity measurement and improvement include definitions of productivity and associated measurement techniques.

In measurement, standard assessment methods and statistical procedures for interpreting information are well known and commonly used. These standard techniques also apply to productivity measurement.

Measurement methods that range from qualitative, or descriptive, to quantitative, or numeric, complement each other. Techniques designed by managers and employees for use in their own department provide the most meaningful reliable results. Results of measurement are important because they can be interpreted and eventually become the foundation of change and/or improvement efforts.

Productivity has many faces. Some faces are easy to recognize. Others are obscure. A good working definition of productivity is very valuable. Without a clear idea of what productivity means in terms of the job, it is difficult to understand the consequences of low, average, and high productivity. For example, managers need to know how well the work efforts of the people they supervise meet goals and expectations of managers further up or down the line. It is equally important to know exactly how each type of performance is rewarded in the organization.

One major productivity problem is lack of agreement on priorities. Identifying problems and assigning priorities can be difficult. Solutions begin to emerge after the true nature and extent of problems have been identified.

Contents

Materials presented encourage you to develop creative ways to examine existing resources and problems, and develop realistic solutions. The steps for achieving these goals are:

- Increasing Awareness—A first step in any problem-solving or change process.

- Understanding Productivity—Includes defining productivity, developing goals, and examining behavior (Chapters 1–3).
- Determining Problems—The specific nature and possible causes of problems are considered. Productivity measures currently used are evaluated (Chapters 4–5).
- Sources of Information—Numerous sources of information exist throughout the organization. Major sources are the person and the job (Chapters 6–7).
- Measurement—Standards, basic measurement methods, and general guidelines are presented (Chapters 8–9).
- Measurement Methods—Descriptive and numeric methods are used to analyze and report individual and group accomplishments. You can develop measures which best fit your own needs, end users' needs, and organizational goals (Chapters 10–14).
- Maintaining and Improving Productivity—Reducing counterproductivity and applying what is known are major ways to increase productivity (Chapters 15–17).
- Practical Applications—Notes, ideas, and summary information from the "Ideas to Remember" section in each chapter provide valuable information for use on the job. You are challenged to create the circumstances and build an environment to foster and maintain productivity improvement (Chapter 18).
- Suggested Readings—Publications in business, psychology, evaluation and measurement, and industrial engineering are listed.
- Answers—Detailed answers provided for each question include examples, cite pertinent literature, and often provide practical solutions.

Major Objectives

Objectives cover a wide range of areas and concerns. You can select important objectives and meet these objectives with varying levels of proficiency:

- Use appropriate productivity concepts and standard measurement methods to assess the effectiveness of current and proposed measurement and improvement techniques.
- Modify and improve productivity measurement and enhancement techniques when new information is available, or when objectives, standards or priorities set initially are changed.
- Understand causes and consequences of low, average, and high productivity, and the detrimental effects of counterproductivity.
- Recognize and use their own unique skills, knowledge, and talents, and those around them to construct ways to improve individual and group performance.

- Consider their own level of productivity, and how it affects subordinates, peers, and managers, and the goals the organization is trying to achieve.
- Develop an understanding of the value of quality in product and service-oriented industries.

When management understands and supports productivity awareness and change efforts, objectives are easier to meet.

How to Use This Manual

Each chapter contains an introduction, the major body of the chapter, references, and ideas to remember. The "ideas" section is for taking notes, recording new ideas, writing reminders, or documenting vital bits of information. These notes can be reviewed and used to develop action written plans for Chapter 18, "Individualized Summaries and Practical Applications."

Certain concepts or themes are repeated and emphasized because they form the core of the manual. These concepts and the reasons for using them are:

- Information on most topics includes descriptive (qualitative) and numeric (quantitative) terms. There is no "best" way to present information. The method used should adequately represent information or data, and fit the needs of the end user. Those responsible for initiating and maintaining change efforts will have to choose the "best" method.
- Operational definitions clarify the meaning of what is being described or measured. This means defining something based on how it is used. People from various disciplines, or those working at the same, or similar jobs, need to agree on what certain important words mean. Precise methods can then be developed and used regularly. This makes it easier to document information, for comparisons and record changes.
- Productivity, achievement, and accomplishment are used interchangeably. Assessment represents the "softer" or qualitative side of measurement. Measurement means the "harder" or quantitative side of appraisal and evaluation.
- The uniqueness of the person is emphasized. Numerous individual differences affect how people react and how they perform their jobs. People and their accomplishments need to be evaluated in their own right.
- A systems approach examines the relationship of input, throughput, and output. Many current measurement systems focus on output, which is "after-the-fact." Productivity may be increased by improving the quality and amount of input. A logical beginning place for

productivity improvement efforts is input. Throughput, such as motivation, is hard to identify, and even harder to measure. The important role throughput plays is underestimated and often discounted.

- The terms reliability and validity appear throughout the sections on measurement. Reliability means consistency in measuring and remeasuring. Validity means that measures do what they are designed or intended to do.
- Indicators show something exists. They are signs, signals, or sources of information. Indicators also measure. Results of measurement can be recorded and interpreted. For example, a thermometer measures and registers temperature. When a person's temperature is monitored for varying periods of time, changes can be detected, and appropriate actions taken. The real value of measurement systems and numbers is in the people and processes used to generate numbers and descriptions.
- Change is constant and inevitable. Managing change is what business is all about. Many fear the unknown aspects of change, and may openly resist change. Major keys to reducing resistance to change are: (1) involve people in constructive ways in all phases of the change process, and (2) introduce change gradually.
- Frames of reference, or ways to view and interpret what is going on, are as diverse as people themselves. Seeing things through the eyes of others broadens views of personal and organizational activities, and affects what people do.
- Quality, a major indicator or definition of productivity, applies to products, processes, and services, and is a major cornerstone of productivity.
- Cross-referencing ties separate sections together, reduces duplication of material, and reinforces what has been learned.

Individual and Group Use

You will derive the most benefit by reading the chapters in sequence. If you "skip around," you will find the question and answer sections valuable ways to obtain specific information and test your knowledge.

Individual Use. Read the chapters in the order presented. Write down answers to the questions before looking them up. Questions sample your unique core of information pertaining to the job and the organization, i.e., determine problem areas, set priorities, make decisions, carry out plans, monitor results, and review or improve plans.

Group Use. Read each chapter and answer questions before discussing them. Share written answers with subordinates, peers, and supervisors. Where possible, have a resource person or knowledgeable group member lead

discussions. If chapters are not completed in sequence, have a capable leader provide continuity.

Increasing Awareness

Increasing "productivity mindedness" is a first step in any productivity measurement and improvement process. Awareness is high when people know what productivity means, and how associated change efforts affect their jobs. Increasing awareness applies to problems and solutions. People who are aware of problems can begin to develop workable solutions. Efforts that focus on work processes in terms of results the organization is trying to achieve are effective.

Example ways for managers to build awareness are strategic planning and goal setting, reinforcing productive efforts, and setting good examples. Maintaining awareness of the value and need of productivity measurement and improvement can include special recognition for high performers, for example.

Raising and maintaining productivity awareness throughout the organization, like any other organizational change effort, takes time—not just days and weeks, but months or years. Productivity can and should be improved.

Productivity Performance of the United States

The Bureau of Labor Statistics (BLS) of the U.S. government is the major source of industrially based data on labor productivity. The BLS defines the various measurement systems used. They report productivity by growth rate, gross domestic product, by industry, by region, and by type of work performed.

Productivity statistics fluctuate, depending on what is measured, when it is measured, and how it is measured and reported. Productivity is evaluated by comparing ratios of output from two different periods, or by comparing a certain ratio with a specific standard, or set of established guidelines or criteria. Comparisons are made between countries, industries, and organizations.

Two of the most comprehensive comparisons of productivity are ratios based on Gross Domestic Product (GDP), and productivity growth rate.

Gross Domestic Product

GDP is based on hours worked, or on number of employees. Comparisons are difficult to make because length of working hours differs from country to country. Compared with America, for instance, the Japanese work longer hours and the British work shorter hours. Another major factor is fluctuating currency exchange rates.

Productivity Growth Rate

For the period 1985–1992, the Bureau of Labor Statistics reported international manufacturing labor productivity growth rates per year were: Japan—3.4%; U.K.—4.5%; Italy—3.1%; U.S.—2.8%; Canada—0.8%; France—2.7%; Germany—1.6%; and Netherlands—1.6%. (Thor, 1993).

Based on international labor productivity (GDP/employee, purchasing power parity), the current average percent growth was 5.5% for Korea; 3.2% for Japan; 2.3% for both Belgium and Austria; 2.1% for Finland; 1.8% for Germany; 0.6% for the U.S.; and 0.4% for Canada.

Service industries now account for approximately 70% of the nation's GNP growth.

In the five or so years since the first edition of this book was published, there is even more opportunity to maximize the use of human resources through proper planning and involvement in improvement programs (not just quality) that are thoroughly understood and supported by everyone in the organization, particularly top management.

The emphasis of the 21st century must be on human factors such as leadership, mentoring, knowing who the customer is, focusing on peoples' special talents, and working in teams. Organizations that increase their productivity growth rate will be ones that put people first—workforce, all types of customers, suppliers, partners . . . stakeholders. They will need to rethink old theories, and consider whether what worked in the past will work in the future.

References

1. Thor, Carl G. *Perspectives '90.* Houston, Texas: American Productivity & Quality Center, 1990.
2. Quinn, James Brian and Gagnon, Christopher E. "Will Services Follow Manufacturing into Decline?" *Harvard Business Review,* November–December 1986, pp. 95–103.

*Thor, Carl G. *Perspectives '93.* Houston, Texas: American Productivity & Quality Center, 1993.

1
Productivity: Viewpoints and Definitions

PURPOSE

- Consider various ways productivity is viewed.
- Evaluate typical ratios and definitions of productivity.
- Construct a general definition of productivity to use as a standard to evaluate other definitions.
- Determine whether the definition could be used in the productivity measurement process.

INTRODUCTION

Many factors affect how people view and define productivity. Perception, knowledge, and experience, for example, influence how productivity is viewed, defined, measured, and improved. A clear, well-focused view helps place the whole productivity issue in perspective.

People in areas such as accounting, economics, engineering, and industrial/organizational psychology interpret productivity in different ways. Each area, or discipline, has its own guidelines and perceptions of how humans, organizations, and machines function in various environments. The common goal of being competitive and maintaining profits requires constant monitoring of return on human and organizational efforts; in other words, success requires productivity measurement.

Measuring productivity reveals how well people and organizations meet expectations or performance standards.

When you know these standards, you can measure specific areas and ultimately enhance productivity. However, you cannot measure productivity until you know what it is.

Most definitions of productivity include profitability, efficiency, effectiveness, value, quality, innovation, and quality of work life. Useful definitions combine unique human and organizational effectiveness variables. Although definitions are the foundation of measurement, definitions may also be the measurement. Standards and ratios are used in most descriptive assessments and numeric measurements of productivity.

Standards, or specific, clearly defined measures of adequacy often form the basis for ratios. Many ratios used to define and measure productivity are of the output/input variety. Simple ratios express the relationship between two similar quantifiable, or countable things by dividing one quantity by the other. For instance, if ten units are produced in five hours, the ratio is 10/5, or 2/1. Ratios should use input and output from the same process, namely both from energy, labor, materials, or capital. Ratios are often used to define and measure productivity.

This chapter presents points of view, standards, ratios, and definitions that will help you better understand productivity in general, and its measurement in particular. Awareness of the broad scope of productivity is the first step in productivity improvement.

VIEWS OF PRODUCTIVITY

Productivity is often considered the result of all personal and organizational efforts associated with the production, use, and/or delivery of products and services. The productivity or accomplishments of people and organizations fluctuate. For instance, we are more or less productive, depending on our job, interests, and motivation. The efficiency of the organization, for example, can be influenced by environmental stability and employee satisfaction. Most efforts to define and measure productivity focus on results or output variables like profit or number of units produced. Productivity is more than results, or output variables, as illustrated in Chapter 3.

Ways to evaluate effort or accomplishment combine numeric (quantitative) and descriptive (qualitative) methods. Quantitative measurement tends to be used in highly structured, repetitive tasks while qualitative assessment is often used in abstract, nonrepetitive, creative tasks. Figure 1-1 illustrates the shift from quantitative measurement to qualitative assessment as the type of task varies from simple to complex, from repetitive to unique, and from well-defined to abstract. Many approaches are a mix of the quantitative-qualitative dimensions (Ranftl, 1978).

A combined quantitative-qualitative orientation is emphasized throughout this book. Both orientations are used in a relative sense. Some procedures and systems are mostly qualitative (Chapters 6, 7, 10, 12 and 15) and others are quantitative (Chapters 8, 9, 11, 13, and 14).

Views of productivity are presented alphabetically, not in order of importance. Accounting, economics, engineering, industrial/organizational, and management are represented (Tuttle, 1983).

Accounting

Accounting data, such as profit/sales, sales/stocks, or profit/employee, are main sources of information in finan-

cial decision making. These data are often readily available, and therefore relatively easy to obtain and convert to standards or ratios. Because accounting data enjoy near universal acceptance, they may be favored over other valuable data.

Financial ratios based on profit, sales, capital, and fixed assets are used to monitor and represent the financial performance of organizations. Most financial ratios are indicators of "business efficiency" in the marketplace. Some indicators represent ratios of sales return on capital employed, or ratios of profit to assets.

Accounting data and financial ratios are standard ways of making comparisons, which can be made at any level in the organization, between organizations, between people, and over time periods of days, weeks, months, or years. Data obtained over varying periods of time reflect changes, illustrate trends, form the basis of predictions, or may be used in other meaningful ways.

The worth of human resources, the most valuable asset any organization possesses, is hard to document in financial terms. Two methods of "cost accounting" human resources are overhead value analysis (Neuman, 1975, 1986) and human resource accounting (Likert, 1967).

Applications of overhead value analysis (OVA) include investigating and reducing overhead, improving non-overhead activities, and enhancing overall productivity. OVA is currently used by several hundred companies in North and Central America, Europe, Australia, and Japan.

Human (asset) resource accounting (HRA) refers to the value of the productive capacity of a firm's human organization and the value of its customer goodwill (Likert, 1967). Despite the logic and precision of design, HRA has met with varying levels of acceptance. The thought that human resources can and should be measured and documented is somewhat uncomfortable, and threatening. However, human resources are an organization's most valuable asset.

Chapter 13, "Profitability," further describes OVA and HRA.

Economics

This approach relates primarily to the production, distribution, and use of income, wealth and commodities. Views range from "macro," or whole industries, to "micro," or small units. Most economic data are based on labor productivity, or number of hours worked, and on amount produced per hour. Data used in economic analyses are usually collected from the bottom-up, beginning at the plant level, going to the industry level, and proceeding to the level of the whole economy.

An efficiency oriented definition is (Tuttle, 1983):

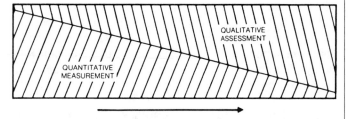

INCREASING LEVEL OF TASK COMPLEXITY, UNIQUENESS, AND ABSTRACTNESS

Figure 1-1. Productivity evaluation. (Reprinted with permission from *R & D Productivity* by Robert Matthew Ranftl © 1978, all rights reserved.)

$$Q = F(L, K, X, T)$$

where Q = volume of output
  F = function, or a variable whose value depends on and varies with that of another quantity or quantities
  L = labor
  K = capital
  X = intermediate products purchased
  T = time

From the practical standpoint, no business can be economically sound and profitable unless products and services are needed in the marketplace, and are competitively priced.

Engineering

There are many separate disciplines in engineering. Engineers working in the productivity area are concerned with applying how human beings think and react to the design, use, and improvement of machines and systems in various environments. Efficiency of people, work groups, or manufacturing processes, for example, is emphasized in a "human factors" approach. Typical questions are: "What is the 'best' way to do a particular job?" "When this best method is used, what standard level of output should be expected, given the production environment, materials, or labor force?"

Engineering definitions recognize that output from a production process is most useful when:

- Output meets quality standards.
- Output is produced before the need for the product has passed.
- Output is consistent with the goals of the organization.

A typical ratio based on engineering data is:

$$\text{Usefulness of a machine} = \frac{\text{Useful work}}{\text{Energy}} = 1$$

This ratio cannot exceed 1.

Standards of performance or usefulness apply equally to people and machines. To illustrate, common standards for a typist are accuracy and number of words typed per minute. A standard for an automobile could be mileage per gallon of fuel used. Joan's typing speed and accuracy and Fred's car mileage can be compared with known, acceptable standards. A standard for Joan is sixty words per minute typed without error. A standard for Fred's car might be twenty-five miles per gallon of gasoline under highway driving conditions. In productivity measurement, two standards for judging efficiency could be past performance history and work sampling (Udler, 1978).

Industrial engineers consider a broad spectrum of activities—work measurement, production control, plant layout, and manufacturing systems, etc.—when seeking to maximize efficiency and economy of effort, and minimize costs. Standards are discussed in greater detail in Chapter 9.

Industrial/Organizational (I/O) Approach

Those having an I/O orientation develop and use performance-based standards or criteria to explain human behavior in organizations. Areas of study include the effect varying work environments, management, peers, organizational climate, and culture have on employee behavior. Carefully developed job standards or criteria are used to compare how well people perform versus how well they are expected to perform. Comparisons are also made within various parts of the company and between similar industries or companies. However, cross-industry comparisons are hard to make because few standardized measuring tools or common methods exist in many industries or professions.

The I/O approach, like that used by family physicians, views people and their environment from a holistic standpoint. Family physicians deal with the health of their patient and the health of immediate family members. Similarly, those in the I/O field deal with employee and organizational "health," such as quality of work life and organizational efficiency and effectiveness. These three topics are discussed later in this chapter.

Management

Management, a general term for "those who manage" or administer, represents a very wide range of philosophies, beliefs, disciplines, and job responsibilities. Managers reportedly plan, organize, staff, direct, control, facilitate, and encourage. Views may represent any of these areas. Managers' views of productivity differ, depending on such variables as their specific roles in the organization, abilities, and knowledge. Like the workforce they supervise, managers are unique. Example views of productivity focus on developing standards, or examining results that are desirable and/or achievable. See box on page 4.

STANDARDS, DEFINITIONS, AND RATIOS

Productivity is an overall statement of the way people and organizations function. Without standards, definitions, and ratios, it is impossible to compare people, jobs, or organizations and determine whether established standards

1. Which view(s) (accounting, economics, engineering, industrial/organizational, management) most closely fits your needs? Does it matter which views are used? Explain.

2. How do these views affect your own understanding of productivity? Is the effect positive? Explain.

are met. These three tools help us describe or assess what is done, how it is done, and how well it is done.

We can't measure anything until we can define it. We can't define anything until we know what acceptable standards or guidelines exist or need to be developed. A first step in any improvement process is to define what is to be assessed or measured. As stated previously, definition can be the same as measurement. Standards, definitions, and ratios play vital roles in all forms of measurement, not just productivity measurement.

Standards

In any profession standards are the basis for developing definitions and constructing measurement systems that range from descriptive to numeric. A broad definition of a standard is something that is developed to use as a rule or basis of comparison to judge quality, quantity, value, content, or extent. According to *Webster's New World Dictionary*, a specific numeric definition of a standard ". . . applies to some measure, principle, model, etc., with which things of the same class are compared in order to determine their quantity, value, quality, etc." A simple definition often used in primarily qualitative areas is ". . . something used by general agreement to determine whether or not a thing is as it should be" (Messick, 1975, p. 955). This definition implies that a non-elastic ruler, or similar basis of comparison, is used to specify "average" or expected level of output or performance. Standards, which can be used in ratios, are particularly helpful when defining quality, profitability, and efficiency. Standards are used in benchmarking.

People like to know how they compare with others. When specific standards for productivity level are known, those being judged either try very hard to find out where they stand, or make up their own standards. In the three examples below, Grace wanted to know where she stood, Mike made up his own standards, and Bill used information to calculate his daily quota:

Example 1. Grace processed medical insurance claims. She wanted to know how she compared with others in her work group. Her supervisor kept saying, "You're doing

fine." Grace knew how many claims she processed each day, but not how many the "average" person processed. Since Grace had no idea where she ranked, she became more and more dissatisfied, and resigned after three months on the job.

Example 2. Mike was the only person selling computer software for a newly formed company. He loved to compete. No sales quotas were to be set for three months until the company got on its feet. Mike recorded the number of sales and number of contacts he made each week, and he tried to sell more software packages and make more contacts than the week before. He competed with himself.

Example 3. Company A, a struggling, upstart computer chip manufacturer, critically and systematically examined and compared Company B, a proven leader in the same industry. "A" benchmarks "B's" best manufacturing and quality control processes against their own. "A" improves its product quality and profitability using "B's" valuable benchmarked data.

GENERAL DEFINITIONS AND RATIOS

This section introduces broad definitions of productivity, discusses ratios, and presents examples of productivity ratios. See box on next page.

Definitions

As definitions change from descriptive to numeric, they are more likely to contain ratios. It is important to know what definitions mean, that they are based on adequate standards, and meet end users' needs. Definitions will contain both quantitative and qualitative elements.

A comprehensive definition is ". . . the ratio of valuable output to input, i.e., the efficiency and effectiveness with which resources—personnel, machines, materials, facilities, capital, time—are utilized to produce a valuable output" (Ranftl, 1978).

3. List three work-related standards by which you are judged.

4. Can these standards be changed to ratios? If so, how?

Beliefs and general statements about productivity based on experience and knowledge are also useful. Of the written responses from 563 chief executive officers and 950 industrial relations officers to questionnaires about productivity (Katzell et al., 1975):

- 90% included quality, quantity of output, output per man-hour, and overall efficiency and effectiveness.

- 70% cited disruptions to normal work flow such as "shrinkage," sabotage, rate of absenteeism, and turnover.

- 60% referred to customer or client satisfaction, job satisfaction, employee loyalty, or morale. See box below.

Ratios

All productivity measurement literature includes ratios, which show the relationship between two similar amounts, or numbers, as when the first number is divided by the second number. Input and output data used in ratios should be based on information from the same process, same job, or same person. For example, Steve's input cannot be compared with Bob's output. When ratios are based on reliable, acceptable standards, and when combined with realistic standards, they form the backbone of the measurement process.

Most output/input ratios use data from energy, materials, capital and labor areas. For instance, a company's energy input should be compared with energy output, not with materials, capital, or labor output.

Financial ratios from sales or profits tell us whether we have been successful and if we are currently successful. Productivity ratios based on number of hours worked or energy used, for instance, tell us whether we will be in a position to compete tomorrow. Table 1-1 shows example productivity ratios from accounting, engineering, industrial/organizational areas, and management (Bain, 1982; Christopher, 1984; Tuttle, 1983; Swaim and Sink, 1984a and Swaim and Sink, 1984b). These ratios are static. They represent "snapshots" at a specific time period. Additional examples of static ratios for sales, supervisory staffs, and "white collar workers" are presented in Chapter 12.

5. My personal definition of productivity is:

6. The definition of productivity accepted within my organization, or within my work group is:

7. The definition of productivity used to evaluate my own performance is:

8. List three concepts or ideas you feel represent productivity.

9. How do definitions in questions 5 and 7 differ?

10. List ratios you would use to measure productivity in your company.

11. Explain why you used these ratios.

12. List the pros and cons of each ratio selected.

Dynamic ratios are used to compare results over two different time periods, for example output/input ratios for July versus August, or Year 1 versus Year 2. Table 11-3 (Bain, 1982) illustrates how dynamic ratios may be calculated and interpreted.

Many ratios and current definitions of productivity come from traditional manufacturing industries, not the rapidly expanding service sector. Service providers and users or customers are good sources of information on standards that can be used in measurement. Typical standards in the service area are the many dimensions of quality, on-time delivery, and customer satisfaction. See box above.

Table 1-1
Examples of Productivity Ratios

General

$$\frac{Output}{Input} \qquad \frac{Output\ energy}{Input\ energy} \qquad \frac{Output\ material}{Input\ material}$$

$$\frac{Output\ capital}{Input\ capital} \qquad \frac{Output\ labor}{Input\ labor}$$

Accounting

$$\frac{Profit}{Sales} \qquad \frac{Profit}{Employee} \qquad \frac{Sales}{Fixed\ assets} \qquad \frac{Sales}{Capital\ employed}$$

Engineering

$$\frac{Effectiveness}{Efficiency} \qquad \frac{Results\ achieved}{Resources\ consumed} \qquad \frac{Useful\ work}{Energy}=1$$

$$\frac{Effective\ output}{Actual\ output} \qquad \frac{Actual\ output}{Potential\ output}$$

Industrial/Organizational

$$\frac{Output}{Input}+\frac{Output}{Standard*} \qquad \frac{Completed\ jobs}{Jobs\ attempted} \qquad \frac{Worker\ output}{Labor\ hours\ input}$$

Management

$$\frac{Management\ output}{Management\ cost} \qquad \frac{Individual\ accomplishment}{Work\ group\ accomplishment}$$

$$\frac{Monthly\ accomplishment}{Standard\ for\ year}$$

* Examples of standards are quality, or on-time delivery of products or services.

DEFINITIONS AND DESCRIPTIONS OF PRODUCTIVITY

Productivity is and will continue to be examined from diverse qualitative and quantitative perspectives. In some cases, standards, ratios, and definitions are used interchangeably. Some productivity measures can stand alone; others are combined with specific variables. Further information on Partial, Total Factor and Multiple Output Productivity Measures is presented in Chapter 14.

The type and scope of definitions are influenced by reason for measuring (training or salary increase), what is being measured (input or output), desired or required form of output (numeric or descriptive), and numerous organizational and personal variables. Major definitions of productivity include profitability, efficiency, effectiveness, value, quality, innovation, and quality of work life (Sink, 1985).

Profitability

Elements of this aspect of productivity include capital, sales, operating costs, information processing, human resources and others, depending on the type of organization. Making and maintaining adequate profit margins is the overall "name of the game," and direction of focus can range from in-house profit centers to foreign competition.

The following ratio looks simple, but data used in the ratio may be hard to obtain:

$$Profitability = \frac{Sales}{Operating\ costs}$$

Profitability can be improved by doing more with less, or producing more and reducing cost. Possible alternatives are cut services, lower overhead, reduce quality, or in government agencies, increase taxes.

A complex definition of profitability containing a number of broad variables (Lehrer, 1983) is:

$$\frac{\text{Product} + \text{Quality} + \text{Service} + \text{Image}}{\text{People} + \text{Tangible} + \text{Money} + \text{Information} + \text{Technology}}$$
Assets

Meaningful data for each variable in this definition are virtually impossible to obtain. The question is "Would the resulting productivity ratio have any meaning?" The answer is "Possibly not." However, the real test is whether the ratio is useful in practice. Chapter 13 covers profitability in greater detail.

Efficiency

Competent performance defines efficiency, namely knowing how to do something and "doing it right." Efficiency is improved when there is more useful output per unit of input. Or, efficiency can be a ratio comparing some aspect of unit performance to the costs incurred for that performance (Tuttle, 1983).

Engineers work in terms of efficiency of various mechanical systems. Industrial engineers, as we have seen, deal with personal and organizational efficiency. Efficiency and effectiveness are similar and efficiency is often considered part of the larger concept of effectiveness.

Effectiveness

Although it is difficult to separate efficiency and effectiveness, effectiveness measures are usually compared with a standard, such as quality or usefulness. The ultimate measure of productivity may be effectiveness (Fitz-enz, 1985). All of the following pertain to either personal or organizational effectiveness:

absenteeism	interpersonal skills
accidents	managerial task skills
cohesion	morale
communication	motivation
conflict	performance
control	planning
cooperation	profit
delegation	quality
development	readiness
efficiency	reliability
flexibility	role and norm congruence
goal consensus	satisfaction
growth	stability
information management	staffing
initiative	turnover
internalization of goals	utilization of environment

Personal Effectiveness. Output variables used as criteria to measure personal effectiveness can be negative-absenteeism, accidents, or turnover, or positive-initiative, flexibility and reliability. When variables have a negative connotation, like absenteeism or accident rates, a low number is highly desirable.

Organizational Effectiveness. Organizational excellence and organizational effectiveness are similar. Effectiveness, or the degree to which an organization achieves its goals (Price, 1977), implies reaching the highest level of performance with the lowest possible expenditure of resources (Jamali, 1984). Creating the greatest good with the least input, a standard definition of productivity, is one of the highest forms of organizational excellence.

Input in the form of capital, labor, energy and materials should be used in the most efficient, productive manner possible. Resources are directed toward objectives that are most prized, i.e., focus on results, do the right thing at the right time, and achieve long-term and short-term goals (Fitz-enz, 1985).

Organizational effectiveness means knowing what to do, what is acceptable, and achieving the "right" goals or objectives. However, determining what is "right" is another story. For instance, a business may be very productive (efficient), but declining markets for its output result in low sales and low profits. Despite high levels of productivity (efficiency), it is not currently effective or successful in the marketplace (Price, 1977).

Basic requirements for organizational effectiveness (Fitz-enz, 1985) include:

- A sound operating philosophy that is communicated to all employees.
- Good planning toward worthwhile objectives.
- A monitoring system that indicates whether or not it is moving toward those objectives in an acceptable fashion. The measurement system plays a crucial part in the last step.

Value

According to Webster's dictionary, value is a fair or proper equivalent in money, or commodities for something sold or exchanged. Other definitions include estimated worth, appraised worth, market price, purchasing power, and replacement costs.

Value and quality are two of the four cornerstones of the successful McDonald's hamburger empire. The other two are service and cleanliness.

Products and services have value only when they are needed or believed to be needed. The major elements that mean "value" to customers or clients may be more a matter of perception than reality. If we believe a certain item has value, for instance, we will continue to use that item, even though quality or value may go down. Perception, not reality, often determines value.

Quality

Conformance to requirements, specifications, or standards characterizes quality. Also, quality indicates the relative worth of products and services, and the efficiency and effectiveness of processes used to produce products and provide services. For example, poor quality performance means that more input or better quality input is needed to produce a specific amount of quality output. Rework, scrap, and waste increase the need for inspection and controls, which in turn require added resources (Belcher, 1987).

From a practical standpoint, quality is a strategic, competitive weapon. When the entire concept of quality is incorporated into product based and service oriented industries, it is easier to attract and retain new business or increase sales in existing markets.

Quality and productivity are inseparable (Christopher, 1984). In 1988, the American Productivity Center located in Houston was renamed the American Productivity and Quality Center to reflect its conviction that quality improvement and productivity are related and occur simultaneously.

It is beyond the scope of this chapter to discuss the relationship between quality and productivity. The relationship varies depending on how each concept is defined. The section on operational definitions (see Chapter 8) provides a mechanism for developing and comparing definitions.

There is a positive relationship between cost and quality, as "doing it right the first time" not only makes sense, but is cost effective.

Some costs of quality are (Crosby, 1979):

- Cost to prevent defects and errors to develop and produce products or provide services associated with quality reviews, preventive maintenance, or supplier evaluations.
- Appraisal costs required to inspect, test, or evaluate products or services, including supplier surveillance, product acceptance, and final inspection.
- Failure costs resulting when products or services do not conform to requirements, such as product redesign, scrap, or warranty charges.

Many quality improvement efforts in assembly-line operations or materials processing operations reduce scrap, minimize rework, lower product liability, and increase customer satisfaction.

Quality improvement is the main target of most human resource development programs. Quality can be the driving force for performance improvement efforts. Corning's Total Quality Management System is noteworthy and includes such principles as meeting customers' requirements, striving to do error-free work, managing by prevention, and measuring by the cost of quality (Wagel, 1987).

Quality, like value, has many meanings. Unique needs and beliefs affect what is seen and believed. Quality is often in the eye of the beholder. The quality theme appears in most chapters. Chapter 14 covers quality in detail.

Innovation

This is the creative process of adapting products, services, processes, structures, etc. to meet internal and external pressures, demands, changes, and needs (Swaim and Sink, 1984b). Innovation may be based on individual task-focused or organizational needs, or may be the result of market pressures, for instance, intense competition. In this case, efforts are directed to perfect or replace a process that already exists, or "supply the missing link."

A numeric way to express innovation involves products marketed (output) per feasible ideas conceived (input) (Swaim and Sink, 1984a), or:

$$\frac{\text{Marketing products adopted}}{\text{Feasible ideas}}$$

Innovation, which in high-tech areas is a common path to success, implies (Drucker, 1985):

- The unexpected success, failure, or the occurrence of an unplanned event.
- Incongruity between reality as it actually is and reality as it is assumed or ought to be.
- Changes in industry structure or market structure that catch everyone by surprise.

Sources for innovation and opportunity involving changes outside the organization (Drucker, 1985) include:

- Demographics, or population changes
- Changes in perception, mood, or meaning
- New scientific and nonscientific knowledge

Quality of Work Life (QWL)

The term QWL is relatively new, but the underlying logic is timeless. This broad, open-ended concept includes work-related factors influencing dedication or commitment to the job and psychological factors.

QWL describes how well people in the organization are able to satisfy important personal needs through their experiences of working and living in the organization (Hackman and Suttle, 1977). When satisfaction is high, commitment to group and organizational goals is also high. To illustrate, a high QWL environment is one in which people are " . . . essential members of an organization that challenges the human spirit, that inspires

13. List the financial indicators used in your organization. Are they good indicators of productivity?

14. At what type of work-related activities are you efficient *and* effective?

15. How does the concept value apply to your job?

16. What could you do to increase your own personal worth as an employee?

17. How could quality of products or services be increased? What contribution does quality really make?

18. In what way are innovation and productivity related? Explain.

19. Can current organizations survive without innovation? Explain.

20. Does your organization have QWL programs? If so, how are they related to productivity?

personal growth and development, and that gets things done. . . ." (Belcher, 1987).

Major dimensions associated with QWL are security, equity, individuation, and democracy (Tuttle, 1983):

- Security—freedom from anxiety concerning physical health, safety, income and future employment.
- Equity—fair and equitable pay, or pay for performance.
- Individuation—extent to which work stimulates the development of unique abilities, namely continued learning, autonomy and full use of skills.
- Democracy—extent to which people's views are listened to and used in decision making, namely, participative management and self-managed work teams.

High-QWL environments are characterized by (Belcher, 1987):

- Employee input to decisions
- Employee participation in problem-solving
- Information sharing
- Constructive feedback
- Teamwork and collaboration
- Meaningful and challenging work
- Employment security

Successful QWL programs consider employees the most valuable of all organizational resources. See box above.

REFERENCES

1. Bain, David. *The Productivity Prescription*, New York: McGraw-Hill Book Company, 1982.
2. Belcher, John G., Jr. *Productivity Plus+*, Houston, Texas: Gulf Publishing Company, 1987.
3. Christopher, William F. "How to Measure and Improve Productivity in Professional, Administrative, and Service Organizations," in *Issues in White Collar Productivity*, Norcross, Georgia: Industrial Engineering and Management Press, 1984, pp. 29–37.
4. Crosby, Philip B. *Quality Is Free*, New York: New American Library, 1979.
5. Drucker, Peter F. *Innovation and Entrepreneurship*, New York: Harper & Row, Publishers, Inc., 1985.
6. Fitz-enz, Jac. "HR Measurement: Formulas for Success," *Personnel Journal*, October 1985, pp. 52–60.

7. Hackman, J. Richard and Suttle, J. Lloyd (ed.), *Improving Life at Work,* Santa Monica, California: Goodyear Publishing Co., 1977.

8. Jamali, Shafique. "Putting a Productivity Improvement Plan Into Action: A Six-Step Plan," in *Issues in White Collar Productivity,* Norcross, Georgia: Industrial and Engineering Management Press, 1984, pp. 64–74.

9. Katzell, R. A., Yankelovich, D., Fein, M., Ornati, D. A. and Nash, A. *Work, Productivity and Job Satisfaction,* New York: The Psychological Corporation, 1975.

10. Lehrer, Robert N. "Using the Concepts," in *White Collar Productivity,* Robert N. Lehrer (ed.), New York: McGraw-Hill Book Company, 1983, pp. 333–345.

11. Likert, Rensis. *The Human Organization: Its Management and Value,* New York: McGraw-Hill Book Company, 1967.

12. Messick, Samuel. "Meaning and Values in Measurement and Evaluation," *American Psychologist,* October 1975, pp. 955–966.

13. Neuman, John L. "Make Overhead Cuts that Last," *Harvard Business Review,* May–June 1975, pp. 116–126.

14. ____. "Overhead: Five Challenges to Conventional Wisdom," *Management Practice Quarterly,* Fall 1986, pp. 5–9.

15. Price, J. L. *The Study of Turnover,* Ames: Iowa University Press, 1977.

16. Ranftl, Robert M. *R & D Productivity,* 2nd Ed., Culver City, California: Hughes Aircraft Company, 1978.

17. Sink, D. Scott. *Productivity Management: Planning, Measurement and Evaluation, Control and Improvement,* Somerset, New Jersey: John Wiley and Sons, Inc., 1985.

18. Slade, Bernard N. and Mohindra, Raj. *Winning the Productivity Race,* Lexington, Massachusetts: D. C. Heath and Company, 1985.

19. Stevens, Craig A. and Wright, Karen. "Managing Change with Configuration Management," *National Productivity Review,* Autumn 1991, pp. 509–518.

20. Swaim, Jeffrey and Sink, D. Scott. "Current Developments in Firm or Corporate Level Productivity Measurement and Evaluation," in *Issues in White Collar Productivity,* Norcross, Georgia: Industrial Engineering and Management Press, 1984a, pp. 8–17.

21. ____. "Productivity Measurement in the Service Sector: A Hotel/Motel Application of the Multi-Factor Productivity Measurement Model," in *Issues in White Collar Productivity,* Norcross, Georgia: Industrial Engineering and Management Press, 1984b, pp. 161–173.

22. Tuttle, Thomas C. "Organizational Productivity: A Challenge for Psychologists," *American Psychologist,* April 1983, pp. 479–486.

23. Udler, A. "Productivity Measurement of Administrative Services," *Personnel Journal,* December 1978, pp. 672–675, 697.

24. Wagel, William H. "Corning Zeroes in on Total Quality," *Personnel,* July 1987, pp. 4–9.

Ideas to Remember

Chapter 1—Answers and Insights

1. Background, experience, and type of job performed affect viewpoints. Views that most closely fit your needs and support your beliefs will be used.

2. Each viewpoint is unique, yet all overlap to some degree. Knowing how other people think, and the type of information they use will increase awareness and understanding.

3. Work-related standards: individual output in the form of sales, production, reports, ideas; company-related standards for goal accomplishment through sales, production, etc.

4. Standards may be changed to ratios if standards are adequately defined. Numeric data are a good way to represent what is important and/or measured. However, not all accomplishments can be represented in numeric form.

5. Personal definitions: output/input, effort, quality, do more with less, do more with the resources you have, work faster, quantity, efficiency, effectiveness, time, QWL, etc. Productivity must be defined before it can be measured.

6. The definition is probably similar to your personal definitions. Specific definitions include product quality, sales, or number of customers reached. Work group: standards, expectations, and quality of goods produced or services provided.

7. Numeric definitions: economics, accounting, or engineering. Descriptive definitions: managerial and industrial/organizational. The "best" definition combines a balance of numeric and descriptive elements.

8. Typical concepts: effectiveness, usefulness, profit, results achieved, or standards or ratios unique to your job or areas of competence.

9. Your personal definitions will focus on positive aspects based on valued achievement, or areas of expertise. However, standard performance appraisal criteria may not reflect true ability. Few people see themselves as others see them. The natural tendency is to inflate one's worth.

10. If tangible products are produced, input and output ratios could be profit, sales, labor, materials, quality, effectiveness, time, energy, and cost. If services are provided, ratios may be customer satisfaction, repeat business, convenience, efficiency, profit, and results achieved.

11. Ratios should provide meaningful, current information based on well defined standards. Supervisors, peers, and subordinates who develop the ratios understand them, and will be more likely to use and improve the ratios.

12. Pros: meets needs, adequate standards, understood, provides meaningful information, or reliable.

    Cons: not broad enough, questionable input data, inadequate for service industry, or outdated information.

13. Financial indicators: sales, profits, return on investment. Financial indicators report past accomplishments. Most reveal nothing about human resources.

14. Efficiency and effectiveness are maximized when people are allowed to do what they are capable of doing. A standard can be used to indicate how well you perform.

15. Value, which is observable and in the mind of the "customer," applies to products and services. "Customers" within (internal) and outside (external) the organization are excellent judges of value. Internal customers are peers or others who work in the same organization. External customers are outside the organization.

    You may be involved in processes that add value to your job, or reduce costs of products or services that do not add value. One example is value engineering, a dynamic team approach having a strong theoretical basis. It uses economic analysis to add value to products, systems, and other appropriate targets of review (Stevens and Wright, 1991). For instance, when used during the development and design stages in the construction industry, plans and efforts not adding value are eliminated. The result is more value for the money, or value added.

16. Increasing personal value: training, career development, continuing education, job enrichment, job rotation, or more opportunity and challenge in your current job, like serving on a cross-functional team.

17. Nearly everything done in the organization could be done better. The real key to quality improvement in products is defect prevention (identifying and rem-

edying problems beforehand), not defect detection (identifying defective products after they are produced). Poor quality service can be summed up in three words, "No one cares."

However, customers are beginning to be taken seriously. Their impact is valued. Some customers have become partners.

Those playing major roles in producing quality products or providing quality services have strong feelings of satisfaction. "Running with winners" is a good motivator. Caterpillar, McDonald's, Maytag, and Hewlett-Packard, are longstanding winners from the quality standpoint. Quality, value, and productivity are inseparable.

18. Productivity is likely to increase when innovative, yet cost-effective approaches are used to solve production or people problems. The endless search for new products and services for which markets exist requires creativity, innovation, and a supportive organizational climate.

19. Survival requires innovation, especially in turbulent economic environments. Maintaining competitiveness in world markets means that technological innovations are produced at a high level of quality and manufactured at a low cost. Examples: semiconductor integrated circuits, electronic packaging, magnetic disks and fiber optics (Slade and Mohindra, 1985).

20. QWL focuses on people's psychological and physical comfort. Most QWL programs (1) have no standard set of principles; (2) stress employee task involvement; (3) strive to preserve worker dignity; (4) try to eliminate the dysfunctional aspects of the hierarchy; and (5) facilitate change.

The number of QWL programs is growing. Properly implemented and administered QWL programs can increase employees' feelings of satisfaction and personal worth, and raise motivation and productivity.

Successful QWL programs (1) consider employees the most valuable of all organizational resources; (2) emphasize employee collaboration and growth; and (3) provide employees with the skills and value orientations necessary to function in a participative environment.

2

Organizational, Group, and Personal Goals

PURPOSE

- Review the major components of the organization.
- Consider how positive and negative forces inside and outside the organization affect productivity.
- Construct short-term, intermediate, and long-term organizational, work group, and personal goals.
- Evaluate the role of organizational planning and goal setting.
- Develop and evaluate realistic solutions to reduce or resolve personal and organizational goal conflict.
- Review general behavioral characteristics of people at work.

INTRODUCTION

Organizations are in a constant state of change. Successful organizations have a clearly developed structure, culture, and climate that employees understand and value. Organizational stability increases when employees understand organizational structure and have assimilated cultural variables unique to their organization. Continuous monitoring of achievement and appropriate, timely revision of goals and strategies keep organizations competitive. Strategic planning may be the one thread that ties organizational efforts and productivity improvement together.

When the sources of personal, organizational, and environmental forces are known, people can take a closer look at their specific roles and use this information to set goals to improve behavior and increase effectiveness.

Making plans, setting goals, and establishing priorities are easier when the importance of commonly performed work-related activities is known. Control is a valuable planning function. There can be no managerial control unless plans, goals, and standards for performance and ways to make changes are clear, complete, and well integrated.

The value of formal planning is greatly enhanced when the chief executive officer takes responsibility for planning, particularly long-range planning. The ultimate test of planning is achieving worthwhile goals. Field and laboratory studies demonstrate that having goals is a major factor in improving performance.

Clearly defined, realistic, short-term, intermediate, and long-term goals help place personal and organizational efforts in perspective. Goal setting identifies employees' self-interests. Productivity should be high under desirable reward systems based on these interests. Successful organizations have clearly defined goals for measuring performance. To have maximum impact, human and material resources should be directed toward worthwhile goals. The organization and its workers are winners when personal goals and corporate interests match (Kelley,

1985). Organizations cannot compete and survive unless all employees know what business they are in. When productivity improvement is tied to business goals, productivity of employees vital to the new technologies is affected in a positive manner (Skinner, 1986).

The ideal productive personality profile is more myth than reality. General characteristics, such as cooperation, facilitation, motivation, etc., encourage productivity in organizations where these traits are reinforced and suitably rewarded.

ORGANIZATION

An organization is a complex system of closely related elements that form a whole. No two organizations are exactly alike. Forces inside and outside the organization affect organizations in different ways. Organizations are affected by internal forces, such as social and political, and by external forces in the environment, for example competition, technology, and market trends. Organizations are in a constant state of change, and must adapt and innovate in order to survive. Conflict is unavoidable. Environmental variables listed in Question #3 of this chapter are prime factors in organizational stability and growth. Change is discussed in greater detail in Chapter 3.

Internal stability of the organization is influenced by how well employees understand organizational structure, and by the extent to which they have assimilated cultural variables unique to their organization. Stability and type of organizational environment can have a dramatic effect on employees. For instance, a stable, friendly environment where people communicate freely is a positive factor.

Each organization, despite its size, has a specific structure, culture and climate, and numerous functions. The formal organization follows guidelines set up in the formal structure. The informal organization, or ''what we say we do,'' represents the true culture of the organization. The number of companies without boundaries is growing (Hirschorn and Gilmore, 1992).

Structure

Organizational charts or diagrams describing how various parts of the organizational system relate to one another are often used to represent organizational structure. Structure incorporates organizational culture, namely, the organization's style, values, norms, and expectations of both the organization and its employees.

Structure, which ranges from formal to informal, affects what people do and how they do it, how they communicate, and how they relate to their peers and supervisors. Formal structures imply ''rules,'' while informal structures are real life interpretations of those rules. Structure has meaning when people perform the various activities associated with achieving goals (Lundgren, 1974).

Formal structure is planned and specified through official channels of communication. Formal structure is static and establishes communication networks in which communication moves up, down, and across, or in any other direction. It spells out authority and responsibility relationships.

Informal structure, which is often unwritten, unspecified, and unplanned, often develops when people interact closely or work in the same group for a period of time. Informal structure may be caused by, or be a reaction to formal structure (Wieland and Ullrich, 1976).

Organizational structure usually refers to the most effective grouping of functions necessary to achieve the organization's objectives. Some desirable attributes of organizational structure (Ranftl, 1978):

- Be catalytic in getting the job done in the most productive manner.
- Never be an end in itself, but only a means to achieve the best possible use of available resources.
- Identify responsibility, decision-making, authority, and performance accountability in a precise manner.
- Be simple, flexible, and adapt to change.

Culture

Beliefs, values, established history, philosophies, traditions, operating procedures, or the organization's personality all contribute to culture. Hiring policies, management style, work climate, remuneration practices, and career development, for instance, reflect culture. The beliefs and personality of chief executive officers are instrumental in shaping an organization's culture.

In general, companies with strong, cohesive organizational cultures are successful, profitable, and have dedicated employees. Southwestern Bell Telephone, Motorola, Proctor & Gamble, and McDonald's are examples of such companies.

Culture can be viewed as an independent variable or input (plans and goals), an intervening variable or throughput (motivation), or dependent variable or output (achievement) (Dessler, 1976). These three variables are discussed in greater detail in Chapter 3, ''A Systems Approach.''

Changing organizational culture in a more positive direction may be one way to establish and maintain a competitive edge. Cultural change may be stimulated from the bottom-up, or top-down, or through human resource development programs, the most common being training.

Conflict

This inevitable part of organizational life has two sides. The positive side-conflict that causes healthy competition can improve the quality of products or services, or stimulate creative solutions to long-standing problems. The negative side-conflict can be disruptive, destructive, stress- ful, costly, and even debilitating. Intensive or prolonged conflict can result in lose-lose, or win-lose situations. Constructive approaches to conflict allow opposing parties to win on some issues. When each party has a sense of accomplishment, negative effects are reduced.

The Organization and Productivity

Positive and negative forces in the organization influence people, processes, and productivity in different ways.

---

1. In the space below draw a very simple picture of your organization. Do not draw a typical organizational chart.
   - Include major activities that take place in your organization, like produce specific products, or provide certain services.
   - Draw a circle inside the organization to represent your own work group.
   - Indicate your position with an X.

2. In the space *inside* the organization write in personal or organizational forces affecting your productivity or the productivity of your supervisor and subordinates—work load, quality control, access to computers, etc.
   - Put a plus (+) beside the positive forces and a negative (−) beside the negative forces. Consider how each force influences you, your supervisor(s), and your subordinates.
   - List the two most important + and − forces below.

   Positive Forces   **Negative Forces**

   _____   _____

   _____   _____

3. In the space *outside* the organization write in personal or organizational forces in the environment affecting your productivity or the productivity of your supervisor and subordinates-economic, governmental, union, consumer, user, or client, etc.
   - Put a plus (+) beside the positive forces and a minus (−) beside the negative forces. Consider how much each force affects your work behavior and that of your immediate supervisor and subordinates.
   - List the two most important + and − forces below.

   Positive Forces   **Negative Forces**

   _____   _____

   _____   _____

4. Evaluate the forces listed in #2 and #3, above. Select five forces having the greatest impact on productivity with the most important force being first and the least important force being fifth. Indicate whether you have some control over these forces, and whether they occur inside or outside the organization. Estimate the probability of being able to change or redirect any of the forces to increase productivity in general.

Forces Influencing Productivity

Forces	Control (Yes/No)	Inside/Outside Organization	Probability of Being Able to Change
_____	____	_____	_____
_____	____	_____	_____
_____	____	_____	_____
_____	____	_____	_____
_____	____	_____	_____

5. List major steps you would take to make best use of the − or + forces affecting productivity the most.

Some forces, like foreign competition and the inflation rate, vary. Few major forces are predictable or totally controllable. Completely unique forces are rare. However, proper planning is required to redirect forces in logical and constructive ways. Misdirected efforts can be costly.

When the amount of control managers have over organizational forces is known, it is a little easier to predict the probability of bringing about personal or organizational change. Change is the core of personal and organizational development. Productivity measurement and enhancement are examples of change efforts. See box above.

Are those who make the goals responsible for implementing them? Where do goals come from? Do people or organizations have goals? Is long-run survival or profit maximization more important? How do productivity improvement efforts and goal setting fit together?

These major issues represent only a small part of planning and goal setting processes. But, efforts to find good answers often result in unexpected, essentially useful outcomes.

PLANNING AND GOAL SETTING

Planning is the first step in the goal setting process. When the organization's mission or purpose is clearly defined and known throughout the organization, it is possible to make better use of human and material resources. This saves time and effort, and should improve the organization's competitive edge.

Plans include a whole framework of actions or objectives that incorporate internal and external constraints and take current circumstances into account. For instance, the positive and negative forces you listed in Questions #2 and #3 could include constraints and may affect goals listed in Questions #6, #7, and #8.

Planning

The major purposes of planning are understanding, control, and prediction.

Understanding. When the importance of commonly performed work related activities is determined, it is easier to use relevant information to set goals and establish priorities.

Planning can also be a form of personal and organizational learning as in developing scenarios. This process involves comparing the world of facts with the world of perceptions. The main purpose of scenarios is to gather and transform information of strategic significance into fresh perceptions (Wack, 1985b). Oil pricing, demand, and consumer and government reactions developed at Royal Dutch/Shell during the 1970s are illustrated (Wack, 1985a). deGeus (1988) presents a 1984 scenario from "Shell" pricing oil at $15 a barrel. The current price was $28, but by February 1, 1986 the price per barrel was $17 and $10 by April, 1986. Shell selected and implemented the best of the existing contingency plans to ease the pain of lowered prices. Oil prices continue to fluctuate.

Control. The organizational control function serves the same purpose as a thermostat. Thermostats regulate or control temperature, for example in buildings, and in cars' heating and cooling systems.

Organizational control systems, like budgeting, scheduling, and performance appraisal, compare accomplishments against established plans and correct or alter deviations to ensure objectives are attained according to those plans. Ongoing administration of the organization, or strategic planning (explained below), literally involves monitoring and adjusting the organization's thermostats according to specific "temperature requirements." The control function and who is in control are very important.

The overall welfare and the ultimate productivity of the whole organization are affected by strategic planning, policy formation, and goal setting. Strategic planning is the process of deciding on objectives of the organization, allocating resources to activities calculated to achieve a set of business goals in a dynamic, competitive environment (Gray, 1986). Most strategic plans reflect technological, economic, political, and social perspectives (Dessler, 1986).

In its current form, strategic planning is a line management function in which staff specialists play a supporting role. Planners contribute information in their own areas of expertise. Line personnel, who are basically responsible for getting the job done, should be included as they have valuable information, skills, and knowledge that can be used in the planning process. Staff specialists, engineers, and systems analysts, for example, have considerable input through their advisory functions. Ideally, all employees should be involved in strategic planning.

Typical strategic plans include setting personnel and financial policies and deciding on new product lines.

Strategic plans have corresponding management control activities of formulating personnel practices, capital planning, and developing new products.

Specific areas of major concern are quality control, reliable delivery, short lead times, customer service, rapid product introduction, flexible capacity, and efficient capital deployment. From a productivity standpoint, the control function enables managers to obtain and use resources effectively and efficiently to achieve the organization's objectives. In this way, productivity increases are linked to business strategies and to action (Skinner, 1985, 1986). Simply stated, managers can help people to do their jobs better.

Strategic plans that are carefully developed and clearly understood provide consistent, effective guidance in decision making and forecasting. Although there have been large expenditures of time and resources on strategic planning in the last 20 years, a growing number of industries and companies are failing to meet their goals, and are lagging behind their competition (Hayes, 1985). The difference between what can and should be done, and how people react to this difference, is the key outcome of the planning process (Grove, 1983).

Prediction. Forecasting predicts or estimates some future event or condition. Forecasting methods can be descriptive, like surveys, or numeric, like economic forecasts. However, the "worth" of prediction tools depends on reliability and accuracy of data. The rate at which the organization's environment changes and the causes of these changes affect the accuracy of predictions.

Goals and Goal Setting

When we set goals, we take control over the direction and nature of the process of change. We often welcome change for the better and fear change for the worse. Setting realistic, achievable, personal, group, and organizational goals and establishing priorities means making difficult decisions. Goal setting and trying to achieve these goals may change the typical way people think, perceive, and behave.

Most goals relate to efficiency, productivity, growth, stability, and financial aspects. Goals often focus on what we know about ourselves and our organization, and on customers and competition in the marketplace. When goals are developed through joint decision making, those involved in the overall goal-setting process develop a sense of ownership in and commitment to the goals. Ownership involves identification and responsibility (Floyd, 1989). People directly involved in goal setting identify with or support the goals they help develop, and will help carry them out. This pride of accomplishment increases the person's willingness to be associated with the finished product, process, or service.

Good goals:

- Are specific and clear enough so that everyone can understand them.
- Can be written down and measured with some degree of accuracy so progress toward them can be determined.
- Indicate periods of time required to achieve them.
- Are realistic, but challenging enough to stimulate motivation.
- Include elements of risk and creativity.
- Are flexible enough so they can be modified to meet changing demands of the marketplace, keep up with technology, reflect trends, or take on a new focus.
- Are compatible with the organization's major purpose or mission.

Goals can be used as standards to assess accomplishment, for example, zero defects in a manufacturing process or increase sales of a product by five percent per month for three months. Concentrating efforts in one major area and making steady gains toward that goal produce more immediate, tangible results than working on a number of less important goals at the same time.

Typically goals differ in purpose, type, complexity, expectations, and time perspectives of those involved in goal setting. Major goals have positive and negative side effects. Goal setting gets better and easier the more often it is done.

Purpose. Goals are criteria or standards used to make and compare decisions and achievement at any point in time. Many goals have a financial basis. Others relate to planning, and controlling, or other management functions.

Personal, job-related goals reflect specific job demands, abilities, and expectations of employees. Many focus on what is done, or on output rather than on ways to achieve goals. The "how" of goal achievement is as valuable as "how much."

Type. Major types of goals are operative, official, tactical, performance, and developmental.

- Operative goals are practical and specific, and relate to the actual operation of the organization; for instance, they pertain to quantity or quality, price schedules, or guidelines for customer service.
- Official goals are general and somewhat vague. They are used in annual reports, corporate charters, and materials written for the public, such as expected earnings on investments.

- Tactical goals are the subgoals that underlie strategic goals, and serve as the plan of action for achieving strategic goals.
- Performance goals are based on specific organizational standards for production, sales, services, etc. Developing and maintaining high quality performance goals is the heart of the productivity issue.
- Developmental goals are associated with growth of individuals in the organization. Expanding and improving capacities or abilities through training is one example.

Complexity. Level of complexity ranges from high-level strategic and tactical goals to lower level goals associated with specific projects and tasks. Also, major goals may consist of a series of subgoals.

Time perspective. Length of time assigned to achieve goals may be as short as a few minutes or as long as 20 or more years. Common time frames are:

- Short-range—less than one year. These goals are specific, for example, increase sales by certain percent each month, quarter, or year.
- Intermediate-range—one to three years. An example is the gradual accumulation of information to make decisions on introducing new product lines.
- Long-range—more than three years, possibly as long as 20 or more years. These are general goals related to the mission of the organization. Such goals must be flexible enough so they can be changed.

When short-term, intermediate, and long-term goals are defined in realistic terms, it is easier to look at successes along the way, and determine the extent to which they have been achieved.

Effective goal setting is efficient; it gets the best results with the least cost and effort. Each organization has subgoals, which are added as the organization grows or changes direction. Goals are more useful when priorities are set for achieving them.

Productivity measurement and improvement are strategic issues. Well-formulated plans for managing productivity that clearly specify time periods required to achieve continuing, long-term improvement are vital to organizational success. However, many companies select goals that are too short term.

Goal Setting and Productivity Improvement

Everyone wants immediate, observable, measurable increases in productivity. Sometimes productivity improvement is seen as a series of annual cost reduction programs in a fixed number of defined projects. Or, some efforts begin by identifying major end result areas and focus mainly on these. Productivity improvement should relate to the strategy, mission, and overall goals of the organization.

Designing and implementing a good productivity improvement program begins with developing sound plans, setting goals, and establishing priorities. Managers who want to measure and enhance productivity and know where to start and what to do have a definite advantage. They begin by taking steps to balance easy to achieve short-term goals against long-term goals. Successfully performing the daily job of getting the work done may appear to meet only short-term goals, but viewed another way, the long-term goal of keeping the business running is being met on a daily basis.

Developing, evaluating, and revising productivity measures is easier when various individual and organizational goals are identified and incorporated into an overall plan. Setting organizational goals involves cooperation, commitment, and compromise. Establishing priorities and adhering to them is critical.

Focusing on only short-term goals and perspectives to bring about immediate productivity increases may initially appear to reduce cost. This focus on episodic thinking may sacrifice employee satisfaction and customer goodwill if quality of products or services is lowered. In some instances, short-term goals, like lowering quality standards to reduce the cost of supplies, may produce long-term losses through customer dissatisfaction and a high return rate. See box below and on next page.

6. List your organization's major short-term, intermediate, and long-term goals. These may include goals related to the marketplace, competition, or expectations of directors or shareholders. Rank what you believe to be management's priority for each goal. Rank priorities 1, 2, and 3 for first, second, and third priorities.

Organizational Goals

Short-Term	Management's Priority Rank	Intermediate	Management's Priority Rank	Long-Term	Management's Priority Rank

7. List the goals of your work group. Rank priorities 1, 2, 3.

Work Group Goals

Short-Term	Priority Rank	Intermediate	Priority Rank	Long-Term	Priority Rank

8. List your personal goals. Rank your own priorities 1, 2, 3.

Personal Work Goals

Short-Term	Priority Rank	Intermediate	Priority Rank	Long Term	Priority Rank
_____	_____	_____	_____	_____	_____
_____	_____	_____	_____	_____	_____
_____	_____	_____	_____	_____	_____

9. Examine all goals ranked number one. List three goals having the greatest potential to increase productivity. State the ''ideal'' goal as it should be. Indicate your plan of action and approximately how long it will take to achieve each goal.

Existing Goal	Goal As it Should Be	Plan of Action	Time to Achieve
_____	_____	_____	_____
_____	_____	_____	_____
_____	_____	_____	_____

10. Describe conflict between your goals, the goals of your work group, and the goals of the organization. Indicate how conflict could be reduced or resolved. Sometimes conflict produces divergent opinions, which may result in new ways to examine and solve problems.

Goal Conflict and Conflict Resolution

Conflict	Ways to Reduce Or Resolve Conflict
_____	_____
_____	_____
_____	_____
_____	_____

People

Although technology and organizations are in a constant state of flux or disequilibrium, many aspects of peoples' behavior, beliefs, and attitudes can be generalized. Typically, people

- Do not change (or want to change) very much, so change should be managed in a manner most likely to result in long range success (Tichy, 1983). An optimistic approach is that ''healthy'' people will change, and with documentation of benefits of changing, more people will change (Lippitt, Lippitt, and Lafferty, 1984).
- Are usually rational, or ''selectively rational'' (Leibenstein, 1980), or compromise between the way they want to believe and the way they feel they must believe. Employees exert more effort when they believe these efforts will further their personal ends.
- Prefer immediate feedback on performance.
- Have a basic need for acceptance.
- Enjoy being recognized for their efforts.
- Want to be rewarded monetarily and non-monetarily for work accomplished.
- Desire latitude in deciding the best method of performing their jobs (self-management).
- Want to derive a feeling of satisfaction on the job.
- Generally want to improve their skills and knowledge.

- Want to feel their work is meaningful.
- Want to pursue their own self interests consistent with their background (Chapter 6) and job demands.
- May see and believe what they want to see and believe. They may ignore reality and fail to accept the views and beliefs of others.

Problems related to managing employees may consume well over half of a manager's time. Also, a small percentage of employees cause most of the problems. This statement is best understood in terms of Pareto's Law (explained on page 41), which implies that 80% of the problems are likely caused by 20% of the employees. Similarly, 80% of persons' feelings of accomplishment may come from projects requiring 20% of their total effort.

Preventive maintenance in the organization, like checking fluid levels in your car, pays dividends. Anticipating the kinds of things that can go wrong improves the chances they will go right.

Employees' knowledge, attitudes, and skills influence productivity. These three broad concepts are covered in greater detail in Chapter 6 (under ''Productivity Indicators'') and in Chapter 7, ''Job Analysis and Job Description.''

People, management, workers, and the company are all the same thing. Every person in the organization must understand the essence of the business; every employee must benefit from the organization's success; and an environment must be created in which this can happen.

---

11. Based on your knowledge and experience within your organization, write down six basic, positive characteristics or traits of ''good'' employees. Rank the most important trait number 1, and the least important trait number 6. Then rank the characteristic (1 low to 6 high) based on how much each influences productivity.

Personal Characteristics and Their Importance to Productivity

Characteristics	Rank	Rank of Importance to Productivity
_____	_____	_____
_____	_____	_____
_____	_____	_____
_____	_____	_____
_____	_____	_____
_____	_____	_____

12. Examine the characteristics listed in #11, above, and indicate whether they are task-oriented (T-O) or social-emotional (S-E). Traditionally, task-oriented characteristics refer to "getting the job done," or being concerned about output or accomplishment (productivity). Social-emotional variables relate to concern about the welfare of the person, recognition of feelings, attitude, etc., but affect goal accomplishment. How many of each type of variable did you list? There were _____ T-O variables and _____ S-E variables. Which is more important? Or, is each set of variables equally important? Explain.

13. If you feel that one group of personality characteristics is more likely to increase productivity, please describe typical situations in which these characteristics could be exhibited.

14. If you feel that one set of personality characteristics is likely to decrease productivity, please indicate typical situations in which these characteristics could be exhibited.

15. What role does time play? Examine answers #6, #7, and #8.

People are mature, and want to grow on the job, and demonstrate these capacities directly related to doing their jobs. Trust is a vital factor. See box on page 21.

How employees' personality characteristics and productivity are related is a unique combination of employee, job, and organizational variables. Most personality characteristics can be classified as task-oriented or social-emotional oriented. The current shift in management style is to a more open or participative approach.

Productive managers generally have productive subordinates. They also share the personality characteristics of competence, providing clear direction, striving for quality, taking initiative, motivating subordinates, sharing information, setting standards, and understanding the nature, purpose and overall goals of the organization.

Is managerial productivity the sum of the productivity of people supervised? What would happen if each year managers had to be reelected by their subordinates? Could managerial productivity and "return on management" be campaign issues? See box above.

Radical changes in organizational structure will occur before the year 2000 (Handy, 1989 and Offerman and Gowing, 1990). Organizational performance is greatly affected by changes in structure, shape, and strategy.

Major factors affecting corporate structure include: (1) globalized markets; (2) instantaneous communcation; (3) political alignments; (4) changing demographics; (5) technological transformations in both products and production; (6) corporate alliances; and (7) flattening organizations due to attrition of the middle managers (Kanter, 1991).

Mergers, partnerships, resource sharing, and other forms of cooperative relationships have dramatically altered the shape of many organizations. New structures will have customers at the top and management at the bottom. Customers, clients, and partners will be the ultimate judges of success.

Organizations are moving toward "M-form," or decentralized, multi-divisional structures having semi-autonomous operating divisions. Each division will be responsible for daily operations (Peters, 1988). Outsourcing, hiring of contract workers, and telecommuting have changed how, when, and where work is done.

Preserving organizational culture in turbulent times enables people to maintain their values, norms, philosophies, and take-for-granted unconscious assumptions that determine perceptions, feelings, thought processes, and behavior (Schein, 1990).

Joint-ventures, cross-functional alliances, and globalization require an understanding of a wide range of organizational cultures. Joint ventures and cooperative managements require contracted relationships, and strategic alliances are increasing (Galbraith and Kazanijian, 1988). The European Economic Community (EC) currently brings together 12 nations and over 320,000,000 people having cultural, ethnic, geographic, political, language, and economic differences.

REFERENCES

1. Bain, David. *The Productivity Prescription,* New York: McGraw-Hill Book Company, 1982.

2. Charner, Ivan. "The Career Passport: Documenting Youth Experience and Making the Job Connection," Washington, D.C.: National Institute for Work and Learning, 1986, 12 pages.

3. "The Career Passport: Documenting Youth Experience and Making the Job Connection," *Career Development,* Fall 1986, pp. 1–3. (Charner's article listed in 2, above, is summarized.)

4. Courtney, Roslyn S. "A Human Resources Program that Helps Management and Employees Prepare for the Future," *Personnel,* May 1986, pp. 32–35, 37–40.

5. deGeus, Arie P. "Planning as Learning," *Harvard Business Review,* March–April 1988, pp. 70–74.

6. Dessler, Gary. *Organization and Management: A Contingency Approach,* Englewood Cliffs, New Jersey: Prentice-Hall, Inc., 1976.

7. ———. *Organizational Theory: Integrating Structure and Behavior,* 2nd Ed., New Jersey: Prentice-Hall, Inc., Englewood Cliffs, 1986.

8. Floyd, Roy. "FOI: Focus, Ownership, and Initiative," *Industrial Management,* January–February 1989, pp. 1 & 13.

9. Galbraith, J. R. and Kazanijian, R. K. "Strategy, Technology, and Emerging Organizations," in J. Hage (ed.), *Futures of Organizations,* Lexington, MA: Lexington Books, pp. 29–41, 1987.

10. Gilmore, John V. *The Productivity Personality,* San Francisco: Albion Publishing Company, 1974.

11. Gray, Daniel R. "Uses and Misuses of Strategic Planning," *Harvard Business Review,* January–February 1986, pp. 89–97.

12. Grove, Andrew S. *High Output Management,* New York: Random House, Inc., 1983.

13. Handy, Charles. *The Age of Unreason,* Boston, Massachusetts, Harvard Business School Press, 1989.

14. Hayes, Robert H. "Strategic Planning-Forward in Reverse?" *Harvard Business Review,* November–December 1985, pp. 111–119.

15. Hirschorn, Larry and Gilmore, Thomas. "The New Boundaries of the 'Boundaryless' Company," *Harvard Business Review,* May–June, 1992, pp. 104–115.

16. Kanter, Rosabeth Moss. "Transcending Business Boundaries: 12,000 World Managers View Change," *Harvard Business Review,* May–June, 1991, pp. 151–164.

17. Kelley, Robert E. *The Gold Collar Worker,* Reading, Massachusetts: Addison-Wesley Publishing Co., Inc., 1985.

18. Leibenstein, H. *Beyond Economic Man,* Cambridge, Massachusetts: Harvard University Press, 1980.

19. Lippitt, Gordon, Lippitt, Ronald, and Lafferty, Clayton. "Cutting Edge Trends in Organizational Development," *Training and Development Journal,* July 1984, pp. 59–62.

20. Lundgren, Earl F. *Organizational Management: Systems and Processes,* San Francisco: Canfield Press, 1974.

21. Ninomiya, J. S. "Wagon Masters and Lesser Managers," *Harvard Business Review,* March–April 1988, pp. 84–90.

22. Odiorne, Robert M. "The Art of Crafting Strategic Plans," *Training,* October 1987, pp. 94–97.

23. Offerman, Lynn R. and Gowing, Marilyn K. "Organizations of the Future," *American Psychologist,* February 1990, pp. 95–108.

24. Peters, T. J. "Restoring American Competitiveness: Looking for New Models of Organizations," *Academy of Management Executive,* 2, pp. 103–109, 1988.

25. Ranftl, Robert M. *R & D Productivity,* 2nd ed. Culver City, California: Hughes Aircraft Company, 1978.

26. Schein, Edgar H. "Organizational Culture," *American Psychologist,* February 1990, pp. 109–119.

27. Skinner, Wickham. "The Productivity Paradox," *Harvard Business Review,* July–August, 1986, pp. 55–59.

28. ———. *Manufacturing: The Formidable Competitive Weapon,* New York: John Wiley and Sons, 1985.

29. Tichy, Noel M. *Managing Strategic Change: Technological, Political and Cultural Dynamics,* New York: Wiley, 1983.

30. Wack, Pierre, "Scenarios: Uncharted Waters Ahead," *Harvard Business Review,* September–October 1985a, pp. 72–89.

31. ———. "Scenarios: Shooting the Rapids," *Harvard Business Review,* November–December 1985b, pp. 139–150.

32. Wieland, George F. and Ullrich, Robert A. *Organizations: Behavior, Design and Change,* Homewood, Illinois: Richard D. Irwin, Inc. 1976.

Ideas to Remember

Chapter 2—Answers and Insights

1. Pyramid-type hierarchies with numerous layers of management are common in most manufacturing industries. Organizational structures with only a few levels of management are Apple Computer and Intel Corporation.

   The picture based on your perception of your job and of your work group should be simple and include several major activities, depending on whether products or services are produced; self, peers, and supervisor(s), and your relationship to them; and separation of your department or work group from the organization as a whole to show your position relative to all the activities of the organization.

2. **Forces Inside the Organization**

   Positive: expanded product line, improved working conditions, increased learning opportunities.

   Negative: poor communication, low level cooperation, lack of management support. With planning and effort, negative factors can be turned into positive factors.

3. **Forces Outside the Organization.** An "environmental scan" may be used to determine these forces. Strategic planners try to determine risks just over the horizon that must be faced in the next five to ten years, and also evaluate opportunities waiting to be exploited. Strategic thinking precedes strategic planning.

   Positive: increased customer demand, better economic climate for research and development, more stable economy, less government intervention.

   Negative: more foreign competition, raw materials more difficult to obtain, union opposition, unskilled work force to hire from, increased taxes.

   Forces difficult to predict are governmental changes due to shifts in administration philosophies, demographic changes resulting from fluctuating population characteristics, social changes, etc. (Odiorne, 1987). These forces affect organizational stability and growth.

4. If forces can be controlled, work behavior may be modified, for example, to reduce absenteeism and downtime, and improve coordination. Budgets, hiring freezes, limited product line, crowded office space are typical, usually temporary limitations, or negative forces.

   Knowing whether forces are inside or outside the organization facilitates formulating plans to examine variables influencing productivity. Forces outside the organization are often beyond organizational control, and will have the lowest probability of change.

5. Steps to use forces to enhance productivity should have the highest probability of change. If you begin with a possible success, even if it is the least important of the five forces, your chance to succeed is better than if you start with a force of higher priority having a lower probability of change.

   Once a force(s) offering the least resistance to change is determined, for instance cost savings or customer service, a possible sequence of steps could be:

   • Increase awareness of need to change.
   • Obtain and analyze feedback from affected employees.
   • Involve affected employees or groups in making decisions regarding the proposed course of action.
   • Implement suggested courses of action and assess possible resistance and make adjustments or necessary changes.
   • Perform followup and make necessary modifications.

6. **Organizational Goals**

   Short-Term: assess current sales; meet or increase production schedules; establish costs associated with delivery of products and services; determine performance milestones for all work and assign clear responsibility for meeting milestones; troubleshoot problems; motivate employees; decrease turnaround time; monitor quality of output; plan and allocate needed space and equipment at optimal locations; and reduce customer complaints.

   Intermediate: plan for cost savings; forecast needs for capital; improve or develop new methods to deliver goods or services; provide relevant job-related training for employees; construct employee selection programs allowing for timely replacement of skilled personnel through attrition; test out new products or services; emphasize the smooth flow between supplier and customer; and fill in gaps to strengthen the organization.

Long-Term: incorporate cost savings into strategic plans, invest in new technology, expand market, introduce new products, invest in human resources, and develop future long-term organizational policies and structures consistent with anticipated trends and changes. National and international affairs and global economy are also important.

General Comments: The goals of most companies are similar, for example, make profit, expand, develop new products, or services, etc., despite the time allowed to achieve them. Some goals will not be achieved unless time limits are imposed. The major issue is to develop realistic goals that can be achieved. The "hard to set" vs. "hard to keep" issue is always present.

No company can ignore short-term goals. Unless managers know the day-to-day job is under control, they will not have the time, or have established the working relationships with their employees to enable them to be flexible, creative, and make good decisions regarding strategic plans.

At one of the recent meetings of the 200-plus member American Productivity Management Association, the preoccupation was with linking productivity gains to business strategy, and developing coherent, detailed, sophisticated programs to achieve those gains.

Priorities: priority ranks are influenced by company policy, organizational culture, and management philosophy. Priorities change over time. It is important to have realistic priorities within the organization, and adhere to them.

7. **Goals of Work Groups.** These goals will be more personalized, but still relate to the specific functions of the organization, including achievement, cooperation, coordination, and sharing information.

Short-Term: need to be cost-effective, increase production, or increase number of customers/clients.

Intermediate: plan and work with peers and supervisors to ensure quality employees, plan to replace aging facilities and equipment, and be alert to new developments and how to exploit them.

Long-term: consider rapidly-expanding technological advances and the extent of their influence (local, regional, or national), develop ways of incorporating productivity into the strategic plans of the organization. Top management should be ac-

tively involved in developing these plans, and provide wholehearted support for all levels of goals.

Priorities: The major goals and priorities of work groups should be similar. Despite shared group priorities, members should apply their unique talents.

General Comments: The amount of difference between existing goals, and goals as they should be affects plans of action. Achieving a balance between what can be done vs. what should be done, considering cost, time and effort, is a critical issue. Personal factors are always involved in any plan of action. Probability of success is important. Some set goals they know they can achieve. Others want a 50/50 chance of success. Highly motivated, competent people often raise their level of goals after each success.

8. **Personal Goals.** Priorities are an individualized matter. Focus, purpose, and direction are important. However, according to well known authorities on motivation, namely Herzberg, Maslow, McGregor, and McClelland, every peak performing person is an obsessive goal setter.

Career Plans: itemize what you plan to accomplish in a given period of time—update skills, acquire new knowledge, develop your career portfolio or passport (Charner, 1986), and begin your professional development program (Courtney, 1986).

Actual accomplishments, not planned accomplishments, are important at performance appraisal time. Ambitious people who set more goals and/or more difficult goals than they can realistically achieve may be appear less productive than the cautious person who sets fewer easier goals, but achieves them all.

Personal Plans: learn more about self, and how to make better use of skills, as in time management, and setting standards for excellence.

Priorities: Job priorities should be clearly defined. Realistic priorities cannot be set unless people know their jobs. Priorities should be based on adequate information.

Personal priorities change over time, particularly during the climb up the promotional ladder. Priorities set are usually affected by factors over which you have varying degrees of control—economy, opportunities for promotion. . . . Without priorities, it is like going on a life-long car trip without a road map.

9. The greater the difference between goals as they are and as they are expected to be, the more difficult the goals are to achieve. Plan what is right, not necessarily affordable, or even possible. Strive toward the ideal. Most goals take longer to achieve than first expected.

10. Conflict may be a series of events related to working with people, or to achieving important goals. Conflict is easier to resolve when real sources (not symptoms) of conflict are clearly itemized and understood. When initial, common reactions to conflict, namely hostility, frustration, and withdrawal have subsided, logical steps can be taken to reduce or resolve conflict. Constructive conflict motivates and even stimulates creative effort. Destructive conflict is harmful, stress producing, and costly.

    Bain's (1982) seven steps describing setting and achieving goals for productivity improvement are well worth reading.

11. Positive employee characteristics could be similar to your own best characteristics. People project or impose their own images on others, and often prefer to work with those having similar personalities and talents. Most characteristics will be desirable personality traits that allow smooth functioning of the organization, enhance communication, or in general result in pleasant, compatible relationships with peers and supervisors.

    How you rank these characteristics is a personal choice. In some instances, subordinates see their supervisors in quite a different light than supervisors see themselves.

    Occasionally, what might be considered negative personality characteristics, such as stubbornness, or don't-give-up attitude, desire to take risks, and non-conformity or originality, may be blessings in disguise. Such a person may serve as a catalyst, or stimulus for others. Productive managers, regardless of their personality characteristics, usually have an equally productive staff. Productive people have high self-esteem, a strong sense of identity enabling them to know who they are and where they are going, a mature social awareness, an internalized sense of values, and persistence in pursuing a problem to its conclusion (Gilmore, 1974). Desir-

able personality characteristics may also reflect a positive, dynamic organizational culture.

12. If you are a task-oriented person yourself, you will have more task-oriented variables than social-emotional variables. The converse is also true. However, females, because of their longstanding roles focusing on concern about feelings, and personal welfare, are more likely to have more social-emotional than task-oriented variables. However, certain jobs require use of one set of behaviors as opposed to the other set of behaviors. Both are equally important-get the job done, and maintain harmony and a spirit of teamwork (Ninomiya, 1988).

13. Personality characteristics contributing to productivity will be ones that maximize one's performance and the performance of those around him. Most characteristics will relate to efficiency, and facilitate work activities-leadership, supervision, communication, and others.

14. Typical situations in which personality characteristics decrease productivity could be inability to effectively deal with job stress, narrow perspective on accepting change caused by a merger, or withholding information from established communication channels.

15. Time plays various roles in the organization. The passage of time, what happens in time, and what "time" means to different people must be considered. Time often means money. However, short-term, poorly planned, cost-cutting efforts typically decrease employee satisfaction, and may even reduce preventive maintenance and discourage effective utilization of employees or equipment, for instance. Some of the best rewards are simply saving time, like minimizing false starts. Meeting deadlines and not keeping customers waiting are highly valued attributes.

    Cycle time originated in manufacturing industries. White collar cycle time is measured by the number of work actions-in-process, or partly completed tasks, divided by their completion rate (see Chapter 14).

    Competitiveness is largely time-based. Eliminating each task or step not adding value to that task shortens cycle time. Time can be a competitive weapon (see Chapter 18).

3

Analyzing Input, Throughput, and Output Variables: A Systems Approach

PURPOSE

- Examine how technology affects productivity.
- Illustrate the way input, throughput, and output affect human and organizational activities.
- Use a systems approach to identify problems.

INTRODUCTION

Systems approaches are one way to describe and place factors influencing personal and organizational behavior in perspective because they examine the relationships between people, jobs, departments, even disciplines. This information can be used to develop an orderly approach to allocate resources, make decisions, or study alternative courses of action, for example.

Systems approaches are popular in many areas—business, engineering, computer science, medicine, education, transportation—but regardless of the area, the major variables are input, throughput, output, and feedback.

Input Variables (also called causal variables) include human/organizational efforts and financial/material resources. These variables are the major determinants of human and organizational behavior, and are often considered the key to improving productivity. They are relatively easy to identify and measure.

Individual Variables—aptitudes, intelligence, attitude, experience, skills, managerial style, values, philosophy.

Organizational Variables—raw materials, capital, equipment, type of structure (formal or informal), purpose, goals, tasks, advertising.

Throughput Variables (also called intervening or process variables) provide information on the feelings and behavior of people, and on the internal state of organizations. Throughput is hard to identify and difficult to measure. Therefore, it is seldom considered a valuable source of information on productivity.

These variables are in a transformational stage, are not readily observed or measured, and are somewhat difficult

28

to identify. The presence of these variables is often inferred from output.

Individual Variables—motivation, perception, trust, expectations, communication, decision making, coaching, counseling, understanding.

Organizational Variables—culture, climate, cooperation.

Output Variables (also called end result variables) are used almost exclusively as major indicators or measures of productivity. They provide after-the-fact information on personal and organizational achievement. Output can rarely be changed unless input is changed.

These variables are readily observed and measured. They are usually reported in numeric terms: financial accomplishments, quantity produced, or number of services provided. Output variables may reveal problems when it is too late to take corrective action.

Individual Variables—sales, customer contacts, customer loyalty, absenteeism, compensation, ideas, patents completed, projects, services provided.

Organizational Variables—return on investment, monetary reserves, level of financial reserves, amount of market share, quality and quantity of products and services, loss from scrap and waste.

The *feedback process* recycles information from input, throughput, and output back into various parts of the system. Generally, modifications or improvements in input usually improve throughput and output.

Successful paths to productivity improvement balance a pure technological and a pure systems approach. This composite approach incorporates a commitment to greater involvement of human resources. Application of technology challenges the organization to consider its own potential for improved effectiveness and efficiency (Heijn, 1982).

The real issue is to understand the potential technology has for affecting personal and organizational variables associated with productivity improvement.

TECHNOLOGY

Technology is the science or study of the practical. Specifically, technology refers to processes or methods that transform inputs into outputs. Technology, a key strategic resource, can be developed in-house, or purchased. The "make or buy" decision depends on need, cost, and availability (Abetti, 1989).

There are two main uses of technology: (1) improve previous technologies, for example the progressive innovation in computer design and miniaturization of computer chips; and (2) as a source of new directions or uses growing out of technology itself, as in gravity-free manufacturing processes in space labs. However, technology has no real value unless it is applied, as in creating wealth or improving the quality of life (Abetti, 1989).

As a tool, technology has positive and negative effects. It may improve the way we think and work. For instance, computers play a unique, pivotal role in developing new processes in manufacturing, materials processing, and information dissemination, retrieval, and storage. From the negative side, adopting and keeping up with technological innovations is expensive in terms of initial outlay for equipment and systems. Disruption of work flow and lost effort due to personal and organizational resistance to change are also costly. The continual need for employee (re)training is costly in terms of outlay. Also, coming up to speed always takes longer than most expect. The large "front end" investment in people, training, software, and equipment usually extends the payout period. Many technologies have limited life, as they will be replaced by new and improved technologies. Technology both aids and hinders achievement.

Rapid technological changes force continuous monitoring of major organizational assets: capital, time, energy, employees, resources, inventory, facilities, etc. Ever-widening technological gaps occur when technological advances occur faster than they are assimilated. Realistic goal setting, a responsive, enlightened management, and a well trained work force help narrow the gap. How well technological advances are understood and applied depends not so much on budget, but on people's acceptance of change. People will be the measure by which our machines will be judged. This is exactly opposite to the way it was in the Industrial Revolution (Bleecker, 1987). See box on next page.

SYSTEMS APPROACHES

Systems approaches are used to develop a framework tying all disciplines or separate parts of the system or organization into an understandable, cohesive whole. A system is a group of components designed to accomplish a particular organization's objective according to a plan.

Systems approaches are perceived as theory, philosophy, management, and analysis. This book emphasizes management and analysis rather than theory and philosophy.

Knowles (1985) states that thinking in terms of wholes or systems is a necessity in an increasingly complex world. Something more comprehensive than the traditional, linear, fragmental approach to planning, problem solving, managing, and evaluating is required.

Figure 3-1 is a typical input-output model of a basic system. Each input is allocated according to a specific operational plan to produce desired output. Inputs of information, energy, and materials are transformed by people and/or machines into products, ideas, or services.

1. List major technologies or technological innovations in your organization. Rank 1 (low) to 7 (high) the relative importance of each technological innovation. Indicate whether each innovation is positive or negative, and estimate the relative cost to adopt/not adopt each innovation.

Technological Innovations: To Adopt or Not

Major Technologies or Technological Innovations	Rank (1 to 7)	+ or − Influence	Relative Cost to Adopt/Not Adopt, $
_____	_____	_____	_____
_____	_____	_____	_____
_____	_____	_____	_____
_____	_____	_____	_____
_____	_____	_____	_____
_____	_____	_____	_____

2. List three technologies or technological innovations that have a positive effect on productivity.

3. List three technologies or technological innovations that have a negative effect on productivity.

The transformation process, also known as what happens in the "black box," is not well understood.

Productivity problems can often be traced to the transformational processes involving people and machines. The potential contribution of the human element of the transformation process to productivity is enormous.

Organizational problems cannot be diagnosed unless one understands the way separate parts of the system function. Knowing how well each part within the organization or system adapts is vital. The organization is in a constant state of change, and internal changes in any part of the system affect other parts of the system.

Using Figure 3-1, for example, if the amount of information increases, existing personnel and machines work faster or more efficiently to produce either more or better ideas. The whole system changes when separate parts change and adapt to the environment. Systems, or organizations, strive to achieve and maintain balance.

Figure 3-2 presents an overall view of the systems approach. Management, applications, and ways to organize resources represent a small part of the whole. Philosophy, theory, and analysis are also vital parts.

Figure 3-3 shows various forms of input, throughput, and output.

Figure 3-4 illustrates the determinants of organizational behavior (input), emergent influences and processes (throughput), and results of organizational behavior (output). Feedback occurs at the input, throughput, and output levels, and is used for measurement and correction. See box on page 32. *(text continued on page 34)*

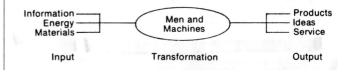

Figure 3-1. Input-output model of a basic system. (From Johnson et al., 1976.)

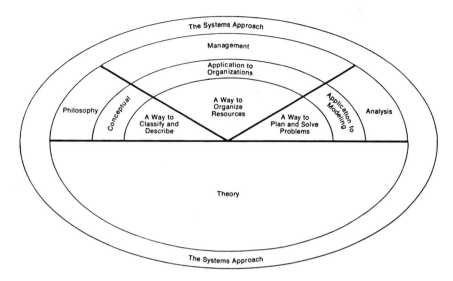

Figure 3-2. The systems approach. (From Johnson et al., 1976.)

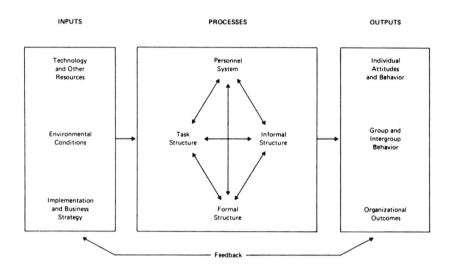

Figure 3-3. An open systems framework of technological change. (From Majchrzak and Klein, 1987.)

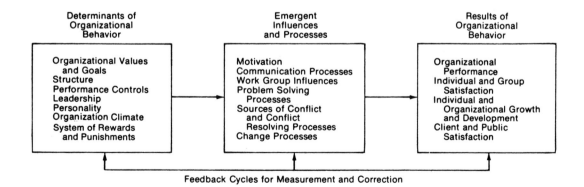

Figure 3-4. Behavioral subsystem of an organization. (From Johnson et al., 1976.)

4. List several typical input, throughput, and output variables affecting technology, the organization, and people.

Input-Throughput-Output Analysis

Concepts Evaluated

Type of Variable	Technology	Organization	People
Input			
Throughput			
Output			

Use the concepts input, throughput, or output to answer the following six questions.

5. Variable(s) measured most frequently _____.
   Why?

   Examples:

6. Variable(s) easiest to measure _____.
   Why?

7. Variable(s) hardest to measure _____.
   Why?

8. Variable(s) currently considered to provide most of the data on productivity are _____.
   Why?

   Examples:

9. Do input, throughput, or output variables have the most potential to influence productivity?

   Why?

10. Classify the following 25 activities as: (input—I, throughput—T, or output—O). Rank (1 is low, 7 is high) the amount you believe each activity influences productivity:

Concept	Variable	Rank of Influence to Productivity
1. Attitude	I/T/O	
2. Leadership	I	
3. Values	I	
4. Coordination	I	
5. Standards	I	
6. Equipment	I	7
7. Trust	I	
8. Motivation	I/T/O	
9. Quantity	O	
10. Group decision making	I/T	
11. Thinking	I/T	
12. Trained employees	I	7
13. Cooperation	I	
14. Performance goals	I	
15. Conflict	I/T/O	
16. Revising	I/T/O	
17. Time	I	
18. Motivation	I	
19. Absence rate	O	
20. Stress	I/T/O	
21. Equipment downtime	O	
22. Organizational structure	I	
23. Processing	T	
24. Quality control	I	
25. Defect prevention	I	

Barnard (1938), president of Jersey Bell Telephone, was one of the first to interpret management in terms of systems. Systems and subsystems of all sizes and descriptions strive to achieve a steady state, or equilibrium. To illustrate, change in one subsystem (marketing) brings about change in other subsystems (sales and customer service). For example, downsizing or restructuring one or more subsystems can throw the whole system off balance.

Feedback joins all parts of the system together. Tapping into feedback links helps determine what is going on in the system. No system, process, or person can function well without feedback. The conceptual tool, "reverse scenario building," enables users to gradually move backwards step-by-step and trace the solution back to the problem. Feedback plays a vital role in each step.

Technology plays a major role in connecting numerous systems together. Basically, technology redefines the speed of change. The amount of traffic on the "information super highway," for instance, will steadily increase over time. In manufacturing, technological advances can offset the the rising costs of scarce resources, or ideally produce more output with smaller input of capital, resources, and labor. A major concern is that unless managers appreciate, understand, and become part of technology, they will be unable to keep pace with the new demands of competition (Jaikumar, 1991).

REFERENCES

1. Abetti, Pier A. "Technology: A Key Strategic Resource," *Management Review*, February 1989, pp. 37–41.

2. Barnard, Chester I. *The Functions of the Executive,* Cambridge, Massachusetts: Harvard University Press, 1938.

3. Bleecker, Samuel E. Personal communication. July 28, 1987.

4. Heijn, Herman J. "Automate the Organization . . . or Organize the Automation?" American Productivity Center, Productivity Brief #14, June 1982.

5. Jaikumar, Jay. "The Boundaries of Business: The Impact of Technology," *Harvard Business Review,* September–October, 1991, pp. 100–101.

6. Johnson, Richard A., Monsen, R. Joseph, Knowles, Henry P. and Saxberg, Borje O. *Management, Systems, and Society: An Introduction,* California: Pacific Palisades, Goodyear Publishing Company, Inc., 1976.

7. Knowles, Malcolm S. "Shifting to a HRD Systems Approach," *Training and Development Journal,* May 1985, pp. 24–25.

8. Majchrzak, Ann and Klein, Katherine J. "Things are Always More Complicated Than You Think: An Open Systems Approach to the Organizational Effects of Computer-Automated Technology," *Journal of Business and Psychology,* Fall 1987, pp. 27–49.

Ideas to Remember

Chapter 3—Answers and Insights

1. Major technological innovations: perform the job faster (computers); streamline assembly line (robots); handling information or information technology; and quality control (optical scanners). In technologically intensive industries, some technologies have limited life. Speed, one measure of efficiency, not effectiveness, is not necessarily a factor in productivity improvement.

   More information, or faster communication may confuse or obscure the real issues. Extra time required to read, assimilate, and react to "excess" information may be uneconomic. Reducing lead time, or getting you closer to customers, or potential customers, for example, is obviously positive. To adopt/not adopt depends on upper management's acceptance, understanding, and wholehearted support. Cost to adopt the "right" technologies is often a major factor. But, can you afford not to adopt them?

2. Technologies having a positive influence on productivity relate to quality control, improving efficiency, or increasing return on investment. But, achieving stated goals and impacting management practices in a positive way are extremely important.

3. Activities negatively affecting productivity: poor employee attitudes; low level quality control; ineffective use of human and material resources; downtime; absenteeism; inadequate on-the-job training; or general inefficiencies.

4. Input-Throughput-Output Analysis. See table below.

5. Output variables are measured most frequently because of ease of measurement and tradition. Quality of goods produced or services provided, number of sales, profit, and cost savings are prime variables.

6. Output variables are currently the main way to represent and assess productivity. Output is easily observed and standards, ratios and formulas currently exist.

7. Throughput variables are hardest to measure because they are difficult to observe. Their presence is inferred from behavior, e.g., motivation, creativity, frustration, stress, thinking, loyalty, and understanding. Throughput variables, like motivation or coordination, can be independent variables. When they change, they cause dependent variables, such as work accomplished, to change.

8. Output, or end-result variables, provide most of the productivity data. Long-standing concern with being able to see output and "measurability" makes them logical, not necessarily valid, reliable candidates. Examples: return on investment, quantity and quality of output in general.

Concepts Evaluated

Type of Variable	Technology	Organization	People
Input	Optical scanners Robots Cellular phones	Capital Culture Materials	Ideas Goals Effort
Throughput	Reasoning Coordination Confusion	Communication Cooperation Stability	Loyalty Motivation Innovation
Output	New product or service Competitive product Satisfied customers	Tasks completed Profit Reputation	Sales per person Cost reductions Turnover

9. Input, or causal variables have the greatest potential to influence productivity. They can be changed by management and the organization. For example, changes in managerial style can produce changes in employee behavior.

Greater emphasis should be placed on input variables. Obviously, what is ultimately produced is primarily controlled by input. Input—effort, quality of human and material resources, planning, budgets, constraints, and other related variables—have a dramatic impact on the way throughput variables and output variables interact. Also, if the nature and quantity of input variables is known, e.g., example, number and expertise of people working on a project, equipment necessary, and budgets required, efforts can be streamlined to maximize results. More productivity measurement and improvement efforts should include a thorough analysis of input or causal variables.

Throughput variables also affect productivity in subtle, important ways. Employee attitudes, beliefs, cooperation, and communication, cause dramatic changes in quality and amount of output.

Output produced and methods used to achieve that output can be evaluated, and results incorporated into the feedback and evaluation process. Then, appropriate changes can be made in the input process. Feedback loops connect output back to input. The cycle is endless.

Writing operational definitions helps clarify meanings. Concepts can be defined according to how they are used. See Chapter 8.

10. See table below.

Concept	Variable	Rank of Influence to Productivity
1. Attitude	I/T/O	_____
2. Leadership	I	_____
3. Values	I	_____
4. Coordination	T	_____
5. Standards*	I	_____
6. Equipment	I	_____
7. Trust	T	_____
8. Intervention	I/T/O	_____
9. Quantity*	O	_____
10. Group decision making	I/T	_____
11. Thinking	I/T	_____
12. Trained employees	I	_____
13. Cooperation	T	_____
14. Performance goals*	I	_____
15. Conflict	I/T/O	_____
16. Revising	I/T/O	_____
17. Time*	I	_____
18. Motivation	T	_____
19. Absence rate*	O	_____
20. Stress	I/T/O	_____
21. Equipment downtime	O	_____
22. Organizational structure	I	_____
23. Processing	T	_____
24. Quality control	I	_____
25. Defect prevention	I	_____

*These factors are also indicators of productivity.

No rankings are provided because of the influence of job demands and employees' special characteristics. You may refer to your ranks at a later time.

4

Analyzing Productivity Problems: Real Problems vs. Symptoms

PURPOSE

- Determine whether problems assumed to be related to productivity are "real," or are symptoms of deeper, more complex problems.
- Establish priorities to deal with productivity problems.

INTRODUCTION

At home and on the job, we often react to symptoms and fail to look for the real causes of problems. Many personal and job-related problems may be seen and treated as symptoms, not real problems. Productivity problems are no different. Determining the source of problems requires skill. Whether we are in the doctor's office or busy at work, the ability to separate symptoms from problems and to see things as they really are, is very important.

Causes of problems can be anywhere within or outside the organization. Team efforts may be needed to identify and resolve these problems.

"FACT VS. FICTION"

It is hard to separate "fact" from "fiction," or real problems from symptoms when dealing with people and their jobs. Symptoms are obvious, and can be described. We can usually assess the severity of a symptom by how much it affects work efficiency, speed, or quality. For instance, symptoms of the common cold decrease one's efficiency. Similarly, productivity is decreased by the symptoms of absenteeism, deliberately slowing work pace, poor attitude, and many other factors. These reactions are symptoms that something deeper is wrong.

Essentially, any events or circumstances decreasing performance level, or overall accomplishment could be labeled "productivity problems." This is why it is vital to determine the exact source of what are initially considered "symptoms" or "problems."

Causes may be outside the organization. For instance, a supplier may occasionally substitute "seconds," which unpredictably lower product quality. Or, a poorly trained "front desk" person may offend customers. Also, long-standing differences may exist between labor and management. Others examples include people who look busy, but achieve little that is constructive; and those who rush through projects but make many errors. The list is endless.

Look past the activities to actions, to results, namely finishing a job or achieving a specific goal. (See Chapter 2, Questions 6, 7, and 8 on goal setting. Chapter 15 provides an opportunity to use key result areas, such as measures of quality, service, or sales.)

Entry-level people have hundreds of ideas about ways to improve or change their jobs and the way work is performed. Companies such as IBM, Four Seasons, etc., make use of this approach, and it is paying great dividends. See box on page 39.

IDENTIFYING AND SOLVING PROBLEMS

Physicians use symptoms (pain, fever, etc.) to make their diagnoses. They reason that fever, for example, has a specific cause. The physician's sequence—blood sample, analysis, diagnosis, and prescribe antibiotic. The best antibiotic is prescribed based on test results. However, if patients do not take the medication, symptoms may remain, and possibly worsen. Accurately identifying a problem is the foundation of a good medical diagnosis. It is also an

aspect of good business. When identifying root-cause problems, not symptoms, one should:

1. Approach the problem in a systematic way, knowing there is an answer.
2. Avoid negatives. Consider ''problems'' as challenges or opportunities.
3. Ensure that concerned parties agree on what the ''challenge'' actually is. This is a good way to separate challenges from symptoms.
4. Determine all possible causes, and write them down.
5. Identify all solutions without evaluation or prejudice. Consider what is right, not necessarily affordable or possible. Assign priorities to solutions.
6. Focus on solutions and how to achieve them.
7. Assign those who handle the solution, or work in the area of concern with the responsibility of implementing it. Concerns could be time, cost or quality.
8. Set deadlines for obtaining solutions and for making decisions. Stick to the deadlines.

Any method of problem solving that has worked in the past can be used. For instance, in brainstorming, a group of five to ten people give many solutions in a short period of time. Ideas that come early may be too obvious. Perhaps

1. List six critical productivity problems. Do these problems occur only within your department, or work group, or throughout the whole organization? Do people or events outside the organization cause problems?

Productivity Problem	Possible Cause	Occur in My Group	Occur Outside My Group
___	___	___	___
___	___	___	___
___	___	___	___
___	___	___	___
___	___	___	___
___	___	___	___

2. Examine each problem above. Write **R** for real and **S** for symptoms. Example symptoms and problems are presented below.

Example 1. Frequent headaches may be a symptom of eyestrain. But, headaches may be stress-related. Taking aspirin is not the solution. Determining the cause of the headaches and reducing tension on the job is one answer.

Example 2. Dick uses up every hour of sick leave as soon as it is accumulated. Dick's boss assumes he is sick. The real problem is that Dick is not challenged by the routine job he has performed for five years. Dick wants to be transferred, or be retrained so he can be eligible for promotion to a higher-level job.

3. From #1, above, select three real productivity problems, beginning with the most important one. Indicate if these problems involve people (employees, customers, suppliers, etc.). Write down how you would solve each problem.

Real Productivity Problems: Who is Involved and How to Solve the Problems

Real Productivity Problem	Involve People (Y/N)	How to Solve Problems
_____	_____	_____
		_____
		_____
		_____
_____	_____	_____
		_____
		_____
		_____
		_____
_____	_____	_____
		_____
		_____
		_____

Put an * by the steps that may be difficult to handle. Your whole program of study or review may revolve around this particular question.

4. Could you have anticipated any of the problems listed in #2, above? If so, list the most critical real problem, from question #3, above. What factors do you routinely look for? If you did not anticipate the problems, or they were beyond your control, write down factors that are important in prevention. Estimate the savings in time and cost that could result.

Applying Preventive Management Skills to Problems of _____

Important Factors in Preventive or Proactive Management	Hours of Time Saved	$ Saved
_____	_____	_____
_____	_____	_____
_____	_____	_____
_____	_____	_____

the 20th idea is one based on considerable thought, and/or incorporates many of the previous ideas. Regardless of how the solutions are generated, the major goal is to obtain useful, practical solutions. Three examples are presented.

Example 1: An exciting new group or team approach to decision making is virtually interactive brainstorming (VIBS). This method is used when it is not practical for team members to meet regularly, but are connected via electronic mail technology.

The first three steps of VIBS are the same as for brainstorming (Osborn, 1941), the Delphi method (Dalkey, 1969) and nominal group technique (Van de Ven and Delbecq, 1974 and Van de Ven, 1974).

Steps are:

1. Define the problem in clear, unambiguous terms. Verify who has the decision-making authority.
2. Communicate the problem to management and to those making the decision. Get their support.
3. Clearly define the scope of the problem in writing and specify the resources needed. Have the project leader sign the document. Include a schedule, milestone chart, and an estimate of time team members should devote to the project. Itemize resources like funds, data, and equipment.
4. Arrange for a temporary electronic mailbox that all team members and the project leader can access. Use the same identification so all communications are anonymous. Teams will have read-and-write privileges and project leaders/facilitators will have delete or erase privileges.
5. Communicate the basics of the project to team leaders. Include a problem statement, historical information, and standard operating procedures for using the mailbox.
6. A sequence to solve problems: (a) collect and group ideas, (b) copy them into the mailbox with balloting instructions, (c) assign weights to each idea, and (d) copy the highest weighted ideas back into the mailbox for the next ballot. Repeat this four-step process until about 75–80% of the members reach consensus. Document the results (Walker, 1994).

Example 2: Cause-and-effect or fishbone diagrams, obviously look like a fishbone. The causes of problems are listed on the bones growing out of the spine. The problem is defined at the ''head.'' This diagram shows how various separate root causes of problems or barriers (not symptoms) might interact, or how possible problem causes relate to one another.

Problems may be traced back to the beginning of the process. There may be many unidentified problems, like poor scheduling, or defective materials.

Team members and senior managers should be involved in all phases of this sequential process. Thomas, Gallace and Martin (1992) present methods to identify, prioritize, and rule out symptomatic barriers and root causes.

Example 3: An increasing number of companies ''empower'' their employees to use their own best judgment to solve problems. Empowerment, which grew out of the social movements of the 1960s and 1970s, is being rediscovered and applied. Companies like the department store, Nordstrom, stand behind their employees' decisions. When properly implemented, empowerment enables and encourages employees to take control over significant aspects of their work and solve problems in a realistic, constructive manner.

REFERENCES

1. Dalkey, N. C. *The Delphi Method: An Experimental Study of Group Opinions,* Santa Monica, California: Rand Corporation, 1969.
2. Osborn, Alex F. *Applied Imagination: Principles and Procedures of Creative Thinking,* New York: Charles Scribner's Sons, 1941.
3. Preziosi, Robert C. ''Perceptions of Roadblocks and Change Management Strategies During Implementation of Organizational Productivity Improvement Projects,'' *Productivity & Quality Management Frontiers-IV,* Vol. 2, edited by Sumanth, Edosomwan, Poupart, and Sink. Norcross, Georgia: Industrial Engineering and Management Press, 1993, pp. 1056–1063.
4. Thomas, Philip R., Gallace, Larry J. and Martin, Kenneth R. *Quality Alone is Not Enough,* New York: American Management Association, 1992.
5. Van de Ven, Andrew H. *Group Decision Making and Effectiveness: An Experimental Study,* Kent, Ohio: Kent State University Press, 1974.
6. Van de Ven, Andrew H. and Delbecq, A. L. ''The Effectiveness of Nominal and Delphi Techniques and Interacting Group Decision Making Processes,'' *Academy of Management Journal,* Vol. 17, 1974, pp. 605–621.
7. Walker, Robert G. ''Virtually Interactive Brainstorming,'' *Industrial Engineering,* September 1994, pp. 20–21.

Chapter 4—Answers and Insights

1. Most productivity problems relate to dealing with day-to-day problems of getting the routine work out: meeting deadlines; making decisions; staying within budgets; keeping up with telephone calls and the flow of paperwork; contacting customers; and keeping customers satisfied. Therefore, improvement efforts directed to what are usually felt to be the routine, daily activities performed by most employees are logical starting places.

   People are often the major sources of problems. Pareto (1848–1923), an Italian economist and mathematician, developed the "Law of Disproportionate Distribution." This law was based on the finding that 80% of Italy's wealth was owned by 20% of the population. This 80/20 proportion is often applied to areas other than economics. Examples: 20% of the employees cause 80% of the problems; managers use 80% of their time to ensure that 20% of the workforce responds to productivity improvement efforts. Machines can be controlled, repaired, and replaced when out-of-date. Humans cannot.

   Possible causes of productivity problems may be classified into general categories:

   • Failure of the workforce (including management) to set goals and/or priorities, and to understand and implement them.
   • Inadequate training and/or experience to perform the job at an acceptable level or standard.
   • Managements' failure to adequately motivate employees through individualized methods, such as praise or recognition for special effort, matching pay with performance, providing opportunity for professional growth and development in areas of expertise.
   • Lack of immediate, constructive feedback on performance.
   • Emphasis on short-term, short-sighted, cost-cutting efforts to look good temporarily, while sacrificing quality, employee morale, and long-term accomplishments.

   Whether any of the problems occur in your group is open to question. You may recognize the same problems in "other" groups, yet fail to recognize or accept them in your own group. Be aware of this common bias.

   Or, problems that are out of your control may need to be addressed some other way—a team effort, a higher-level contact from your own company, or a sharing of the problems with those who caused the problems or who know more about the possible causes than you do.

2. Only you will know whether the problems are real or represent symptoms. The main point is to critically examine the cause of each problem. If people do not acknowledge problems exist, or downplay them, refer to these difficult areas as "opportunities" or "challenges." This reduces or eliminates a negative approach.

3. Most problems involve people. Machine-related or technical problems are often easier to solve, and probably cost less in terms of time, effort, and money, than solving "people problems." Problem resolution should be a joint effort—people causing the problems should know they are exhibiting non-productive behavior. Ask "offenders" how to solve the problems, as they will have good answers. They are worried about the problems, too. The fact that you are concerned is a major step in the right direction.

   Solving problems requires following a logical series of steps with those causing the problems:

   1. Jointly identify problems.
   2. Work together to develop alternative solutions.
   3. Consider and implement the best alternative(s) to solve problems.
   4. Jointly evaluate your solutions.
   5. Modify solutions accordingly, and look back at the original problem identified in Step 1. See how effective you and your employees were at solving the problem. It may be necessary to modify procedures and go through the whole process again.

4. If you are not a proactive thinker, and don't do preventive maintenance (on cars), or preventive management by anticipating problems (on the job), you could be in the majority. Unfortunately, it takes about six times longer to correct an error than to do it right the first time.

Preventive management is proactive management. Planning ahead and anticipating possible problems saves time, effort, and reduces costly errors. This means: (1) have a feel for what has happened in the past, (2) anticipate what may happen, and (3) have strategies or plans ready to solve problems when they occur. Remember the old proverb, "An ounce of prevention is worth a pound of cure."

If productivity improvement efforts are to be successful, it is vital to identify the organizational barriers and have the capability to overcome these barriers. Preziosi's (1993) discusses perceptions of roadblocks and change management strategies that can be used to enhance the success of productivity improvement projects. Identifying roadblocks in advance and selecting corresponding ways to maximize success of change efforts illustrates proactive management.

However, skill in anticipating problems will grow as you become more aware of productivity problems and learn more about your employees' unique talents, needs, attitudes, and work behavior. Anticipating what may happen requires special effort. You will soon begin to learn what kinds of situations are most likely to produce problems. Knowing employees' stress levels, for example, will allow you to make good predictions or better guesses about who can't meet deadlines, or who works well under pressure.

The largest savings of time and cost will come from proper planning, which includes setting goals (Chapter 2) and establishing day-to-day priorities for the most frequently performed activities. History repeats itself, and so do problems. An old proverb states that if your only tool is a hammer, you tend to see every problem as a nail.

Ideas to Remember

5

Evaluating Status Quo Productivity Measures

PURPOSE

- Determine major job-related activities and analyze how each contributes to goal achievement.
- Examine usage, value, and estimated level of accuracy of existing productivity measures and relevance of current measurement systems.
- Consider ways to implement existing productivity measuring systems.

INTRODUCTION

Methods used to measure productivity based on primary job activities usually yield meaningful results. Although such repetitive activities are intrinsic to the job, are they being performed productively, i.e., efficiently and effectively?

Measuring productivity is an art and a science having the major variables of time, energy, cost, personal and organizational receptivity. How often measures are used, how much they contribute, estimated level of accuracy, approximate cost, time to implement them, and receptiveness of supervisors and subordinates provide a broad data base for further action. At the very least, measurement efforts focus awareness on the need to develop better measures, or on the need to measure in the first place.

Measurement is only one way to examine and document productivity. The mere act of measuring is not enough.

Concepts and methods used to measure numerous job-related factors can be applied to productivity measurement. Using operational definitions and understanding the basics of measurement (both Chapter 8), and setting standards (Chapter 9) are basic to measuring productivity.

EVALUATE WHAT YOU HAVE AND/OR DESIGN NEW MEASURES

The concept of standards was introduced in Chapter 1. As our "yardstick," it will appear in many forms throughout this book. Standards are used to evaluate people, processes, products, and events in our own lives. People develop their own standards and believe in their own systems, but many have difficulty explaining their systems to others.

The standards of "above average," "average," or "below average" are familiar. However, each has many meanings. Without some type of standards that people understand, it is difficult to document activities. Measurement can be an illusive process. Therefore, methods for measuring employees' productivity and judging the quality of products and services may be undocumented. However, faith in existing systems does not mean they are adequate, and an adequate system is necessary. So, it is important to "take stock" periodically of your own productivity measurement methods.

Productivity Measurement Inventory

A productivity measurement inventory can be a detailed listing of past and present measurement methods, complete with results and recommendations, but in this chapter, it is simply a list of important productivity elements—performance appraisals, various records of individual and group achievement, gainsharing, profit sharing, or meeting quotas or goals on a consistent basis. Additional sources of information are goals, budgets, mission statements, etc.

Inventories can include tangible and intangible factors and have financial overtones. Here, however, tangible means obvious, and intangible means "less than obvious." Both types should be included in the inventory.

Reviewing and evaluating factors or items for the inventory are themselves learning experiences. For instance, thinking through what exists, and what has been done makes it easier to evaluate the worth of what has been measured, and the reasons for measuring. Often this is a positive, encouraging step. It definitely raises awareness. We usually have more resources than we first think we do.

Developing an inventory also raises awareness. It encourages a second look at goals and accomplishments. Measurement systems are often built into goals, or vice versa. How else would goal achievement be realistically determined?

"Reinventing the wheel" is pointless if perfectly acceptable productivity assessment techniques already exist. But, making the wheel run smoother, faster, or even connecting it to other wheels does increase productivity.

Answers to questions presented in this section are the first steps in the inventory process.

Keeping an inventory may be listed in your "Ideas to Remember" section. It may even appear again in Chapter 18, "Practical Applications."

Designing New Measures

It is seldom feasible or realistic to measure all personal and organizational efforts. Deciding which ones contribute the most to productivity takes effort. How do we know which activities to measure? Precedent and creating new methods are the major ways.

Precedent. It is easier to copy what has been done previously than to change. One approach is to use what worked for others. In jobs that share common content, using existing methods is a beginning point. Frequently, existing methods can be specifically adapted for your own purpose. Although no two people, jobs, or organizations are exactly alike, certain similarities do exist.

Creating New Methods. Resistance to change and inertia ingrained in the organization may have to be overcome. Although new measures are hard to construct, researching new areas and working with supervisors and peers to develop new assessment systems is a good learning experience. Efforts directed to creating new measurement methods increase awareness of the need for measurement in general, and create an opportunity for employee involvement. Creating new methods is a major focus of the rest of this book.

Any new method must have a team orientation. Training, counseling, coaching, or mentoring teams is very different from traditional supervision of "subordinates." Developing measures for team performance and linking reward programs to overall business strategy are very challenging endeavors.

Time devoted to training, either as a team member or team leader, may initially hinder day-to-day work output. However, people learn from each other, as in one-to-one teaching and mentoring. Cross-training, which enables people to do each other's jobs, builds versatile teams. Individuals and teams become more valuable the longer they work together.

Team members are good judges of each other's abilities. However, unless the work climate is based on honesty, openness, and trust, very little information will be shared with supervisors or with team members.

Team results may be downplayed and individual efforts emphasized. Putting group goals above individual goals often requires a complete change in thinking and managing. "Lone rangers" who do not want to work with others find it hard to adjust to teamwork.

A longstanding problem is to determine equitable individual pay for group performance, for example gainsharing. (See Chapter 15 and Major Keys to Improving Productivity, Chapter 19). Team-based compensation, variable pay, skill-based pay, and other innovative compensation programs can be used for various teams and industries.

How long will team concepts last? Schrage (1995) predicts the next step after "teamwork" will be collaboration, a relationship amplifying peoples' individual talents and training.

The following questions will help you gather information for your productivity inventory, and stimulate you to improve existing methods, or develop new ones. Answers to these questions can be used to answer various job-related questions in Chapter 11. See box on following page.

REFERENCE

1. Scharge, Michael. *No More Teams,* New York: Currency/Doubleday, 1995.

1. List major, constructive activities you perform during the course of the day . . . month. Rank difficulty level (1 is low . . . 7 is high) of each activity. Indicate the approximate percent of time spent in each activity and its contribution to organizational goals. If productivity measures exist for these activities, record the percentage of time each measure is used.

Assessment of Job-Related Activities

Major Activities Performed on the Job	Level of Difficulty (1 . . . 7)	% Time Spent in Activity	% Contribution to Goals	% Use of Measure
_____	_____	_____	_____	_____
_____	_____	_____	_____	_____
_____	_____	_____	_____	_____
_____	_____	_____	_____	_____
Average _____	Total _____	Total _____	Total _____	

2. List methods to measure productivity used in your organization. Indicate how often each is used. Estimate the percentage each measure contributes to productivity data, and the percentage of time methods are "accurate."

Productivity Measurement: Usage, Contribution, and "Accuracy"*

Method of Measuring Productivity	How Often Used (%)	Estimated % Contributed to Productivity Data	Estimated % of Time "Accurate"
_____	_____	_____	_____
_____	_____	_____	_____
_____	_____	_____	_____
_____	_____	_____	_____
_____	_____	_____	_____
_____	_____	_____	_____

*"Accuracy" is approximate, but will include reliability and validity (Chapter 8).

3. Select one method from #2. The method of measuring productivity is_____. Write down steps that have been taken, or should be taken, to implement this method. Indicate the approximate cost, and the time to implement each step. Rank estimated levels of employee and supervisor receptivity on a scale ranging from 1 (low) to 7 (high).

(continued on next page)

Implementing Productivity Measurement—Part I

Sequence of Steps	$	Time to Implement	Rank of Employees	Receptivity By Supervisors

4. Did you experience problems in #3, above? If so, explain how you would remedy these problems.

5. Select a second method from #2, above. The method of measuring productivity is_____.
Write down steps that have been taken, or should be taken, to implement this method. Indicate the approximate cost and the time to implement each step. Rank estimated levels of employee and supervisor(s) receptivity on a scale ranging from 1 (low) to 7 (high).

Implementing Productivity Measurement—Part II

Sequence of Steps	$	Time to Implement	Rank of Employees	Receptivity by Supervisors

6. Did you have any problems in #5, above? If so, explain how you would remedy these problems.

7. Examine both methods and determine how they are the same and how they are different. Which is the better method? Why? Explain how methods could be improved or changed.

8. Has the growth of teams and your involvement in teams changed the way you measure and improve productivity?

Ideas to Remember

Chapter 5—Answers and Insights

1. Major job-related activities, difficulty level, and time spent in each activity differ in product-based and service-based industries. In productivity-based businesses, focus should be on quality, quantity, facilitating efforts, and maximizing use of time, effort, resources, and capital. In service-based industries, activities emphasize customer orientation, repeat business, and market expansion.

   All levels of difficulty are expected for each job. If too much time is spent in "easy" jobs, you may feel unproductive and unfulfilled. Also, such tasks could be delegated, provided they get done.

   You may/may not feel you contribute much to organizational goals. Possible reasons for low contribution: unclear picture of goals: your position is one of support, so no direct contribution is possible; or you underestimate your worth.

   In general, the highest percentage of use of each productivity measure should correspond to major activities, time spent, and contribution to goals, Or, usage should be directly related to difficulty level, time, and contribution to goals. Check to see if methods used most frequently are also ones that contribute the most to productivity data, and have the highest estimated level of accuracy.

2. Ways to measure productivity in your organization should include a balance of quantitative and qualitative techniques.

   Common measures used on a continuous basis include performance appraisals—quantity and quality of output, comparing both with a specific, accepted standard, and other measures of efficiency and effectiveness.

   Others could be financial indicators, return on investment, sales, profit, absenteeism, employee turnover, waste or scrap, satisfied employees or customers, customer goodwill, and employee loyalty.

   If methods used add little to productivity data, either you are looking in the wrong place, or using inappropriate measuring techniques. Productivity goes beyond what is observed. It can become a way of life and become a part of the organization's culture, like "Think ZD," (Zero Defects). How people communicate with each other, share infor-

mation, and accept and understand their specific roles in the organization are important.

The estimated percentage contributed to productivity data varies between and within organizations. Measures used most frequently usually contribute the most. But, do they provide what is needed? If not, assessment methods need a second look.

Determining level of "accuracy" is difficult. There is no good way to do this without determining whether data are reliable (consistent) and valid (do what they are supposed to do) (Chapter 8).

Standards used to compare obtained vs. estimated level of accuracy may need to be checked. Estimates may be satisfactory, if assessment methods have been used for an extended period of time, and are felt to be doing the job.

Methods to measure productivity will be diverse and include various ratios, standards, definitions, measures of efficiency, effectiveness. . . . Usage, contribution, and estimated level of accuracy are related. Ideally the "best" methods should be ones that contribute the most to productivity data and are accurate.

3/5. After selecting the method to measure productivity, the following sequence of steps provide guidelines:

   a. Examine existing records for standards or baseline comparisons for specific jobs, e.g., projects completed by hour . . . month, budgets, cost estimates, customers served, customer complaints, etc. Cost can be minimal—only a few hours of your time. However, the time peers and supervisors spend away from the job, and the disruption of workflow should be considered.
   b. Ask employees who are evaluated by the method in question whether they feel it is satisfactory. If you provide sincere encouragement, employees will give good suggestions for improvement.
   c. Increase awareness of the need to measure.
   d. Analyze various components and their impact on the situation.
   e. Encourage support from peers and supervisor(s).
   f. Focus on benefits of the system.
   g. Stress that if methods are inappropriate, they can be altered to produce the least possible resistance to change.

h. Monitor on a regular basis.
i. Revise and improve constantly; incorporate new ideas into methods of measurement so techniques remain current and reflect exactly what is going on in the job.

Problems may relate to gaining support of upper management, lack of employee understanding of the necessity of the program, employee participation, or setting priorities.

4/6. Most problems relate to initial resistance or reluctance of employees to productivity assessment, including fear of the unknown. Such a program takes considerable patience and perseverance. Most programs require a minimum of six months to get started. If employees are provided with logical reasons, are involved in the process, and believe they can be helped, they will likely be cooperative. Management support is crucial.

Use a logical, step-by-step approach to identify problems and symptoms. Study alternatives and select and implement the "best" ones. Reevaluate and review each step, and then start all over again with the new information you have obtained.

Ask those having problems with the system for help. People like to know they are needed. Remember, the person doing the job is the best judge of how it should be done, which improvements to make, and how improvements can be made.

Problems may be employee resistance and fear of the unknown—new procedures are always threatening. People like to feel secure, and achieve a comfortable state of equilibrium.

7. Experience provides good answers. Sometimes our first efforts are good because we try hard. But, later efforts may be better due to previous experience solving similar problems, and because we are willing to use input from others. "Best" methods minimize implementation time or cost, or are proven methods employees and supervisors like.

8. Working in a group requires talents that support and motivate group accomplishment. Individual efforts may be downplayed so the greater goals of the group can be achieved. Measurement of productivity will be primarily on group output. Productivity measures presented in Chapters 12–15 provide useful information.

Due to wide individual differences in performance and motivation, even in homogeneous groups, what motivates one person will not necessarily motivate all group members.

One of the greatest discrepancies is between what people do and how they are paid. Determining pay scales and bonuses for individuals is seldom easy. The issue becomes even more complex when a person's pay is based, either partially or totally, on group accomplishment. Profit sharing and gain sharing are two standard group-based alternatives discussed in Chapters 12, 13 and 17.

6

Major Sources of Personal Productivity Information

PURPOSE

- Identify and analyze major sources of job-related information and obvious indicators of productivity.
- Examine typical examples of "hard" and "soft" data.
- Increase awareness of people's uniqueness.
- Consider the ways individual differences affect productivity.

INTRODUCTION

Work in progress, or completed work, is a prime source of productivity information. Supervisors use job-related data to compare employees' levels of performance. Better judgments are made when behavior being assessed is based on a wide range of possible sources.

Numerous sources of personal and job-related information are used to develop productivity indicators. Indicators (Chapter 1, page 2) signal progress toward the achievement of objectives. Some productivity indicators are based on observable behavior, others on inferences and assumptions about behavior. Behavior is endlessly complex.

A systems approach is used to put individual differences in perspective, and to illustrate their potential. Improved input in the form of more experience, better attitude, and increased knowledge improves the amount and quality of output. Similarly, improved throughput in the form of enhanced motivation and stable personality has a positive effect on output. Applying significant information to individual differences to raise performance level is definitely worthwhile. Stressing employees' unique abilities and talents allows full use of skills.

The search for good, representative information to use in measurement covers (1) standard data sources currently recognized and used throughout the organization; (2) commonly recognized output-oriented sources; and (3) valuable, underutilized, unique information having great potential for increasing productivity.

STANDARD DATA SOURCES IN THE ORGANIZATION

In most organizations, information sources come from the work location. But, this is not always the case. Some data come from interpretations of what goes on. Other data come from partial, undocumented, unreliable information based on minimal contact. Typical information sources include samples of work produced, meeting goals or quotas; performance appraisals; performance records; interviews; personal opinions; and assessment centers.

Samples of Work Produced

Quantity and quality of goods and tangible services are output variables and are relatively easy to define. Intangible services, or activities difficult to describe and document include counseling, coordinating, negotiating, and customer goodwill. Samples of work should be random, yet adequately represent goods or services in question.

Developing and maintaining viable standards or criteria to evaluate quality is a formidable, universal effort beyond the scope of this book.

Meeting Goals or Quotas

Most types of planned results, or tangible descriptions of output, are goals. However, standards, or acceptable ranges of achievement, must be specified for each goal. How well achieved goals (results) match standards set for goals is a direct measure of productivity. Goals range from immediate to long-term.

Results for typical manufacturing industries involve sales, effectiveness, quality, efficiency, service, and financial return. See Figure 6-1.

Results for service and product-oriented industries may be the same—in return on investment. Results for service industries relate to customer complaints, determining who repeat customers are, on-time delivery, and other service-related indicators. Results for product-oriented or materials-processing industries are often number of units, quality of products returned, and other significant variables.

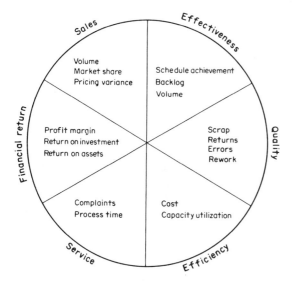

Figure 6-1. Key end result areas for managers and employees. (From Bain, 1982.)

Performance Appraisals

More is written about performance appraisal than about any other method of obtaining information on employees. Despite the renewed interest in the potential of performance planning and review, there are three major limitations: (1) a performance appraisal is one of the most critical, and probably poorly performed of all managerial functions; (2) appraisals are frequently unstandardized, arbitrarily rated, and not uniformly interpreted; (3) despite the fact performance reviews are a way of life in most organizations, few employees or managers look forward to them.

There are legal constraints on performance appraisal as specified in Title VII of the Equal Employment Opportunity Act of 1964 and subsequent guidelines of the Equal Employment Opportunity Commission (Odiorne, 1984). It is important to be very clear about exactly what performance is expected. Goddard (1989) cites specific cases involving litigation on promotion, discharge, layoff, and merit pay.

Performance appraisals may be an ongoing activity, or held regularly—every three to six months or once a year. Results-oriented appraisals are based on job performance, not on personal traits and personality characteristics. What is done on the job is important.

A well-constructed, regularly administered performance appraisal that employees understand and accept has great potential for increasing productivity. Performance appraisals emphasizing positive aspects, or generally favorable outcomes in the form of constructive feedback, a raise, or promise of a raise or promotion that is ultimately given, are motivational. Appraisals accompanied by career counseling and career development have added positive impact (Bianco, 1984).

Performance planning and review, as evidenced by increased interest in performance appraisal, are often considered by managers to be the best ways to accomplish objectives.

The overall purpose of performance appraisal systems is to assess present and potential performance and provide constructive feedback to enhance employees' performance, and ultimately improve individual and organizational effectiveness, or productivity.

Performance Records

The following are examples of performance records (Phillips, 1983):

- Absenteeism
- Accident Costs, Accident Rates
- Break-in Time for New Hires
- Budget Variances

- Complaints, Employee & Customer
- Costs, Overhead
- Costs, Unit
- Dollar Savings on Equipment
- Downtime
- Efficiency
- Employees Promoted
- Errors, Employee
- Grievances
- Inventory Adjustments
- On-time Shipments
- Overtime
- Percent of Quota Achieved
- Production Schedules
- Productivity
- Project Schedule Variations
- Rejects, Scrap
- Reports Completed
- Supervisor Bonuses
- Tardiness
- Terminations, Employee
- Time Card Corrections
- Total Output
- Turnover
- Work Backlog
- Work Stoppages

(From Phillips, 1983, p. 89)

Most variables represent the major types of results of Figure 6-1. The majority are numeric output variables, such as days absent, hours of overtime, or number of rejects.

What type of appraisal to use depends on the person's abilities and type of job performed, as well as the general philosophy and needs of the organization. Existing procedures and standards used in performance appraisal dictate how evaluations are performed. Much can be done to increase the overall acceptance and credibility of the performance appraisal process. "Performance appraisal, at all levels of the organization, must be an integral part of any plan of action designed to improve productivity" (Bain, 1982).

The complexity of information obtained from performance appraisals ranges from informal, or highly subjective, to formal, or highly objective, for example, from a brief hand-written "report card," to a detailed assessment.

Results of formal and informal performance appraisals are used to make decisions on factors directly affecting productivity, such as:

- Motivating employees to improve performance in areas identified as being weak.

- Serving as a basis for selecting employees to participate in training and development activities.
- Providing feedback to employees being evaluated.
- Reinforcing existing company culture.
- Awarding merit pay increases and promotions.

Will performance appraisals continue in their present, somewhat eclectic state, or will they become more task specific? Admittedly, specific tasks are easier to evaluate than broad, general ones, but there are more of them.

Compensation programs are based on the need to appropriately gauge and reward performance. Performance monitoring is a continuous process that provides immediate feedback on an individual and organizational level. Performance monitoring can be used in compensation programs as a "yardstick" to measure goal attainment and individual and group performance improvement. Could monitoring be an improvement over a once-a-year performance appraisal? Time will tell.

Interviews

Most appraisal or performance interviews are unstandardized. They provide information on numerous areas hard to assess by other means. Information about performance, including constructive feedback, can be freely exchanged by supervisors, peers and subordinates.

The major hazard in relying heavily on interview data are that information is colored by the perspectives and personality of the interviewers, and by the person being interviewed. Interviews often contain self-report data that are difficult to verify. Comparing or validating what employees say (qualitative) with performance (quantitative) poses problems.

For instance, Don tells Lloyd what he thinks Lloyd wants to hear. Lloyd does not realize this.

Frequently, attitudes, biases, and perceptions color what is said and heard. "It is not what you show, but what is seen. . . . Not what you say, but what is heard. . . . Not what you mean, but what is understood." (*The Better Work Supervisor*, 1984).

One effort to standardize performance reviews is the "scorable interview test," as applied to hiring (Mercer and Seres, 1987). This "test" contains a number of standard, or core questions commonly asked in interviews and questions that are developed specifically for clients' needs. Those planning to use the interview go through a comprehensive three-day training session. For example, Nuecor Steel of Charlotte, North Carolina uses it to hire first-line supervisors. Since introducing the 26-item scorable interview for hiring purposes, Hinkley & Schmidt, a Chicago-based firm in the bottled water industry, decreased turnover from 50% to 26%. This was an annual savings of $140,000 (Mercer and Seres, 1987).

Chapter 10 presents examples of specific types of interviews and various kinds of questions that could be used to elicit specific types of information.

PERSONAL APPRAISAL BY SELF, PEERS, AND SUPERVISORS

Most people are relatively good judges of their own performance at work and away from work. We often use our own subjective, built-in measuring systems to compare ourselves with others.

The person, not the job, is to be evaluated. Obtaining, processing, and reporting information on employees is no simple task. When various sources of data are combined, meaningful, unbiased assessments usually result. Two major problems associated with assessment are lack of agreement on the exact purpose of the appraisal and failure to develop and adhere to uniform guidelines. Chapter 9 presents information on Basic Guidelines for Measurement.

Self Appraisal

As is commonly known, self-report may be distorted due to differences between what managers need to know (fact), and what employees want to reveal about themselves and believe their managers want to hear (fiction).

Throughout their school and college years, young people have compared themselves with classmates. They know their relative positions through class standings and grade-point averages. Joining the working force does not reduce this desire to compete and compare.

Employees hungry for feedback on performance can be creative in their search for feedback on their own performance. This is what Jim did.

During his early lunch hour away from the office, Jim phoned his supervisor to inquire whether the position advertised three months ago, which he now filled, was still available. When told there was no opening, Jim asked several questions about the performance of the person currently in the position. The supervisor, who did not recognize Jim's voice, said the person was a productive, valued employee. There are more realistic ways to obtain performance data, but Jim wanted immediate feedback.

Peer Appraisal

The "peer information line" is seldom tapped. Peers have continuous contact at work, know each other's work habits, ways of thinking, communicating, and getting along with others. Peers use their own personal ranking system to see how they measure up against other employees. They also know the "pecking order," who is most likely to get a promotion, and who is a promising candidate for advanced training.

Given the opportunity, a group of peers could provide considerable information about associates' abilities. Information from peers is likely to be valid, reliable, and practical. However, using peer information may be considered a violation of confidence. Until people in the organization begin to trust, respect, and understand each other, useful information obtained from peers will remain untapped. Fooling a peer is difficult!

Supervisor Appraisal

Data on employees can be obtained, for example, from observation, direct questions, review of complete projects, and analysis of results in general. These data may be recorded and used in numerous ways, as in performance appraisals, or later discussed with workers. Because of difficulty in obtaining quantitative information, supervisors may go to great lengths to obtain subjective information. A balance should be sought between quantitative and qualitative data. Hard facts based on employee output can be compared with what peers say about employees, and what employees say about themselves.

Information on employees' skills and abilities also comes from informal contacts—at lunch, carpooling, or company-sponsored activities. Supervisors who occasionally "step down" from their supervisory roles to talk freely on a one-to-one basis with their subordinates learn surprising things: Phyllis is a top Amway salesperson; Mark is president of his PTA group. Given an opportunity, both could use their coordinating and facilitating skills in their jobs.

One way to determine the overall attributes of employees, or more specifically how employees could be judged, is to determine how good they are as a boss, and how good they are as a subordinate (Sandler, 1984).

Assessment Centers

Assessment centers were first used by the Office of Strategic Services and the British War Office during World War II to select officers. Assessment centers have been used by Sears, J. C. Penney, General Electric, IBM, AT&T, Sohio, and many other companies to evaluate and select literally hundreds of thousands of managers.

The multiple peer-superior rating methods used in the center are based on many types of input data. Examples are management games, in-basket exercises, mock selection interviews, and leaderless group discussions. Observers are trained to use numerous assessment techniques, such as simulations under controlled circumstances. All relevant data, including assessors' judgments, are discussed in evaluation meetings (Glueck, 1978). Results are reported and used in ways similar to in-house performance appraisals.

Having an independent, non-biased organization or group perform assessments reduces the need and cost of having trained evaluators in the organization. Despite the purported overemphasis on interpersonal skills, assessment centers are considered very useful tools to evaluate and select managers. See box on next page.

RECOGNIZED SOURCES OF PRODUCTIVITY-BASED INFORMATION

Observing and documenting primary job activities are beginning steps in measuring productivity. Observable indicators of performance are usually output variables. Previous chapters stressed that not all behavior is observable, but may be inferred from input and throughput.

Indicators

Indicators are devices that measure, or record, and visably indicate. Each activity in the organization has measurable signs or indicators. Some indicators are harder to observe and measure than others. Some examples include your car's gas and temperature gauges, which provide valuable, continuous information on current status; and financial analysts who use specific economic-based indicators to make informed decisions on various types of investment opportunities for their clients.

If you feel you lack good indicators of personal and organizational productivity, ask your supervisors, peers, or subordinates, or develop them yourself. See box on next page.

Hard and Soft Data

Data can be described as hard or soft. The amount of hard and soft data used to develop productivity indicators is mostly a matter of availability of information and personal choice. Indicators should meet acceptable standards of validity and reliability (see Chapter 8).

Hard Data. Hard data represent measurements, and are presented as rational, undisputed facts (Phillips, 1983) that are typically classified as costs, time, and quality. These data come from input or output, are easier to collect, and are often more desirable and useful than soft data. Examples of hard data are as follows:

Output
Units produced
Tons manufactured
Items assembled
Money collected
Items sold
Forms processed
Loans approved
Inventory turnover
Patients visited
Applications processed
Students graduated
Tasks completed
Output per manhour
Productivity
Work backlog
Incentive bonus
Shipments

Time
Equipment downtime
Overtime
On time shipments
Time to project completion
Processing time
Supervisory time
Break in time for new employees
Training time
Meeting schedules
Repair time
Efficiency
Work stoppages
Order response
Late reporting
Lost time days

Costs
Budget variances
Unit costs
Cost by account
Variable costs
Fixed costs
Overhead cost
Operating costs
Number of cost reductions
Project cost savings
Accident costs
Program costs
Sales expense

Quality
Scrap
Waste
Rejects
Error rates
Rework
Shortages
Product defects
Deviation from standard
Product failures
Inventory adjustments
Time card corrections
Percent of tasks completed properly
Number of accidents

Soft Data. Soft data are often subjective, and difficult to define, collect, and analyze. Much soft data are of the throughput variety and are typically classified as work habits, work climate, feelings/attitudes, new skills, development/advancement, and initiative. Assigning dollar values to soft data is questionable because it is often considered a less credible performance measure than hard data. Examples of soft data are as follows (Phillips, 1983):

Work Habits
Absenteeism
Tardiness
Visits to the dispensary
First aid treatments
Violations of safety rules
Number of

New Skills
Decisions made
Problems solved
Conflicts avoided
Grievances resolved
Counseling problems solved
Listening skills

(text continued on page 56)

1. Analyze your own job. Review the major sources of personal productivity information from your job description or performance appraisal. Indicate the percent of time used for each source. Rank the estimated value of the source, and acceptance by subordinate (you) and your supervisor. This exercise can be repeated with any subordinate-supervisor combination.

Sources of Personal Productivity Information

Sources	% Time Used	Rank of Value of Source	Rank Acceptancy Subord.	Super.
Samples of Work Produced	_____	_____	_____	_____
Meet Goals or Quotas	_____	_____	_____	_____
Performance Appraisal	_____	_____	_____	_____
Performance Records	_____	_____	_____	_____
Interviews	_____	_____	_____	_____
Personal Appraisals by:				
Self	_____	_____	_____	_____
Peers	_____	_____	_____	_____
Supervisors	_____	_____	_____	_____
Assessment Centers	_____	_____	_____	_____
Total Percent _____ **Average**		_____	_____	_____

2. List activities performed in the organization that are obvious signs or indicators of personal productivity. Include at least two input, two throughput, and two output variables. What type of measures are associated with these productivity indicators? If so, who measures them?

Measures Associated with Major Productivity Indicators

Major Productivity Indicators	Measured in Organization Yes/No	By Whom?
_____	_____	_____
_____	_____	_____
_____	_____	_____
_____	_____	_____
_____	_____	_____
_____	_____	_____

communication
breakdowns
Excessive breaks

Reading speed
Discrimination charges
    resolved
Intention to use new skills
Frequency of use of new
    skills

PERSONAL VARIABLES CONTRIBUTING TO PRODUCTIVITY

The study of individual differences, a separate field of investigation in psychology, dates back over one hundred years to Galton (1822–1911), a half-cousin of Darwin (1809–1882), and Cattell (1860–1944). Galton's book, *Hereditary Genius,* and his work in quantitative measurements, including statistical correlation, are world-renowned. Cattell made major contributions in perception and individual differences.

Work Climate

Number of grievances
Number of discrimination
    charges
Employee complaints
Job satisfaction
Unionization avoidance
Employee turnover

Development/Advancement

Number of promotions
Number of pay increases
Number of training
    programs attended
Requests for transfer
Performance appraisal ratings
Increases in job effectiveness

Uniqueness, as reflected by individual differences, is a product of learning and behavior. Although major factors such as knowledge, skills, and attitudes impose limits on human performance, opportunities to develop one's full potential should not be limited.

Feelings/Attitudes

Favorable reactions
Attitude changes
Perceptions of job
    responsibilities
Perceived changes in
    performance
Employee loyalty

Initiative

Implementation of new ideas
Successful completion of
    projects
Number of suggestions
    submitted
Number of suggestions
    implemented

The number of individual differences or human factors selected covers major areas in assessment. People are unique and exhibit a wide range of individual differences. Appropriate use of these differences, as applied to proper job assignment, for example, should maximize productivity (Meister, 1989).

---

3. Select two input, two throughput, and two output measures from #1, above. Indicate whether data on which each productivity indicator is based is "hard" or "soft." Data from some indicators may be hard *and* soft, particularly for throughput variables.

Classification of Major Productivity Indicators

Major Productivity Indicator	Soft Data	Hard Data
Input Variables:		
_____	_____	_____
_____	_____	_____
Throughput Variables:		
_____	_____	_____
_____	_____	_____
Output Variables:		
_____	_____	_____
_____	_____	_____

4. List major productivity indicators for the job you currently perform.

    - State whether they are input (I), throughput (T), or output (O) variables.
    - Classify them as hard or soft data.
    - Estimate personal level of satisfaction with these indicators (1 is low . . . 7 is high).

Major Job-Related Productivity Indicators

Major Productivity Indicators	I, T or O	Hard or Soft Data	Satisfaction Level (1 . . . 7)
_____	_____	_____	_____
_____	_____	_____	_____
_____	_____	_____	_____
_____	_____	_____	_____

5. Do productivity indicators accurately represent job performance? Explain.

What Is Measured?

Performance as a whole is impossible to assess unless major factors contributing to individual differences are known and measured. The relative importance of these factors is subjectively weighted to determine whether there is a good match between what is available and what is needed.

Individualized preferences for food, clothing, housing, cars, and other aspects of daily living dictate a person's lifestyle. In the same vein, individual differences become prime factors in job performance.

Although preferences and behavior may change over time, certain individual differences, such as ability, attitude, interests, and personality remain relatively constant throughout life. Individual differences impose limits on human performance. One of the first steps in increasing human performance is understanding the magnitude and nature of individual differences.

Brief descriptive information is presented in the following sections for each major classification of individual differences. Order of presentation is alphabetical, and the amount written about each area is unrelated to importance.

In some instances, descriptions are short because considerable information exists in that area.

Age

The influence of age is difficult to determine because of the varying impact of the aging process on sensory ability, particularly on vision, hearing, and memory. Evaluations and subsequent decisions must be made on an individual basis. The "youth" versus "experience" controversy will remain unresolved. The "general aging of the work force," or the rapid growth in the 40 to 60 year age group cannot be ignored.

Aptitude

A common definition is innate or acquired capacity, ability or talent in a specific area, such as reading, mathematics, mechanical, music, art or clerical. Aptitude tests are used to determine current level of aptitude, as required by job placement, and predict success in various occupations, training courses, or jobs.

There is a strong, positive relationship between ability and performance (Hunter and Schmidt, 1983). To illustrate, data from 515 validation studies based on general cognitive, perceptual, and psychomotor abilities were examined. The positive relationship between ability and performance shows that cognitive abilities predict performance in jobs.

Aspiration Level

Expectations of accomplishment in undertaking everyday activities, or in choosing life goals, differ widely. Level of aspiration is influenced by success or failure in attaining goals. People who know their abilities develop levels of aspiration closely related to those abilities. Those performing successfully at a certain level of difficulty usually raise their level of aspiration after each success. The old saying, "nothing succeeds like success," is very appropriate. The strength of motivation is at a peak when the probability of success is .50. This represents a 50-50 chance of success/failure (Hampton, Summer, and Webber, 1978).

Attitude

Attitudes are likes or dislikes, or positive or negative evaluations about some aspect of the world (Hilgard, Atkinson, and Atkinson, 1979). Definitions often include emotional, learning, and social components. Attitudes are acquired early in life from a wide range of sources, namely, family, school, friends, peers, and work groups, etc. Age, ethnic, political, geographic, and sex-based differences in attitudes are the most common.

Despite the relative stability of attitudes, they are hard to measure, and even more difficult to change. Surveys, questionnaires and self-report are primary indicators of attitudes. No single attitude survey meets the specific needs of the user. Methods to determine the strength of variables influencing attitudes must be developed, and results interpreted and conveyed back to supervisors. But, attitude surveys are difficult to construct. Survey results are based on self-report, an information source of questionable reliability and validity. Knowing employees' attitudes toward certain work-related and closely-allied current issues is extremely important.

At work, attitudes influence employees' perceptions of jobs, reactions to subordinates, peers, and supervisors, and affect expectations for being rewarded (pay, promotion, etc.) for performing their jobs.

There is strong evidence that attitude and performance are related (French, 1978 and Phillips, 1983). Most employees with a positive attitude toward work in general outperform those with negative attitudes. Although positive and negative attitudes are contagious, their impact on performance is rarely considered.

Behavior

Job performance combines employees' interpretations of what supervisor(s) and peers want, and what employees believe to be their jobs.

As discussed previously, most productivity measures are based on tangible, readily observed, measurable behavior or output. Emphasizing output handicaps those whose personal output depends on work efforts of others, or whose jobs do not have tangible output, as in coordinating material or human resources.

Beliefs and Values

A belief is a statement about the world that a person thinks is true (Hilgard, Atkinson, and Atkinson, 1979). Values, like attitudes, begin to develop in childhood, and are learned or acquired primarily from people who are admired, or with whom the person identifies, such as parents, relatives, friends, teachers, or other professional persons who play a meaningful role in a person's life. Fortunately, most identification is positive.

In industry, values are transmitted by stories, myths, and legends, all of which constitute company culture. Belief and value systems are extremely important components. Successful organizations maintain a sound set of beliefs on which actions and policies are based. For instance, companies must faithfully adhere to these beliefs if they want to provide excellent customer service.

The relative achievements of employees are influenced more by the drive, spirit, and basic philosophy of the organization than by technology, organizational structure, economic resources, innovation, or timing. The major issue in productivity relates to the strength of employees' beliefs in the organization's precepts and how these beliefs are carried out.

Communications Skills

These skills are basic to any job. Being a good communicator is a particularly important attribute. The whole work process revolves around communication in general, like keeping people informed, providing accurate feedback, and not withholding valuable information. Also, the effectiveness and efficiency of the communication process, and the reliability of the information conveyed affects human and organizational productivity.

Energy and Health

Level of energy used at work depends on physical and mental health and attitude, which in turn affects productivity. Wellness, which includes health promotion and disease prevention programs, is a relatively new concept. Exercise facilities and amount of money spent on exercise demonstrates national health consciousness.

"Wellness" promoted at Tenneco Oil Company is expected to have a 10- to 15-year payback when exercisers in their 20s and 30s start with good fitness habits. By keeping good habits throughout the critical 50- to 60-year-old period, expensive, possibly life-threatening problems can be reduced.

In 1985, 1,400 of Conoco's 2,000 Houston-based employees initially screened enrolled in their company's wellness program. The 1987 study based on responses of 606 participants who returned questionnaires revealed a strong positive relationship between exercise and work productivity (Rudman and Steinhardt, 1988).

The opposite side of the coin of "wellness" is illness. Approximately 3,000,000 to 7,000,000 of the 100,000,000 employed Americans use some form of illicit drug on a daily basis, and more than 53,000,000 use drugs occasionally. Between 5,000,000 to 10,000,000 of the work force suffers from alcoholism (Quayle, 1983). Herzlinger (1989) indicated the number of problem drinkers may be as high as 18 million. Despite the hazards of smoking, 50 million Americans smoke (Herzlinger).

Distressing statistics compare "sick" versus "average" employees (Quayle, 1983):

- The absentee rate of employees with drug or drinking problems is 16 times greater than the average employee.
- The accident rate is four times higher.
- One-third more sickness benefits are used.
- Five times more compensation claims are filed while on the job.
- 40% of industrial fatalities and 47% of industrial injuries can be traced to alcohol abuse.

In September 1984, the National Institute of Mental Health reported 19% or 43,000,000 American adults suffered from mental or emotional problems.

In 1984, cardiovascular disease alone cost an estimated $64.4 billion in treatment and lost output. This cost alone is roughly equivalent to the total budget of twelve large U.S. states. For instance, a reduction of only 1% in cardiovascular disease would save more than $640 million a year (Herzlinger and Calkins, 1986).

In 1987, health care benefits increased to 35.3% of employers' total benefit expenditures. This represented an increase of 3.2% over 1986. For this same period, health care costs were 9.7% of payroll costs, an .8% increase over 1986 (Harper, 1988).

The answer to health problems and rising costs is prevention. Generally, well-adjusted, healthy people make productive, reliable, low-risk employees. Ideally, total wellness, or the health of the entire person, including wellness of body, mind, and spirit, should be emphasized.

Expectancy

Expectancy, a subjective estimate of what may happen, is a major factor in motivation and productivity. A classic example of expectancy is the Pygmalion effect, which was introduced by George Bernard Shaw in his 1912 play, *Pygmalion*. This play was transformed into the perennially popular musical, *My Fair Lady*. Henry Higgins initially treated Eliza as "baggage," but Professor Pickering always treated her as a lady. When Higgins raised his expectations, Eliza performed unpredictably, but became a "high society" lady.

The Pygmalion effect observed in management was expertly documented by Livingston (1969). This effect is a case of self-fulfilling prophecy, which causes subordinates from whom supervisors expect more to actually perform better (Baxter and Bowers, 1985). Business world examples indicate:

- Managers' expectations and treatment of subordinates largely determines subordinates' work performance and career progress.
- Superior managers have the unique characteristics of being able to create high performance expectations that most subordinates fulfill.
- Subordinates frequently do what they believe they are expected to do.

Experience

There are an increasing number of 40- to 65-year-old people in the work force. Some retired early and started new careers. Not all organizations want to pay for experience. Experienced people overqualified for their current jobs can move into other areas where their talents can be better utilized. There is now less room at the top than ever before for the young, fast-rising executive.

Interests

Skilled people are seldom motivated to perform well unless they are interested in their jobs. No reasonable amount of money or encouragement keeps employees doing a job they dislike. They may perform a disliked job for a period of time, but frustration and resentment will grow, and efficiency decreases. They are likely to change jobs or leave the company.

Intelligence

Intelligence (IQ) means mental ability, scholastic ability, or potential. IQ, a relative term, is often reported as being in a specific range, as "above average," for instance.

There is no demonstrated relationship between intelligence and productivity. However, how employees apply specific mental abilities, or use their potential to work more efficiently and effectively, is important.

Knowledge

Knowledge is vital in rapidly expanding, technologically based environments. Many employees lack the necessary basic skills to perform their jobs at an acceptable level. Some are overwhelmed by technology, while others are unable or unwilling to apply existing skills or knowledge.

Functional literacy rates are approximately 95% for Japan and 80% for the U.S. Studies of scientific competence and literacy among American adults revealed that only 5% qualified as scientifically literate.

Companies are reported to spend more than $40 billion on nearly 8 million student-employees, or $5,000 per year on education. This exceeds the amount spent by all four year colleges or institutions of higher learning in the U.S. (World of Work Report, 1985).

The American Society of Training and Development estimated that corporations spend $300 million annually on remedial programs alone (Magnus, 1986).

Learning Style

Of the many approaches to learning, the individualized approach designed to meet learners' needs (Ludwig and Menendez, 1985) supports ideas in this book. Learning style is affected by most variables cited here. The fact that no two people learn exactly the same way has challenged educators throughout history. However, diagnosing and meeting these needs constitutes "lifelong learning."

Holistic learning (Meier, 1985) and holistic education (Rinke, 1985) are possible ways to examine the dilemma of learning. Holism is a functional, integrated, and generalized model of education focusing on whole teaching-learning situations. The teaching-learning strategy is varied to meet the needs of the learner (Rinke, 1985). On-the-job behavior and predicted accomplishment depend on ability to learn and apply what is learned.

Level of Schooling

Level of schooling differs widely. There is usually a positive relationship between educational level and pay. Exceptions are overqualified and some part-time persons.

The high illiteracy rate in general poses major problems for business and industry. The size of this problem is staggering. According to Harold McGraw, Jr., Chairman of the Board of McGraw-Hill, Inc., an estimated 25 million American adults 17 years old and older are termed "functional illiterates." Many cannot read. Most read only up to a third or fourth grade level. The majority have problems completing job applications, comprehending newspaper headlines, and understanding a medicine bottle warning label. More than 45 million adults have such limited basic skills in reading, writing, and arithmetic they are marginally able to cope with their daily environments (McGraw, 1987).

Two possible solutions are to train employees in basic skills and hire better qualified personnel. Both are being done. Many organizations provide training directly, or support it indirectly through tuition, or time off from work. Better selection procedures are needed. Assumed discrimination based on employment testing is one issue.

Education can become a way of life. At IBM, for instance, on any given business day, nearly 18,000 of more than 389,000 employees worldwide attend a class or work on self-study courses. This represents about five million student days a year, or about the same schedule as a major university (Fairbairn, 1989).

Life-Style

Numerous variables affect life-style, namely personality, energy and health, interests, beliefs, values, and home and work environment. There is evidence to support the relationship between life-styles and self-assessed productivity. For instance, people who incorporate regular exercise into their life-style are generally more productive (Dahl, 1985).

Bob Ealing, manager of Conoco's Health and Fitness Center in Houston, believes exercise and productivity are related. Ealing (1985) reports that those who exercise are already a select group who have incorporated exercise into their life-styles.

Motivation

A comprehensive definition of motivation is the process of arousing actions, sustaining the activity, and regulating the pattern of activity; or, once you get started (aroused), you keep on going (sustain activity) at a certain pace (regulate speed). Motivation includes the inner control of behavior, specifically physiological conditions, interests, attitudes, and aspirations.

Motivation cannot be observed directly, but inferred from behavior. It is a good example of a throughput variable. For example, people bored with their jobs usually have low motivation. Although they look busy, they may not really be performing meaningful work. The illusiveness of motivation challenges those trying to develop reliable, valid measurements.

A small, positive relationship exists between motivation and productivity. This relationship is hard to document. Supporting evidence comes from high achievers or people working with high achievers. High achievers exhibit the following behaviors (Williams, 1978):

- Achieve impressive results, usually overfilling their position.
- Work long and hard, and make personal sacrifices frequently.
- Seek out rather than avoid problems.
- Solve difficult problems.
- Make the right decisions most of the time.
- Initiate action.

Information on motivational differences can be applied (Hampton, Summer and Webber, 1978)

- To analyze jobs to determine the types of behaviors needed to perform them successfully.
- To review prospective candidates for behavioral or motive patterns that indicate high motivation.
- To select a prospective candidate when ability and other differences do not favor one specific candidate. Differences in motivation may be the deciding factor in selection, or may serve as the basis for promotion . . . termination.

Motor Skills

Tests of motor skills measure speed and coordination of movement, fine and gross motor skills, and perceptual, spatial, or mechanical functions. Numerous reliable, valid tests are available. Some tests are designed "in-house" for specific jobs.

The relationship between high-level motor skills required on the job and productivity is generally positive, provided all other job-related variables, and individual differences such as interest, attitude, motivation, and ability remain constant.

Personality

The most unique feature anyone possesses, other than physical appearance, is personality. Personality refers to the whole individual. It is affected by attitudes, interests, intelligence, motivation, and many other distinctive characteristics.

Surface personality traits represent freely expressed, observable characteristics, for instance, pleasantness, sociability, nervousness, or friendliness. Rating scales, questionnaires, or other pencil-and-paper techniques measure these traits.

Inner personality traits consist of "depth factors," and include fears, desires, aspirations, and other concepts relating to the self. Many people are totally unaware of their inner personality traits. These inner traits are often unconscious, and difficult to define and assess. Interviews, individual personality assessments, or other relatively unstructured situations like discussions, meetings, or team efforts reveal inner traits.

Selecting employees based on compatible or complementary personality and job-related traits may be unrealistic in terms of effort and expense. Smooth-running teams should be productive. Conflict can reduce productivity and damage interpersonal relationships.

Temperament

Personality and temperament are related. Temperament is the unique way people think about and organize their feelings and actions. Temperament represents an overall manner of responding to people and various factors in the home and work environment. A consistently pleasant temperament is obviously a positive influence anywhere.

PERSPECTIVES ON ASSESSMENT OF INDIVIDUAL DIFFERENCES

Organizations use various methods to assess employees. Methods range from well standardized, accepted tests used on a national basis to ones developed for specific jobs within the organization. The Equal Employment Opportunity Commission's "Guidelines on Selection Tests" (published in the *Federal Register*) has affected the type and number of employment tests used. The major issue focuses on assumed discrimination based on abilities.

There is no one best assessment method, just as there is no one best theory of management or ideal set of characteristics ensuring success. Knowing capabilities of employees, and how closely their abilities match jobs to be performed, is a great help to any manager. The closer the fit between employees' motivation and interest in their jobs, skills and job requirements, the higher the productivity is expected to be.

Assessment information is used primarily to identify potential, however actual problems associated with decreased productivity may be determined. Knowing how and when data will be used is extremely important. Some information may be used once a year, while other information may be used daily.

A cautionary note relates to information on career counseling or promotion. This information should be obtained, analyzed, reported, and recorded with considerable care. Confidentiality is a continuing, major concern.

How information is reported influences its ultimate usefulness. If only numeric data are provided, and no reference points, such as average scores, or expected range of scores required for successful performance on the job are reported, data become meaningless.

Numeric data cannot readily be transformed into descriptive statements, or conversely, in order to conform to the format required in the personal record. Similar issues are discussed in Chapters 7 and in Chapters 10 and 11 on qualitative and quantitative information, respectively. See box below.

There is increasing evidence that cognitive or reasoning ability tests combined with either assessment center results or with standardized personality tests increase the validity of predictions of job performance (Hunter, 1986 and Hunter, Schmidt, and Judiesch, 1990). Cognitive ability is the best predictor of performance in most employment situations. Varied scientific studies present the same conclusion: intelligence and aptitude tests are positively related to job performance (Barrett and Depinet, 1991).

---

6. Sources of major types of individual differences on which productivity information is obtained are mostly input and throughput variables. Some variables, like personality and motivation, could be both. Input and throughput combine to produce output, behavior, or performance.

    List three major job components you perform most often. Rank (1 is low . . . 7 is high) the importance of the role each individual difference variable plays. Omit individual differences that do not apply.

Job Components

#1_____ #2 _____ #3 _____

Major Classifications of Individual Differences

Individual Differences	Rank #1 Job Component	Rank #2 Job Component	Rank #3 Job Component
Age			
Aptitude			
Aspiration level			
Beliefs & values			
Behavior			
Communication			
Education			
Experience			
Intelligence			
Interests			
Knowledge			
Level of schooling			
Attitude			
Common sense			
Energy & health			
Expectancy			
Learning style			
Motivation			
Personality			
Temperament			
Life-style			
Motor skills			

6. (continued) For each of your three job components, indicate which individual differences variables were: input #1 _____ #2_____#3_____; throughput #1_____#2_____#3_____ ; output #1_____#2_____ #3. What does this mean?

REFERENCES

1. Bain, David. *The Productivity Prescription,* New York: McGraw-Hill Book Company, 1982.

2. Barrett, Gerald V. and Depinet, Robert L. "A Reconsideration of Testing for Competence Rather Than for Intelligence," *American Psychologist,* October 1991, pp. 1012–1024.

3. Baxter, Gerald D. and Bowers, John K. "Beyond Self-Actualization: The Persuasion of Pygmalion," *Training and Development Journal,* August 1985, pp. 69–71.

4. Bianco, Virginia. "In Praise of Performance," *Personnel Journal,* June 1984, pp. 40–48, 50.

5. *The Better Work Supervisor.* Concordville, Pennsylvania: Clement Communications, Inc., March 19, 1984, p. 1.

6. Dahl, Tor. *World of Work Report.* Vol. 10, No. 1, 1985.

7. Ealing, Robert. Interview with author, November 4, 1985, at Conoco's Health and Fitness Center, Houston, Texas.

8. Edwards, Mark R. "Implementation Strategies for Multiple Rater Systems," *Personnel Journal,* September, 1990, pp. 130, 132, 134, 137, 141.

9. Equal Employment Opportunity Commission, U.S. Civil Service Commission, U.S. Department of Labor and U.S. Department of Justice. "Uniform Guidelines on Employee Selection Procedures," *Federal Register,* No. 43, 1978, pp. 38290–38315.

10. Fairbairn, Ursula F. "Lessons in Education at IBM," *Personnel,* April 1989, pp. 12, 14, 17–18.

11. French, Wendell L. *The Personnel Management Process,* 4th ed., Boston, Massachusetts, Houghton Mifflin Company, 1978.

12. Gass, Jerry and Prince, Charlene. "Family of Measures: A Tool for Continuous Improvement," in *Handbook for Productivity Measurement and Improvement,* William F. Christopher (ed.) and Carl G. Thor (ed.), Cambridge, Massachusetts: Productivity Press, Sec 4.8.1–4.8.12, 1993.

13. Glueck, William F. *Personnel: A Diagnostic Approach,* Dallas, Texas: Business Publications, Inc., 1978.

14. Goddard, Robert W. "Assessment: Is Your Appraisal System Headed for Court?" *Personnel Journal,* January 1989, pp. 114–118.

15. Hampton, David R., Summer, Charles R. and Webber, Ross A. *Organizational Behavior and the Practice of Management,* Glenview, Illinois: Scott, Foresman and Company, 1978.

16. Harper, Douglas C. "Control Health Care Costs," *Personnel Journal,* October 1988, pp. 64–70.

17. Herzlinger, Regina E. and Calkins, David. "How Companies Tackle Health Care Costs: Part III," *Harvard Business Review,* January–February 1986, pp. 70–80.

18. Herzlinger, Regina E. "The Failed Revolution in Health Care—The Role of Management," *Harvard Business Review,* March–April 1989, pp. 95–103.

19. Hilgard, Ernest R., Atkinson, Rita L. and Atkinson, Richard C. 7th ed. *Introduction to Psychology,* New York: Harcourt Brace Jovanovich, Inc., 1979.

20. Hunter, J. E. and Schmidt, Frank L. "Quantifying the Effects of Psychological Interventions on Employee Job Performance and Work-Force Productivity," *American Psychologist,* April 1983, pp. 473–478.

21. Hunter, J. E. "Cognitive Ability, Cognitive Aptitudes, Job Knowledge, and Job Performance," *Journal of Vocational Behavior,* 29, pp. 340–362, 1986.

22. Hunter, J. E., Schmidt, F. L., and Judiesch, M. K. "Individual Differences in Output Variability as a Function of Job Complexity," *Journal of Applied Psychology,* 75, pp. 28–52, 1990.

23. Livingston, J. S. "Pygmalion in Management," *Harvard Business Review,* July–August 1969, pp. 81–89.

24. Ludwig, John and Menendez, Diane. "Effective Communication through Neurolinguistics," *Training and Development Journal,* March 1985, pp. 44, 46, 48.

25. McGraw, Harold W., Jr. "Adult Functional Illiteracy: What to Do About It?" *Personnel,* October 1987, pp. 38–42.

26. Magnus, Margaret. "Training Futures," *Personnel Journal,* May 1986, pp. 60–63, 66–71.

27. Meier, David. "New Age Learning: From Linear to Geodesic," *Training and Development Journal,* May 1985, pp. 40–43.

28. Meister, David. *Conceptual Aspects of Human Factors,* Baltimore, Maryland: Johns Hopkins University Press, 1989.

29. Mercer, Michael W. and Seres, John J. "Using Scorable Interview 'Tests' in Hiring," *Personnel,* June 1987, pp. 57–60.

30. Nobile, Robert J. "The Law of Performance Appraisals," *Personnel,* January, 1991, p. 7.

31. Odiorne, George S. *Strategic Management of Human Resources,* San Francisco: Jossey-Bass Publishers, 1984.

32. Phillips, Jack J. *Handbook of Training Evaluation and Measurement Methods,* Houston, Texas: Gulf Publishing Company, 1983.

33. Quayle, Dan. "American Productivity: The Devastating Effect of Alcoholism and Drug Abuse," *American Psychologist,* April 1983, pp. 454–458.

34. Rinke, Wolf J. "Holistic Education: An Answer," *Training and Development Journal,* August 1985, pp. 67–68.

35. Rudman, William J. and Steinhardt, Mary, "Fitness in The Workplace: The Effects of a Corporate Health and Fitness Program on Work Culture," *Health Values,* March/April 1988, pp. 4–17.

36. Sandler, Leonard. "The Successful and Supportive Subordinate," *Personnel Journal,* December 1984, pp. 40–45.

37. Teal, Thomas, "Service Comes First: An Interview with USAA's Robert F. McDermott," *Harvard Business Review,* September–October, 1991, pp. 116–127.

38. Williams, J. Clifton. *Human Behavior in Organizations,* Cincinnati, Ohio: South-Western Publishing Company, 1978.

39. World of Work Report. "Corporate Classrooms: A Degree of Difference," Vol. 10, No. 4, 1985, pp. 5–6.

Ideas to Remember

Chapter 6—Answers and Insights

1. The following are obvious signs of personal productivity:

   • Meet the required standards for output.
   • Satisfactory completion of projects on time.
   • Operate equipment in a manner demonstrating required levels of competence (speed, accuracy, minimum waste, etc.).
   • Above average number of satisfied, repeat customers.
   • "Good" employee performance appraisals.
   • Justifiable recommendations for promotion.
   • Good level of performance supported by verbal report from employees who state they are performing well.
   • Meet sales quotas, enlarge sales territory with expanded product line and show a profit within the minimum number of months.
   • A profit center with a profit, satisfied employees, and understanding, supportive management.
   • Demonstrable evidence that employees are satisfied, and get along well with their peers and supervisors.

   Percentage of time used should be over half. Rank will vary, depending on the credibility and use of sources. Acceptance will vary, but with any good program, subordinates' and supervisors' ratings should be similar.

   Examine available data to see what you have before starting out in a new direction. Supervisors at the various levels in the organization have access to most productivity information, and know approximate levels of productivity. Employees themselves also have a good idea of how they compare with their peers. Peers are also good judges of productivity.

2. Major productivity indicators were listed in #1, above. Sources of personal productivity information similar to the those listed exist for organizational productivity, for instance, make a profit, show growth, reasonable return on investment, or have stability. These may overlap with personal indicators. However, they may not currently be measured in any logical, systematic manner. Data may already exist for most of your company's productivity indicators, but it may be mostly financial. Measurement may be ongoing in most departments.

3. Selection of input, throughput and output measures:

Major Productivity Indicator	Soft Data	Hard Data
Input variables		
listening skills	X	
new ideas	X	
budget		X
trained work force		X
Throughput variables		
communication	X	
motivation	X	
stress caused by long work day		X
delay caused by assembly-line problems		X
Output variables		
attitude	X	
satisfied employees	X	
items assembled		X
services provided		X

   Hard throughput data are difficult to define. As previously mentioned, throughput usually refers to an unstructured, formative state in which little is clearly defined.

4. When productivity indicators are based only on what is seen or observed (output) by supervisors, some of the most valuable, but hard to obtain sources of information (throughput) are eliminated. What is visible could be just the tip of the iceberg.

   Attitude, which can be input, throughput, or output, for example, has a tremendous impact on productivity. Input variables in the form of effort exerted, experience, and educational background are invaluable. As a minimum, productivity indicators should represent not only input, throughput, and output areas, but also reflect the impact of forces outside the organization (Chapter 2), because environment, economy, government intervention, and competition, to mention only a few, play critical roles.

Classifying indicators as "hard" or "soft" data provides information on usage, viability, and ease of measurement. However, real or imaginary satisfaction with productivity indicators is a major issue. Equally important is the fit between what is expected and what actually occurs. What is said and what is meant may be two different things.

Is productivity measurement philosophical or political? Perhaps both. Negative reactions to measurement in general should be minimized. Quality of assessment technique is directly related to quality of later decisions.

5. Productivity indicators may appear to be good representations of what is done. But there is more to a job than doing only what is measured, or measurable. As jobs, people, processes, and technology change, so will productivity indicators. Productivity can be perception, an attitude, a way of reacting . . . even an illusion of competence.

   Objectives of performance appraisals designed to assess behavior should be: (1) clear; (2) have measurable, work-based standards; and (3) reflect the changing nature of the job performed and work place. Good two-way communication is essential during the interview/appraisal processes.

   Assessment techniques, like the multiple rater performance appraisal (MRPA) system replace the evaluation done by only the supervisor (Edwards, 1990). By using more than one evaluator, individual biases are reduced or eliminated. Westinghouse, Fidelity Bank, and Arizona State University are a few of the organizations using MRPA.

   Performance appraisals must be based on factors directly related to the job. To illustrate, the Uniform Guidelines on Employee Selection Procedures have been adopted by EEOC the and by several federal agencies. The EEOC requires employers to validate any selection procedure or criterion "used as a basis for making employee decisions" that have an adverse impact on a protected group (Nobile, 1991).

   United Services Automobile Association (USAA) is the fifth largest personal auto insurer and the sixth largest homeowners insurer in the United States. By basing people's evaluations on key end result areas, the reliability and validity of assessments are increased. Key results areas of the 7,500 employees in the Property and Casualty Division of USAA, in descending order or priority, are: (1) service; (2) profitability and financial strength; (3) competitive advantage; (4) operating efficiency and productivity; (5) loss control; (6) human resources; and (7) growth. This important division generates 75% to 80% of USAA's revenue, (Gass and Prince, 1993 and Teal, 1991).

6. Some individual differences, like age, energy and health, and learning style, are equally important in all job components. As your job changes, the rank you assign to individual differences will change. Attitude, beliefs, and values play major roles in all work-related and personal endeavors.

   Input variables, particularly those relating to education, acquisition, and demonstration of skills, can be improved through training and development.

   Throughput variables are less likely to be influenced or modified by behavior change efforts, and may be considered, for better or for worse, to be quite resistant to change.

   Output variables—downtime, reports completed, rejects, absenteeism, etc.—are cited early in the chapter. Output, such as level of performance, can be dramatically lowered by poor quality input and throughput.

7

Job Analysis and Job Description

PURPOSE

- Evaluate various sources of job-related information.
- Consider the role core, unique, and expanding job components play in motivation and productivity.
- Describe and analyze major job functions.

INTRODUCTION

The usefulness of a job analysis and a job description depends on how well they are constructed, who constructs them, and how they are applied. Job analysis overlaps job description, and both improve understanding of the human resources function. Job analysis usually comes first and focuses on work requirements, including data (information, facts, etc.), people (skills, abilities, etc.), and equipment (computers, robots, etc.). A job description is a word picture setting out specific duties, responsibilities, and organizational relationships for a given job.

Job analysis and description are more complete when employees and their supervisors develop them jointly. Working together improves the quality of decisions on sharing and delegating job components, and on the skill level needed to perform the job. A close fit between employees' abilities and jobs performed usually means efficiency and motivation are high.

Job analysis can be used to: (1) improve quality of job descriptions, mainly in hiring and promotion; (2) broaden the scope and relevance of job descriptions; (3) provide data sources for productivity measurement; and (4) establish guidelines for increasing motivation through better match of job skills and job requirements.

SOURCES OF INFORMATION

The more closely peoples' unique talents match their jobs, the higher their efficiency is expected to be. Disinterest, poor attitude, or not being challenged at work, are some of the many reasons for decreased productivity. Job analysis and job description are excellent major sources of information on performance. How rigidly job analyses and job descriptions are followed and implemented within the organization differs widely.

Job Analysis

Job analysis is a common basis for job descriptions. It is one of the least understood, but most important functions of the personnel administrator and manager. Job analysis functions are often tied in with compensation.

Glueck (1979) proposed seven major job analysis methods. Information from these methods can be used to develop standards or indicators of behavior:

1. Examine and compare previous job analyses or job descriptions of similar jobs.
2. Observe the employee performing the job (Chapter 6).
3. Interview the employee and/or supervisor (Chapter 6).
4. Have the employee answer specific structured or open-ended questions about the job (Chapter 6).
5. Check the log, diary, or records kept by the employee.
6. Record job activities—audio, video, or other means if consistent with company and federal guidelines.
7. Analyze equipment design information from blueprints or design data relevant to the job.

Methods 1, 4, and 7 are quickest, but less reliable than other methods. Methods 2, 3, 5, and 6 are more accurate, but could require extra effort, time or expense.

Job analyses should be performed by qualified persons having extensive knowledge of jobs being described. Those doing the jobs should have input and be allowed to critique the final product. Employees whose jobs are being analyzed know more about their jobs than anyone else.

Major issues are implementing job analysis methods and legal concerns. A comprehensive study of job analysis systems in nine separate geographic locations revealed that few organizations have done full-scale program evaluations or determined the costs and benefits of job analysis functions (Levine, et al., 1988). Problems of accessibility to records and confidentiality are also critical issues. Faith in the value of job analysis is growing, but legal pressures for accurate documentation are also increasing.

Job Descriptions

Job descriptions are one of the organization's most important information resources (Grant, 1988). Length of job descriptions range from one- or two-page summaries of basic tasks performed on the job to mental images of a job that needs to be done. Generally, the shorter the job description the more complex the job, and the greater the latitude a person has in performing it, such as vice-president of sales. Some of the longest, most narrowly defined job descriptions can be for assembly line, or piece-rate jobs having specific production limits or quotas.

Ideally, people are hired to perform jobs outlined in job descriptions, but, for numerous reasons, job descriptions may be out-of-date, incomplete, or non-existent. Admittedly, job descriptions are hard to write. Components of varying positions do not fit into neat classifications. For example, writing job descriptions for technical professionals—engineer, systems analyst or R&D scientists—is difficult because of the depth and breadth of the various tasks

performed. However, trying to function without any form of job classification is no answer, either. Classifications do provide yardsticks for goal attainment, and are good stepping stones toward measurement.

Job descriptions are used in (1) human resources planning; (2) job design; (3) performance appraisal; (4) employee selection and placement; (5) career planning; (6) compensation (Wright and Wexley, 1985); (7) motivation in general, including non-monetary rewards; (8) facilitate changes in work design and task assignment; and (9) assessing skills, knowledge, education, experience, etc. (Grant, 1988).

Job descriptions are valid (measure what they are supposed to measure) to the extent they accurately represent job content. The likelihood of hiring and retaining qualified employees increases when accurate complete job descriptions are used.

Job descriptions are written in terms of (1) job titles, (2) job purpose, (3) work flow, (4) specific, established goals, (5) expected results, or performance standards to be achieved, (6) duties and responsibilities, and (7) functions to be performed. Plachy (1987) provided practical information on writing job descriptions. Woods and Dillion (1985) presented a detailed example of a job description and a job rating scale. Basic personnel texts also cover this area.

Asselin and St. John (1986) discusses a two-phase system—Phase One clarifies a manager's role by constructing a job description consisting of major responsibilities and measures and standards of performance; Phase Two provides a guide to achieving goals by developing an annual performance plan and support for that plan. Methods for reviewing progress at prearranged intervals and annual performance appraisals are discussed. Performance planning and appraisal are the heart of the system.

Like job analysis, the "best," or most "accurate" job descriptions are developed jointly by the person doing the job and those trained in developing and writing job descriptions. Job descriptions should reflect changes in employment selection and hiring practices, organizational and governmental guidelines, and technological advances. Ultimately, job descriptions make their way into performance appraisals. For instance, job descriptions based on established performance standards can be compared with employee performance using qualitative (Chapter 10) and quantitative (Chapter 11) approaches.

CORE, UNIQUE, AND EXPANDING JOB COMPONENTS

It is easier to analyze jobs that are divided into smaller units, or components. The role each component plays in performance is examined before measuring performance level. Jobs can be divided into three components—core,

Table 7-1
Summary of Relationship of Importance of Core, Unique, and Expanding Components to Job Difficulty and Motivation

Type of Component	Typical Tasks Performed	Difficulty Level	Importance	Implications for Motivation
Core	Routine, often manual operations *Example:* typing, processing forms, or repetitive assembly-line work	Low, but often meaningful, or enjoyable in proper work environment. Can be shared or rotated with others of similar abilities to expand knowledge of a wide range of core tasks.	Vital to overall goals of organization, and essential to staying in business.	• Rotate to minimize demotivational effects of routine. • Crosstraining to allow for sharing or changing jobs. • Reward and recognize good performance to maintain productivity. • Can be delegated and/or taught.
Unique	Specific to education, training, and/or experience, and depend on ability and skills. *Example:* medicine, accounting, fine motor coordination, verbal fluency	Moderate to high for all levels, but unique to profession or discipline.	Forms the major part of a job or profession. Provides the diverse skills and abilities organizations and businesses require.	• Most training and development efforts are in area of expertise. • Forms nucleus of the job. • Job analysis and description are based on this area. • Gives job performer identity, i.e, uniqueness
Expanding	Relates to personal growth and development in profession or area of expertise. *Example:* create new products, use novel approaches, perform forefront research, generate creative ideas.	Demanding, but challenging. Can require near constant attention and effort to remain current.	Allows creativity and innovation, feelings of high-level accomplishment which are very motivational, and extremely rewarding.	• Highly motivational. • Stretches personal and professional abilities. • Fosters creativity and innovation, i.e., self-actualization. • Cannot be delegated or taught.

unique, and expanding tasks as summarized in Table 7-1. Most of the working day is spent in core activities. Varying amounts of time are devoted to unique activities. Only a small percentage of time focuses on expanding

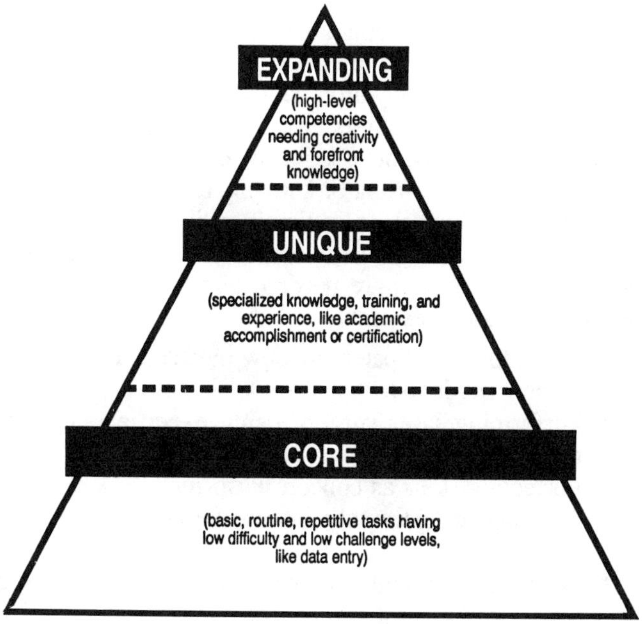

Figure 7-1. Core-Unique-Expanding Model.

tasks. However, people do move back and forth between the three levels.

The Core-Unique-Expanding (C-U-E) model is a fact-based, experience-based representation model (Figure 7-1). It describes and illustrates methods to define, group, and analyze specific types of work activities (Smith, 1993a, 1993b).

Core Components

People with the same or very similar job descriptions perform common core tasks, such as typing, routine paper work, or small parts assembly, for instance. "Core" implies the center, or major area. Employees doing the same core jobs can work at different locations in the same company. They may have different job descriptions, even though they do the same core tasks. Also, people in different companies throughout the world perform similar routine or core tasks.

To illustrate, both pilots and data-entry clerks use similar levels of skills to enter numeric data in their computers. Differences are not in the level of skill required to enter data, but in amount of time spent entering data. Airline pilots or flight engineers spend a small percentage of time entering flight data. Clerks may spend 90% of their day entering data from numerous sources.

Typical core tasks include:

- Entering existing data into computer.
- Reading mail.
- Jogging, riding bicycle, or lifting weights.
- Driving car at 55 mph on the highway.
- Looking for a misplaced file folder.

Major components of core tasks have varying levels of complexity. Core components performed by a janitorial service, for example, require less skill and thought than core components performed by an accountant. Core components for janitors are very different from those of accountants. However, core tasks play important roles for janitors and accountants.

We all perform core tasks and these tasks often consume more time than we are willing to devote to them. Core tasks, which can readily be taught or delegated to other employees, expand employees' experience, as in job sharing, job rotation, or cross-training. This concept is also used in various training programs that stress "master the basics first." Those mastering numerous core components have a good understanding of these core components and how they fit together.

Employees who apply this expanded knowledge become more valuable at not only the level at which they are working, but also when promoted. Tasks can be shared or rotated frequently to minimize the demotivational effects of routine and to provide additional learning opportunities.

Employees may resent performing what they perceive to be routine tasks, and if routine tasks are a major part of their daily job, resentment may grow. New employees in particular should not be assigned only core tasks. Core tasks can be rotated among employees, or delegated. However, if assigned only unique tasks, workers may appear unproductive while trying to learn or acquire new job skills.

Sales clerks, receptionists, and other "front-line" employees are often a customer's or client's first contact with an organization. These key people who repeatedly perform core tasks share a major responsibility for keeping customers satisfied and companies in business. Because of high visibility in some core jobs, people at this level should be appropriately recognized and encouraged to maintain their "personable," front-line images and high performance.

However, the repetitive nature of most core tasks makes them potential candidates for "computerization" or automation. Automation is "good" or "bad" depending, among other things, on whether you are affected. Cost, temporary disruption of work flow, and associated training costs could also be problem areas.

Unique Components

Unique job components are based primarily on educational background, experience, training, or specific certification. They cannot be readily assigned to others. For example, mechanical engineers, musicians, and accountants each have separate fields of general and specific information and expertise to:

- Redesign catalytic converter.
- Play musical instrument in symphony orchestra.
- Analyze cash flow data.

Judgment, intuition, and a special combination of skills based on gradual accumulation and application of knowledge separate core and unique tasks.

Unique skills are relatively easy to identify. Most people are hired based on these skills, i.e., physicians, engineers, nurses, auditors, etc. Unique skills can be acquired or expanded through college courses, on-the-job training, continuing education, independent study, or other ways. Much training and development occurs in this area.

Below average performance in unique component areas may be caused by poor job skills, inadequate training, or failure to stay current. In some areas of specialization, unique skills can become dated rather quickly. The half-life (time for half of something to disappear or be used up) of many technical degrees is approximately five years. Staying competent means updating skills frequently. Lack of unique skills and knowledge obviously lowers productivity.

Expanding Components

These tasks require continuous acquisition and application of new information to existing unique job components or skills. People in many professions—engineers, surgeons, attorneys, systems analysts, etc., must not only remain current in their fields, but continually expand their information base. For most, using or knowing how or when to use the latest technological innovation is critical.

Expanding tasks grow in breadth and scope as new products and services are needed, and new technologies developed. Examples are:

- Developing and patenting new mechanical processes or new products.
- Performing laser surgery using experimental techniques.
- Perfecting skills as concert performer.
- Creating an extremely innovative advertising campaign.
- Producing computer chips with twice the storage capacity of closest competitor.

Maintaining high-level competence requires self-discipline and often independent study. Keeping current and improving expanding skills involves personal or company support and expenditure of time, effort, and money.

Enabling employees to perform expanding tasks has tremendous potential for increasing motivation and productivity. Although most employees reportedly prefer to perform at this demanding level most of the time, it is seldom economically feasible or practical.

Performing expanding or complex tasks is highly motivational for new graduates and upwardly mobile young employees. Involvement with expanding tasks approaches the self-actualization level, the highest of Maslow's hierarchy of needs.

Few jobs in traditional companies either require or allow employees to function at this level much of the time. Work loads are often concentrated in core and unique areas. However, every job that allows some time for expanding tasks will foster creativity and innovation.

SKILLS INVENTORIES

Skills inventories can range in complexity from a mental list to a computerized printout. They can focus on the past (basis for standards), present (performance appraisal), and future (job training) (Washing and Boveington, 1986). Inventories that sample and monitor a broad range of skills required and used on the job become useful documents.

Before assigning jobs, types and required level of skills should be determined.

Major uses of skills inventories are in (1) human resources planning, (2) career development, (3) internal recruiting (4) individual career planning. Inventories are particularly useful at performance appraisal time. To illustrate, knowing the difficulty level of job components lets the supervisor assign some easier tasks to new employees. Difficulty level can gradually be raised as new employees gain skill and experience. Reilly and DiAngelo (1988) outline ways to redesign jobs to meet employee's specific needs.

The U.S. Department of Labor *Dictionary of Occupational Titles* is an excellent source of information containing more than 40,000 titles and 25,000 actual job descriptions. This resource could be used to develop skills inventory systems.

Courtney (1986) presents a detailed description of a human resources management program for assessing, planning, and developing employees' professional and management skills.

The Core-Unique-Expanding tasks (CUE) method aids in developing general skills inventories or data bases on employees. This information will supplement existing biographic and demographic data, for instance, job titles, job assignments for each job title, career goals and objectives,

---

1. Write a brief description of five major job functions or components for your own job.

2. Select three of the most important job components and write them below. Develop a brief operational definition for each job component. (See Chapter 8 for operational definitions.) Indicate whether job components are mostly knowledge (K), ability (A), or skills (S). Specify whether components are core (C), unique (U), or expanding (E). Estimate the approximate percent of time spent in each activity.

Analysis of Job Components, Type and Level of Skills Used

Job Components	Complete Description or Operational Definition	(K,A,S)	Level C,U,E	% Time Each Level
_____	_____	_____	_____	_____
_____	_____	_____	_____	_____
_____	_____	_____	_____	_____

3. The following 16-item Analysis of Job Components has the same first five questions as # 2. Subsequent questions relate primarily to productivity.

Job Analysis and Its Relationship to Productivity Measurement

Categories	Job Components		
	1	**2**	**3**
1. Brief description	_____	_____	_____
2. Operational definition	_____	_____	_____
3. Knowledge (K), Abilities (A), or Skills (S)	_____	_____	_____
4. Core (C), Unique (U), or Expanding (E)	_____	_____	_____
5. Percent time performed	_____	_____	_____
6. Rank* amount of time to learn	_____	_____	_____
7. Rank complexity level	_____	_____	_____
8. Rank importance to job	_____	_____	_____
9. Rank importance to company objectives	_____	_____	_____
10. Rank estimated current productivity level	_____	_____	_____
11. Rank desired productivity level	_____	_____	_____
12. Rank motivating potential	_____	_____	_____
13. Rank contribution to company profit	_____	_____	_____
14. Current way of measuring productivity	_____	_____	_____
15. "Ideal" way of measuring productivity	_____	_____	_____
16. Other	_____	_____	_____

*A 7-point scale (1 = low . . . 7 = high) is to be used throughout. To increase reliability of ratings, each point on the rating scale may be operationally defined (Chapter 8).

appraisal ratings level of skills and knowledge and general and specific training. See box on page 71.

This analysis summarizes and classifies major job components. It can be used to obtain pertinent information on numerous jobs. This data base can be used to develop measures or indicators of productivity.

REFERENCES

1. Asselin, Gerald A. and St. John, Walter D. "Promote Productivity: User-Friendly Management," *Personnel Journal*, December 1986, pp. 40–47.

2. Bloom, B. S., et al. *Taxanomy of Educational Objectives, Handbook I. Cognitive Domain,* New York: McKay, 1956.

3. Courtney, Roslyn S. "A Human Resources Program that Helps Management and Employees Prepare for the Future," *Personnel*, May 1986, pp. 32–35, 37–40.

4. Gagne, R. M. *The Conditions of Learning,* New York: Holt, Rinehart and Winston, 1965.

5. Glueck, William F. *Foundations of Personnel,* Dallas, Texas: Business Publications, Inc., 1979.

6. Grant, Philip C. "What Use Is a Job Description?" *Personnel Journal*, February 1988, pp. 44–53.

7. Levine, Edward L., Sistrunk, Francis, McNutt, Kathryn J. and Gael, Sidney. "Exemplary Job Analysis Systems in Selected Organizations: A Description of Process and Outcomes," *Journal of Business and Psychology*, Vol. 3, No. 1, Fall 1988, pp. 3–21.

8. Plachy, Robert J. "Writing Job Descriptions that Get Results," *Personnel*, October 1987, pp. 56–63.

9. Reilly, Bernard J. and DiAngelo, Joseph A. "A Look at Job Redesign," *Personnel*, February 1988, pp. 61–65.

10. Smith, Elizabeth A. "A Conceptual Model for Introducing Quality into Measurments of White-Collar Productivity," *Productivity & Quality Management Frontiers-IV,* Vol. 1, edited by Sumanth, Edosomwan, Poupart, and Sink. Norcross, Georgia: Industrial Engineering and Management Press, 1993a, pp. 391–398.

11. _____. "Operationally Defining Quality of White Collar/Knowledge Work," *Proceedings of the European Organization for Quality,* Vol. 1, Helsinki, Finland, June 14–18. 1993b, pp. 286–291.

12. _____. *Creating Productive Organizations,* Delray Beach, Florida: St. Lucie Press, 1995.

13. Washing, Harry A. and Boveington, Kurt W. "How Useful Are Skills Inventories?" *Personnel*, June 1986, pp. 13–14, 16–17, 19.

14. Woods, James G., and Dillion, Theresa. "The Performance Review Approach to Improving Productivity," *Personnel*, May 1985, pp. 20–27.

15. Wright, Patrick M. and Wexley, Kenneth N. "How to Choose the Kind of Job Analysis You Really Need," *Personnel*, May 1985, pp. 51–55.

Ideas to Remember

Chapter 7—Answers and Insights

1. Job components selected should relate to major activities performed. They will represent core, unique, and expanding activities. Table 7-1 provides examples.

   Gagne (1965) defines and describes five domains of the learning process. The domains are: motor skills; verbal information; intellectual skills; cognitive strategies; and attitudes. Bloom's (1956) cognitive (thinking), affective (feeling or emotion), and psychomotor (movement) categories are commonly used to describe learning and behavior.

2. The three job components selected will probably be unique or expanding, although they could be core activities that keep you employed and companies in business. Operational definitions will help clarify the exact nature of job components. Whether components are classified as knowledge, attitude, or skills depend on your job. Total time spent in all activities should be at least 50 to 75%. If not, some major components have been omitted, or your job is very diverse.

3. The 16-item analysis expands on #2. Information from all items for three job components can be used to prepare a job description and a job analysis. There are examples in most personnel texts. Articles by Grant (1988), Plachy (1987), and Washing and Boveington (1986) are particularly helpful.

   Other ways job analysis and description can be helpful are in redesigning jobs to meet new needs, to keep up with technological or work place changes, or as a basis for determining skill-based or knowledge-based pay. Remember, jobs and people are both variable. People change, and so do jobs.

   The C-U-E model is used to: (1) examine various types and levels of work skills, processes, and outcomes; (2) provide a systematic way to identify, describe, document, and group personal skills, ability, and knowledge; (3) compare and rank major work content along ten dimensions; and (4) assign work-related variables to Core, Unique, or Expanding areas.

   This model is used to analyze and compare results of work processes and outcomes along 10 work-related dimensions: range; type; cycle time; complexity; structure; standards; sequence; motivating potential; control; and value added functions.

   Practical applications are: (1) improve decisions on job placement, training, career development, and self-assessment, among others; (2) streamline and upgrade work from Core (routine) to Expanding (highly motivational) activities, increase job satisfaction and productivity; and (3) provide a solid, fact-based and experience-based format for building quality or other important standards and competency-based variables into work activities (Smith, 1995).

8

Basics of Measurement

PURPOSE

- Develop operational definitions for productivity and productivity indicators.
- Consider the role reliability and validity play in measurement.

INTRODUCTION

The more clearly and thoroughly a concept is described, the more precisely it can be measured, and the more confidence one has in the value of the measurement.

Rating scales arrange variables or concepts in order, and assign numbers to attributes of persons, processes, products, and services that are being measured.

Reliability means stability or consistency of results. When the same or similar methods of measuring peoples' performance gives comparable results over a period of time, methods are considered reliable. The time period between mesurements can range from one day to many years. Measurement systems are valid if they measure what they are supposed to measure (content validity), and are based on sound theories or logic (construct validity) that support the findings of other systems (concurrent validity). Information from measurement systems can also be used in prediction (predictive validity).

OPERATIONAL DEFINITIONS OF PRODUCTIVITY

When people ask, "What do you mean?" they usually want explanations or definitions. Some statements like "Your performance is fine" or "I need it soon" are meaningless without further explanation or additional details.

Definition. An operational definition describes a concept in terms of how it is used and what it really means.

Purposes
- Increases precision of descriptions and measurements of concepts.
- Enables users to develop definitions unique to people, jobs, professions, situations, and points of view.

Advantages
- Reflects knowledge and feelings of those developing it.
- New definitions can be compared with existing ones, revisions made, and "best" ones selected.
- Agreement on meanings increases probability that concepts defined are used and understood more uniformly.
- Definitions are used with increasing frequency, i.e., in industrial management and industrial engineering.

75

Practical Applications

- Increases understanding of concepts underlying productivity by improving objectivity, reliability, validity, and precision of measurement in information or data sources.
- When definitions of productivity are firmly established, behavior, performance, and level of productivity can be evaluated using approved criteria developed with operational definitions.

Examples

- Feedback and revision processes associated with a systems approach help keep definitions current. Definitions in greatest need of revision are those affected by constantly changing variables, namely technology, economy, etc.
- Supervisors and subordinates who jointly develop operational definitions for performance appraisals increase their understanding of the whole productivity process. Through involvement, they experience a sense of "ownership" in the definitions, and become more committed to use what they helped develop.

Cautions

- Readily available, observable output-based information sources should not be overused. Additional valuable sources are input and throughput.
- Although newly developed, some detailed definitions may be too narrow or limited. They can be broadened to make them more usable.

Assumptions. Those being measured or those doing the measuring:

- Have or can develop adequate definitions of productivity.
- Desire to become involved, and begin with his or her own job.
- Accept and use newly developed definitions, or use existing ones, provided they are of high quality, and are willing and able to evaluate and improve them.
- Have the understanding and support of supervisors and upper management.

Procedures for Developing Operational Definitions

The following procedures could be used (1) in existing work or problem-solving groups, or (2) with those who are unable to meet as a group. With appropriate approval and organizational support, users can develop their own ways to distribute, collect, and revise information. An "awareness" campaign emphasizing positive factors may be needed to reduce resistance to change.

The following steps list only what is to be done, not how it is to be done:

1. Each person in the group writes out definitions of productivity concepts or indicators commonly used in the organization.
2. All definitions (there may be over 50) are reproduced and distributed to each person. At least one hour is allowed for the group to critique and select the "best" ten or more uniformly understood definitions.
3. Each person operationally defines each point on the 5-point to 7-point rating scale.
4. Each person rates each definition on the operationally defined 5-point to 7-point rating scale.
5. Definitions with the highest rankings are selected by individual votes, or consensus.
6. Definitions are used to develop indicators or measures of important variables representing productive activities.
7. After definitions have been tested, the quality of the resulting definitions, and the effectiveness of the procedure are evaluated by those developing and using the definitions. Subsequent revisions are made, transcribed, and circulated to appropriate persons. This procedure enhances the quality, usefulness, and precision of the definitions.

    These definitions can be used to develop productivity indicators or productivity measures. Once the merit of using operational definitions has been demonstrated, use and enthusiasm should increase.
8. When the definitions have been used for a long enough "test" period, the overall effectiveness of the procedure is determined. Revisions are made and circulated. Progressive revisions will enhance the quality and usefulness of the definitions. Revision and review may be done on a regular basis for extended periods of time. See box on next page.

RATING SCALES, RELIABILITY, VALIDITY, AND CORRELATION COEFFICIENTS

This section is a brief introduction to rating scales, reliability, validity, and correlation coefficients. Detailed information is readily available in publications on tests and measurements, and in statistics books.

Rating Scales

We all have our own systems of judging and making comparisons. Rating scales help us classify and describe people, events, or things in more precise ways.

Definition. Rating scales are sets of rules for assigning numbers to observations, information, behavior, etc.

1. Develop an operational definition for the best two major productivity indicators listed in Chapter 6.

2. Develop an operational definition for one major productivity indicator from:
   - Input
   - Throughput
   - Output

3. Refer to your definition of productivity (Chapter 1). Redefine it using operational terms.

Purpose
- Express estimates of attributes of things or personal traits in descriptive or numeric form.

Types
- Nominal—divide variables into specific groups or categories, for example, job classification, race, or sex.
- Ordinal—attributes of people, products, processes, services, etc. are arranged in order, or ranked from lowest to highest.
- Equal-Interval—does not have a true zero; the differences between all intervals are the same, as in the Fahrenheit temperature scale. For example, the difference between 72°F and 73°F is the same as the difference between 32°F and 33°F.
- Ratio—is the same as the interval scale, but has an absolute zero point, for example, a ruler.

Reliability

A poorly running car is unreliable, and its performance may be unpredictable or inconsistent. People, processes, and products can also be unreliable. Developing reliable measures is a detailed, time-consuming process usually requiring training in evaluation and measurement techniques, and/or statistics.

Definition. Reliability is a measure of consistency throughout a series of measurements, observations, or repeated activities.

Types
- Test-retest or measure-remeasure—the same test or set of measures is used with the same person or group on two different occasions.
- Alternate forms—two or more tests, measures, or observations are used on the same people and results examined. If there are three measures, there will be three scores: 79, 81, and 80. If results are nearly the same, behavior is considered consistent.
- Split-half—the same test or set of measures is divided in half so that each person has two scores, for example, odd-numbered questions versus even-numbered questions, or first half of the test versus the second half of the test.

Reporting Reliability

Reliability is expressed as a coefficient, r. It represents the relationship between two or more variables. (See ''Correlation Coefficients'' later in this chapter for more detail). Appropriate statistical tests (not presented here) are used to determine whether data from reliability studies are statistically significant.

Validity

Using valid methods increases confidence in the value of results. Valid systems ''do what they are supposed to do.'' However, valid measures take time to develop.

Training in evaluation and measurement and statistics is very helpful.

Definition. Validity represents how closely a measuring instrument measures what it is supposed to measure.

Types

- Face Validity—what is seen and done is measured. If your latest performance appraisal did a good job of assessing your abilities, face validity is high.
- Content Validity—the extent to which techniques measure exactly what they are designed to measure. Typing tests should measure typing speed and accuracy.
- Construct Validity—the degree to which the measurement technique uses the theory or concepts on which it is based. Operational definitions help develop better descriptions of meaningful or task-relevant concepts. For example, a test measuring ability to write computer programs in the desired computer language really measures factors basic to understanding and that language.

    Information used to establish construct validity can be obtained from (Phillips, 1983):

    (a) "Experts" in the field.

    (b) Correlations between the concept measured and the construct to be measured.

    (c) Logical deductions based on representative information available.

    (d) Data from criterion groups (a set of groups on which specific information on productivity rate, for example) is already known.

- Concurrent Validity—represents the extent to which a measuring instrument agrees with the results of other instruments used at approximately the same time to measure the same characteristics (Bain, 1983). People doing well on a small-parts dexterity assessment, for instance, should also perform well on a job requiring fine motor coordination.
- Predictive Validity—the extent to which a measure can predict future behavior or results (Bain, 1983). If, for example, the productivity indicator is high sales, a measure to predict excellence in sales could be constructed. If assessments of aptitudes of people applying for sales positions predicted they would become successful salespersons, and those same salespersons had high-volume sales, predictive validity would be high.

Reporting Validity

Validity is expressed as a coefficient, r. This coefficient represents the relationship between a certain skill and a specific criterion, for example. Appropriate statistical tests (not discussed here) are used to see if results of validity studies are statistically significant (see following section on "Correlation").

Practical Applications

- When construct validity is high, the foundation provided by indicators or measures is strong from conceptual, planning, and practical standpoints.

---

4. Develop an operational definition for each point on the 7-point rating scale used throughout this book. You may use these definitions to increase the precision and reliability of your own rating system.

5. How reliable are measures of performance used to assess the work you perform?

6. In what way do the following apply to your job?
   - Content validity
   - Predictive validity
   - Construct validity
   - Concurrent validity

- When concepts of validity are applied to the organization, a criterion of meeting production standards correlates highly with the production goals of the organization. Organizational goals are validated by satisfactory performance. It is assumed goals are meaningful, realistic, and consistent with sound financial policies.

Cautions

- Ideally, validity coefficients should be as high as possible, although the real issue is not necessarily how high validity coefficients are, but knowing when to accept/reject them.

Correlation Coefficients

Correlation coefficients represent the amount of relationship between two or more variables. Correlations range from -1.0 (maximum negative relationship) through zero (no relationship) to $+1.0$ (maximum positive relationship). **Purpose.** Correlation coefficients are used to report reliability and validity coefficients. Data are reliable or valid if coefficients are statistically significant. Coefficients that are not statistically significant may provide enough data to show trends. Determining statistical significance is beyond the scope of this book (see Suggested Readings).

REFERENCES

1. Bain, David. *The Productivity Prescription,* New York: McGraw-Hill Book Company, 1982.

2. Phillips, Jack T. *Handbook of Training Evaluation and Measurement Methods,* Houston, Texas: Gulf Publishing Company, 1983. (Chapter 9 on ''Data Analysis'' provides excellent background on analyzing data and using basic statistics, for instance frequency distributions, statistical inference, tests of significance, and other related areas.)

3. Schippmann, Jeffery S., Hughes, Garry L. and Prien, Erich P. ''The Use of Structured Multi-Domain Job Analysis for the Construction of Assessment Center Methods and Procedures,'' *Journal of Business and Psychology*, Summer 1987, pp. 353–366.

Chapter 8—Answers and Insights

1. Operational definitions for major productivity indicators:

   - Effectiveness—able to complete 40-hour assignment on time with minimum problems (2 minor ones) and few changes (less than 5 areas questioned by supervisor).
   - Innovation—produced 6 new suggestions for work improvement to reduce waiting time for supplies; decrease downtime; fill orders 10% faster.

2. Operational definitions for:

   - Input—mental energy (increased concentration, better listening skills, focus more effort in areas of greatest need), work at 80% of capacity for 35 hours per week.
   - Throughput—attitude (think positively, look for optimistic outcomes, discount negatives).
   - Output—increase customer satisfaction (follow up customer complaints, observe service customers receive, obtain input from customer surveys), minimize mistakes and redoing projects by preparing a detailed ''game plan'' (including alternatives) in advance, and following it.

   Baselines for performance should be available. Operational definitions need to include some numeric data or rating scale values above the baselines for various activities. Otherwise, behavior operationally defined will not be above the baseline, or above ''average.''

3. Unique answer, but probably expanded on concepts of efficiency, effectiveness, standards for output, satisfied customers, sales, etc. Operationally defined rating scales may be used to increase the precision of definitions. As you continue to reuse and rewrite your definition, your knowledge and skill will increase, and definitions will become broader and more precise.

4. Operational definition for 7-point rating scale: usually the middle (4) as neutral or average; 1 and 7 are the extremes; 2 and 6 are less extreme; and 3 and 5 are ''below'' and ''above'' average, respectively. Schippmann, Hughes, and Prien (1987) provide the following detailed descriptions of rating scale values:

A.
''Difficulty to Acquire'' (Tasks)

For each activity or task consider the *difficulty* an employee would have to acquire proficiency to perform the task. Our interest here is not whether an individual has an opportunity to learn how to perform a given task but rather the difficulty the individual would have in learning to perform a task with proficiency. Use the following scale to make your judgments:

1— This task is very easy to learn how to perform. Proficiency is acquired in a very short time.

2— This task is easier than most others to learn. Proficiency can be acquired in a relatively short span of time without any great degree of difficulty.

3— This task is about average difficulty to learn compared to other tasks.

4— This task is harder to learn than most others. It can take a fairly long time to develop proficiency.

5— This is one of the most difficult of all tasks to learn or perform. It requires a great deal of time and/or practice to develop proficiency.

B
"Where Acquired" (Job Skills)

For this operation consider *where* an individual would *acquire* each job skill. You are to judge whether the job skill is learned on the job or before entering the job. Use the following scale to make your judgments:

1— The job skill can only be learned on the job. A new person on the job could not be expected to have this job skill.

2— The majority of the job skill might be learned on the job, but the new worker might be expected to have learned some of it elsewhere.

3— The job skill may either be learned before entering the job or while on the job.

4— The majority of the job skill must be learned before entering the job but a worker may learn more of it while on the job.

5— A worker must have the job skill before entering the job, and it cannot be learned on the job.

C
"Importance" (Job Skills)

In this operation you are to indicate the *importance* of various statements of knowledge, skill, or ability required for performance in your job. For each job skill statement, proceed in the following manner. First, consider whether a job skill is required for full job performance. If the job skill is *not* required, then you should *not* mark the answer sheet for that item. However, if the job skill is required, then decide how important that job skill is to full job performance and fill in the circle that corresponds to your judgment. Use the following scale to make your judgments:

1— This rating indicates that the job skill has minor or incidental importance for job performance. It is not essential to the whole job, but useful for some minor part of the job.

2— This rating indicates that the job skill is desirable and useful for some minor part of the job but is not necessary for successful performance of the whole job.

3— This rating indicates that the job skill is moderately important to successful performance in either the whole job or some relatively major part of the job.

4— This rating indicates that the job skill is very important to successful performance on the whole job or a significant part of the job.

5— This rating indicates the job skill is critically important for successful job performance for the whole job.

5. Reliability is a matter of consistency. You are the best judge of whether your performance is consistent, and whether personal or professional problems detract. Reliability is increased if a standard evaluation format is used and results compared. This assumes there is a standard format that is changed infrequently.

Reliable results don't just happen. Training and experience are necessary if reliable, valid results are to be obtained. Some people will need practice working together in order to develop reliable guidelines and standards. When there is agreement on standards, methods, and interpretation, then reliable, consistent results will be obtained over a period of time.

6. Validity as applied to the job:

- Content—Your job and what you are trained to do are the same, or your performance appraisal is based on what you actually do.

- Predictive—Screening tests (usually aptitude) may show you have excellent training in computer programming, for instance, and you would be predicted to do well in this same area.

- Construct—The numerous activities in the work place are supported by acceptable, industry-wide findings and research, etc.

- Concurrent—Specific skills and abilities are required to perform your job. You possess these talents, as demonstrated by previous work experience and certain screening tests you may have taken.

Prime questions in establishing validity—"Are we doing what we are supposed to do?" "Are we getting what we expect to get?" "Are our assumptions about customers' needs valid?" Benchmarking efforts are of little value if operational definitions are not valid. Exactly what is being "benchmarked" must be expressed in precise, clear terms that people understand and can communicate accurately to others. Follow-up activities to validate results include interviewing clients, surveying customers, or comparing results with accepted standards. Benchmarking efforts and achieving validity are closely related.

Ideas to Remember

9

Measurement Standards and Guidelines

PURPOSE

- Consider the important role standards play in measurement.
- Evaluate guidelines basic to measurement
- Examine various forms of rater bias.

INTRODUCTION

Standards are used to compare any type of outcome, or behavior. Setting standards is a critical first step in measuring productivity. Specific or implied standards exist for every job. Information used in personal productivity standards comes from the person doing the job, from "evaluators," and from various existing data sources within and outside the organization. Standards change as the job changes.

Most assessment techniques are based on methods used in evaluation and measurement. Data analysis techniques are primarily from statistics and mathematics.

Rater biases, which occur in any judgmental process, adversely affect measurement and interpretation. Common biases, whether a result of personality conflicts, perceptions of raters, or persons rated, can affect the quality and value of ratings. Objectivity and reliability increase when sources of rater biases are known, and conscious efforts made to minimize distortions.

STANDARDIZATION AND STANDARDS

Standardized methods are highly refined in many manufacturing and scientific investigations. Standards (see Chapter 1) form a firm foundation for measurement in any field of investigation and can be unique to the job, person, organization, and industry. But, some standards, like professional certification exams, apply equally to all persons in the same professions, for instance, physicians, nurses, engineers, and teachers.

Consider the confusion in measurement when the length of an English king's foot was accepted as a "standard foot." When sizes of successive kings' feet changed, measurement systems changed. What would happen if automobile and computer manufacturing processes were unstandardized? What about athletic events? The Indianapolis 500?

Standards vary in precision. In the military, for example, exact, documented performance standards or codes, are well known and enforced. Scientists use specific standards and procedures to initially perform a study, repeat the study, and compare results. Repeating the study under exactly the same controlled conditions increases the reliability of results. In labor-management relations, however, standards for "a fair day's work for a fair day's pay" provoke heated discussions. Resulting negotiations may/may not be successful.

What Established Standards Allow Users to Do

Practical applications are normally presented last. When they come first, readers can evaluate the value and possible use of the information presented. Major practical applications of standards—

- Set fair, uniform procedures for observation, data collection, analysis, and interpretation in general. Establishing high standards for reliability and validity further enhances the value of results. Determining whether performance has changed is impossible without standards. Those being evaluated know whether the standards are fair.

- Enable different supervisors to use the same method (observation, interviews, etc.) to measure (with operationally defined standards) specific attributes (quality of service or product), and obtain comparable (within acceptable limits), reliable results. When supervisors and subordinates work together on standards, both learn and respect the other's views.

- Provide specific measures or descriptions of acceptable limits or conditions for current accomplishments, benchmarks, goals, or expected outcomes. When standards are set, steps toward improvement can be determined and documented. Remember the non-elastic yardstick of Chapter 1? See box below.

BASIC GUIDELINES FOR MEASUREMENT

The following guidelines are only a beginning. They set the tone for all efforts related to data collection, beginning with increasing awareness of the need to measure and ending with completed projects. Guidelines cover broad, general areas. They are not presented according to order of importance.

Completeness

Productivity indicators used to assess performance should be based on an "adequate" number of input and output variables known to separate productive from non-productive behavior. What does "adequate" mean? It means different things, depending on need. Many forms of what initially appears to be non-productive behavior may be creative, ground-laying work for which there is no immediate payoff. If major "core," "unique," and "expanding" parts of jobs (Chapter 7) are used as a basis of productivity assessments, resulting measures should be relatively complete.

Inclusiveness

Productivity measurements may be directed to service, production, manufacturing, or materials processing activities. A bottom-line concept of monetary or intrinsic value is implied.

In sales or service-related activities, productivity measures normally center on satisfied, repeat customers; purchasing; inventory; management; production control; data processing; personnel; and finance.

In manufacturing and materials processing industries, productivity measures reflect unique variables primarily related to: quality; quantity; effectiveness; efficiency; innovation; equipment; facilities; on-time delivery; and end user satisfaction.

---

1. In the space that follows list some of the basic standards you have used in any form of measurement. Could these be used in productivity measurement? If not, write down two standards that do relate to productivity measurement.

How often are standards used, and how likely are they to work?

Standard	Percentage of Use	Probability of Working
_____	_____	_____
_____	_____	_____
_____	_____	_____
_____	_____	_____

Comparability

Assessments of productivity, like Olympic records, are relative measures that change over time. Olympic records are made to be broken. So are productivity records.

Comparisons of productivity level are made over hours, days, weeks, or even years. Productivity measures contrast one time period with another time period, and use an objective or an acceptable standard, like output per given unit of time, that is understood (Bain, 1982). A typical standard may be output per given unit of time.

The productivity of two different organizations is hard to compare, as different standards, goals, and criteria are used in measurement. Expense and effort involved in setting standards, and making comparisons is high.

Readily Understood

People for whom the measures are designed need to understand them. If they helped define and develop realistic, achievable measures, they are more likely to understand and use them.

Understanding and accepting any method of measurement takes time, particularly when productivity is such a vital part of peoples' lives. Employees' failure to understand, or be informed of the purpose and use of assessment methods, is a major problem in any form of measurement.

Acceptable to Those Involved

Are measures acceptable to management, to the evaluator, and to those being evaluated? Measures should be endorsed and wholeheartedly supported by management. Acceptance may be initially difficult to achieve, but once achieved, should be maintained. No one can be convincing unless they believe in themselves, and in the products used, or services provided.

Consistency of Use

Measures used on a consistent, scheduled basis become a way of life in the organization. Obtaining consistent data is imperative, particularly when specific standards have been set, and comparisons are made on a predictable basis. An example is using performance appraisals on a predictable basis such as twice a year.

Reasonable and Fair Standards

Standards that are reasonable and fair are highly motivational. When used on a continuous basis, and updated accordingly, standards remain current, yet reflect changes in job descriptions, responsibilities, and performance.

Standards should have a realistic and achievable baseline that can be achieved at least half of the time. Motivation is highest when the probability of success, or likelihood of achieving the standard, is .50, or equal chance of success or failure (Hampton, Summer, and Webber, 1978).

Involve Those Doing the Job

Those doing the job should have considerable say regarding the best way to perform the job. They know their jobs better than anyone else. Time, effort, resources, and cost of involvement are worth considering. The cost of not getting employee involvement may be staggering.

Performance Evaluated on Site

People exhibit peak performance where they are most comfortable—in their own surroundings. Typical ways to measure include various qualitative methods (Chapter 10), and on-site performance, namely informal, semi-formal, and formal methods (Chapter 11).

Statistical Considerations

The following are statistical considerations for ensuring that acceptable data gathering, analysis, and reporting methods are used to obtain reliable, valid results.

- Samples of data from variables or indicators known to adequately measure productivity should represent a cross-section of input, throughput, and output variables (Chapter 3). Reliability and validity (Chapter 8) are equally important.

- Small differences can be detected and assessed. This feature is especially important in determining comparable worth, and in making decisions on hiring or promotion where there are many equally well qualified candidates.

- The accuracy of any measurement system should be related to its end use. Generally, the standard for a simple activity performed 20 minutes a day need not be as accurate or comprehensive as a standard developed for a complex activity regularly performed for several hours a day. Exceptions are short-term activities crucial to the success of the whole effort, like adhering to the daily 20-minute preventive maintenance schedule on equipment worth millions of dollars.

Cost-Effectiveness

- Resulting measures should be cost-effective in terms of using existing data sources, provided they meet minimum standards for measurement. But, using available data does not imply data are meaningful or current. Up-to-date records must be reviewed and concerned people in positions of authority consulted before any new measures are designed.

- Measures are either cost-effective, or if not immediately cost effective, can be shown or predicted to be cost effective in a reasonable time period.

- Measures should require a minimum of paperwork to administer, interpret, and record information. Economy of time and effort is imperative. Unfortunately, productivity assessment is often an "add on" to most jobs, not a major, routine daily activity.

Flexibility

- Flexible measurement systems change as job content, responsibilities, and employment practices change. A large "core" of commonly used measurements will ensure sufficient carry-over so that important variables assessed previously can still be measured. Certain core measures can be used for individuals and/or groups in formal or informal settings.

Practical Issues

All of the following are based on common sense.

- Measures should be as simple as possible, particularly when first introduced. Complex measures may be rejected by those not well versed in mathematics or statistics.

- Work, products, or processes over which employees have some control should be included. Without control, employees lack "ownership" or involvement in the work process, and are seldom motivated to perform above a minimum level.

- Employees need to understand what productivity means in terms of their jobs. Employees improve their performance when there is something in it for them—some monetary or non-monetary reward, or special incentive.

- It is the daily routine—maintaining the inventory, satisfying customers, completing reports, and keeping current, accurate records of cash flow—that keeps a company in business. What appears to be routine work (traditionally performed by "Indians"), is the most important work in organizations. In recent times, some "Chiefs" have had careers shortened by economic reversals, cutbacks, or layoffs.

- There is no better score-keeping mechanism than the score card a golfer carries around (Tarkenton and Company, 1983). Similarly, most employees know how well they perform their jobs. They carry some type of mental productivity "score" around in their heads. People who mentally keep score know how their scores have changed over time, and also how meaningful their scores are to the whole work effort.

- Interruption of work flow should be minimized. Ideally, productivity measures are built in to the job itself and are part of the organization's strategic plans. This is the ultimate test of any measurement system.

- More effort should be directed to assessing input, one of the keys to solving the productivity problem. Input variables (effort, enthusiasm . . . experience), and throughput variables (motivation, creativity, and cooperation) are often excluded because they are hard to define, observe, and measure.

  The endless need for immediate information sacrifices long-term perspectives, particularly if data are needed quickly. The easy way out is to focus on tangible, available, readily measured output behavior. Time versus need is a constant problem in productivity measurement.

Unique Characteristics

- Techniques varying in complexity level should be designed to meet the unique needs of employees, their jobs, and the organization at a specific point in time. For example, when an organization is small and expanding rapidly, new products and services are added. As a result, employees perform a wide range of jobs. When the company matures and stabilizes, the nature of jobs and the measurement systems change. General productivity measures developed during the early stage of an organization's life may be quite different from those developed several years later. The organization and the measuring systems changed, and employees also changed. Very few things are constant. See box on following page.

SOURCES OF RATER BIAS

Nearly everyone has difficulty evaluating others and writing down their assessments. Errors creep in. Being totally objective is difficult. When people are aware of their biases or prejudices, inconsistencies, and misperceptions are decreased. Supervisors who make a concerted

2. Which of the guidelines do you currently use or plan to use? Where do you use or plan to use them?

Using Basic Guidelines for Measuring Productivity

Guidelines	Use (Yes/No)	Where?
1. Completeness	_____	_____
2. Inclusiveness	_____	_____
3. Comparability	_____	_____
4. Readily understood	_____	_____
5. Acceptable to those involved	_____	_____
6. Consistency of use	_____	_____
7. Reasonable and fair standards	_____	_____
8. Involve those doing the job	_____	_____
9. Performance evaluated on site	_____	_____
10. Statistical considerations	_____	_____
11. Cost effectiveness	_____	_____
12. Flexibility	_____	_____
13. Practical Issues	_____	_____
14. Unique characteristics	_____	_____
15. Other: (list)		
_____	_____	_____
_____	_____	_____

effort to be objective are not only better judges of people, they gain the respect of their subordinates.

The following are major sources of rater bias.

Inter-Rater Reliability

If several raters evaluate the same person using the same rating scale, and the same evaluation criteria, the employee should receive very similar ratings from each rater. But, this is not always the case.

Inter-rater reliability can be improved if those devising the rating system agree on the meaning and value of productivity indicators to be measured. One simple way is to increase agreement by using operational definitions (Chapter 8). Other better, but more time-consuming and costly ways are specific training programs or closely supervised work experiences.

Doing Merit Ratings in Absentia

Basing performing ratings on memory, or on indirect or insufficient information is common; for example, the supervisor doing the rating may have little daily contact with the person being rated.

Personal Influence of Biases

Biases are influenced by personality, experience, and educational background. Everyone has biases, but most are unaware of them. Prejudices and preconceived notions color what is seen, heard, and done. Odiorne's classic examples of seven types of "halo effect" are extremely revealing (1979):

"Halo Effect." When managers rate an employee on several traits, they usually rate in terms of an overall impression, or halo of goodness or badness. Employees who perform well on a specific assignment do not neces-

sarily perform equally well on all assignments. This tendency to generalize is relatively common.

- Compatibility—the tendency to rate employees we know and like, or ones with a pleasing personality (probably like our own personality), higher than they deserve.
- Effect of past record—it is assumed that employees who perform well in the past will continue to perform well.
- Recency effect—employees who functioned extremely well last week or yesterday can offset longstanding mediocre performance. This bias is also known as the "Santa Claus" effect.
- High potential effect—one employee's record on paper may be overrated compared to tangible work accomplishment.

- No-complaints bias—the supervisor treats no news as good news. If there are no problems, everything is fine. The employee who pesters the supervisor, but performs at a high level, is rated lower than the silent, solitary dud.
- One-asset man—the supervisor will unknowingly tend to over-rate the glib talker, the nicely dressed employee, or the employee with the advanced degree.
- Blind-spot effect—supervisors do not see certain types of defects or limitations if the deficiencies resemble their own shortcomings. Also, supervisors who think on a grand scale and do not pay attention to details may not appreciate a detail person.

Odiorne (1984) discusses the reverse of the "halo effect"—the "horns effect." Examples emphasize the negative aspects of behavior, recent failure, undesirable

3. Look through each of the following and indicate common instances where these biases occur. Use a 7-point scale (1 is low, 7 is high) to rank the extent of control you have over each of these biases.

Occurrence and Control Over Rater Biases

Biases	Where Bias Occurred	Extent of Control Over Biases
1. Compatibility		
2. Effect of past record		
3. Recency effect		
4. High potential effect		
5. No-complaints bias		
6. One-asset man		
7. Blind-spot effect		
8. Logical error		
9. Central tendency error		
10. Personal bias		

4. Did you recognize any pattern to your biases?

5. What do you plan to do about rater bias?

personality traits, and contrary, uncooperative subordinates.

The following biases are general and occur fairly often:

- Logical error—A supervisor assumes that certain desirable or undesirable traits always go together. If employees are pleasant and polite, the supervisor is more likely to see them as having other desirable characteristics, like being honest and outgoing.
- Central tendency error—This error occurs when a supervisor ignores the variability among employees, or the traits of one employee, and rates all employees as ''good,'' ''fair,'' or ''average.''
- Personal bias—Supervisors may select, promote, or single out people much like themselves for special consideration. Or, just the opposite may occur. Supervisors may have difficulty getting along with people who are like themselves, and fail to recognize the similarities. See box on previous page.

REFERENCES

1. Bain, David. *The Productivity Prescription,* New York: McGraw-Hill Book Company, 1982.
2. Hampton, David R., Summer, Charles E., and Webber, Ross A. *Organizational Behavior and the Practice of Management,* Glenview, Illinois: Scott, Foresman and Company, 1978.
3. Odiorne, George S. *MBO II: A System of Managerial Leadership,* Belmont, California: Fearon Pitman, 1979, pp. 235–250.
4. _____. *Strategic Management of Human Resources,* San Francisco: Jossey-Bass, Publishers, 1984.
5. Tarkenton and Company. ''Managing for Productivity and Quality,'' Atlanta, Georgia: Tarkenton & Company, 1983, pp. 1–5.

Ideas to Remember

Chapter 9—Answers and Insights

1. General standards: financial, academic, sports, political, mechanical, etc.

   Productivity standards: achieve work goals—immediate (meet daily requirements); intermediate (growth on the job); or long-term (continue to master new skill or knowledge areas). Others include quality, quantity, satisfied customers or clients, sales, and commissions, etc.

   All standards should have base periods and base rates (Chapter 11) and ranges of "average" levels of achievement; and combine some unique aspects with some job-related, company-wide standards.

   If you or your organization have not developed any specific productivity assessment programs, standards necessary to "survival," or those required for reporting purposes may be the only ones used. Acceptance and support of management is a critical factor. "Ownership" in the standard or assessment method is very important. Standards are meaningless unless they are used and accepted.

   Although quality is one of the many definitions of the broad concept of productivity, more and more standards relate to measuring, maintaining, and improving quality. Examples are ISO 9000 standards, numerous quality improvement programs, and the steadily growing array of quality awards. (See Chapter 14.) Standards for customer service are very inconsistent. Some progressive companies, like the mail-order house, L. L. Bean and the Westin hotel chain, have made excellent progress in raising and maintaining high standards of customer service.

2. Although each is important, no one guideline fits all needs. It is impossible to develop measurement systems that use all guidelines. Various combinations of guidelines apply at different stages of the measurement process. If you were to rank each guideline, ranks and usage would change over time.

3. Answers reflect personal bias, and how these biases affect judgments of others. Controlling or eliminating biases is difficult. Recognizing them in ourselves and in others is important. Biases are acquired early in life, and are reinforced, for instance, by authority figures with whom we have major contact. Like attitudes, biases are difficult to change. With effort, the influences of biases can be reduced.

4. If there is a pattern to your biases, can you control them? Reducing the use of bias is a personal matter.

   Biases are built in to the way people think and act. People who acknowledge their biases and try to understand them are more likely to change or modify their biases. Feedback from team members or close associates can help identify patterns and gradually reduce the negative effects of biases.

   Biases in assessing or evaluating people can be reduced or even eliminated if some of the same concepts used to establish and maintain reliability and validity are applied.

5. Possible ways to control or reduce biases:
   - Have other persons rate the same person or activity, and compare results (inter-rater reliability).
   - Look through the list on page 87 each time you rate people, and try to be more objective. You may exhibit rater bias in specific areas, or with certain persons.
   - To increase awareness, write down the types of people, events, or things that bring out your biases. When you make judgments, you can double check to see how obvious your biases are.
   - Ask someone to work with you. Our own biases can be recognized by others more readily than we can recognize them in ourselves.
   - Use operational definitions to specify exactly what you are rating. Defining each point on the rating scale (Chapter 8) is a possibility.

10

Qualitative Assessment

PURPOSE

- Consider various sources of qualitative information.
- Develop unique, comprehensive ways to analyze diverse qualitative information.

INTRODUCTION

Qualitative measurement methods permit one to group and examine diverse information that eludes most forms of precise measurement. Data from these methods help validate quantitative measures. Qualitative methods are useful sources of a wide range of descriptive information.

If obtaining meaningful, work-related information disrupts normal performance, simple qualitative approaches are a good first step, particularly in new or developing programs. When general procedures for measuring productivity have been established, assessments may gradually become more formal or quantitative. Qualitative and quantitative (Chapter 11) methods augment each other.

Due to the evolutionary nature of work, established standards for routine assessment need constant revision and updating. Qualitative information may require specialized, often creative methods of evaluation, interpretation, and prediction. Information value is always enhanced when appropriate standardized methods of analysis are used.

SOURCES OF QUALITATIVE MEASUREMENT INFORMATION

Qualitative methods use deduction, or involve reasoning from general principles to logical, specific conclusions. Common sources of quantitative information include documents, interviews, case studies, decision-making models, goal-free evaluation, and utilization-focused evaluation (Patton, 1980). Each can stand alone.

It is important to convey to those being assessed that information gathering efforts are positive steps in the overall productivity assessment and improvement process. With continued use and feedback on changes and improvements from employees and their supervisors, the best parts of each source become obvious. Gradually, common elements will begin to form the basis of qualitative measurements.

Documents

Existing documents or records are a valuable source of information on past accomplishment. Base lines, trends, successful, and unsuccessful events are revealed. Originals of questionnaires, transcribed interviews, surveys, notes, or other documents should be kept in a safe place for future reference. Copies of documents can be made for immediate use. Rough notes, complete with quotes, side remarks, even personal notations, are very revealing.

A well-documented series of activities has additional meaning when examined at a later date. Context, or work setting, personal beliefs, and perceptions play major roles in interpretation. History repeats itself. Productivity history also repeats itself. Documents may be prophetic; even provide suggestions for improvement. People use personal diaries, notes, work-related incidents, and other information in their autobiographies. Similarly, documents could form the core of an organization's "autobiography of productivity."

Interviews

This data source is somewhat limited because participants and staff can report only their perceptions and interpretations of what was discussed. Viewpoints and perceptions are often distorted by personal bias, anxiety, politics, or lack of awareness.

Audiotaped or videotaped interviews can be examined at a later date. People being "taped" must be informed. Cost, time, and confidentiality limitations make taping a impractical alternative in most work settings.

Interviews range from open-ended to highly structured. Documented responses become valuable resources. Conversational interviews in a relaxed setting take more time, but are often very valuable. Because of differences in style, context, and biases, no two interviewers obtain the same results. (See "scorable interview test" in Chapter 6, and "reliability" in Chapter 8.)

Example questions include:

Experience-Based or Behavior-Based Questions. These are productivity oriented questions such as "If I followed you through the day, what would I see you doing?" "What is the most important part of your job?" "What part of your job takes the most/least time?"

Opinion/Value-Based Questions. These are thinking and interpretive process questions—"What would you like to see happen?" "How could you improve communication . . . cooperation in your work group?" "How much emphasis is put on producing quality products or providing quality services?"

Feeling-Based Questions. These are questions directed at understanding emotional responses underlying experience and thoughts—"Do you feel anxious, confident, frustrated, etc.?"

Knowledge-Based Questions. These are questions on factual information on established job-related factors—"Why is this performed?" "What is important?" "Would additional training help you perform your job better?"

Time-Frame Questions. These help determine when certain activities occur, or if there are specific routines, or deadlines, e.g., complete projects, deliver services, or interface with clients and customers. Deadlines are a baseline for accomplishment.

Types of questions asked and how they are interpreted is critical. Are answers taken at face value? Is content analyzed in any predictable, standardized manner? Were rating scales used to put data in perspective? Were operational definitions used to clarify specific issues? Precision in documenting all information, whether it comes directly from questions or from information generated from questions, is very important.

Case Studies

This detailed method gathers and organizes relevant material for the "one of a kind" activity. A specific person or set of activities is studied in detail, data analyzed, and events explained.

Continuous, gradual additions of information to case studies demonstrate changes in performance, and, for instance, document when "problems" first occur. Such information can be applied to individualized education and training programs for career development, and for self improvement.

Decision-Making Models

The kinds of decisions to be made dictate the type of model selected. Methods of making decisions should be consistent with guidelines used to construct the model. Information used in the model should represent a broad range of areas so that valid, reliable decisions or predictions can be made. For example, activities, options, and actions are investigated to determine how evaluation information could help do the job better. Validity of models depends on theories and information used to construct them, and on the value of the data used. Models should also be reliable, and give consistent results when used in the same or similar situations. Models and decision making are very broad areas, and will not be discussed further.

Goal-Free Evaluation

This inductive, wholistic method uses data from a broad array of actual effects or events. It aids in determining how well certain effects or actions are demonstrated. Measurable real effects and outcomes, not alleged effects, are important. What people really do, not what they appear to do, is critical (Patton, 1980).

Purposes of goal-free evaluation are to (Patton, 1980):

- Avoid the risk of missing important unanticipated outcomes by using too narrow a focus.

- Remove negative implications of discovering or revealing unanticipated or potentially negative, yet very important major effects.
- Eliminate resulting perceptual and rater biases.
- Maintain objectivity and independence in all assessments.

Goal-free evaluation methods require you to:
- Gather data directly on what is being done.
- Assess effectiveness without focusing only on output or stated goals.
- Consider the role and value of input and throughput.

Description and direct experience of what is being observed is emphasized. Those using this process are open to whatever information or data are obtained. They can change their focus when necessary, as there are alternate ways to achieve the same, or comparable results. To use the analogy of travel by car, there are many ways to get where you want to go, some shorter than others. Getting to your destination is often more important than how you got there. See box below.

ANALYZING QUALITATIVE INFORMATION

The main types of methods used in analyzing qualitative information are process; individualized outcomes; formative evaluation; summative evaluation; multimethods approach; "triangulation"; utilization-focused evaluation; and "other." Qualitative assessments draw primarily from psychological measurement, educational psychology, industrial engineering, and statistics.

Process Evaluations

In this type of evaluation the process affecting how a product or outcome is produced or results are achieved

---

1. Think of a social gathering where you met a very interesting, dynamic person with whom you enjoyed talking. Did you use any of the qualitative methods presented in this chapter to examine his/her beliefs and accomplishments? If so, list them. If you described this person to someone else, did you use qualitative descriptions?

2. Review the five ways used to obtain behavioral information. Indicate the percent usage, and rank (1 is low . . . 7 is high) how often each method is used, and how cost-effective it is in assessing on-the-job accomplishments. List and rank "other" data sources used in your organization.

Qualitative Methods Used on the Job

Qualitative Method Used	Percent Time Used By			Rank (1 low . . . 7 high)	
	Peer	Self	Supervisor	Cost	Effectiveness
Documents	_____	_____	_____	_____	_____
Interviews	_____	_____	_____	_____	_____
Case Studies	_____	_____	_____	_____	_____
Decision-Making Models	_____	_____	_____	_____	_____
Goal-Free Evaluation	_____	_____	_____	_____	_____
Other:	_____	_____	_____	_____	_____
_____	_____	_____	_____	_____	_____
_____	_____	_____	_____	_____	_____
Percent Totals	_____	_____	_____		

3. How confident are you of expanding the scope of methods in #2, above? Which methods will you use and why/why not?

4. Will you compare results from qualitative and quantitative assessment (Chapter 11) methods before making important decisions on employees? If so, how you will do this?

5. List specific on-the-job behavior that can best be tapped with qualitative measurements. Estimate and rank the effectiveness and comprehensiveness of each behavioral factor listed.

Behavioral Factors in Qualitative Measurement

Behavioral Factors	Rank of Effectiveness (1 . . . 7)	Rank of Comprehensiveness (1 . . . 7)
_____	_____	_____
_____	_____	_____
_____	_____	_____
_____	_____	_____

is examined rather than the end result. Understanding and describing the internal dynamics of operations as they relate to people, products, and services are emphasized. For instance, techniques used in sales presentations are studied rather than the number of sales made. To obtain an overall perspective, information about salespersons and the various methods they used would be obtained from customers, supervisors, peers, and suppliers. A thorough process analysis would include specific details about methods or processes employed. How many different techniques were used, and the merits of each could be examined later.

Process evaluations are developmental, descriptive, continuous, flexible, and inductive (Patton, 1980). Processes are often considered throughput, such as attitude, trust, or motivation. For example, separating and looking at all processes contributing to good customer service is difficult and time-consuming, but essential in order to improve service. Need, time, and budget dictate how extensive each effort will be.

Evaluation processes, like those used by detectives, search for major patterns, characteristics or changes in patterns or activities. Clues, inconsistencies, and even loose ends become additional sources of information. Expected outcomes and actual outcomes can be examined and compared.

Unfocused, unstructured methods allow strengths and weaknesses of what is being examined to be of equal value. This means it is not necessary to develop hypotheses about the nature or sources of strengths and weaknesses. Specific elements that contribute to success can be determined, and incorporated into a sales promotion program, for instance, and factors detracting from successful endeavors can be eliminated. Similarly, different ways of analyzing qualitative data may produce similar conclusions. Working with qualitative measures is a challenging, creativity activity.

Individualized Outcomes

These methods are designed for specific people, services, or expected outcomes. Outcomes are different for different people. Extra effort used to sample a person's abilities, knowledge, and skills pays dividends. Just as no two people are exactly alike, methods are designed to accommodate varying backgrounds and experience levels of persons or processes being evaluated or measured. There are many different ways to do the same thing, as in job training, health care, even individualized insurance, and health benefits programs.

Formative Evaluation

This method of assessment is used to gather information throughout a particular process or project. For instance, this beginning-to-end sequence focuses on quality as applied to people, services, and products. Information is regularly "fed back" to employees. Constructive, task-relevant feedback is critical early in an employee's career, or when a new employee gradually adjusts to a new job, or newly created position having few guidelines.

Also, the early phases of product development may be evaluated and then revised for the purpose of providing constructive feedback on improvement.

Summative Evaluation

Summative information comes at the end of a project, or assignment, or time period. Although information may be readily available at any time, summative means sum, or end. Most performance appraisals and evaluations of effectiveness of training programs are summative.

Multimethods Approach

No one method is totally complete. Added together, diverse sources of qualitative information can provide a complete picture. To establish reliability, a major goal of assessment techniques, different forms of the same measure or test, or nearly identical measures, are compared. If these measures produce the same or almost the same results, the level of reliability is relatively high.

If results of various approaches measure what was intended (content validity), and agree with on-the-job performance, for instance, concurrent validity is expected to be high. A series of methods could also be used in prediction (predictive validity).

Triangulation

This method arranges diverse types of data into a cohesive whole. Major factors are source and type of data, and investigator perspective and bias. Triangulation is one of the many ways to analyze and put order into various types of quantitative information.

In triangulation, the evaluator can guard against the accusation that a study's findings are simply an artifact of a single method, a single data source, or a single investigator's "bias" (Patton, 1980).

Utilization-Focused Evaluation

This strategy is based on need. Content is not decided in advance. First steps are to identify and organize specific decision makers and information users, for example, supervisors, customers, clients, and peers, and find out exactly what they need. Typical questions are: "What difference would new information make?" "What would you do if you had an answer to that question?"

Any established method may be used if its prime focus is on utilization. Content that emerges from what is studied is emphasized. No method is worth doing well if it is not needed.

"Other" Methods for Analyzing Qualitative Information

The "catch all," non-threatening nature of this category makes it a valuable source of information. I learned the importance of "other" during a week-long cancer education program for nurses. Because this was a first-time program, it was necessary to obtain as much feedback as possible. The evaluation was quantitative (rating scales) and qualitative (open-ended questions), and included the category of "other." Responses to "other" written by course participants were very informative, and covered topics ranging from critiques of specific content areas and instructors to physical limitations of the classroom.

My job was to analyze and present findings to the program director. Comments and suggestions from "other" were very helpful, and were used to improve the program. In 15 years of use, "other" has provided a wealth of valuable information in many areas the author has evaluated.

Unscheduled, free-time activities, namely lunch hours, coffee breaks, or casual discussions, could constitute the unwritten "other." Valuable sources of information also come from subordinates, peers, supervisors, clients, and customers.

Although meanings, patterns, and importance of work-related activities vary, there is general stability as evi-

6. Compare the use of formative versus summative evaluation in your own job. Could/would you change how you are evaluated, particularly your performance appraisal?

denced by predictable reactions to everyday events. Knowing where differences are, and why there are differences, is the real issue. Interpreting open-ended categories, such as "other," requires divergent thinking, and novel, creative approaches. See box above.

Cautions

If agreement on what is seen, or documented is low, people may not be viewing the same behavior, or are using different ways to report what they see. Becoming a trained observer requires attention to detail, and involves specific training and practice. Specialized training focuses on developing and adhering to precise criteria for observing, documenting, and interpreting actual behavior, or records of behavior. If two or more independent observers see, report, and interpret the same qualitative data, and obtain comparable results, findings are considered reliable. This procedure establishes a basic level of inter-rater reliability, and raises credibility of results.

CHANGING DESCRIPTIVE CATEGORIES INTO MEANINGFUL SOURCES OF INFORMATION

Psychological interpretation applies an alternate frame of reference or language system to a set of observations or behaviors. The ultimate purpose is to make them easier to manipulate (Levy, 1963). Simply stated, psychological interpretation changes what is seen into words that describe something that can be measured.

People have unique ways of observing activities, and describe or interpret them the best way they can. Descriptive statements (Step 1) are based directly on observations, or on reliable, valid data from observations. Step 1 becomes the base for making interpretations (Step 2), and developing predictions (Step 3). These three steps illustrate how basic information is changed into predictions about behavior. Predictions must have solid foundations.

The remainder of this chapter is devoted to building a strong foundation for analyzing behavior. This process requires considerable knowledge of the person and the job performed.

The following example illustrates this three-step process.

Step 1: Statements. Bill, a five-year employee, writes more than his share of high quality, comprehensive reports in a short period of time. He is very dependable. He often helps others complete their projects. Bill's work record is above average.

Step 2: Interpretations. Bill is: (1) highly motivated; (2) competent; (3) writes well; and (4) has above average word processing skills.

Step 3: Predictions. Bill's level of performance (productivity) will remain high and may increase if he receives appropriate recognition and encouragement from his supervisor(s). Bill will profit from career development. See next page.

The Observation-Interpretation-Prediction System

Dana (1966) proposed three increasingly complex levels of observing and thinking: Level I, Level II, and Level III. Level I comes from facts or data from observations, records, verbal report, and various other sources. Level II is based on ideas, or perceptions about an orderly arrangement of facts from Level I. Level III consists of theories or predictions based on Level II. An interpretation of Dana's (1966) method is as follows:

Observation—Level I (based on a sound foundation of facts).
- Stays close to data.
- Deals with specific events.
- Uses precise statements about people, behavior and events.
- Events are likely to be true.
- Focuses on actual relationships of people, processes, and events.

Interpretation—Level II (makes broad, general interpretations based on Level I facts).
- May go beyond data to include patterns or trends.
- Focuses on broad categories of events.

7. Apply the same process used with Bill to your own behavior. Make specific, somewhat detailed observations of your own behavior, and write them down. Also write down one interpretation and one prediction.

Own Behavior

Observations _____

Interpretation _____

Prediction _____

8. Refer to #7, above. To answer this question, apply the three simple steps used with Bill to a wider range of your subordinate's behavior. These steps are changed into broader categories or levels ranging from simple and general, to more involved and specific. They are: Observations—Level I, Interpretations—Level II, and Predictions—Level III.

Make observations about your subordinate's behavior, and write them below. Make interpretations and predictions, and write them below. Is the behavior productive?

Subordinate's Behavior

Level I—Observations _____
_____

Level II—Interpretations _____
_____

Level III—Predictions _____
_____

• Uses general statements about people, behavior, or events.
• May be based on biases of interpreter.
• Uses assumptions about relationships of people, processes, and events.

Prediction—Level III (makes predictions based on Level II interpretations).
• Constructs hypotheses.
• Develops theories.
• Makes judgments.
• Considers consequences.

The logical, carefully documented progression from Level I to Level III is one way to use readily available descriptive or qualitative information and increase its value by making it more meaningful and relevant to the person and the job performed. At the end of this process, Level II information is sufficiently refined to be used in Level III. When specific behavior and behavior patterns have been determined, it is then possible to use information in Level III in predictions.

This procedure applies to all levels of employees, even customers. For instance, supervisors may find this method, or an adaptation of it, useful at performance appraisal time. Groups may use it in team training or team building efforts. In proper use, this system can help users refine available information and develop testable hypotheses about behavior. Being able to predict how employees will perform, or how customers will react, is very worthwhile.

Predicting performance = Predicting productivity

Brief statements from the Level I, II, and III methods are described in detail as follows:

Level I. This is the broadest category. It contains raw data, and statements of observed facts. For example, everything a person does on the job could be observed—mannerisms, facial expressions, movements, essentially any form of interaction with others.

Work experiences, educational background, and numerous abilities and traits in the form of individual differences (Chapter 6) could be included. Operationally defining data in Level I makes the transition to Level II easier. At work,

9. Refer to #7, above. Develop a broader group of observations, interpretations, and predictions for your own behavior.

Own Behavior

Level I—Observations   _____

_____

Level II—Interpretations   _____

_____

Level III—Predictions   _____

_____

behavior is affected by the type of task being performed. Some behavior is erratic, while other behavior is very predictable and constant. Level I data could be gathered all day. Or, observations could be made randomly, or at specific time intervals. Observers, peers and supervisors who are either trained, or know exactly what to look for, could obtain this information.

The method used to observe and record behavior should be unbiased. Information obtained needs to be presented in a form that is easily understood. Chapter 8 criteria on validity, and reliability apply.

Level II. This middle category involves developing summaries to classify or group similar descriptive Level I observations or bits of information together. Considerable thinking and reasoning is needed to understand the broad range of surface behavior. The hard work of assimilating information and developing realistic, meaningful categories comes at this level. Supervisors and peers who know the job and how it should be performed can do this. Indicators of productivity could actually be Level II concepts, or could be developed from information developed for this level. Time and effort invested pay off as Level III predictions are easier to make. Also, predictions are more likely to be valid when they are based on a sound foundation.

Level III. All information from Levels I and II is integrated into a meaningful whole, or series of summary predictive statements. The value of Level III depends on how well Level I and Level II data have been collected and put together. Level III statements are broad, yet testable. Level III information supports Level II assumptions, trends, and interpretations.

If Level III findings are reliable and valid, they could be used in job descriptions, in interviews, or incorporated into performance appraisals. Or, statements about a person (employee, supervisor, or customer) could become the basis of predictions or hypothesis to be investigated later.

If typical Level III behaviors represent the "productive person," it could be hypothesized that people exhibiting similar "productive behaviors" should also be productive. This is a longstanding, controversial hypothesis. But, based on experience, most productive behavior is contagious. See box.

REFERENCES

1. Dana, Richard H. *Foundations of Clinical Psychology,* Princeton, New Jersey: D. Van Nostrand Company, Inc. 1966.

2. Levy, Leon H. *Psychological Interpretation,* New York: Holt, Rinehart and Winston, Inc., 1963.

3. Patton, Michael Quinn. *Qualitative Evaluation Methods,* Beverly Hills, California: Sage Publications, Inc., 1980.

4. Smith, Elizabeth A. "The Role of Qualitative Information in Productivity Measurement," *Industrial Management,* March–April, 1991, pp. 19–22, 24.

Ideas to Remember

Chapter 10—Answers and Insights

1. Qualitative methods: observation and possibly interview. You relied heavily on self report. If you compared verbal ''notes'' with others, your descriptions and interpretations should be reliable, and unbiased. Your descriptions may focus on accomplishments.

2. Usage will vary, depending on the nature of the job. A method presented will help increase your skills of observation, interpretation, and prediction. Compare total percentages for peers, self, and supervisors. Methods used most often should be ones with the highest effectiveness ranking, and affordable cost. ''Other'' may be methods you or your organization have developed. You are the best judge of their value.

3. Confidence relates to level or status in the organization, and how secure people are in their jobs. Introducing new concepts takes time. Employees may resist such attempts at change. Qualitative methods selected should receive high rankings on reliability, and cost effectiveness.

4. Comparisons are always helpful, and increase concurrent and predictive validity. Thoroughly understand information from both forms of assessment methods. Write down basic observations or raw data, develop some categories or concepts describing these observations, and then use this information to make predictions or recommendations. Factors may come from observations, documents, records, or any number of sources (Smith, 1991).

5. Qualitative—motivation, attitudes, loyalty, perceptions of the job, positive feelings about the organization in general, getting along with co-workers, accomplishment, achieve future goals, etc.

   It may be difficult to list factors because they overlap. Examine the first two factors listed. Are they the ''best,'' or simply the first ones to come to mind? Sometimes, the more we think about something, the better our ideas become. Last could be ''best.'' Answering this ''preview'' question will be easier after reading Chapter 11 on Quantitative Methods.

   The role of behavioral factors is easier to determine if adequate records exist, and if these factors are used in the organization. If ranks of effectiveness and comprehensiveness are high, you have probably selected good, representative factors.

6. Like most people, you probably prefer formative evaluation. This method offers more opportunity for constructive, ongoing feedback, and enables employees to modify or change their behavior. However, formative evaluation is more time consuming, as it takes more effort because more personal contact and additional record keeping is involved.

7. Observation: spends lots of time with customers making sure they receive good service.

   Interpretation: customers come first.

   Predictions: person oriented, good listener, and problem solver.

8. Observations: high work output; likes to work alone; dislikes interruptions; intense; serious; spends little time in group activities.

   Interpretations: job as computer programmer requires long periods of intense concentration; is highly motivated to perform; takes work seriously; is very likable, but not particularly social.

   Predictions: highly dependable; very productive; high quality output with few mistakes, so is always given the difficult, high-priority jobs that have definite deadlines.

9. Observations: easily interrupted by co-workers; neglects paperwork to some extent; likes customer contact; enjoys telephone contact with current and prospective customers.

   Interpretations: a "people" person; likes immediate feedback or knowledge of results provided by frequent customer contact; often discusses peers' work-related problems.

   Predictions: good supervisory material; could be a facilitator, and spend more time encouraging others to do their best (be productive).

   Answers to #7, #8, and #9 were primarily positive. However, this same procedure could be used to predict what is least likely to happen. Predictions can be positive or negative.

11

Quantitative Measurement

PURPOSE

- Consider existing data sources.
- Develop and evaluate data gathering systems.
- Select various ways of presenting data that meet employee and organizational needs.
- Evaluate various ways to measure productivity.

INTRODUCTION

Everyone measures and is measured. Knowing what to measure is as valuable as knowing how to measure. A sound foundation for measurement is equally important as a sound foundation for office buildings or homes. Good measurement systems, like well designed and constructed buildings, can be changed and improved.

Meaningful measurement and constructive feedback of results is essential to personal and organizational success. Existing measurement systems that balance available sources of achievement-based information from records and reports against new measurement methods serve two purposes. One, their broad range of content combines the old and the new; two, they are less expensive than totally new methods, as they can be expanded, and improved, not totally replaced.

Availability of data, need for measurement, type of job being evaluated, and skills and background of those involved affect the choice of measurement methods. Any measurement system is a form of control.

Employees need to understand what productivity means in terms of their jobs, including standards, base periods, and base rates. It is important to judge whether the results provide useful, constructive information that is used in the best interests of employees. Ultimately, these "rulers of accomplishment" are used to compare results, and recommend improvement in general.

SOURCES OF QUANTITATIVE MEASUREMENT INFORMATION

Work-related accomplishment is measured and documented in some form in every organization. Obvious sources are employees themselves, and detailed, well-maintained records. Data acquired on a daily basis gradually adds to the store of available information. Data can be analyzed for patterns, discrepancies, or trends. Records of personal and organizational achievement can be direct sources of productivity based information, for instance productivity indicators.

How much information exists, how reliable it is, and whether it is in a usable form affects the type of assessments used. The "best," most reliable, valid, and representative sources of personal and job-related data should form the basis of productivity measurement.

Availability of data or currently preferred productivity indicators should not dictate the choice of assessment methods. Guidelines on measurement and standards (Chapter 9) and qualitative assessment (Chapter 10) still apply.

The following are examples of existing sources of information on accomplishment. In this instance, accomplishment implies behavior, which may/may not be productive. Information sources are not listed in any particular order of importance.

Personal

- Log of past and present activities and accomplishments from performance appraisals, or other records.
- Standards based on job analyses and descriptions.
- Employees' beliefs about peers' and supervisors' expectations.
- Hiring standards when employee was hired, including major performance criteria discussed in the interview.
- Qualitative information from observation, notes, interviews or other relevant sources ultimately affecting productivity.
- Demonstrated need for training based on substandard performance and output and employees' requests for training and development.

Organizational

- Limitations or itemization of what cannot be done, or cannot be done well enough to be cost effective.
- Comparisons of stated goals of department, division . . ., organization with accomplishments.

Customers

- Unfilled needs of customers (within and outside the organization), clients, suppliers, retailers, subcontractors, etc.
- Errors, rejects, scrap, waste, returns, repairs, malfunctions, customer or client complaints, etc.

METHODS TO OBTAIN PRODUCTIVITY-BASED INFORMATION

There are many ways to obtain productivity-based information. Methods selected often consider cost, time, and availability of valid, reliable measures. But, equal emphasis should be on the unique abilities of employees, and on the specific nature of the job being performed.

Some may feel that numeric methods are too structured, and require information difficult to "put a number on." Admittedly, sources of information for numeric standards may be subjective. Chapter 10, Qualitative Assessment, laid the groundwork for this chapter.

Any progress made in the numeric area of measurement has a positive effect on productivity improvement. We can't improve anything until we can measure it. We can't tell whether or not we have improved it until we measure it. The circle is endless.

Example methods presented are: (1) job analysis and standards (Table 11-1); (2) top-down, and bottom-up approaches; (3) direct and indirect; (4) informal; (5) semi-formal; and (6) formal.

Ratios are often used to determine numerical information on productivity. A step-by-step method to develop performance ratios is presented.

Job Analysis and Development of Standards for Productivity Measurement

Step-by-step directions for completing Table 11-1 follow. Each job or task is classified according to skill level (core, unique, and expanding concepts as described in Chapter 7). Difficulty is ranked on a 7-point scale. Tasks are then examined in terms of how often something occurs (frequency), how much effort is used to do it, and how long it has been performed. Weights assigned to each of these categories help place in perspective job standards to be used in productivity measurement.

Measuring achievement begins with a complete analysis of jobs performed on a consistent basis, including skills required and difficulty level. Determining the most important dimensions of jobs makes creating better measures easier.

Information is more meaningful when the person whose job is being evaluated and that person's supervisor complete Table 11-1 independently. Then, they compare results. Information used in this table applies equally to all levels of jobs from manual to professional. For jobs having easily identified skill levels and readily observed performance, numeric approaches are simple, as in counting units completed, telephone calls handled, or machines repaired. In more complex jobs, particularly those requiring communication and coordination, specific performance measures are harder to determine and document. However, patterns supporting the job descriptions (Chapter 7) do exist and will emerge.

Keeping standards current is important due to the changing nature of jobs, technological innovation, and other factors. Standards may vary within the same organization.

The following steps correspond to the column of Table 11-1 having the same number.

Table 11-1
Job Analysis and Development of Standards for Productivity Measurement

Job/Task	Skill Level C, U, E*	Rank Difficulty Level (1–7)	% Time Performed	Weight Base of 10	% Effort Used	Weight Base of 10	Length of Time Performed	Weight Base of 10	Standards 1st Choice	2nd Choice	3rd Choice
1**	2	3	4	5	6	7	8	9	10	11	12

* C = Core, U = Unique, E = Expanding   ** Numbers 1–12 are used to describe content (see pages 101–103).

Comments _____

Recommendations _____

Date _____   Job Evaluated _____

1. **Job/Task.** Select major jobs or tasks performed from the original job description for the job. If there is no job description, one should be made. The description should be kept current. Information on "core" "expanding" and "unique" job components (Chapter 7) could be used. List jobs or tasks actually performed on a frequent basis. If this information is not readily available, an activity or work log covering a week of typical activities may be used. However, this log will change as the focus of work changes over time. Any new methods of performing the job, or additional tasks should be added, and new standards developed accordingly. Obviously, tasks become more difficult as job complexity increases.

2. **Skill Level Required.** Classify each job into core (C), unique (U), or expanding (E) job components. Chapter 7 may be consulted.

3. **Difficulty Level.** Rank difficulty level using a 7-point scale, or use scales developed in your organization. To further increase precision, employees and supervisors may want to develop operational definitions for each point on the scale.

4. **Frequency.** Determine how often each job or task is performed. Although this may initially be based on estimates, frequency should eventually come from observations, or documented behavior. As data accumulate, percentages can be used. Percentages may not total 100, as it is unrealistic to list all the jobs or tasks performed.

5. **Assign Weights.** Using the percentages determined in #4, assign a weight to each job or task. The highest percentage receives the highest weight. Weights can be based on a total of 10 or multiples of 10.

6 & 7. **Effort.** Determine how much effort goes into each job, and then assign weights using the same logic and methods of #5.

8 & 9. **Time.** Measure the length of time the task is performed, and base this number on at least a typical

1. Use Table 11-1 to analyze major jobs or tasks you perform every day. Develop three standards for each job or task. (You may want to write answers on a photocopy of Table 11-1 and save the original for later use.)

week. Sampling is necessary. It is uneconomic to observe for a whole week. Assign weights as before.

10, 11, & 12. **Standards.** Standards exist for every job. However, it is common to develop ones specific to your needs. Employees and supervisors may develop them together. Some standards are industry wide, while others relate to a particular job.

If work group members are doing the same job, and their supervisor(s) feel they are working at an "acceptable" rate, each person should meet the standards most of the time. Unrealistically high standards will seldom be met. If standards are too low, employees can always meet them. In this case, they will not be motivated to work harder.

Flexible standards, or different levels or ranges of acceptable performance within the same standard, allow for individual differences in experience, motivation, and ability. Also, inexperienced, newly hired people busy learning the job cannot be expected to immediately perform at the same level as experienced people.

The three columns for standards allow space for listing first, second, and third choices. However, different levels of the same standard may be recorded. This would be helpful when people are either new on the job, or are learning the job.

Standards are used to determine how performance contributes to the whole company effort. Most standards are used to detect changes in output variables, and to establish base rates or other specific criteria for comparison purposes. When realistic standards have been developed, accomplishments of individuals, groups, and departments can be compared. However, not all standards should be based on tangible accomplishment or on output variables.

Raising input standards (experienced workforce, positive attitudes, high motivation, etc.) should increase the quality and amount of output. Placing higher standards on throughput variables in the form of good communication, trust, and cooperation affects quality and accomplishment in a positive manner.

Standards developed in Chapter 9 and behavioral factors in Chapter 10 are helpful in completing Table 11-1. Reference to standards is made throughout this book.

The method of Table 11-1 makes it possible to examine jobs and find overlapping areas. Overlap in core areas is most common. As discussed previously, these core areas contain more routine tasks than do unique or expanding areas. Also, it may be possible to determine what jobs can be shared, or rotated.

Usually, job standards need clarification. Many employees operate under assumed guidelines, and never really ask about them. Knowing the guidelines or standards for a job is like knowing the rules of a game. There is no way to compete effectively without knowing the rules. Imagine trying to play Monopoly without knowing the rules! See box.

Top-Down Versus Bottom-Up Approach

These methods examine how well workers achieve organizational objectives and goals.

In the top-down approach, major sources of data consist of output variables—measures of cost, time, and effort as obtained by line management (Nolan in Lehrer, 1983).

In the bottom-up method, statements of goals and objectives are used to clarify the organization's mission and strategies. This method is extremely useful and commonly used. Each role in the organization is analyzed. Individual contributions are integrated with organizational objectives, strategies, and missions. This approach provides an opportunity for individual commitment. Resulting evaluations of individual performance can be used for performance evaluations, career counseling, or in other constructive ways (Nolan in Lehrer, 1983).

Direct Versus Indirect

Direct approaches use observation and measurement of on-the-job performance.

Indirect methods are usually subjective and include verbal reports from supervisors, peers, and subordinates.

Subjective reports may lack supporting information, and contain inferences, assumptions, or hearsay.

Use of both methods is often a personal preference. Availability and intended use of the information are major considerations.

INFORMAL, SEMI-FORMAL, AND FORMAL WORK MEASUREMENT METHODS

Nolan's detailed discussions of these three major methods (Lehrer, 1983, pp. 111–158) are condensed in the following:

Informal

These unstructured methods may have a qualitative base, as in interviews, documents, or case studies. Information obtained can be used to support findings from other sources. Methods discussed are historical data, short-interval scheduling, and wristwatch time studies.

Historical Data. Past performance records, sometimes considered the simplest form of work measurement, show accomplishment, not what should have been done. Work will have been measured in some numeric form, such as units of production or accomplishment. Rating scales, or other basic numeric data originating in production information provide benchmarks, or guidelines, not inflexible standards or criteria for comparing future production or performance.

Short-Interval Scheduling. This is primarily an approach, not a technique. A predetermined amount of work performed throughout the day is measured. An example is number of units produced during a 5-minute interval at specific time periods during the working day. Sometimes follow-up procedures are needed to determine how methods may be improved, or changed to sample a broader range of behavior.

Wristwatch Time Studies. These studies are also known as a "big brother" approach. Possible problems are that people who are watched do not work at a realistic rate. One time they may be nervous and perform poorly. Another time they may work briefly at a high level to make an impression.

Observers who are not trained in precision techniques may make timing or recording errors. Judgment errors, or bias may also creep in. Inter-rater reliability is a critical issue.

Information obtained may be incorporated with existing methods, or serve as the basis for developing new methods of measurement.

Semi-Formal Methods

Work sampling and time-ladder studies distinguish productive time from non-productive time.

Work Sampling. This method is based on observations of employees at work. Amount of work performed is reported in meaningful units—projects, letters written, phone calls made, services rendered to customers, or sales finalized. These units can be analyzed and compared. Simple tasks are easier to observe and amount of output readily added up. Because of the diverse nature of some complex activities, it is very difficult to adequately sample behavior and obtaining meaningful results.

Standards are easier to develop for assembly-line jobs than for jobs requiring numerous activities. Standards are acceptable only when those being observed are not slowed down or handicapped by poor performance of those further up the line, or by bottlenecks, for instance.

Work accomplished is compared with statistically valid tables or performance standards developed for a specific classification of work, for example, number of transistor components assembled during a given time interval. Data obtained are based on counted output, or on observations made by an unbiased observer during the same period of time.

Time-Ladder Studies or Self-Logging. This is a participative approach to work measurement. Employees must have a clear understanding of the purpose of measurement. Employees record or log what they are doing, when they are doing it, and the amount of work completed during a set period of time. A list of activities being performed is prepared. It is then possible to use this list to determine how time is spent, what activities are performed, and how much work is processed. Information obtained by this technique could be used in Table 11-1.

Formal

Highly structured, repetitive tasks are best suited to quantitative measurement (Ranftl, 1978). Time and motion studies and stop-watch studies are examples.

Time and Motion. Frederick Taylor, the "father of scientific management," and Frank B. Gilbreth, and his psychologist wife, Lillian, pioneered the study of time and motion in the early 1920s. Movie cameras recorded every movement made, enabling detailed qualitative and quantitative studies to be performed.

Videotaping now serves this same purpose. Although time consuming, and possibly expensive, it provides complete documentation of all performance. Employees

2. Of the sources of information just presented, which ones have you used, and why/why not? List other useful methods. Rank value (1 is low . . . 7 is high) of each as a source of productivity data.

Sources of Information on Productivity

Source	Use	Rank Value	Ways to Analyze Data
Top-Down versus Bottom-Up			
Direct versus Indirect	_____	_____	_____
Informal:			
Historical Data			
Short-Interval Scheduling	_____	_____	_____
Wristwatch Time Studies	_____	_____	_____
Semiformal Methods:	_____	_____	_____
Work Sampling			
Time-Ladder Studies or Self-Logging	_____	_____	_____
Formal Methods:	_____	_____	_____
Time and Motion			
Stopwatch	_____	_____	_____
Other (List):	_____	_____	_____
_____	_____	_____	_____
_____	_____	_____	_____

who view their own videotapes, and later discuss them with their supervisor(s), will derive considerable benefit from constructive feedback. However, videotaping employees, monitoring, or electronically tracking their phone calls with clients/customers, or counting number of keystrokes made by data entry clerks, is an invasion of privacy issue (Vittolino, 1987). Also, close, often unannounced scrutiny can contribute to increased stress levels, fear, and even hostility.

Stopwatch Studies. These can be more formal than the "wristwatch" time studies previously described. However, the same principles apply. Major criteria include adequacy of sampling periods and reliability of recording and reporting methods. See box.

DEVELOPING NUMERIC STANDARDS

There is a vast difference between having good data available for use and deciding where to look for information. Standards can provide ranges of numbers that can be used to examine performance. For instance, standards

established for a particular task may be used to determine whether a person doing that same task is performing it at a "poor," "average," or "excellent" level.

Table 11-2 shows how data can be used to develop standards, or averages that can be used in various statistical tests of significance. Selected data from an assembly-line operation are presented. Base rates and base periods are discussed and illustrated.

Table 11-3 shows how simple productivity ratios and other related ratios and index numbers are developed. Explanatory notes accompany the table.

Constructing a Table

Begin with data from output (number of products or services) provided during a specific time period, and number of people required to produce them. Averages or standards can be computed. Also, statistical tests for descriptive data can be performed. Other criteria or standards could relate to cost, quality, on-time delivery, demand, or fluctuating work flow.

Table 11-2
Summary of Units Processed, People on the Job and Reject Rate

Day	Total Processed	People on the Job	Average	Total Rejects	Average Rejects
2	280	14	20.0	19	1.36
7	315	15	21.0	29	1.93
23	164	10	16.4	33	3.30
Total	759	39	57.4	81	6.59
Average	**253**	**13**	**19.1**	**27**	**2.20**

Table 11-3
Calculating Ratios and Indexes from Basic Data

	Base Period Amount (1)	Base Period Index* (2)	Following Period Amount (3)	Following Period Index† (4)
1. Output, units	50,000	100	81,900	163.8
2. Hours	5,000	100	6,500	130.0
3. Compensation	$30,000	100	$42,250	140.8
Ratios:				
4. Output per hour (line 1 ÷ line 2)	10	100	12.6	126.0
5. Compensation per hour (line 3 ÷ line 2)	$6.00	100	$6.50	108.3
6. Unit employment costs (line 5 ÷ line 4)	$0.60	100	$0.516	86.0

* The index for the base period (column 2) is normally not shown as it is in this example, but instead is "understood" as being 100.
† The index for the following period (column 4) is derived as follows: (column 3 ÷ column 1) × 100. Indexes may also be calculated by dividing one index by another, as is shown in lines 4, 5, and 6.
(Bain, 1982, p. 54)

Record each person's performance. There will be variations, as some will perform better than others, or have different "error" or "reject" rates. Also, there may be many reasons for not meeting "quotas."

Table 11-2, an abbreviated table, summarizes output and number of rejects in a 15-person department. For illustration purposes, averages are used as standards.

On Day 2, 280 units, or 27 more than overall average of 253 units, were processed by 14 people. There were 19 rejects, or 8 less than the overall average of 27. The 1.36 average reject rate per person (19/14) was below the 2.20 overall reject rate.

On Day 7, 315 units, a record number, were produced by 15 people. This average of 21 units per person was 2

more than the overall average of 19.1. There were 29 rejects or an average 1.93 rejects per person.

On Day 23, 10 people produced 164 units, far below the average of 253. Average output per person was 16.4. There were 33 rejects, or an average of 3.30 per person, considerably higher than the overall reject rate of 2.20.

There is ample room for speculation about what really happened. One scenario is presented. Day 23 could have been a Monday or a Friday. Mondays and Fridays are characterized by slow start up, and early slow down, respectively. Variations in the daily amount produced reveal general trends. Is it possible for the smallest number of employees working that month to have the highest reject rate on Day 23? The obvious answer is to do more sampling the next month, pick trends, and compare results. Examining what is not done may provide as much, if not more data, as looking at the positive side. In any event, causes of low productivity may be traced to individuals, groups, products, or services. The ultimate goal is improved quality and productivity.

Determine a Base Period

A base period is determined by comparing present productivity ratios with a previous period, or base period. The base period should be a normal period, uninfluenced by unexpected events, such as seasonal fluctuations or vacation periods. It should be long enough to determine whether work efforts are about what would be expected.

Comparisons are made over a specific period of time, or against minimum accepted standards of human and organizational performance. The main question is, "Have we improved or regressed compared with the base period? How much change has occurred?" Knowing why change occurred and how much change occurred is important (Bain, 1982).

An index number is the percentage added to or subtracted from 100. A general form for an index is:

$$\text{Index} = 1 \pm \frac{\text{Current} - \text{Base}}{\text{Base}}$$

Index numbers (numerator and denominator) are calculated using the same base period. If the base unit is incorrect, all measurements will be incorrect.

Amount of change is often expressed in percent (Bain, 1982):

$$\text{Percent change} = \frac{\text{Current period} - \text{Base period}}{\text{Base period}} \times 100$$

Example 1: Current period = 110; Base period = 100

$$\frac{110-100}{100}=\frac{10}{100}\text{ or }10\%\text{ improvement}$$

Change is also expressed as an index by adding to, or subtracting from 100.

Example 2: If production is 115 units for the current period and 100 units for the base period, "high level" effort could be:

$$\frac{115-100}{100}=\frac{15}{100}\text{ or a }15\%\text{ increase}$$

Similarly, if production was 85 units for the current period, and 100 units for the base period, the 15% decrease would represent "low level" effort. Employees' performance records can be compared over periods of time, changes noted, and future performance estimated.

Advantages of indexes are:

- Percentages are easy to calculate.
- Trend lines can be plotted.
- May be converted to other indexes.
- Makes comparisons with government statistics possible, such as the productivity index produced by the Bureau of Labor Statistics (Bain, 1982).

Table 11-3 compares base periods with following periods for the purposes of calculating ratios and indexes (Bain, 1982). See box below.

Ratios

Most ratios are output/input. This form of ratio is used throughout this book. This is a typical "engineering" ratio, that cannot exceed 1.0. However, when it is more comfortable or meaningful to work with numbers greater than 1.0, the ratio used is input/output.

Some ratios do use output/output to compare results of two different time periods, as illustrated on the following page.

In any event, determining exactly what goes into a ratio is the essence of productivity measurement. Developing criteria for productivity ratios is like deciding on what you want in your next car. Performance, reliability, and economy are major factors in most car purchases. The same is true for ratios of output/input.

Information from input and output must be from the same process. In manufacturing industries, the costs of materials, labor, equipment, and overhead are well known. In service industries, input is difficult to quantify, as in the effort used to make a sale, or please a demanding customer.

Without methods of comparison, ratios are meaningless. Existing indexes and base rates representing past and present performance may already exist. Variations in job performance, or organization-wide fluctuations caused by variables within (cash flow) or outside (increased foreign competition) the organization require built-in flexibility.

Standards developed throughout the organization, or in industries performing similar activities or producing the same or nearly the same products are needed. Typical standards in service, manufacturing, and materials processing industries could be identical—quality, on-time delivery, and meeting user's criteria.

Some industries have established performance standards for tangible, numeric measures of output. The specific nature, use, and interpretation of these standards varies between industries, and within units or departments of the same organization. Valid, and reliable criteria, standards, or base rates used in ratios greatly increase their value. See box on next page.

---

3. Are base rates or indexes used in your organization? If so, list them. If not, could existing information on productivity be used to develop indicators or be converted to base rates or indexes? Explain.

4. Are Tables 11-2 and 11-3 primarily for blue collar output? Could similar tables be developed for white collar productivity? Explain.

5. Refer to Table 11-1. Select three of the most representative standards, and rank reliability (R) and validity (V) on a 7-point scale. Briefly describe information to be used in each ratio before writing it down.

Developing Productivity Ratios from Standards

Job/Task	Rank of R	V	Ratios Description	Numeric
1.				
2.				
3.				

The following ratios illustrate definitions of productivity—efficiency, effectiveness, financial, and economic data:

Effectiveness and Efficiency

$$\frac{\text{Projects completed}}{\text{Projects attempted}} \qquad \frac{\text{Recommendations made}}{\text{Recommendations followed}}$$

$$\frac{\text{Obtained output}}{\text{Potential output}} \qquad \frac{\text{Output}}{\text{Input}} + \frac{\text{Output}}{\text{Standard*}}$$

Sales

$$\frac{\text{Sales}}{\text{Operating costs}} \qquad \frac{\text{Customer purchases}}{\text{Customers contacted}} \qquad \frac{\text{Ideas generated}}{\text{Ideas adopted}}$$

Economic Viewpoint

$$\frac{\text{Output 1990/Input 1990}}{\text{Output 1989/Input 1989}} = \frac{1.1}{1.0} \text{ or}$$

1.1/1.0 = 1.10, representing an annual increase of 10%

General All-Purpose

$$\frac{\text{Total output}}{\text{Sum total of identifiable inputs}}$$

* *Base rate=quality, timeliness, or criterion level of performance.*

From a systems view, is typical input data readily available? Is it easy to measure? Agreed on by managers? Tangible? Is output data readily understood by those who need it? Does it fit an existing format, for instance, personnel, or engineering? Is output constant enough that it can always be reported in the same format? Are input and output from the same process? Answers to all questions should be, "Yes." Now, for the next question.

Who decides what input and output variables are used in ratios? Those doing the work, their peers, and supervisors should develop, test out, critique, and improve the quality of information used in performance ratios. Group effort also facilitates the communication process, primarily by reducing misunderstanding.

Table 11-4 presents common information sources for ratios in the manufacturing and in service sectors. In manufacturing and materials processing industries, amount of raw materials, and associated equipment and labor costs are known. Depreciation of equipment, inventory, and labor are usually fixed costs. They may not be easy to compute. Amount of output or number of tangible products customers purchase is relatively easy to determine.

In service areas, input is often labor-intensive. Input is primarily directed to many types and levels of customers or clients. Results of consumer surveys often bring about changes in input, for instance, the need for a new product.

Where is throughput? The presence of throughput is inferred. Inferences can be wrong, or misleading. Throughput variables often relate to personal feelings about the job performed, and reflect beliefs and values of peers, management, atmosphere of the workplace, and organizational culture. Throughput, an important, yet often ignored variable, can literally make a project sink or swim. See box, #6.

6. Where does throughput appear in productivity ratios? How could throughout affect your ratios?

Table 11-4
Sources of Information for Ratios in the
Manufacturing and Service Sectors

Manufacturing	Service
Input	
• Raw materials (steel, wood, cement, hydrocarbons)	• Customer demand (food, medical, travel)
• Labor	• Advertising or promotion
• Capital	• Effort to contact customers
• Equipment	• Letters, phone calls, use media
Throughput	
• Transformation of raw materials into products	• Make service appealing (cost, quality, availability)
• Monitoring all stages of product development process	• Strategize, demonstrate, facilitate to sell service to customers
Output	
• Product completed according to specific standards	• Quality service that meets customer/client standards
• Cost to manufacture is known	• Customer goodwill intangible and difficult to compute
• Equipment used depreciates	• Major expense advertising

Table 11-4 information can be generalized to other areas or adapted to meet specific needs, such as materials processing or packaging.

Steps to Develop Performance Ratios

The following ten steps are general, and apply to measuring most change efforts. If workable ratios exist, test them out using the following system. If you do not have performance ratios, complete all ten steps with estimates or hypothetical information to work out the "bugs."

1. List persons at various levels within the organization who should be involved, if only to increase awareness. Begin with your own department. Peers can assist you, and critique your efforts. Status reports, and final summaries of findings help peers in their own efforts.

2. Review various activities and functions for which you are currently responsible. Keep personal, departmental, and organizational goals in mind. Do not start with a preconceived notion of what you want to find and stop looking when you find it.

3. Determine the best method to obtain input data. In manufacturing, data will be classified into well-established categories, and be relatively easy to obtain. Data should be valid and reliable. In the service sector, input data is often effort exerted and time spent. Throughput could be thinking, learning, and motivation. Output is projects completed or sales finalized. Methods to obtain data include observation, interviews or other direct measures of on-the-job performance, analysis of reports and other documents (Chapter 10), and monitoring team efforts.

4. When a data collection method is selected, or a new one developed, determine how closely indicators relate to achievement of personal, group, and organizational goals. An optimum balance between qualitative and quantitative measurement and how each complements the other is important.

5. Operationally define input, throughput, and output (Chapter 8).

6. Identify information required to construct productivity ratios. Determine how and where information is to be obtained. Make sure information is current, and reflects any changes in job requirements, level of person performing the job, or work procedures.

7. Define standards or specific levels of performance to be achieved. Standards must adequately sample behavior, and provide meaningful, reliable, and valid information. Company-wide, industry-accepted, or other appropriate standards should be evaluated.

8. Numeric values must increase when performance improves. If this does not happen, there is something wrong with the measuring system. Employees need to know how increased effort improves results. If the same set of output/input ratios have been used for years, determine why. They could be perfectly fine, or outdated.

Possible problem areas:

- Some complex jobs may initially require considerable monitoring to determine exact components.
- Separating team and individual output may/may not be necessary.
- Some goals are so long-term that short-term accomplishment of minor goals is accepted as the standard.
- Determine which goals are most critical to organizational success.
- Consider how to handle misdirected or scrapped projects for which productivity ratios usually decrease over time.
- When products or services provided by an organization change or cycle during a specific period, it is hard to develop comparable productivity for this "mix." Labor resources for each product or service can be included. Bain (1982) has helpful suggestions.

9. Compare information from ratios with other standards of performance. The amount of monitoring will gradually decrease as projects become more firmly established.

Ratios selected may not be representative. How do they compare with accomplishment ratios of those in similar departments, or with industry-wide standards or trends? Rapid technological advances are important. There are always better, faster, and cheaper ways to do things, but will they work for you? Is implementing them in the best interests of employees? Are they cost-effective from an all-round standpoint?

10. Review accomplishments and start all over again. This is similar to completing the feedback process, and then starting all over again at the beginning. Developing productivity ratios is a never-ending job, as once basic measures are obtained, new ones may need to be added. This means developing new ideas. No one measure lasts forever. See box below.

Profit Motive

Profit motives may be overriding factors in productivity measurement. Logical measurement and reasoning processes are used to determine whether divisions within companies are either profitable or demonstrate that their products or services currently are, or will be in demand. Profit centers, which are essentially self supporting, are typical examples. Profitability is discussed in detail in Chapter 13.

Statistical Procedures

In the early stages of developing measures, hand-held calculators having statistical notation are adequate. Usual procedures to develop measures include computing means or averages, standard deviations, Z-scores, and doing t-tests.

Later, analyses of variance, x^2, rank-order correlations, least-squares estimates, and linear regression may be used to do more detailed analyses. Complex correlations, for instance, product-moment, multiple, partial, and biserial, usually require relatively sophisticated statistical notation for calculators, or a statistical package or program for computers. Software in statistics can be readily obtained. (See Suggested Readings for selected texts.)

Meta analysis, a versatile quantitative statistical method, organizes and extracts information from large masses of data that are hard to analyze any other way. Combining results of independent studies makes them easier to view and to understand. When results of weaker studies are combined with stronger studies, specific

---

7. Review the 10 above steps. Outline your steps below. Use estimates or hypothetical data. If you are assessing your subordinates or team members, see the whole process through their eyes. Or, write procedures for your supervisor or team leader to evaluate you.

patterns meriting further investigation can be detected. To illustrate, two similar sets of data with slightly different independent variables (two performance appraisal ratings on the same person), or two similar (productivity) indicators can be averaged. Then, different patterns of behavior that appear in similar indicators can be determined.

Meta analysis is often used in social research (Rosenthal, 1984). Other uses are to determine the validity of personal evaluations, and in medical research to determine trends or follow up intriguing leads on causes of diseases.

Statistical calculations used in meta analysis are: correlation coefficients, r's; standard normal deviate, Z; and probability, p. Many meta-analysis models use cumulative probabilities, significance testing, inferential methods (analysis of variance), multiple regression, and homogeneity statistics. These methods are based on the notion that a certain amount of variation in sizes of effects is due to sampling error (Hunter and Schmidt, 1989)

Methods of Displaying and Reporting Data

Simple ways to display numeric data include tables, graphs, charts, and numerous types of computer-generated graphics, including matrices. Remember, one picture is worth a thousand words! Appropriate statistical analyses increase the credibility of data.

Data that are readily available to employees enable them to respond to information on their own performance, or on their group's performance. Data can take the form of status reports, updates, modified standards, or even changes in job descriptions, or in technical procedures. Usually, data reporting formats are well established in most organizations.

Results of qualitative assessment methods (Chapter 10) support, or even validate quantitative measurements. The author often uses this dual technique in evaluation studies.

The ultimate purpose of any measurement method is to obtain reliable, valid results to make comparisons and predictions, and to improve decision making. Information coming from a wide range of sources must be analyzed using the most appropriate method.

Systematic quantitative and qualitative measurement brings order, structure, and meaning to information and/or data. Smith (1991) contrasts the characteristics of qualitative and quantitative data along 10 dimensions, such as sources of data, role of evaluator, method, data analysis techniques, reliability, and validity, among others. (See Suggested Readings section for additional references.)

REFERENCES

1. Bain, David. *The Productivity Prescription*, New York: McGraw-Hill Book Company, 1982.

2. Hunter, John E. and Schmidt, Frank L. *Methods of Meta-Analysis,* Newberry Park, California: Sage Publications, 1989.

3. Nolan, Robert E. "On Work Measurement," in *White Collar Productivity,* Robert N. Lehrer, Ed., New York: McGraw-Hill Book Company, Inc., 1983, 111–158.

4. Ranftl, Robert M. *R & D Productivity,* 2nd Ed., Culver City, California, 1978.

5. Rosenthal, R. *Meta-Analytical Procedures for Social Research,* Beverly Hills, California: Sage Publications, 1984.

6. Smith, Elizabeth A. "The Role of Qualitative Information in Productivity Measurement," *Industrial Management,* March–April, 1991, pp. 19–22, 24.

7. Vittolino, Sal. "The Ticklish Issue of Monitoring," *Human Resource Executive*, October 1987, pp. 18–21.

Ideas to Remember

Chapter 11—Answers and Insights

1. A "reduced size" table with answers could be included. Or, basic guidelines could be given. Determining skill and difficulty levels for various jobs place jobs in perspective with respect to the whole organizational effort. Assigning weights also helps develop priorities. The thinking process required by this question produces insights that would not normally occur, and could not be explained in the chapter.

   Developing standards may also require brainstorming with peers having similar jobs. Diversity of opinion may mean different interpretations of the same jobs. People do perform the same job in different ways. Agreement on standards for core jobs should be relatively easy, but only one person may be performing unique jobs.

   Standards for unique jobs may require input from peers who have similar background and training, and who are performing the same or a very similar job, for instance systems analysts. Industry standards for accomplishment will be available on job classifications, expectations for various experience levels, etc.

   Standards for expanding jobs will be specifically designed for each person. Established standards will eventually have to be quantified if they are included in productivity assessment efforts.

   Mental standards for expanding jobs may be sufficient, but everyone likes to know how they compare with others. Tangible measuring systems with specific levels of achievement are motivational, however many people are not self-motivated and often need encouragement from peers and supervisors. Supervisors will know the standards of their subordinates, so they will provide needed reinforcement. Without goals, accomplishments lack meaning.

   Completing Table 11-1 involved considerable effort. In many instances, standards may be concepts or ideas, not specific measurements that can readily be changed to ratios. Qualitative approaches, such as observation, interviewing, and examining the real "core" of jobs increase understanding of jobs in general. Job-related personal yardsticks for developing ratios can be verbal at first, but they should be clearly defined, written down, and later used as a basis for evaluating performance.

   If your answer is well researched and realistic, your peers and supervisors may be interested in it. If so, you have already saved yourself and your organization about six months of work.

2. Sources of information are probably bottom-up historical data, and if the job can be readily defined, some direct observation. More semi-formal than formal observations will be used. Time-ladder can be done on your own. Most data analyses will be based on averages, standard deviations, and tests of significance.

3. Many organizations have base rates or indexes for financial data. There are numerous other industry-wide base rates—number of customers handled per hour, sales quotas, interest rates, ROI, etc. Nearly any form of quantitative data can be converted to base rates or indexes.

4. Tables 11-2 and 11-3 are not necessarily for blue collar output. Similar tables could be used for any form of quantifiable data from all levels of employees. Examples: amount of work accomplished, quality of product or service, customer satisfaction, various financial variables, repairs, defects, accidents, downtime absenteeism . . . etc.

5. Typical standards from engineering and management are presented. Ratios can be based on numeric data from sources presented below, and from data from tables similar to Tables 11-2 and 11-3.

   Engineering: Routine or core engineering tasks monitor status of currently functioning equipment: standards include downtime, cost of maintenance per major piece of equipment, and repairs.

   Unique task—compare performance of personally recommended, newly purchased equipment with comparable older, operative units.

   Expanding task—compare monthly progress on equipment redesign.

   Management: Routine task—complete usual reports to meet requirements.

   Unique task—schedule for training staff on new computer system on time.

   Expanding—acceptable progress on feasibility study to recognize and reward high performers with non-monetary incentives.

Ratios will be the usual output/input for specific areas of concern.

6. Throughput does not appear in productivity ratios. The importance of throughput, for example motivation, flexibility, and honesty, is often ignored, or taken for granted. An automobile's throughput is also taken for granted. The power of the motor, and the way the transmission, brakes, and steering mechanisms work cannot be seen, but they respond when needed. Like throughput in the automobile, little attention is paid to human and organizational throughput unless something breaks down.

7. Answers will reflect your own organization, ideas, and methods. Additive or synergistic effects of working together can produce something better than the sum of the separate efforts used to produce it.

The opposite can occur, too. Failure to cooperate or poor job skills can reduce overall group efforts.

Quantitative and qualitative methods cover a broad spectrum of performance. Measurements and ratios that have an element of built-in flexibility can incorporate unexpected events and adequately reflect changes in work and in the work place.

Are results in a form that is easily understood? Can results be conveyed to management? The ultimate test is whether measures and results provide valuable information that can be realistically applied to increase the quality, efficiency, and effectiveness of the way work is usually done.

Additional information on developing productivity measures is presented in Chapters 12–15.

12

Productivity: Human Resources

PURPOSE

- Examine the varied roles managers play.
- Evaluate selected methods of examining productivity of managers and their subordinates.
- Develop families of measures to assess productivity of individuals and groups.
- Consider ways to implement measuring systems within the organization.

INTRODUCTION

Whether managers plan, organize, staff, direct, control, and/or facilitate group efforts, all want to increase output/input ratios. These ratios may represent profits, sales, or other types of accomplishment. The goal of increased productivity is the major issue. Productivity of people working alone and in groups is affected by the effectiveness and skills of their managers. Generally, productive managers have productive subordinates.

The changing nature of the work force, technological innovations, and many other factors alter how managers function. Accountability and performance are beginning to be more important than the color of peoples' collars. What is done and how individuals and groups achieve organizational goals is the real issue.

Rapid, continued growth in the service sector has moved customers closer to managers. Turning the organization chart upside down theoretically puts customers on top. When the needs and input of customers within and outside the organization are put first, the way work is perceived, scheduled, and accomplished is changed. Internal and external customers are good judges of the quality of products and services.

One way to measure productivity of human resources is a "family of measures" approach. This technique provides a wide array of methods that can be used directly or adapted to meet the unique needs of the user. What is learned in using this method is just as important as the outcome.

DISTRIBUTION OF THE WORK FORCE

The Bureau of Labor Statistics estimates that those classified as executives and managers, professionals, and sales, administrative, and support personnel make up approximately 55 percent of the work force. This figure could rise to 90 percent by the year 2000 (American Productivity Center, 1987).

Compensation of white collar workers totaled $800 billion in 1982, or about 70 percent of industry's annual payroll including factory labor (Brisley and Fielder,

114

1984). In the 1990s, the annual payroll is expected to reach $1.35 trillion (Kelley, 1985).

What about the productivity of those doing "blue" and "white" collar jobs? Booher (1986) indicates that during the last two decades increases were 90 percent for blue collar workers and 4 percent for white collar workers.

Is this because many "blue" collar jobs are automated and computerized? It could be, but what about "white" collar workers? White collar workers reportedly spend 21 to 70 percent of all working hours on paperwork, including preparing, reading, recording, interpreting, filing, and maintaining information (Booher, 1986).

Is paperwork unproductive? It appears to be a necessary evil. It often "comes with the territory." Inefficiencies associated with paperwork, or with any other work-related efforts, can be symptoms or problems.

The main focus of this chapter is not paperwork, but to provide alternative ways to examine the diverse nature of work in general, and document what is done in a way that leads to measurement. Numerous methods are described and illustrated. Methods selected will change over time, depending on specific individual, group, and organizational needs.

A logical starting point is to begin with what management does. Steps along the way include a survey of subordinate-manager activities; a "family of measures" approach; a look at administrative productivity; and the special methods you develop for your own use.

THE MANY FACES OF MANAGEMENT

Management can be a random, fragmented process. But, actually, many activities follow set guidelines and do meet certain expectations. Managerial activities include:

- Supporting work-related needs of persons supervised.
- Doing varying amounts of routine tasks.
- Following company policy or conforming to existing organizational culture.
- Being a knowledge specialist.
- Allocating resources, manpower, money, capital, and time, a non-renewable resource.
- Handling existing or recurrent crises, which take their toll in time and energy.
- Serving as role models.
- Gathering and disseminating information.

New challenges caused by changing work-force beliefs, technology, and environmental variables affect management's perceptions and reactions. Managers who develop workable strategies to cope with these challenges will be effective.

Typical trends influencing the workplace relate to people, the organization, and technology as follows:

People

- A growing self-directed work force that needs support rather than direct management. Responsibility and credit go directly to those performing the tasks.
- Hiring generalists who have a broader range of skills than specialists.
- Steadily growing number of temporaries, including leased personnel.
- A more educated, more demanding, self-assured work force that is not necessarily motivated by the usual monetary incentives.
- Downsizing, or getting the same (or larger) job done with a leaner work force.
- Growing recognition of the value of human resources.

Organization

- Diversification or remaining competitive to stay in business.
- Customers' needs for new products and services.
- Organizational size and maturity tend to limit productivity growth (Bain, 1982).
- Increases in the service sector to 68 percent of the nation's gross national product and 71 percent of its employment (Quinn and Gagnon, 1986).

Technology

- Automation of routine administrative functions.
- Move toward an information and service economy, and away from the familiar product-based economy.
- Costs, frustration, and downtime associated with rapidly increasing pace of technology and automation.
- Use of systems approaches and systems-oriented capabilities to optimize inventory management, materials handling, and distribution; operation layout; process flow; and scheduling (Crandall, 1986).

EXAMINING PRODUCTIVITY

Ways to examine productivity include goal setting (Chapter 2); systems approach (Chapter 3); the core-unique-expanding (CUE) method (Chapter 7); and individual differences (Chapter 6). Profitability (Chapter 13) is one of the most standard, yet debatable, ways to look at productivity in general.

The consistent, underlying theme of productivity improvement is to get more output with less input, or maximize goods and services provided while minimizing human and material resources.

The following methods presented in this chapter are:

- A subordinate-manager activities survey that considers the effect input, throughput, and output have on individual and group accomplishment.
- An adaptation of a "family of measures" approach.

- Christopher's Administrative Productivity Index, which originated at Intel Corporation.
- Others to be developed by the reader.

SUBORDINATE-MANAGER ACTIVITIES

The single most important job of managers is eliciting peak performance from their subordinates (Grove, 1983). Coaches fill similar roles in sports.

Effectiveness and output of subordinates reflect the effectiveness and output of their managers. One way to examine the activities of managers and their subordinates is presented in the following section.

Subordinate-Manager Activities Survey

Table 12-1 provides an opportunity to summarize and rank managers' major activities as viewed by their subordinates, peers, and supervisors. Three adjacent levels (of management) can be compared.

When any survey or measurement method is used on a continuous, predictable basis, results from different periods of time can be compared. When activities are measured three or four times, for example, and results examined, patterns will begin to emerge.

Examination of the results of the survey presented in Table 12-1 will reveal patterns or consistencies in managerial activities and unique occurrences. Ranking the

importance of major activities helps place them in perspective, and provides information on what activities are most valuable.

Example uses of this survey include the following:
1. Employees and their managers complete the survey separately, and then discuss results. Differences in the way each major activity is ranked on overall quality of performance are compared with specific performance standards.
2. Group members complete the survey separately, and discuss results in their own group. Results are summarized, and presented to the appropriate level(s) of management.
3. Specific output, throughput, and input are examined. Individuals and group contributions are compared with overall performance standards, and results shared with individuals, groups, and various levels of management. A survey is not worth much if the results are not shared and used.

Steps to complete the survey are presented in the following section. Quality is used as the example standard that is most closely linked to productivity. Quality begins with people. However, efficiency, effectiveness, profitability, or other indicators, could also be used as productivity standards. Standards that are understood and accepted by those using them are used with greater enthusiasm than standards selected by other means.

Table 12-1
Evaluation of Managerial Activities by Subordinates, Peers, and Supervisors

Major Managerial Activities	Rank	Output Group	Output Indiv.	Throughput Group	Throughput Indiv.	Input Group	Input Indiv.	Overall Performance Standard of Quality	Overall Rank Extent Managers Met Standard
1	2	3 ±	4 ±	5 ±	6 ±	7 ±	8 ±	9	10

Name of Person Rated _____ Completed by: Supervisor _____ Peer _____ Subordinate _____

Steps to Complete the Survey. Each step is explained. The number of each step corresponds with the column number in Table 12-1.

1. List major managerial activities.
2. Rank managerial activities in order of importance.
3. Under "Output" indicate which managerial activities listed in Column 1 apply to improving quality of group output. The way to use the unnumbered +/− Column is explained in #10, below.
4. Under "Output" for individual, indicate which managerial activities affect quality of individual output. List positive and negative influences.
5-6. Use the same procedure as in #3 and #4 to indicate which managerial activities affect quality of group and individual "Throughput."
7-8. Use the same procedure as in #3 and #4 to indicate which managerial activities affect quality of group and individual "Input."
9. Write out the overall standard used to judge manager's influence on improving quality of group and individual output, throughput, and input. Each standard should be reliable and valid.
10. In the space to the right of Columns 3–8, indicate whether managerial activities have a positive (+) or negative (−) effect on overall productivity or achievement of groups and individuals. Compare the overall quality standard(s) of Column 9 with managerial activities listed in Column 1, and evaluated in Columns 3–8. In Column 10, rank (1 is low . . . 7 is high) how well managers' activities in general meet the standard of quality, thus increasing the quality of group and individual performance.

Comments. If supervisors, peers, and subordinates agree on what managerial activities actually are, and on what tasks are important, all have similar views of priorities and standards. If there is little agreement, priorities, standards, and expectations may need to be redefined or reevaluated. However, some managers are better with groups than with individuals. Although managerial style and activities may differ, meeting the accepted standards for performance, namely, quality, effectiveness, and efficiency, is the main issue.

Even though output is seen as a tangible result, throughput plays a vital role. Input affects throughput and output. Managerial activities and needs of customers inside and outside the organization are part of the input. Often, increasing the quality of input, and maintaining the quality of throughput improves the quality of output.

If the overall rank of the extent to which managerial activities meet specific, valid, reliable standards is high, productivity is probably high. If overall ranks are low,

standards may lack validity, i.e., they do not adequately represent what they are supposed to represent. Also, standards may have low reliability, and give inconsistent results when used repeatedly in the same setting.

A "family of measures" approach is one way to look at various levels of work performed by a wide range of people, including managers.

A FAMILY OF MEASURES

A family of measures consists of similar or related concepts that are grouped together. Each family of measures should serve a specific purpose, and have relevance and interest in its own right (Thor, 1987a). Families of measures may be developed for various aspects of performance, for example, effectiveness, quality, or any other standards associated with overall accomplishment. Typical uses and purposes of a family of measures are as follows:

Uses	Purpose
Self	Self-tracking or job analysis over time to provide feedback on individual performance.
Work units or peer groups	Discuss and compare individual and group job content to minimize overlap.
Subordinates and supervisors	Compare three adjacent, vertical levels of management—the same, above, and below.
Open-ended survey	Gather information from specific sources, or at random throughout the organization, and select (consensus or other methods) measures best representing work accomplishment.

This method helps the user describe all major work activities regardless of content. People for whom the family of measures is being developed help select the activities to be included. Selecting measures and determining similarities within and between jobs can be done by group discussion. Common parts of jobs, whether performed by managers or subordinates, can be examined, tried out as possible measures, revised, and included in the family.

Considering and eventually selecting major activities for a "family" is a valuable learning experience. Ranking activities provides insights that are not obtainable any other way.

Direct and Indirect Families of Measures

There are direct and indirect families of measures (Thor, 1985). Each is explained briefly.

Direct Productivity Measures. These are used in screening, planning, and control functions. Each of these functions is extremely broad, and represents major organizational activities. Needs of users should be defined clearly.

Screening relates to specific criteria for assessing staff and evaluating general and specific operations of the organization. Screening measures apply to employment, quality control (minimize scrap, waste, and redoing), reducing downtime, cost control (labor or machine hours, units of energy), statistical process control, and quotas for sales.

Planning and goal setting were presented in Chapter 2. Major issues in planning are understanding the nature of work and setting priorities. Goal setting involves taking control over the direction and nature of the change process. Monitoring progress toward goals, following standards, and completing projects on time underlie most goal setting. Major goals relate to scheduling, budgeting, growth, and increasing productivity.

External control applies to timely and precise instructions for the work force. *Self control*, which refers primarily to self-directed work efforts, is a part of the attitude and training of workers.

Indirect Productivity Measures. These apply to raising awareness, feedback on performance, and motivation. Specific examples are efforts that encourage positive results, such as cooperation, communication, and decrease turnover and absenteeism. Behavior resulting from the influence of indirect measures is what is important (Thor, 1985).

Sources of Information for a Family of Measures

In certain jobs, families of measures may be broad and cover numerous activities, functions, or operations. In jobs having specific, clearly defined tasks, several "families" may be needed. If families of measures are developed for closely related jobs, similarities will result. Combining appropriate families will broaden their scope making the end result more comprehensive.

The most meaningful information for the family comes from a cross-section of users, including employees, their supervisors, customers, and clients. Focus should be on major or key services provided to customers or users.

Qualitative and quantitative information comes from performance appraisals, job descriptions, and many other existing forms of available data. Information can also be generated by brainstorming, or by various other group processes.

Existing measures should reflect changes in the job, in work relationships, and in methods of recording and reporting achievement. Updating becomes a continuing task. Measures are only as good as they are useful. All measurement is an intervention. Intervention brings about change (Thor, 1985).

Selecting a Family of Measures

Selection criteria are the same for any other productivity standard or measure. Main criteria include reliability, validity, and other standards and guidelines (Chapters 8 and 9). Although there is no one "best" indicator or measure of productivity, those that are simple, practical, and meet needs of end users are valuable.

Question 1 (in box on next page), can be used to obtain information on a consistent basis, perhaps monthly, or quarterly. Changes in activities, ranks, customers, and productivity measures can be monitored, appropriate changes and improvements made, and results documented. With continued use, an information base for a family of measures will result. See box on next page.

Individuals and groups can use the sample survey instrument on page 120. The questions cover the job and job performance, and intended use of measures within the family of measures. Specific information on standards, use, and form for reporting results can be applied on the job. Steps to complete the survey are:

1. List the major product, service provided, or process performed.
2. Indicate the area from which information for the "family" comes. Information may be a specific job, profession, or series of tasks critical to productivity.
3. Record whether information is *provided by* supervisors, subordinates, groups, or self. Also record whether information is *used to evaluate* supervisors, subordinates, groups, or self.
4. Determine major outputs. If managers are being evaluated, information from Columns 3 and 4 of Table 12-1 may be helpful.
5. Write down the major "tools" used by various levels of people as they perform their jobs. Tools may range from unique mental ability, namely, imagination in primarily creative and innovative endeavors, to computers.
6. List assumptions related to commonly held beliefs or expectations about the person performing the job, the job itself, or specific organizational variables. Standards for output, quality, or other important

1. Answers can be given for self, group, or supervisor(s), and results compared. Comparisons can be made on a one-to-one basis or in group discussions. When responding for self, circle "Self," for group, circle "Group," and for supervisor(s), circle "Supervisor(s)."

Information for a Family of Measures for Self, Group, or Supervisor

Major Activity or Job	Rank	Service/ Product/ Process	Type of Customers Internal	External	Proposed Productivity Measure
___	___	___	___	___	___
___	___	___	___	___	___
___	___	___	___	___	___
___	___	___	___	___	___
___	___	___	___	___	___

- List five of the most important activities consistently performed by the person or group for whom measures are being developed.
- Rank the importance of each activity to individuals, groups, or organizational achievement or productivity. You may have more than one ranking for each activity.
- Indicate if major outputs are services, products, or processes. Example processes are materials processing, data processing, report preparation, etc.
- Record whether customers are internal (inside) or external (outside) the organization. It may be helpful to name customers, or group customers according to specific services or products needed or used.
- Write down the proposed productivity measure to be used in the family of measures. This measure should meet various standards or criteria for "good" measures.

concepts may be included. Assumptions are affected by internal organizational and external environmental variables.

7. Indicate whether "core," "unique," or "expanding" tasks (Chapter 7) are measured. Core measures should be relatively constant, and be essentially the same for all people performing similar tasks. Unique measures will differ as they relate primarily to the skills and abilities needed on the job. Expanding measures like those for creativity may be hard to develop.

8. State whether the measures are firm and remain constant over time, or flexible. Consider whether measures need to be updated and modified as the job and the skills of the person performing the job change.

9. Record whether the measures could stand alone, or if they need to be combined before being considered for the family of measures.

10. Indicate whether the measures are for group or individual use.

11. Write down other factors not previously covered.

12. List four or five measures to be used in the family. The specific family of measures should cover most activities considered to affect work behavior, and ultimately, productivity. Answers to Question 1 (in box) may be helpful.

    Give the specific standards, i.e., base rate, range, average, or level of satisfactory accomplishment. Indicate whether the measure is direct (D), or indirect (I). State who uses the measure. Give the numeric form for reporting results, as in ratios, or percents, or a brief description.

Sources of Information. The following are typical activities and standards for eight major work areas. Coordinating, although presented last, is involved in all activities throughout the organization:

Sample Survey

1. Product, service, or materials processing _____
2. Area (job, profession . . .) _____
3. Completed by: supervisor, subordinate, self, or group (circle one). To evaluate: supervisor, subordinate, self, or group (circle one).
4. Major output _____
5. Major "tools" _____
6. Assumptions _____
7. Measures core, unique, or expanding tasks _____
8. Firm or flexible _____
9. Could stand alone _____
10. Use for group or individual _____
11. Other factors _____
12. Use above information to complete the following:

Measure	Specific Standard(s)	D/I	Used by	Form for Reporting Results
___	___	__	__	___
___	___	__	__	___
___	___	__	__	___
___	___	__	__	___

Product-Based or Materials Processing
Typical Activities: maintain work flow, meet standards, preventive maintenance, access to adequate inventory.
Standards: quality, minimize rejects, reduce downtime, prompt delivery.

Service-Based Jobs
Typical Activities: coordinate, motivate employees, monitor, anticipate changing needs, encourage, facilitate, troubleshoot.
Standards: customer satisfaction, value (include costs), reliability, on-time delivery, transactions per hour, ability, product needed in marketplace.

High Tech Jobs
Typical Activities: create, assimilate new information, focus on task, apply knowledge, divergent thinking, use expertise, maintain "cutting edge."
Standards: self direction, maintain schedules, profitable and usable end result, keep up standards, quality, quantity.

Finance
Typical Activities: monitor financial variables, chart cash flow, keep up daily routine, maintain "old"

customers, get new customers, report to board of directors, expand services offered, increase financial base.
Standards: accuracy, completeness, meet guidelines or specifications, cost effective, meet end users' needs, use understandable format for reporting, conform to industry standards, timeliness.

Sales
Typical Activities: research potential market, know product or service provided, understand customers, mediate in problem situations if customers are not satisfied, coordinate.
Standards: meet sales quotas, satisfy customers, company makes profit, meet own "success" standards, expand territory.

Engineering
Typical Activities: solve problems, improve products, services or processes, design and create, convey information, apply unique and expanding skills and training, maintain resources ranging from reports to equipment.
Standards: profitable end result, worthwhile, usable end result, e.g., reports, patents, buildings, machines, quality product or service, reliable product or service,

adhere to guidelines, e.g., safety, blueprints, designs, specifications; minimize scrap, waste . . . downtime.

Assembly-Line
Typical Activities: cooperate, maintain work flow, minimize errors, reduce waste and scrap, output per hour.

Standards: downtime, equipment use, routine preventive maintenance, labor costs per unit of productivity, overtime.

Coordination
Typical Activities: facilitate, communicate, provide needed resources, mediate, motivate.

Standards: efficient, meet end users' needs, cost effective, timeliness, smooth operations.

Although these activities and standards are primarily output variables, most activities in the high tech area are input. As stated in previous chapters, output variables are easier to measure, are used more often, and are commonly accepted. Throughput variables, as illustrated in coordinating and sales activities, are difficult to quantify and measure. Input variables play a major role in productivity improvement efforts.

Activities are not presented in any order of importance. Activities and standards are simply lists of commonly used variables appearing in the productivity measurement and improvement literature.

Close inspection of the activities and standards reveals common elements. Many major work activities and standards are the same or similar. The standards of quality and quantity appear throughout this workbook. They began their life in Chapter 1 as definitions of productivity. Other broad standards, such as value, cost, and reliability, are commonly accepted and used throughout the organization.

Standards are really "rulers." To be used as rulers, the units, or specific levels of attainment must be stated in clear, precise terms, or measurable units, such as hours worked, projects completed, or units sold. Also, each organization, division, department, or section must further define standards with sufficient precision that resulting measurements mean something to the person being measured, and to those measuring. Typical standards and their descriptions are:

Quality—attitude, knowledge, and skills, materials, processes
   Value—manufacturer, provider, and end user
   Quantity—transactions/hour
   Customer—loyalty and satisfaction
   On-time delivery—meets users' specifications
   Cost—competitive, affordable, based on value
   Consistent and reliable—quality is dependable
   Change as demand changes—updated when necessary

Support systems—equipment, human resources, etc., are fully functional

Accountability—stand behind product or service. See box on next page.

Other Sources of Information on Families of Measures

Thor (1987a) describes a family of measures model, or matrix, for measuring productivity in a maintenance department, and (1987b) applies a family of measures concept to integrate gain sharing and white-collar productivity measurement.

Felix and Riggs' (1983) detailed presentation on productivity measurement by objectives includes partial and total productivity measures. They present specific steps to complete their objectives matrix, and ways to "normalize" measures, and develop weighted productivity criteria.

OTHER QUANTITATIVE PRODUCTIVITY MEASURING TECHNIQUES

Examples from Intel (Main, 1981), Christopher (1982, 1984), and Kristakis (1983) are presented in some detail. Christopher's method discusses administrative productivity indicators, and manufacturing productivity indicators. Kristakis (1983) presents a way to examine office productivity.

Developing and Using Administrative Productivity Indicators (APIs)

The following API was developed at Intel Corporation (Christopher, 1984). Ways Intel uses API are written up in *Fortune* (Main, 1981).

Developing an Indicator. API is the single overall measure quantifying how successfully a unit achieves its purpose. API is useful when work output is physical, measurable, or countable. When API is monitored over time, you know where you were and where you are. You can set meaningful objectives for where you intend to be in the future (Christopher, 1984).

$$API = \frac{\text{Work output}}{\text{Labor hours input}}$$

1. Develop APIs using answers from the following questions (Christopher, 1983):

   - What is the key purpose of the unit?
   - What is the unit organized to do?
   - What is the major transaction flow?

- What is the end product or service?
- Who are the customers for what is produced?
- What is the value to the customer?

2. Identify the physical output of products or services, which helps determine whether the unit has achieved its purpose. Examples include:

Physical Things	Action Performed
employees	hired
invoices	paid
analyses	documented
work order	completed

3. Test the selected work output. Has work been done? Has the purpose has been achieved?

4. Define the input measure(s). The major input is person/hours of work, although energy, materials and capital could be included.

   According to Main (1981), at Intel, routine jobs that are likely candidates for productivity improvement are simplified. Job functions are spelled out in detail, studied, and reassembled logically.

   A productivity index based on output is set up just before simplification begins. One such example is:

$$\frac{\text{Physical output in units}}{\text{Hours of work}}$$

An example from accounting based on accounts payable:

$$\frac{\text{Number of payment vouchers processed}}{\text{Hours worked}}$$

A quality index ensures that quality, not quantity, prevails. Quality indexes, which will not be discussed further, could be based on a number of errors, for example. In accounting, there is no point in increasing the number of outputs, namely vouchers processed, if there are numerous errors.

Using an API to Measure Productivity. By reversing the traditional output/input ratio:

$$\text{API} = \frac{\text{Labor hours input}}{\text{Units of output}}$$

---

2. Indicate whether the family is for work group, individuals, or self. List jobs or tasks to be measured. Write down five activities for the family of measures covering most operations, or functions affecting work behavior, and ultimately productivity. List the standard, base line criteria, or acceptable performance level for each activity. Indicate whether the purpose of each measure is direct or indirect. State who uses or will use measures and standards.

A Family of Measures

For: Work group, individuals, or self (circle one)
Jobs/tasks to be measured _____

Activities in Family	Standards	Purpose Direct	Indirect	Used By
_____	_____	_____	_____	_____
_____	_____	_____	_____	_____
_____	_____	_____	_____	_____
_____	_____	_____	_____	_____
_____	_____	_____	_____	_____

3. How could information from #2 be used on the job? Develop a plan that either you or management could use to monitor and increase productivity of managers and people they supervise.

The "hours per unit" (HPU) makes it possible to do labor cost calculations. This helps with staffing and capacity planning, and provides benchmarks to monitor productivity change.

When administrative units reduce HPU, productivity increases. The base period, or "going in" HPU, is used as a standard to compare current status of productivity and predict future trends. API can then be expressed as HPU.

Where capital input is significant, API is represented by:

$$API = \frac{\text{Work output}}{\text{Labor input} + \text{Capital input}}$$

If there is more than one input in the denominator, partial productivity measures can be calculated and monitored for administrative and service units. Formulas are:

$$\text{Labor API} = \frac{\text{Work output}}{\text{Labor input}}$$

$$\text{Capital API} = \frac{\text{Capital input}}{\text{Labor input}}$$

Meaningful steps toward achieving future goals can be taken if API is monitored over time, records kept, and past ratios and current ratios compared.

Christopher's (1984) multiple output productivity measures are discussed in Chapter 14.

Developing Productivity Measures for Manufacturing

These methods are best suited to productivity in a manufacturing plant where labor hours, materials, energy, and capital are critical variables (Christopher, 1982). Ideally, plant productivity measures that are developed and monitored through a participation process can be communicated through open discussions or dialogues. This enables employees to learn and understand how measures for their unit contribute to overall management. But, specifically they should know:

- How outputs determine success, and how these outputs are measured.
- How inputs are used to produce these outputs, and how they are measured.
- The relative importance of labor hours, materials, energy, and capital.

Specific steps required for each unit to develop, review, and revise productivity measures for their unit are listed here. Christopher recommends using a dialogue process to:

1. Define the desired output.
2. Determine the most useful measure of this output.
3. Identify and measure inputs.
4. Develop appropriate productivity measures (outputs in relation to inputs).
5. Report measures for the relevant reporting period (hour, shift, day, week, month, quarter), and monitor trends over time.

Measuring Office Productivity

Kristakis' (1983) five-step method outlines how individual offices can independently perform their own productivity evaluation and improvement activities by following these steps:

1. Write down major work processes from start to finish, including input, output, human resources and labor, materials, equipment, and information.
2. Rank work in order of greatest productivity improvement potential.
3. Break down selected work processes into detailed operations.
4. Evaluate work process operations with the intent of improving productivity.
5. Determine operations whose improvement offers the largest return, e.g., saves time and justifies equipment.

Then, follow specific procedures for implementing results.

4. Could the productivity of a wide range of people with various "colors of collars" performing the same or similar activities be assessed with the same family of measures?

Table 12-2
Example Decriptions and Ratios of Performance Variables

Performance Variables	Methods of Measurement
Sales	
• Customer contacts ranked by likelihood of sales:	$\dfrac{\text{Number successes}}{\text{Number of attempts}}$
• Total customers contacted daily compared with eventual sales:	$\dfrac{\text{Units sold}}{\text{Sales quotas}}$
Supervisory Staff	
• Ratings of job satisfaction:	Attitude survey
• Difference between actual and desired achievement levels:	$\dfrac{\text{Actual} - \text{Desired}}{\text{Desired}}$
• Total time in major activity known to affect productivity (coordinating, planning, listening, facilitating . . .):	$\dfrac{\text{Productive} - \text{Unproductive}}{\text{Productive time}}$
• Management productivity:	$\dfrac{\text{Management output}}{\text{Management cost}}$
"White Collar Workers"	
• Difference between attempted and completed projects:	$\dfrac{\text{Attempted} - \text{Completed}}{\text{Attempted}}$
• Rank of accomplishment on key money-making projects:	$\dfrac{\text{Monthly accomplishments}}{\text{Yearly standard}}$
• Comparison of individual with work group accomplishment:	$\dfrac{\text{Individual accomplishment}}{\text{Work group accomplishment}}$
• Comparison of standards for separate work units within:	$\dfrac{\text{Time standard unit A}}{\text{All units in A}}$

Table 12-2 contains brief descriptions and ratios of performance variables for sales, supervisory staff, and "white-collar workers" in general.

DATA ANALYSIS

Analyzing and reporting data using appropriate statistical procedures (Chapter 11) increases credibility and usefulness. Means, standard deviations, χ^2, regression analysis, and multiple linear regression are appropriate techniques.

It will be necessary to develop an acceptable format for input, storage, and retrieval of data. Confidentiality of information could be a concern.

The relationship among several independent, or input variables (hours worked, resources used, budget allocated), and dependent or output variables (quality, number of units produced) can be computed.

Economic measurements based on staffing or cost comparisons may be used to compare achievements or contributions of one group with another. (See Chapter 13 on Profitability.)

IMPLEMENTATION

The general problems listed in this section have been discussed before, but are worth repeating. Anticipating problems increases the effectiveness of many intervention programs.

Typical steps to implement a productivity measurement program are outlined. Brief descriptions do not mean steps can be done quickly or easily. Accomplishing some steps will take considerable effort for extended periods of time. Specific, written plans and several alternatives for each area examined can be very helpful.

1. Make sure satisfactory methods of measuring productivity do not already exist. Records having adequate information may be examined and qualitative and/or quantitative assessments constructed.
2. Determine problem areas on your own first, then work with others.
3. Perform needs assessment(s).
4. Reevaluate problem areas: yours and those of others in similar jobs, units, departments, or levels in the organization.
5. Raise awareness, beginning in areas of primary concern. Awareness may also precede Step 1.
6. Obtain feedback from those affected and from other reliable sources.
7. Develop assessment methods.
8. Move slowly and refine and improve assessment methods as you progress.
9. Build flexibility into processes used to develop the program and into the assessments that are developed.
10. Use group decisions and decision-making practices.
11. Obtain commitment from appropriate levels, particularly upper management.
12. Incorporate feedback to improve results.

The first positive results usually include discovering routines, and identifying core jobs and responsibilities. The way each person performs the same job (process or throughput variables) may be more important than end results.

Problem areas usually include the following, although anticipating problems increases the effectiveness of many intervention programs: Overcoming or reducing resistance to organizational change, specifically the culture, structure, and communication networks. Personal resistance takes many forms—reluctance to cooperate; fear of what may happen, or fear of the unknown; misuse of information; misunderstanding; demotivational aspects; dislike of feedback; and invidious comparisons.

REFERENCES

1. American Productivity Center. *Issues and Innovations*, Houston, Texas, 1987.
2. Bain, David. *The Productivity Prescription*, New York: McGraw-Hill, 1982.
3. Booher, Dianna. "Don't Put It in Writing," *Training and Development Journal*, October, 1986, pp. 46–51.
4. Brisley, Chester I. and Fielder, William F., Jr. "'Unmeasurable' Output of Knowledge/Office Workers Can and Must be Measured," in *Issues in White Collar Productivity*, Atlanta, Norcross, Georgia: Industrial Engineering & Management Press, 1984, pp. 1–4.
5. Christopher, William F. "How to Develop Productivity Measures That Can Improve Productivity Performance," Special Report, Stamford, Connecticut: Productivity, Inc., 1982, pp. 1–8.
6. Christopher, William F. "How to Measure and Improve Productivity in Professional, Administrative, and Service Organizations," *Productivity Yardstick,* Vol. 3, No. 5, 1983, pp. 3–10.
7. Christopher, William F. "How to Measure and Improve Productivity in Professional, Administrative,

Ideas to Remember

and Service Organizations," in *Issues in White Collar Productivity*, Atlanta, Norcross, Georgia: Industrial Engineering & Management Press, 1984, pp. 29–37.

8. Crandall, Richard E. "Applying Industrial Engineering Techniques to Service Industries," *Industrial Management*, May–June, 1986, pp. 13–16.

9. Felix, Glenn H. *Productivity Measurement with the Objectives Matrix*, Corvallis, Oregon: Oregon Productivity Center, 1983.

10. Felix, Glenn H. and Riggs, James L. "Productivity Measurement by Objectives," *National Productivity Review*, Autumn, 1983, pp. 386–393.

11. Grove, Andrew S. *High Output Management*, New York: Random House, 1983.

12. Kelley, Robert E. *The Gold Collar Worker*, Reading, Massachusetts, Addison-Wesley Publishing Company, Inc., 1985.

13. Kristakis, John. "Short Method Makes Frequent Evaluation of Office Productivity a Realistic Objective," *Industrial Engineering*, December, 1983, pp. 48–50.

14. Main, Jeremy. "How to Battle Your Own Bureaucracy," *Fortune*, June 29, 1981, pp. 54–58.

15. Preziosi, Robert C. "Productivity Management Competencies: Differences in Managerial and Organizational Assessments," *National Productivity Review*, Spring 1986, pp. 174–179.

16. Quinn, James Brian and Gagnon, Christopher E. "Will Services Follow Manufacturing into Decline?" *Harvard Business Review*, November–December, 1986, pp. 95–103.

17. Teal, Thomas. "Service Comes First: An Interview with USAA's Robert F. McDermott," *Harvard Business Review*, September–October, 1991, pp. 116–127.

18. Thor, Carl. "Productivity Measures: Tailored for Effectiveness," American Productivity Center. *Manager's Notebook*, Vol. 2, No. 3, 1985, pp. 1–4.

19. Thor, Carl G. "Measuring the Maintenance Department," *Productivity Brief*, No. 57, American Productivity Center, 1987a.

20. Thor, Carl G. "Knowledge Worker Gain Sharing," *Productivity Brief*, No. 61, American Productivity Center, 1987b.

Chapter 12—Answers and Insights

1. Answers depend on activities or jobs performed, type of organization, and on the resulting services, products, or processes. A "people" orientation is high in service industries. Needs and types of customers also affect what is done on the job.

   Activities taking most of the working day may not be the ones most important to goal achievement. Also, activities should not be listed simply because they can be measured.

   If you write down five or six activities, important common elements will emerge. Common elements can be ranked in terms of overall contribution to individual, group, and organizational productivity.

   Proposed productivity measures should meet usual criteria (Chapter 8–11). They should also provide information to improve productivity, and increase the value or worth of human resources in general.

2. Specific families of measures will be unique to the job, and possibly to people or groups being assessed. Families listed may be similar to major work areas cited in text. Most activities performed should be included in one or more families of measures.

   Standards may be descriptive, and contain operational definitions. Standards may be either numeric, for instance, ratios, base rates, or other numeric formulas.

   Ideally, standards should include examples of direct measures (screening, planning, and control functions) and indirect measures (awareness raising, feedback, and motivation). Use of both direct and indirect measures provides a balance.

   The family of measures used by a specific group should be developed, critiqued, and updated by that same group. Users may be managers, those performing the job, or peers. Or, they may be used as standards for performance, as in professions requiring licensing, certification, or accreditation.

   "Suppliers," or those providing raw materials or other forms of supplies are vital to many manufacturing, materials processing, and service industries. Suppliers may not be informed of "user's" specifications and requirements.

   Customers are also important end users. Measures need to meet customers' needs, and serve the purpose(s) intended. Measures that fit a specific framework for presentation, documentation, etc., that is readily understood, will be easy to communicate to upper management, and others.

3. Information from #2 can be used to monitor activities on a regular basis, ranging from daily to quarterly. Purposes include performance appraisals (raises, promotions, assignment to specific work groups or task forces, etc.); improving and/or changing current work methods on activities usually performed poorly (substandard performance); assessing effectiveness and efficiency of performance in general; monitoring customer complaints; and checking for bottlenecks in assembly-line type operations; etc.

Classify activities or standards according to some specific method: "always the same, or core," "change predictably . . . change unpredictably," range from simple to complex; performed by specific people or groups, etc.

A plan to monitor and increase productivity of those supervised could be:

- Obtain base-line measures or descriptions of acceptable or average performance if such information is not already available. These could be existing standards.
- Survey the needs and expectations of in-house customers and those outside the organization, ask questions, or observe.
- Have subordinates, peers, and supervisors rank work activities in order of importance. Important, critical activities or jobs can be determined.
- Estimate the approximate amount of time, effort, and cost of implementing the family of measures.
- Anticipate possible sources of resistance, or areas of difficulty. Begin with the path of least resistance. To maximize successes, focus on an area known for successes.
- Be patient, as any change is anticipated as a form of control. Unknown aspects are always feared, so communicate freely and openly about your goals and expectations.
- Ask others to help you. Those who develop a sense of ownership, or involvement with the project, will become loyal supporters.
- Don't give up. Any small changes in a positive direction are definite accomplishments. Most productivity improvements begin as small, almost imperceptible gains. Over extended periods of time, small gains, when added together, end up being significant.

4. People throughout the organization perform some common activities, functions, or operations: try to use time efficiently, cooperate, communicate, facilitate, motivate, and learn. However, these activities are throughput variables, which are difficult, but not impossible, to measure and document.

Common elements will be input variables—number of hours worked, level of skill, effort, etc. Certain activities or variables in families of measures may change, but the name of the family remains constant. This constancy makes the whole concept of related factors one of the predictable elements in productivity measurement.

The concepts of core, unique, and expanding tasks may help with the grouping of tasks into certain specific areas.

Example 1 illustrates use of a FOM. Example 2 describes a model designed to measure managerial performance. Key results areas were first discussed in Chapter 6.

Example 1: At United Services Automobile Association (USAA), key results areas are: service; profitability and financial strength; competitive advantage; operating efficiency and productivity; loss control; human resources; and growth.

Teal (1991) outlines how USAA uses a family of measures (FOM) in merit evaluations. In 1986, USAA began to develop their FOM to provide performance feedback that is periodic and timely. Measures are: (1) quality; (2) quantity of work completed; (3) service timeliness; (4) resource utilization (percent of available hours the group actually spends working; and (5) customer satisfaction. Separate reports are developed for the unit, department, and aggregate levels. Employees receive these reports on the 15th of each month. Reports are analyzed from the macro and micro perspectives. Employees understand their own performance report and are able to analyze it.

Example 2: Preziosi's (1986) Model of Productivity Management Excellence was based on survey results from sixty managers. This model, or blueprint, consists of a set of precise task-performance statements. These competence statements can be used in the measurement of managerial performance.

13

Profitability

PURPOSE

- Examine profitability from specific numeric perspectives.
- Evaluate the role of a human resources accounting system.
- Consider the relationship of quality and profitability.

INTRODUCTION

Financial data may be considered a prime source of information on the worth of the organization. Recommendations to cut overhead, increase profits, even eliminate product lines and reduce the work force, are based on standard, well known financial data.

Is there any reasonable way to determine the value of employees' contributions? Value can be monetary, but value applied to human resources includes knowledge, good work ethics, loyalty, dedication, trust, and much more. The relationship between productivity and profitability becomes more complex when the human element is considered.

Making a profit is a very realistic goal. Does making and retaining profits mean the organization is productive? Probably. Of the various ways to examine profitability, those including a human element are beginning to be taken seriously, for instance Neuman's Overhead Value Analysis, and human resource accounting.

There is growing acceptance of the relationship between profitability and quality. The importance of quality is emerging as a major issue, particularly in customer service. How well is the price of quality really understood? We are likely to know more about the high price of poor quality.

Financial data, like any other information, is critical to organizational success. It will be of limited value unless it is communicated to organizational decision makers. Equally important is presenting it in a format decision makers understand, which in practice is, unfortunately, rarely ever accomplished adequately.

ROLE OF PROFITABILITY

Accounting or financial reporting systems are a major form of management control. Return on investment, i.e., earnings divided by investment, is a prime control technique indicating one measure of organizational success. However, emphasizing rates of return, and ratios of direct and indirect costs excludes other important financial and operational indicators. For example, employee worth is seldom considered.

Balance sheets itemizing total monetary assets, total liabilities, and stockholder equity are commonly used. Assets and liabilities are used to make comparisons within and outside of the organization. But, balance sheets represent only monetary variables, not human resources.

Qualitative views of costs and quality are based mainly on prevention of defects, as in quality control in manufacturing, or in planning functions in general. Setting standards for the delivery of quality services and products can minimize the costs of correcting errors after they have occurred, replacing merchandise, or giving discounts because of poor service.

Profitability is the "name of the game in business," but not the entire game (Albanese, 1978). Operating a business profitably is basic to survival and growth. Showing a "profit" applies equally to profit and non-profit organizations. Non-profit organizations direct financial and human resources to social welfare, legislated programs, philanthropy, or support of worthy endeavors for which they were formed. Ordinarily, non-profit organizations, in particular, want to get the most service or value per dollar spent.

Profits are never more effective as a measure of an organization's success, or lack thereof, as when they do not exist (Albanese, 1978). Major organizational efforts directed to optimizing, or maximizing profits, are "satisficers." "Satisficing" implies a certain amount of searching until a satisfactory, not an optimal, alternative is reached (Leavitt, 1978).

Sources of increased profits may be hard to pin down. They may be qualitative, or based on subjective information that does not fit into neat categories on balance sheets, such as new product lines, expanded inventory systems, highly trained sales forces, knowing your competition and creatively segmenting your customers, or streamlining and enhancing promotion and marketing procedures.

Ways to increase profits appear deceptively simple, but often involve the whole organization to increase income, reduce overhead, or both. Promotion costs, for instance, are often increased to bring about more sales. Or, cost-cutting efforts can lower the quality of products and services, and adversely affect end users. Knowing when and where to cut corners is an art and a science.

DEFINITIONS OF PROFITABILITY

Most definitions of profitability are ratios. A simple ratio is:

$$\text{Profitability} = \frac{\text{Sales}}{\text{Operating costs}}$$

In manufacturing and materials processing industries, major factors are costs associated with capital investments, raw materials, direct labor, and manufacturing overhead. Ratios can be used to compare capital, indirect costs, materials, or overhead to direct labor. But, if ratios are used incorrectly, they can create more problems than they solve (Slade and Mohindra, 1985).

The following example ratios illustrate one way to represent efficiency. However, differences in ways to determine direct and indirect labor costs and compute capital may make these ratios more misleading than helpful.

$$\frac{\text{Indirect labor costs}}{\text{Direct labor costs}} \text{ and } \frac{\text{Capital}}{\text{Direct labor}}$$

Capital investment changes when new tools and technologies are introduced into production. The ratio increases as industries become more capital intensive (Slade and Mohindra, 1985), but this is not necessarily desirable.

Additional example ratios are:

$$\text{Earned standard cost} = \text{Actual production} \times \text{standard cost}$$

$$\text{Efficiency of operation} = \frac{\text{Earned standard cost}}{\text{Actual payroll cost}}$$

$$\text{Production efficiency} = \frac{\text{Total earned man-hours}}{\text{Actual hours worked}}$$

Profit is also the difference between the net price and the actual cost to customers. Costs to suppliers include presale, production, distribution, and post-sale service costs. Other considerations are customer behavior and management of customers (Shapiro, Rangan, Moriarty, and Ross, 1987).

A complex definition of profitability, which is also a multiple-factor measure, includes variables associated with direct labor costs, machine time, inventory, and other related variables:

$$\frac{\text{Product} + \text{Quality} + \text{Service} + \text{Image}}{\text{People} + \text{Tangible} + \text{Money} + \text{Information} + \text{Technology Assets}}$$

In principle, multiple-factor ratios bring numerous input and output factors together. But, these complex ratios are not particularly useful in practice. Some problems relate to difficulty in precisely defining and measuring each factor. The real issue is, "What does the ratio really mean, and how could it be used?"

Profitability is more than reducing expenses, increasing sales, or gaining a larger market share. Retaining profits is a never-ending battle. Retained earnings are affected by competition, economic climate, customer goodwill, government controls, intervention or quotas, existing market or need for products or services provided, trained work force, employee morale, sabotage, strikes, etc. Profitability also involves keeping track of the true rate of inflation of each input and output.

For example, in service industries, profitability is closely related to strategic concepts of the business. Included are such operational variables as response time, number of services/square foot, value of service/hour, completeness of information (insurance forms), number of complaints, intensity of cross-training, or employees' rates of learning.

The following numeric approaches are but a few ways to look at profitability.

NUMERIC APPROACHES TO PROFITABILITY

''Without a good cost accounting system, it is management by anecdote'' (Shapiro, Rangan, Moriarty, and Ross, 1987). Most financial indicators of profitability have their basis in accounting, but most of today's accounting practices were developed before 1925.

Selecting major business performance variables considered important to profitability and following their performance is a critical first step in any assessment process. Although any number of financial variables could be selected, the six discussed by Christopher (1982) are very representative. Changes in profitability at the operating income level result from some combination of change in sales volume, price, product mix, new products, variable costs, and fixed costs.

For example, Mead Corporation examined capital allocation, people management, and asset management. They considered these indicators to be key profit-influencing variables. In 1972, Mead did an extensive audit of product lines and market segments to determine where to introduce cost-effective leadership. Mead's program resulted in a return on total capital that increased from 4 percent in 1972 to 11.2 percent in 1976 (Gale, 1981).

Other important methods to obtain and present financial information are profit and loss statements, payback periods, discounted cash flow, cash and marketable securities, receivables, inventories, current assets, and value of equipment. Software is readily available.

Major ways to analyze and present financial data selected for further discussion are return on investment (ROI), return on controllable assets (ROCA), balance sheets, overhead value analysis (OVA), and Financial Accounting Standards Board.

Return on Investment (ROI)

ROI, which originated in finance and accounting fields, is only one method in a series of financial analysis tools. It is a valid technique for measuring past productivity. In

the example, as in real life, earnings can be either pre-tax, or after tax:

$$\frac{\text{Pre-tax earnings}}{\text{Investment capital}} \text{ or } \frac{\text{After tax earnings}}{\text{Average investment}}$$

ROI is one of the best control methods indicating capital efficiency or the absolute and relative success of a company. Capital efficiency can be compared within departments, and with other organizations. These comparisons show how profitability, cost patterns, investment, working capital, and financing vary between the same or different industries. To illustrate, decisions to mechanize/automate have long-term effects on ROI because large, initial financial investments; employee training; and updating and maintaining equipment are needed.

Too much emphasis on investments required to maximize rate of return may sacrifice other equally important goals. Exclusive use of ROI may reduce or overwhelm excellent non-financial indicators.

For instance, ROI does not distinguish between the measurement of financial performance of a manager of a profit center and that of the organizational unit being managed. Profit center performance is measured in absolute terms, while the manager's performance is measured in relative terms. Managers in companies using ROI will try to maximize the ratio, and may make suboptimal decisions, or even scrap perfectly good assets (Dearden, 1987).

Return on Controllable Assets (ROCA)

This method evaluates how effectively controllable assets are managed. ROCA is compared with income statements, operating ratios, and financial ratios. Valuable information to control costs helps determine areas of greatest leverage to increase profits and productivity (Slade and Mohindra, 1985). This method could be subject to error if the ''institutionalized'' assumption is that non-controllable assets are not controllable!

Balance Sheet

Table 13-1 is a sample balance sheet analysis and shows major assets and liabilities for companies from six different industries (Slade and Mohindra, 1985). Areas of profitability leverage vary greatly between businesses. Data from balance sheets provide clues on where to cut or increase costs, save money, and increase profits.

Separate financial indicators can provide misleading information when unsupported by other valid data. To illustrate, balance sheets are used in combination with the profit-and-loss statement and, on occasion, with the sources-

Table 13-1
Sample Balance Sheet Analysis

	Equipment Leasing	Commercial Bank	Electric Utility	Supermarket Chain	Advertising Agency	Auto Manu-facturer
Cash and marketable securities	9.4%	28.0%	0.2%	12.0%	18.0%	8.4%
Receivables	18.4	67.3	1.7	3.1	61.1	6.6
Inventories	6.5	—	1.4	39.5	—	25.1
Other current assets	—	0.4	0.6	3.0	8.9	3.9
Plant and equipment (net)	60.3	2.7	95.5	41.3	9.8	43.7
Other assets	5.4	1.6	0.6	1.1	2.2	12.3
Total assets	100.0	100.0	100.0	100.0	100.0	100.0
Notes payable	—	6.9	2.9	6.8	—	5.1
Accounts payable	4.4	77.3	0.8	25.0	46.4	23.7
Accrued taxes	8.2	—	0.5	1.0	2.3	3.6
Other current liabilities	1.9	5.2	1.7	7.3	10.1	0.7
Long-term debt	58.0	1.1	50.1	3.8	3.3	4.6
Other liabilities	4.3	2.5	2.4	3.6	—	7.1
Preferred stock	8.1	0.2	9.4	—	—	—
Capital stock and capital surplus	7.1	4.3	26.1	37.7	6.4	6.2
Retained earnings and reserves	8.0	2.5	6.1	14.8	31.5	49.0
Total liabilities and stockholder equity	100.0	100.0	100.0	100.0	100.0	100.0

* (Slade and Mohindra, 1985)

and-uses-of-funds statement. Equally important are the accounting standards and rules used. See box on next page.

Overhead Value Analysis (OVA)

OVA was developed at McKinsey & Company in the early '70s. According to Neuman (1986a), "OVA provides an efficient discipline for scrutinizing all of the many thousands of activities that make up overhead. It identifies all the areas where cuts can safely be made, and provides a framework for balancing costs against quality and value."

OVA is a bottom-up process using input from the lowest level in the organization. It encourages the involvement and commitment of all levels in the organization. The core of OVA is that every management level is equally involved. Managers directly concerned with OVA agree to list and rank every feasible cost-saving service-reduction effort in order of importance. Top management's job is to decide which options to implement.

In the last ten years, OVA has become a powerful tool to help companies reduce or eliminate unnecessary work and increase productivity. In addition, it is currently being used by several more visionary companies to find ways to effectively strengthen and enhance overhead resources for direct profit improvement.

OVA has been used in almost all industries, such as automobile, airline, banking, insurance, machine tools, and electronics. This process, as indicated in Chapter 1, has been successfully implemented in North and Central America, Europe, Australia, and Japan. In most cases, companies have saved between 15 to 25 percent of their overhead costs (Neuman, 1986a). For example, financial results of one OVA program conducted in 1986 resulted in $31 million in immediate savings and $33 million in additional savings on a base of roughly $180 million in costs studied (Neuman, 1986b). This project requires further study.

The ten operating principles of OVA are (Neuman, 1986a):

1. The focus is on work tasks, on what is produced at what costs, and how it relates to the business objectives. The focus is *not* on how well people perform.

2. The value of end products and services are determined through structured interaction of suppliers and receivers (users).

3. Management sets specific overreach targets or "stretch" goals in order to push thinking to challenge everything.

4. Line managers at lowest levels are given the prime responsibility for generating cost-savings ideas.
5. Top management is committed to and heavily involved in the program.
6. A comprehensive human resource plan is developed that facilitates all feasible ways to reduce or redeploy human resources without excessive disruption or terminations.
7. Effective communications are stressed throughout, both top-down and bottom-up.
8. Overhead redeployment reduction is consistent with overall company strategy and priorities.
9. Management at all levels examines *all* indirect activities throughout that organization, as well as cross-company expenses, for instance, employee expense accounts, use of telephone services, company cars, attending conventions, management perks, etc.
10. Definite time-lines for accomplishing the program are set as short as operationally possible, perhaps three to four months.

Table 13-2 illustrates a process for identifying options for reducing overhead (Neuman, 1975, p. 121) by requiring the user/manager to list major end products or services, and then decide on a method to reduce overhead. The six methods of reducing overhead in Table 13-2 range from eliminate to substitute. Examples of end products or services are reports, forms, analysis, advice, and deci-

sions. Managers throughout the organization obtain ideas from subordinates, peers, and the organizations with whom they most typically interact. The act of gathering ideas and information implies cooperating and sharing, and encourages systematic, innovative thinking. The resulting data base provides invaluable information in budgeting.

Making OVA Work: Implementing the Process. Neuman (1986b) summarizes the six sequential phases of OVA, beginning with preparation and ending with implementation. Major phases in each step are presented:

1. **Prepare for the Program**
   - Establish a steering committee.
   - Select and train a coaching task force comprised of upper level management.
   - Form all non-production departments into OVA units, each representing 15–30 people.
   - Develop baseline budgets consisting of a breakdown of total annual operating costs for each OVA unit.
   - Set an overreach cost-reduction target, usually 40 percent of the baseline budget.
   - Decide on seeking cost-increase ideas as well.
2. **Develop the Data Base**
   - Define each unit's missions, the basic activities that support the missions, and the end products produced.
   - Allocate manpower and baseline costs among the end products.

---

1. List major areas where costs savings could be made. Rank (1 is low . . . 7 is high) areas according to their affect on productivity. Indicate whether costs savings are "quick fixes." Indicate whether the effect on output is positive (+) or negative (−).

Variables Influencing Profits

Areas Where Possible Cost Savings Could Be Made	Rank	Quick Fixes (Yes/No)	Effect on Output + or −
_____	____	____	_____
_____	____	____	_____
_____	____	____	_____
_____	____	____	_____

2. Select the most important area from the above list. Develop a logical, cost-effective plan to improve profits and quality.

Table 13-2
Identifying the options

End products or services	Options for reducing overhead					
	Eliminate	Defer	Reduce quality	Reduce amount	Reduce frequency	Substitute
Reports					•	
			•			
	•					
Forms			•			
				•		
					•	
Analysis						•
			•			
Advice	•					
		•		•		
			•			
Decisions		•				
	•					
						•

* (Neuman, 1975)

- Summarize costs for each activity and mission.
- Identify services and activities across department lines that have cost-reduction potential.

3. Generate and Evaluate Ideas
- Generate large numbers of ideas for workload/expense reduction through 40 percent.
- Establish challenge groups of suppliers *and* receivers of services to evaluate cutback ideas and suggest additional areas.
- Each unit manager summarizes all comments and evaluations of cost-reduction ideas.
- Have reduction ideas reviewed by next level of management.

4. Review and Decide
- Unit managers present all ideas to the OVA steering committee.
- Steering committee reviews all recommendations and makes final cost-reduction decisions.

5. Plan Implementation
- Send all approved ideas back to unit managers.
- Unit managers plan implementation and gain steering committee approval.
- Each implementation plan must include:
  —A full description of the approved idea.
  —Specific steps required to implement it.
  —A timetable for completion of each step.
  —The expected dollars and cents reduction in the unit's monthly budget.

6. Implement
- OVA unit managers implement the ideas.
- Periodic progress reports submitted to management.
- Make changes in how overhead is managed day to day.

Three parallel programs can be used to implement the six phases of OVA:

1. Manpower Redeployment—A human resources planning committee is assigned the task of developing strategies for dealing with freed-up human resources. Redeployment and procedures options include, but are not limited to: filling legitimate needs for workers; work-sharing; retraining; accelerating attrition through voluntary actions, terminations, etc.

2. Communications Strategy—A communications coordinator is selected to develop strategies and implement actions to inform employees of the program's objectives and to gather employee feedback, ideas, questions, gripes, throughout the program.

3. Integration—The OVA program is designed to integrate selected elements of the process into the day-to-day operations of the business in order to change how overhead will be managed in the future.

Additional information on OVA includes a case study and a section on determining whether OVA is for you (Neuman, 1983). Much of the data used in OVA has its basis in accounting, and requires a sound knowledge of the variables centered in reporting and control systems. Managers who are not accountants may be overwhelmed by the procedures, sources, and value of data required.

Financial Accounting Standards Board

A financial reporting method developed by the Financial Accounting Standards Board gives a picture of a company's true economic resources, obligations, and prospective cash flow (Hawkins, 1984). Although the Board's proposals have positive and negative impacts, using standardized, recommended methods will increase the validity, reliability, and objectivity of financial statements.

Other Methods of Reporting Financial Information

Other numeric ways to report information include a company's economic resources, obligations, and prospective cash flows (Hawkins, 1984).

Many methods, such as a utility analysis, are done by industrial/organizational psychologists. A utility analysis examines cost savings associated with employment testing and putting a dollar value on job performance.

Two additional sources of information are estimating the dollar value of performance (Eaton, Wing and Mitchell, 1985), and measuring the economic impact of human resource programs (Rauschenberger and Schmidt, 1987).

Few methods of reporting financial indicators consider the importance of human resources. One exception is human resources accounting.

Human Resource Accounting (HRA)

As mentioned in Chapter 1, HRA is one way to put a monetary value on human resources. HRA, also known as human asset accounting, was developed by Likert (1967), who states, "Human asset accounting refers to activity devoted to attaching dollar estimates to the value of a firm's human organization and its customer goodwill."

Three major assumptions underlie HRA: (1) basic characteristics of the organization can be measured, as with a survey; (2) characteristics measured predict future performance; and (3) that performance can be converted to a dollar value.

The following practical step-by-step ways to apply HRA are logical and broad in scope (Flamholtz, 1985):

1. Calculate the cost to recruit, select and hire employees.
2. Evaluate management training programs to measure costs and benefits in dollars and cents.
3. Measure productivity, and motivate, reinforce, and reward employees to increase productivity.
4. Predict, measure, and reduce employee turnover.
5. Compare costs and benefits of layoff, replacement, and relocation decisions.

By discounting backwards in time, a dollar figure can be assigned to the value of the human organization. Terms used are similar to those for capital budgeting.

HRA can provide management with evidence for not cutting human resources and/or their budgets whenever a financial crisis occurs (Bowers and Stambaugh, 1986).

Few experiments have been done to measure the investment costs and losses in human resources (Koontz, O'Donnell, and Weihrich, 1980). Such extensive studies are difficult to do.

The real test of any system is daily use. HRA appears to have no linkage to the overall business purpose and its customers. Whether HRA will become an accepted tool remains to be seen.

COSTS AND QUALITY

Quality, one of the definitions of productivity (Chapter 1), essentially is conformance to specific standards. Quality has a price. It is expensive to introduce and maintain. The cost of quality permeates all productivity improvement efforts.

Quality built into services or products is the most meaningful and cost-effective in the long run (Suzawa, 1985). Quality can also be inspected in, but this is "after-the-fact." When products have already been completed, inspection is the only alternative.

A *Forbes* article, "What Price Quality?" (November 17, 1986) helps place the quality-cost problem in perspective:

"Product quality draws salutes and lip service, but how much attention does it really get? Not as much as it deserves, if a Gallup Poll of nearly 700 U.S. executives for the American Society for Quality Control (ASQC) is any indication. An impressive 41% ranked quality the most critical issue for the next three years, and 57% judged it more important than profit, cost or product scheduling. But even more (70%) missed badly on its cost, estimating that the price of product development, warranties, returns, etc., added up to 10% of gross sales. Companies that have concentrated on quality control say it is 20% to 30%. Two-thirds of the respondents thought they would get back $3 or so for every $1 invested in quality within the first three years, but the ASQC says the actual return can be much higher. The executives also rated the quality of U.S. products better than they thought consumers would. 'That is dangerous,' notes James Houghton, chairman of Corning Glass and a quality control expert. 'You ought to listen to your customers.' Perhaps more dangerous, 64% called complaints the best way to measure quality, a sign that they chose to wait for trouble instead of heading it off. Finally, 15% of those polled saw no link between productivity and quality, ignoring the fact that quality can save rework, spoilage, inventory and other costs." See box below.

Cost of Quality

Skinner (1986) observes a positive relationship between cost and quality: "When low cost is the goal, quality often gets lost. But when quality is the goal, lower costs do usually follow."

Managers who believe quality and cost are related begin by making the long-term investment in people and equipment necessary to improve product quality and reduce costs (Leonard and Sasser, 1982).

Good quality yields a higher (ROI) for any given market share. As quality goes down, so does ROI. Improving product quality in this instance is a profitable activity (Garvin, 1983).

Table 13-3 summarizes Quinn and Bhatty's (1984) narrative about the cost of quality. This tabular format

compares qualitative and quantitative dimensions for prevention, appraisal, and internal and external failure within a manufacturing environment. I added the qualitative-quantitative dimension.

Materials are inspected and procedures monitored throughout the product development process. Internal failures are errors occurring before delivery of products, labor, and additional overhead caused by defective products. External failures are errors occurring after delivery to customers. Internal and external failures cost money, and often take the form of complaints, repair, returned goods, or product liability, including litigation.

Example: Graphs illustrating how conformance to quality and costs of quality control are related can be applied in various industries. The twelve steps to examine the cost of quality are described in considerable detail, but are here simply listed below (Quinn and Bhatty, 1984):

1. Identify the quality problem.
2. Develop and analyze the distribution of quality costs.
   - Draw up the department's personnel worksheet.
   - Draw up the department's activity worksheet.
   - Develop the cost of quality summary worksheet.
   - Develop the cost of quality report.
   - Analyze the cost of quality report and the distribution of quality costs.
3. Determine the different error types.
4. Determine how the errors are generated.

---

3. List indicators or variables measuring quality. Rank how well they measure quality. Does your company justify whether these methods are cost-effective? Include the approximate percentage of emphasis your company places on the variables listed.

Variables Affecting Profits, Quality, and Cost-Effectiveness

Variables Influencing Quality	Rank Measure of Quality (1 to7)	Justify Cost-Effectiveness (Y/N)	Percent of Company Emphasis
_____	_____	_____	_____
_____	_____	_____	_____
_____	_____	_____	_____
_____	_____	_____	_____
_____	_____	_____	_____
_____	_____	_____	_____

Table 13-3
Cost of Quality*

Category	Qualitative	Quantitative
Prevention	Hire qualified workers, plan and develop quality standards, job training . . . continuing education.	Eliminate or reduce the number of defects by qualitative methods, primarily training and quality standards, such as manuals.
Appraisal	Develop and implement specific methods to evaluate workers, product design, and delivery of goods and services.	Detect errors by inspecting, verifying, auditing, checking, monitoring and keeping adequate, up-to-date records.
Internal Failure	Find and correct errors before delivering products to customers or providing requested services.	Rework, redo, scrap, wasted time, and additional use of equipment, or extra man hours.
External Failure	Correct errors after products or services are delivered to customers with possible loss of customer good will and/or image in the marketplace.	Cost of redoing, scrap, penalties, compensation paid, interest payment on late deliveries, cost of investigation, and cost of lost customers.

* Adapted from Quinn and Bhatty, 1984.

5. Determine which function(s) are responsible for/contribute to internally-generated errors, or those made by own employees, as in crediting the wrong account.
6. Establish specific reasons for errors made by the different functions.
7. Formulate solutions for elimination and/or reduction of errors.
8. Establish specific reasons for externally-generated errors, for instance delivery of wrong repair part.
9. Formulate solutions to eliminate/reduce externally-generated errors.
10. Develop a timetable for implementation of solutions.
11. Establish improvement targets.
12. Monitor the working of the program.

Example (IBM): Suppliers must commit to improving their own quality. This means submitting their plans to purchasers, as done in IBM's Total Quality program at Research Triangle Park, North Carolina (American Productivity Center, 1987).

Example (Federal Express): In the past five years, Federal Express has reduced the average cost per express transaction by more than 5 percent annually. Their definition of quality as "improved management" helped bring about these savings (Smith, 1987). They were one of four winners of the Malcolm Baldrige National Quality Award in 1990.

Monitoring Work in Process

Work monitoring is a very significant concept, particularly in areas where results are not immediate, as in start-up periods. "Work-in-process" inventories that are kept current document progress on various stages of work efforts. People doing the job are good at estimating how well they are doing and how much work remains. Keeping track of attempts, and unfinished tasks can be very revealing in terms of cost and lost effort. Frustration and demotivational effects caused by trial-and-error approaches used in new or experimental projects are seldom considered.

Example (Hewlett-Packard): They simplified the calculation of work-in-process in only a portion of the company. An estimated 100,000 accounting entries per month were eliminated (Baker and Huang, 1986). See box below and on next page.

4. Is profitability, a readily-measured, easily-observed output variable overemphasized? Could OVA, or concepts underlying OVA, be useful in your organization? Explain.

5. How could human resource accounting be used in your organization?

6. Are your current or alternative preventive management techniques, like preventive maintenance of equipment, cost effective? If so, list preventive management techniques most likely to reduce cost.

7. When you ask someone else, perhaps from your own company, for a specific product or service, do you know the real costs in terms of time, effort, and money? Internal or external "vendors" may exert extraordinary effort to please longstanding customers.

   Clarifying exactly what customers want may let an equally valuable product or service be substituted for less cost. Think what it costs the supplier to provide exactly what you want, or they think you want. Perceptions are not always accurate. List some of your experiences in this area.

8. Are employee stock ownership plans, as one way of sharing in the monetary control and management of a company, likely to increase? What impact do they have on personal and organizational productivity and on the financial future of the organization?

9. What effects do poor hiring practices, destructive conflict, turnover, absenteeism, etc., have on overall profitability?

10. Could human resource departments become profit centers?

Ideas to Remember

REFERENCES

1. Albanese, Robert. *Managing Toward Accountability for Performance*, (rev. ed.), Homewood, Illinois: Richard D. Irwin, Inc., 1978.

2. American Productivity Center. "Total Quality: When 'Good Enough' Isn't Good Enough Any More," *Productivity Improvement Bulletin*, May 10, 1987, #709, pp. 5–6.

3. Baker, William M. and Huang, Phillip. "Group Technology and the Cost-Accounting System," *Industrial Management*, May–June, 1986, pp. 24–26.

4. Blakeslee, G. Spencer, Suntrup, Edward L., and Kernaghan, John A. "How Much is Turnover Costing You?" Personnel Journal, November, 1985, pp. 98–103.

5. Bowers, David G. and Stambaugh, Leslie Krauz. "Making Organizational Surveys Pay Off," in *Targeting Change: Organizational Development*, Conard N. Jackson, Ed., Alexandria, Virginia: American Society for Training and Development, 1986, pp. 41–47.

6. Brownstein, Andrew R. and Panner, Morris J. "Who Should Set CEO Pay? The Press? Congress? Shareholders?" *Harvard Business Review*, May–June, 1992, pp. 28–32, 34–35, 38.

7. Christopher, William F. "How to Develop Productivity Measures that Can Improve Productivity Performance," *Special Report*, Stamford, Connecticut: Productivity, Inc., 1982, pp. 1–8.

8. Dearden, John. "Measuring Profit Center Managers," *Harvard Business Review*, September–October, 1987, pp. 84–88.

9. Eaton, N. K., Wing, H. and Mitchell, K. "Alternate Methods of Estimating the Dollar Value of Performance," *Personnel Psychology*, 38, 1985, pp. 27–40.

10. Flamholtz, Eric G. *Human Resource Accounting*, San Francisco, California: Josey-Bass Publishers, Inc., 1985.

11. *Forbes,* "What Price Quality?" November 17, 1986, p. 10.

12. Gale, Bradley T. "Can More Capital Buy Higher Productivity?" in *Behind the Productivity Headlines*, pp. 155–163. Boston, Massachusetts: Harvard Business Review, 1981.

13. Garvin, David A. "Quality on the Line," Harvard Business Review, September–October, 1983, pp. 64–75.

14. Grove, Andrew S. *High Output Management*, New York: Random House, 1983.

15. Hawkins, David F. "Toward the New Balance Sheet," *Harvard Business Review*, November–December, 1984, pp. 156–163.

16. Koontz, Harold, O'Donnell, Cyril and Weirich, Heinz. *Management*, 7th ed. New York: McGraw-Hill Book Company, 1980.

17. Leavitt, Harold J. *Managerial Psychology*, 4th ed., Chicago: University of Chicago Press, 1978.

18. Leonard, Frank S. and Sasser, W. Earl. "The Incline of Quality," *Harvard Business Review*, September–October, 1982, pp. 163–171.

19. Likert, Rensis. *The Human Organization: Its Management and Value*, New York: McGraw-Hill Book Company, 1967.

20. Mercer, Michael W. "The HR Department as a Profit Center," *Personnel,* April 1989, pp. 34–36, 39–40.

21. Neuman, John L. "Make Overhead Cuts that Last," *Harvard Business Review*, May–June, 1975, pp. 116–126.

22. _____. "Gaining a Competitive Edge Through Participative Management of Overhead," in *Handbook of Business Planning and Budgeting*, New York: Van Nostrand, Reinhold, 1983, pp. 444–485.

23. _____. "OVA: Avoid the Slash-and-Burn Approach to Overhead Reduction," *Management Practice Quarterly*, Summer, 1986a, pp. 2–6.

24. _____. "Overhead: Five Challenges to Conventional Wisdom," *Management Practice Quarterly*, Fall, 1986b, pp. 5–9.

25. Pine, Judith and Tingley, Judith C. "ROI of Soft-Skills Training," *Training,* February 1993, pp. 55–58, 60.

26. Quinn, Michael P. and Bhatty, Egbert F. "Cost of Quality and Productivity Improvement," in *Issues in White Collar Productivity*, Georgia/Norcross: Industrial Engineering and Management Press, 1984, pp. 151–160.

27. Rauschenberger, John M. and Schmidt, Frank L. "Measuring the Economic Impact of Human Resource Programs," *Journal of Business Psychology*, Vol. 2, No. 1, Fall, 1987, pp. 50–59.

28. Rosen, Corey and Quarrey, Michael. "How Well is Employee Ownership Working?" *Harvard Business Review,* September–October, 1987, pp. 126–128, 132.

29. Shapiro, Benson P., Rangan, V. Kasturi, Moriarty, Rowland T., and Ross, Elliot B. "Manage Customers for Profits (Not Just Sales)," *Harvard Business Review*, September–October, 1987, pp. 101–108.

30. Skinner, Wickham. "The Productivity Paradox," *Harvard Business Review*, July–August, 1986, pp. 55–59.

31. Slade, Bernard N. and Mohindra, Raj. *Winning the Productivity Race*, Massachusetts: Lexington Books, 1985.

32. Smith, Frederick W. "Q=P: A New Management Paradigm," *Quality*, October, 1987, pp. 24–27.

33. Spencer, Lyle M., Jr. *Calculating Human Resource Costs and Benefits*, New York: John Wiley and Sons, 1986.

34. Suzawa, Shoichi. "How the Japanese Achieve Excellence," *Training and Development Journal*, May 1985, pp. 110–112, 114–117.

Chapter 13—Answers and Insights

1. *Input variables*: various financial variables, planning, employee training, preventive actions, or adopting some form of control or standards to develop products or deliver services, and quality of equipment. *Throughput*: loyalty, trust, motivation, customer goodwill and others difficult to justify. *Output*: sales promotions, quality or speed of delivery of products and services, competition, imposed regulations or quotas, or economy.

2. Most indicators will be output. Greater improvements, although they may be long-term, come from controlling input. Emphasizing quality is logically a first not a last step, and therefore becomes input, not output. Throughput plays a major role, but is seldom considered.

   Steps could include: Be sure of your facts; use data based on at least a two- to six-month period; document causes of decreased profits; pick an area that has the highest probability of being changed or improved; increase awareness; communicate what you are doing to those involved; take small steps and evaluate outcomes; take larger steps as you and your program become accepted and better known; demonstrate, where possible, the first possible evidence of increased quality and profits; monitor and provide feedback on a regular basis.

3. Variables affecting profit in service areas: customer satisfaction; repeat usage; errors; daily, continued demand; etc. In product-oriented areas: scrap, waste, redoing, warranties, value, etc.

   Your company may not feel they need to justify their major outputs if they are making an adequate profit, and current products or services are in demand. The common trap to avoid, though, is the comfortable assumption that "business as usual" will continue indefinitely. It is imperative to continually challenge the underlying assumptions about products and services; markets; competitors; customers; environment, etc. Unless this is done, it is impossible to lead change or react to change in order to profitably survive.

   Percent of company emphasis on certain variables differs between and within different parts of the same company.

4. Skinner (1986) suggests profitability, a universal standards of success, is overemphasized. Reports of financial worth and cash position can be interpreted many ways. Monetary variables are readily understood, but are not the only variables on which sales, mergers, or buyouts are based. Use of OVA, or comparable methods, provides meaningful information on cost and profitability through problem identification, and also in budgeting.

5. HRA can be used in recruiting, selection, and hiring personnel; evaluate training programs; predict, measure and reduce turnover; compare costs and benefits of layoffs, and measure and increase productivity. Consult Flamholtz (1985) for specific details. See Pine and Tingley (1993) for ROI.

6. Preventive management implies that managers anticipate possible happenings. Examples are advance planning (with subordinates), "trial runs," or pilot projects.

7. Determining exactly what you or someone else needs is the real key to saving time and money, obtaining quality products and services, and having satisfied customers. Written specifications, including substitutions and their costs, are a first step. This will initially take time, but is cost-effective. Users and suppliers do each other financial favors by working together.

Customers, clients, and end-users can be long-term assets, particularly when they are "partners," or part owners. Partnering is useful when "start up" is time-consuming or costly. Close relationships between vendors or suppliers and customers required by maintaining high quality standards, at competitive costs, is also a form of partnering. Customers' demands for products manufactured using specific quality standards binds customers to quality suppliers. Partners and suppliers may be worlds apart or in the same office.

8. Since 1974, when Congress enacted the first of a series of tax measures designated to encourage employee stock ownership plans, the number of employee-owned companies has grown from about 1,600 to 8,100. The number of employees owning stock has increased from 250,000 to 8 million (Rosen and Quarrey, 1987). Appropriately designed and administered employee incentive programs have always been good motivators. Employee ownership should be a positive influence on productivity and financial stability.

In the late 1980s, steel, airlines, trucking and construction industries took active roles to save jobs mainly by buying plants, avoiding strikes. Employee ownership is growing as at Penneys and Wal-Mart. Atmos Energy, a utility company, is 15% owned by employees and 5% owned by management.

By the year 2000, employee ownership in public corporations is predicted to be more than 15% in one-quarter of all public corporations (Brownstein and Panner, 1992).

9. All decrease overall profitability. Hiring practices can be improved, and turnover partly controlled (Blakeslee, Suntrup, and Kernaghan, 1985). Destructive conflict has untold negative effects.

10. Human resource (HR) departments can become profit centers when HR managers begin to use a profit-focused planning model, such as those used in sales, marketing, and finance. Mercer (1989) proposes: (1) Determine the business problem and its cost; (2) Develop an HR oriented solution and determine its cost; (3) Calculate the resulting dollar-improvement benefit, and (4) Compute the cost-benefit ratio. Mercer presents case examples and detailed planning models.

Work sheets, and financial formulas for assessment are available (Spencer, 1986).

Companies that survive the increasingly turbulent times will be ones with good human relations and good leaders.

14

Quality

_____

PURPOSE

- Provide an overview of the quality movement.
- Present the major variables in service-based and product-based industries.
- Evaluate and compare the major factors in service-based and product-based industries.
- Discuss ways to achieve, maintain, and improve quality.

INTRODUCTION

There are hundreds of ways to view and describe quality. Quality is one of the concepts used to define productivity. Chapter 2 also lists profit, quantity, efficiency, effectiveness, value, innovation, and quality of work life.

There are at least as many variations of quality improvement programs as there are organizations pursuing quality, and it is this array of views and interpretations that is a prime source of excitement, confusion, and frustration.

Any clear picture of quality must be based on customers' needs, perceptions, expectations, and standards. This picture should also incorporate the organization's vision, mission, and goals and the people in it. Quality improvement efforts must shift the distribution of power to those actively doing the work, namely empower them. Also, the reward system must be made more equitable so the match between pay and performance is closer.

Unfortunately, what is rewarded gets done.

A common metaphor used in the ever-increasing literature on quality is being on a road or taking a continuous journey. The quest has no end point. People on the road cannot see the end. They will meet people coming and going. A few will have stopped. Some will be tired. Several will be eager to start the exciting trip. However, no one will have completed the journey. Achieving and maintaining quality is a lifelong endeavor.

One type of quality program may work as planned, but it may not work the same way twice. When similar programs are used repeatedly, success is not guaranteed.

Quality assessment and improvement efforts are primarily tools designed to bring about positive change. Over time, the initial, inevitable resistance to any change effort can be slowly and systematically reduced through employee involvement and commitment from top management.

Tools and method should never be selected before the purpose of the change effort is understood and described in precise terms. Efforts that put tools and methods before purpose do a disservice to both employees, customers, and to the organization. This is where intelligent leadership comes in. The real purpose of quality assessment and improvement should never get confused with the tools and methods.

The number of "quality tools" and copies of these tools grows daily. Some tools are reinvented so many times they all begin to look alike. Tools are not responsible for the outcomes of programs on quality, or any other program. People are. Even the best tools fail in the hands of inexperienced people. Lessons can be learned from experienced tool handlers, or from proven leaders.

It is vital that the real purpose of change efforts be considered carefully and from many perspectives. Quality can be achieved in ways not requiring full-blown quality programs, or perhaps not even a quality-based program at all. Possibilities are: encouragement and support of creativity; improved open, honest, two-way communication; alternate reward systems that tie remuneration directly to individual and/or team results; skills-based training; recognition programs promoting employment loyalty; improved internal management; changing the company culture, among others. As stated in the preface, the major issue in productivity is how well people work together.

Major factors affecting how quality is perceived and handled in the organization and beyond are: (1) current status of quality; (2) definitions and examples of quality; (3) history of the quality movement illustrated by selected examples; (4) quality in product-based and service-based industries; (5) direct and indirect indicators of quality; (6) factors affecting quality; (7) customer focus; (8) designing quality assessment and improvement program; and (9) quality issues in perspective.

CURRENT STATUS OF QUALITY

The concept of quality is beginning to permeate most organizations. Programs to achieve and maintain quality represent a normal distribution of achievements ranging from pessimism, frustration, and failure, to optimism, enthusiasm, and glowing results. Are we getting all the quality we are paying for? The normal distribution of answers is: Yes. Maybe. No. Only time will tell.

Some organizations have always believed in quality. Longstanding reputations and equally long periods of delivering quality services and products help forge the reputation for quality, such as that of Procter & Gamble. Maytag stresses "ten years' trouble-free operation" (Peters and Waterman, 1982). The reputation for quality is often earned slowly and at considerable cost. The gradual evolution of quality in Ford Motor Company's Taurus automobile is a steadily evolving success story that began more than 10 years ago.

It is estimated that from 25–50% of a manager's time is spent on some form of quality endeavor. Reportedly, these managers directed their organization's quest for quality.

Some organizations have reached their goals for quality before being side-tracked. Others took a round-about path, but are now going in the general direction. A few are still trying to figure out when to start and what road to take.

Pockets of quality are spreading, often in unpredictable places. Change takes place slowly. Resistance to change is natural. Change always starts very slowly and gradually gains speed. No one can escape the growing emphasis on quality or permanently hide from change. Customers are demanding quality. Some are receiving it more often now than in the past. The customer may end up winning (Desatnick, 1994).

The need to address quality in meaningful ways is gaining momentum. Slash-and-burn decisions some top management make to minimize costs erode change and improvement programs in general, not just quality. The staying power and patience to wait the three to ten years for payoff appears long, but generally is worth the wait.

The continuous journey to achieve and maintain quality must be in the mind sets of those starting their partly unchartered quality travels. Motorola, as we will see, achieved a specific level of high quality, and constantly strives to improve it. Continuously raising quality standards is at the core of all quality initiatives. However, quality begins and ends with the customer. Whether we know it or not, we are alternately customers and suppliers in our own organization and in our community.

Major players on the quality front are customers, clients, consumers, suppliers, manufacturers, partners, vendors, and people of all levels who work with products and services. They may live and work anywhere in the world.

Concepts cannot be defined in precise terms unless people using them totally understand what the concept means in work-related terms, like jobs, customers, mission, and goals. There are wide individual differences in the way people view and achieve quality. A person's professional background, work experience, even attitude, have a major impact on their views and responses to change efforts. Once people basically agree on precisely what quality means, the hard part is communicating these concepts to others in familiar terms. Open, two-way communication and operational definitions to state and clarify meanings (Chapter 8) are a good way to start.

Quality programs range from inspirational to full-blown, successful organizational efforts. Ironically, the title of the book written by Thomas, Gallace, and Martin (1992), *Quality Alone Is Not Enough,* sums up the quality issue. Winning strategies in quality programs come from the minds of leaders, and from everyone in the organization.

However, not all is positive on the quality front. Unless the quality concept is incorporated into the vision, mission, and strategic plans of the organization, and supported throughout the organization, quality efforts will likely fail.

The need for quality is often a response to negatives—unmet customer expectations, lost opportunities, high cost of rework, and shrinking market share, for instance.

VIEWS, DEFINITIONS, AND EXAMPLES OF QUALITY

Achieving and maintaining a desired level of quality are overlapping processes in any organization. Achieving quality is more than avoiding all factors that reduce quality or add to non-quality. Maintaining quality requires planning, effort, detecting problems, and knowing what customers need and can afford. Satisfying customers can be a very hard, often thankless work.

It is important who reviews the results of quality programs and how these results are interpreted and presented. Much can be added or lost in the analysis, write-up, presentation, and interpretation of results, particularly if they are not what was expected. Last, but by no means least, how does the customer view, interpret, and use results? In the final analysis, the elements and expectations of the quality improvement process are defined in terms of the customer.

Quality can not be separated from manufacturing, design, marketing, sales, or training. Quality should be at the core of everything we do, wherever and whenever we do it. Improvement and profitability are main ways to gauge quality. It is no longer enough to manage *for* quality, but *by* quality.

Overall definitions of quality are grouped into three major areas: (1) views of quality; (2) standards set by customers and other end users; and (3) operational definitions in service and product sectors.

Views of Quality

How people see quality is influenced by perceptions, expectations, beliefs, values, experience, training, culture, and myriad other important factors. Those within and outside the organization see quality in slightly different ways.

The following are example views of quality from within the organization.

Chief executive officer—total quality management
Management information system—continuous process improvement
Engineer—zero defects in manufacturing
Receptionist—sufficient accurate information to answer questions
Personnel department—quality of work life
Human resources—training and development
Accountant—cost savings
Employee—empowerment
Customer—exactly what I want when I want it (quality + timeliness)
Private citizen—no new government taxes in community

---

1. List the quality-related issues or problems you currently face. Do you work alone, or in a group? Is there a method or process to effectively deal with the problems or issues? If so, describe the method. If not, describe the methods you would like to use.

Issue or Problem	Solve by Self or Group	Methods Used	Methods to be Designed
_____	_____	_____	_____
_____	_____	_____	_____
_____	_____	_____	_____
_____	_____	_____	_____
_____	_____	_____	_____

Definitions of Quality

Major definitions of quality are based on: (1) conformance to standards; (2) timeliness; (3) fitness for use; (4) customer focus; (5) marketplace; and (6) service-based and product-based sectors.

Conformance to Standards. A common definition is the degree to which a service or product conforms to a predetermined set of requirements (Crosby, 1979). Standards, like design specifications, or quality standards for raw materials used in manufacturing, are often made explicit in advance. This means meeting or exceeding standards created or designed by clients, customers, partners, or any one of many end users or stake holders. It also means anticipating the needs of a variety of customers and end users, and providing quality services and products, sometimes by surprise, other times by design.

Standards may originate with the developer, internal customer, external customer, end-user, vendor, supplier, or partner, or be one-of-a-kind as in a prototype. Other standards may be agreed upon as in ISO 9000 Series Standards, or similar standards for quality.

Example 1: ". . . meeting the customers' requirements the first time, correctly, and all the time" (excerpt from September 1992 interview between Glavin and the editor of the "Face-to-Face" column of *Management Review).*

Example 2: In manufacturing or materials processing industries, quality may be inspected in (proactive) or faulty products scrapped (reactive). It is expensive to inspect quality into products and services. In theory, inspection creates nothing, but is an essential part of maintaining and improving quality. Some alternatives to low quality products are to let them go, reject, redo, sell for less, or balance "seconds" against customer goodwill.

$$\text{Quality} = \frac{\text{Number of damaged units produced}}{\text{Total number of units produced}}$$

Example 3: Cost of non-conformance, or the cost of not doing things right the first time. For instance, cost estimates could be as high as 20% of sales. The cost of quality can be viewed from the standpoint of prevention, appraisal, internal failure, and external failure.

Contact with or knowledge of "customers" may be low. "Doing it right the first time" eliminates costly and time-consuming trial-and-error approaches. Unfortunately, creativity that thrives on intelligent risk taking may be reduced or eliminated when experimentation and learning by doing are prevented or discouraged.

However, it is seldom possible to afford the time or the cost not to "do it right the first time." The major question is, "What is right?" Customer patience, for instance, can no longer be sacrificed. Although costs usually increase with trial-and-error efforts, many people learn by these random methods.

Timeliness. No one likes waiting for goods or services. A product or service having extremely high quality is of little or no value if it is late. Many customers many even want you to anticipate their unpredictable needs.

Time is an inelastic commodity. It cannot be bought or sold. Often the greatest personal rewards, even cost savings in terms of lost efforts or false starts, come from simply saving time.

White-collar cycle time is a relatively new concept. It is measured by the number of partly completed tasks, divided by their completion rate.

Fitness for Use. Juran's real concern is for the user. Users can operationally define fitness using terms that are easy to understand and convey. An operational definition for quality is conformance, durability, or availability when needed.

What the Customer Says It Is. Feigenbaum's brief definition says it all—the customer is king.

Increasingly, customers want manufacturers and suppliers to have ISO 9000 Series certification. These relatively new international standards for quality management and quality assurance gradually evolved over a period of years. They were developed jointly by the international agency for standardization comprising national standards bodies of about 100 countries. ISO 9000 is discussed in the following section.

Customers doing business with manufacturers and suppliers having ISO 9000 quality assurance standards for products feel they have a quality advantage. In a similar vein, companies in the United States that have won the Malcolm Baldrige National Quality Award are much sought after as suppliers.

This decade and possibly the next decade are the era of customer sovereignty. Desatnick (1994) discusses the nine major attributes that successful role models in service companies share. All attributes are based on meticulous attention to detail, as demonstrated by customer-oriented value system, quantitative measures to monitor the effectiveness of service policies, practices and procedures, training support, and outstanding employee relations. A later section deals with customer focus.

Determined in the Marketplace

Customers, competition, and cost often determine quality in the marketplace. Decisions based on cost only mean purchasing a cheaper, inferior product. Quality can be where you find it. However, customers know what quality is. As previously discussed, quality can range from fact-based to perception-based. Products and services may have extremely high quality, but without demand in the marketplace, nothing is sold.

Some of the best known, current top service providers include longstanding service-oriented companies: RCA, Avis Auto Rental, Walt Disney, McDonald's, Westin hotels, and Hartford Insurance (Desatnick, 1994).

In all phases of business, not just quality, everyone, at one time or another, is either a customer or supplier. The customer/supplier role comes as a revelation to most people. Ultimately, everyone in the supplier-user chain is responsible for delivering, maintaining, and evaluating quality.

Operational Definitions of Quality

Of the total work force in the United States, about 70% provides services and 30% provides products. In general, service industries are growing more rapidly than product-based industries.

An increasing number of product and service combinations, like computers and supporting software, are crossovers. In these instances, customers interface with both service and product components. For better or for worse, the quality of hardware may be judged entirely by the quality of software. Knowing exactly who suppliers and customers are, and what they provide, enhances product/service crossover relationships.

Another possible area for confusion is the connection between internal customers and their internal suppliers within the organization, perhaps even in the same work group. These groups may have difficulty believing they need to meet each other's guidelines or standards for quality. There is always danger in taking each other for granted.

Operational Definitions of Quality in the Service Sector. It is very important to specify quality or other standards like excellence, customer satisfaction, delivery time, or value on the accept/reject scale. Specifications may be implied, verbal, or documented. Agreement and documents let suppliers and customers determine whether their criteria or level of acceptance are being met. It is not always possible or realistic to rely on salespersons or company representatives to convey the true message of quality.

Once the mechanics of quality are understood, a similar process of operationalizing concepts associated with contracts can be set out. Then, objectives and policies can be established, resources allocated, and cost estimates made.

With practice, employees can design customer-friendly methods to handle customers' problems. Over time, customers will supply a broad range of challenges and information on quality. This rich source of data can be documented and form a solid base of practical information that could become part of a manual. No methods are fool-proof, so constant updates and revisions reflecting changes in customers' requirements and services provided are necessary.

Operational Definitions of Quality in the Products Sector. Management, employees, customers, and vendors each have slightly different views of quality. They will understand quality best from their own perspectives. When they see quality as their customers see it, they can do a better job of meeting current quality standards. By being proactive, they can anticipate future events.

The following examples of operational definitions of quality use measures of output or hard data. Two different levels of significance follow:

Example 1: Motorola's definition of quality is Six Sigma, or 3.4 defects per million. This single metric for quality is total defects per unit. Motorola continues to reduce this defect rate (Tadikamalla, 1994).

2. Define quality as you see it. Your definition may differ from the way it is defined in your organization or in your work group. Using an operational definition may help increase the precision of your definition.

In 1988, Motorola, Inc., was one of the first to receive the Baldrige award. Motorola attributes much of its success in quality improvement to this program. McFadden (1993) illustrates the components of a Six-Sigma quality program using numeric tables, graphs, and statistical calculations.

Example 2: Using the Two Sigma level (slightly less than 5 defects per hundred), Gable (1991) estimated that in the following year, 14,208 defective personal computers would be sent out; 55 malfunctioning automatic teller machines (ATMs) would be installed; and 268,500 defective tires would be shipped.

The Quality Glossary lists over 150 concepts directly related to quality, associated statistical methods, and has an extensive bibliography (Bemowski, 1992).

HISTORY OF THE QUALITY MOVEMENT

This brief review includes Deming, Juran, Feigenbaum, Crosby, two well-documented efforts, and representative literature. A history of quality should include a quote from Aristotle, "Quality is a habit, not an act."

Deming

W. Edwards Deming is known for statistical process control (1920s–1930s), sampling and statistical methods in Japan (1940s–1960s), and overall quality (1960s–1990s). His prime concern was on Total Quality Management (TQM) as a culture or "philosophy of management." Major concepts underlying the Deming philosophy are to strive for continuous improvement in satisfying customers and reduce the variation in products and services. One of his strongest beliefs was that if TQM were to succeed, top management must make a commitment to creating a supportive organizational culture. After a long and illustrious career, Deming died on December 20, 1993 at the age of 93.

Deming's fourteen points, or principles directed toward continuous improvement, are summarized (Walton, 1986):

1. Create a constancy of purpose for improvement of product and service. The aim is to become competitive, to stay in business, and to provide jobs.
2. Adopt the new philosophy that is free of defects, delays, and mistakes.
3. Cease dependence on mass inspection to achieve quality.
4. End the practice of awarding business on the basis of price tag alone.
5. Improve constantly and forever the system of production and service.
6. Institute modern methods of training.
7. Institute modern methods of supervision.

8. Drive out fear so everyone may work effectively.
9. Break down barriers between departments so everyone in every area works as a team.
10. Eliminate numeric goals, slogans, and posters seeking new levels of productivity without improving methods.
11. Eliminate work standards that prescribe numeric quotas.
12. Remove barriers that rob people of the pride of workmanship.
13. Institute a vigorous program of education and retraining.
14. Put everyone in the company to work to accomplish the transformation.

Walter A. Shewart, a statistician at Bell Telephone Laboratories in New York, developed the Plan-Do-Check-Act cycle in the early 1950s. This cycle, also known as the Deming cycle, is used to create programs to help implement the above 14 points. The cycle has been modified over the years, and may continue to evolve.

Descriptions of the accompanying seven deadly sins take the form of negative restatements of his fourteen points (Deming, 1982, 1986).

1. Lack of constancy of purpose.
2. Emphasis on short-term profits.
3. Evaluation by performance, merit rating, or annual reviews of performance.
4. Mobility of management.
5. Running a company on visible figures alone.
6. Excessive medical costs.
7. Excessive costs of warranty, fueled by lawyers that work on contingency fees.

Deming proposed three major keys to quality improvement:

1. Understand and use statistics to identify variations produced in processes, products, and services. Only then can causes of variations be studied and eliminated.
2. Management is responsible for quality.
3. All work is performed as part of a system that should be organized in various ways to satisfy customer requirements.

Many organizations have adopted TQM. It is probably the best known management approach to long-term success through customer satisfaction. TQM has been either tried or applied in numerous industries, university (Potocki, Brocato, and Popkick, 1994), and government settings.

Walton (1986) presents an excellent overview of Deming's life and work. Sashkin and Kiser (1993) discuss

TQM in detail. Smith (1993a & 1993b) evaluate the role of TQM in the public sector.

Juran

Joseph M. Juran was born in Romania in 1904 and came to the United States in 1912. Reportedly, the modern quality movement that began in the United States about 1951 can be traced to Juran. He went to Japan several years after Deming. Both made similar lecture and consulting tours. For the last 50 years, Juran has been a leading proponent in defining and shaping quality (1992). A focal point of Juran's approach is (1) quality planning, (2) quality control, and (3) quality improvement through quality management. His major efforts pertain to ways to implement concern for what the customer wants.

He proposes using a "quality planning road map" to plan, coordinate, and integrate a concern for quality into all operations of the organization. (Juran and Gryna, 1993).

His five quality checkpoints form the core of TQM. They illustrate the relationships between internal and external suppliers and internal and external customers. Checkpoints are:

1. Obtain accurate, timely information about customers needs, wants, and expectations.
2. Determine whether the product or service is ready for delivery. This step is often the main focus of so-called quality control activities.
3. The site of production or work activity is given an overall evaluation.
4. Quality of incoming materials is inspected to ensure that the expected level of quality is present.
5. Input materials, parts, and supplies are designed and produced to specifications.

Suppliers and vendors work together to ensure desired levels of quality are reached and maintain, perhaps even exceeded, as in continuous quality improvement. For example, in 1988, Procter & Gamble (P&G) established a partnership agreement with Wal-Mart. P&G now has more than 120 sales, purchasing and data processing teams working with its customers (Sashkin and Kiser, 1993).

Juran feels that the 20th century is one of productivity and the 21st century will be one of quality. There will be partnerships with suppliers and customers, and with the work force, like self-directing teams and joint improvement projects (Juran, 1994).

Feigenbaum

Armand V. Feigenbaum introduced the term "total quality control," or TQC, in his classic article, "Total Quality Control." This breakthrough article was published in the November-December 1956 issue of *Harvard Business Review*. His book by the same name was published in 1961. One of Feigenbaum's latest areas of emphasis is on the quality of education and America's competitiveness (1994).

TQC integrates the quality-development, quality-maintenance, and quality-improvement efforts of various groups enabling production and service to provide full customer satisfaction at an economical level (Spitzer, 1993a & 1993b); or, maximize customer satisfaction at the most economical level.

To illustrate, inter-functional teams in marketing, engineering, purchasing, and manufacturing share the responsibility for all phases of design and manufacturing. These teams follow the new products through design control, incoming material control, and product or shop-floor control.

Crosby

Philip B. Crosby was the main impetus behind the Martin Company's Pershing missile discussed in the following section.

Crosby (1979) advocates "quality is free." It costs less to build it or do it right the first time than to repair it later. Most efforts to improve quality occur at the bottom of the organization. Crosby's concerns are that there is no really agreed upon definition for quality, and people develop their own definitions of quality. When they meet their own expectations for quality, they stop trying to improve. His subsequent work and his reputation for quality are well known (Crosby, 1984, 1986, 1988, 1989).

Examples and Tools of Quality

Three different ways to achieve and maintain quality are summarized: (1) The Martin Company's goal of "zero defects;" (2) International Quality Study; (3) Malcolm Baldrige National Quality Award; (4) ISO 9000 Standards; and (5) benchmarking.

The Martin Company. This company built the Pershing Missile for the U.S. Army. Several incidents highlight the achievement of "zero defects." The end of the story is that in December 1961, a Pershing missile with "zero discrepancies" was delivered to Cape Canaveral.

The events in the story begin with the U.S. Army's challenge to Martin's general manager at Orlando, Florida to deliver the first field Pershing missile one month ahead of schedule. Martin's manager promised this missile would be perfect—have no hardware problems or document errors, and be fully operational 10 days after delivery. The current norm was 90 days or more. In the next two months, the Martin mode of operation was "build it right the first time." There would be no time for the usual inspections.

In February 1962, Martin delivered a perfect missile on time. It was fully operational in less than 24 hours. Following this positive experience, Martin management told employees that "zero defects" was the only acceptable quality standard. This standard was instilled in the work force through special events, training, and by posting quality results.

The International Quality Study (IQS). This massive, international study of management practices was done jointly by Ernst & Young (1991 & 1992) and the American Quality Foundation (AQF).

The American Society for Quality Control (ASQC) was formed in 1946. Deming was a charter member. In 1987, ASQC formed AQF, a separate nonprofit, executive-led group. On January 1, 1994, leadership of the AQF was returned to ASQC.

The mission of AQF is to support the long-term development and promotion of total quality improvement. AQF's focus is global, national, and personal, including national, public, and economic concerns. Other efforts include promoting the integration of the human side of the quality equation into existing and new quality practices (Benson, 1991).

The primary purposes of the IQS study: (1) use results to develop an inventory of "best" practices and (2) identify and study new trends and directions.

Data came from a comprehensive study of management practices of over 500 companies in the automotive, banking, computer, and health care industries in Canada, Germany, Japan, and the United States (Bemowski, 1991).

Data were collected from January through August of 1991. A team of executives and managers at each company completed the written survey that addressed more than 100 different assessment areas organized into 5 major sections, and more than 900 specific management practices. Completing the survey required a minimum of 5 executives and managers at least 20 hours. This effort yielded a total of more than 1.5 million pieces of information. The response rate to the survey was very high—84%.

The survey was designed to collect data that could be analyzed vertically, horizontally, and longitudinally. The vertical analysis allowed data to be compared at different levels in the organization. The horizontal comparison allowed comparisons across functions, beginning with suppliers and ending with follow-up with customers. The longitudinal approaches allowed quality practices to be assessed over varying time periods.

Major results cover employee involvement, customer focus, strategic planning and process improvement.

1. *Employee Involvement.* Current employee involvement in quality-related teams was 5% for German companies; 15% for Canadian companies; 16% for U.S. Companies; and 40% for Japanese companies.

   Businesses in U.S., Canada, and Germany expect to increase the level of employee involvement. Japanese companies expected to stay about the same. Quality performance in all countries will likely be used more often as a criterion for compensating employees. For instance, in the U.S. more than half of the companies expected to use measures of quality as a basis for pay.
2. *Customer Focus.* About 40% of the businesses in Canada, Japan, and the U.S. place primary importance on customer satisfaction in strategic planning. About 22% of the German businesses do so. Japanese companies are three times as likely as North American businesses to always or almost always (defined as more than 90% of the time) translate customer expectations into the design of new products and services. German businesses are twice as likely as North American businesses to do so.
3. *Strategic Planning.* The percentage of businesses indicating the importance of competitor comparison in the strategic planning process were 32% for Japan; 29% for the U.S.; 25% for Canada; and 5% for Germany.
4. *Improvement.* The percentages of businesses indicating they always or almost always use process simplification were 47% for Japan; 19% for Canada; 12% for the U.S.; and 6% for Germany.

   Results of the study show quality is a common language. "Quality tools transcend the language barrier, but their application is clearly cultural" (Bemowski, 1991). Readers are encouraged to follow the results of this study either through forthcoming literature or by reading the publications of Ernst & Young.

The Malcolm Baldrige National Quality Award (MBNQA). The scope of MBNQA is broad. Only a brief history and description are provided. Pertinent literature reviews are cited.

The MBNQA was introduced in 1987 by the United States Congress in honor of Malcolm Baldrige, Secretary of Commerce (1981–1987). The award was created by Public Law 100–107 and signed August 10, 1987. The original purpose listed in the award criteria was to "... test all elements of a total quality system." In 1989, the purpose was changed slightly to "... permit the evaluation of the strengths and areas of improvement in the applicant's quality system and quality results." The core of the "Baldrige" has remained constant over the years.

The MBNQA introduces a standard for understanding the overall scope of quality and quality improvement. This award also provides a common reference for quality policies and practices. Application criteria are published each year by the National Institute of Standards and Technology, United States Department of Commerce, Gaithersburg, Maryland.

Major objectives are:

1. Help stimulate American companies to improve quality and productivity while obtaining a competitive edge through increased profits.
2. Recognize and spotlight accomplishments of companies that improve the quality of goods and services.
3. Establish guidelines and criteria that can be used by a wide range of organizations to evaluate quality and their own quality improvement efforts.
4. Provide guidance to other American organizations wanting to learn how to attain high quality. Make available detailed information on how to change culture and strive for eminence.

The 1993 and 1994 categories and associated number of points out of a total of 1000 are:

1. Leadership—95 points
2. Information and Analysis—75 points
3. Strategic Planning—60 points
4. Human Resources Development and Management—150 points
5. Management of Process Quality—140 points
6. Quality and Operational Results—180 points
7. Customer Focus and Satisfaction—300 points

Point values in each category have changed little since 1988. For example, leadership dropped from 150 points in 1988 to 90 points in 1992. Also, customer satisfaction, the most heavily weighted area, has always been 300 points, or 120 points higher than the next highest category. Winning the award means performing many customer-related activities well. It is even more important to know which ones are *not* performed well, and how and when to improve them. Involving everyone in the organization in customer satisfaction is the real key.

A core process used in the MBNQA is benchmarking. Ideally, descriptions of major terms, concepts, and standards should be defined in clear terms that are readily understood. Use of operational definitions is one way to achieve this clarity.

A historical review of the "Baldrige" includes (De Carlo and Sterret, 1990; Garvin, 1991; Harvard Business Review's Reader's Debate, 1992; and Neves and Nakhal, 1994).

Garvin's (1991), "How the Baldrige Award Really Works," is a detailed, insightful article describing the award, scoring, selected results from the General Accounting Office study, and processes used by prospective applicants. Responses to Garvin's article ranged from positive to negative. Responses from 21 expects in quality were published in the "Debate" section (*Harvard Business Review*, 1992).

Beginning June 1992, *Quality Progress* published a six-part series of monthly articles titled on each of the six categories of the MBNQA.

Beginning January 1993, *Quality Progress* published a five-part series of monthly articles on leadership in TQM. All were based on *Leadership for the Quality Transformation* (Johnson, 1993).

Neves and Nakhai (1994) present figures and a table illustrating:

(1) changes in the Baldrige award process from 1988–1994; (2) examination categories and their point values; and (3) comparisons of the quality framework from 1988 through 1994.

The "Baldrige" is evolving and changing to reflect a broader focus on customers in the service sector. This award has generated a great deal of interest in quality and spin-off awards by various organizations and governments.

A brief history of the Deming Prize (Japan), the Baldrige Award, and the European Quality Award is outlined by Nakhai and Nevess (1994). The number of spin-off awards in American industries and government is growing. The Baldrige award plays a pivotal role in increasing awareness of quality and of providing a mechanism to assess and compare achievements along numerous dimensions. Despite its critics, the spirit and content of the Baldrige award have encouraged and reinforced quality programs in positive ways. Health care institutions can now apply.

ISO 9000 Standards. The International Organization for Standardization (ISO) federation was founded in 1946 to promote the development of international manufacturing, trade, and communication standards. The Technical Committee of the Geneva-based ISO was responsible for developing the standards in the 1980s. Standards were released in 1987. This committee has grown to include hundreds of experts from around the world.

The purpose of ISO 9000 is to guide the development of a stable measurement process, allowing areas requiring increased control to be identified. Simply stated, ISO 9000 is based on two phrases, "Say what you do, do what you say" (Beardsley, 1994).

ISO 9000 was originally developed for customer-supplier audits. As designed, standards provide a means to effectively document elements of the quality system used to produce and maintain quality products and services.

The ISO 9000 Series is a set of five individual, but related international standards on quality management and quality assurance. The ISO is the international agency for standardization. It is currently made up of national standards bodies in approximately 100 countries. Standards were designed primarily for manufacturing industries, but are being redesigned and expanded for service industries.

To register under ISO 9000, a company's full range of manufacturing and customer service processes must be audited. An independent third-party registrar certifies that the quality system, as documented and implemented, meets the requirements of ISO 9000.

A major first step in working toward ISO 9000 acceptance is writing a quality manual. The general policies, procedures, and practices of an organization are documented. There are five types of manuals, or tiers.

- Tier 1 contains the overall policy statements issued by top management.
- Tier 2 is a quality manual documenting ways to meet requirements at one site of a company's multi-site location, for example. Ways to meet the management responsibility would also be documented.
- Tier 3 is a single site manual containing a detailed description of requirements actually met at the main office of the site.
- Tier 4 is a departmental or line function or activity group manual. It is usually a detailed manual—processes techniques, technical details, descriptions of methods, etc.
- Tier 5 is the detailed operating procedures manual. It is often the starting point for assembling and organizing the documentation supporting the existing (or future) quality system described in the manual.

These standards have been adopted by NATO, the United States Department of Defense, the American Society for Quality Control, the American National Standards Institute, nearly 100 countries around the world, about 2000 European companies, and by a growing number of American-owned and American-based companies.

ISO standards are an important requirement for companies doing business throughout the U.S., Canada, Europe, and numerous other countries around the world. Customers use this quality system as a check and balance report card to increase confidence and decrease the expensive resources commonly implemented to insure quality. ISO

standards lock quality into both supplier and customer (Marquardt, 1992).

The five standards:

- ISO 9000 shows how to use the other four standards in the series. It provides guidance for selecting the proper model. This standard focuses on twenty aspects that are subject to rigorous auditing during the certification process. Example areas include: management responsibility, quality system, process control, quality records, and statistical techniques.
- ISO 9001 is the widest and most comprehensive standard. It provides guidance for the selection and use of quality management and quality standards. This standard quality system requirements needed to develop a contract between parties, like demonstrate a suppler's capability to design and supply the desired product. It covers all phases of documenting operations within an organization—design, production, installation, service inspection, testing, training, and others.
- ISO 9002 covers production, installation, and servicing. It is used to detect and correct problems in contract negotiations between supplier and purchaser.
- ISO 9003 covers ISO 9002 but adds the final product inspection and testing the buyer specifies in the contract.
- ISO 9004 provides planning and implementing guidance to manage producers' products and services. This standard can be used to develop and implement internal quality systems, as in quality management and associated quality systems elements.

The ultimate goal is to provide better quality products and services for a competitive cost. With ISO 9000 assurance, customers can be reasonably sure they are getting competitively priced, quality products.

Specific benefits of the standards are: (1) builds customer confidence; (2) reduces customer auditing; (3) meets customer requirements; (4) provides a competitive advantage, as in international trade; and (5) marketing tool.

At Johnson Controls, obtaining ISO certification was good business practice. The pre-certification activities helped infuse formal managers with daily operations of the plant and reestablished and formalized the plant's basic quality practice. The twin disciplines of documenting and auditing quality practices closed the corrective or rework loop (Farahmand, Becerra, and Greene, 1994).

U.S., Far East, and European officials are concerned with credibility, particularly when ISO standards are used in marketing (Zuckerman, 1994).

ISO 9000 supplements TQM and may be a starting place for comprehensive quality efforts (Townsend and Gebhardt, 1994). Successful TQM efforts will have a quality system that resembles ISO 9000. Reportedly, TQM programs can make minor changes and meet ISO 9000 registration requirements (Corrigan, 1994).

Overall, achieving ISO registration enhances insight into the entire organization that might not have been achieved any other way. How and why you are/are not satisfying your customers is revealed. The process lets your customers know you have gone through the introspection necessary to assure them that you can and are providing what you say you are (Beardsley, 1994).

ISO standards and procedures undergo continuous revision. It is important to know the purpose behind ISO certification before starting the program, or any quality-based program for that matter.

ISO 9000 certification is no guarantee of success. Going through the step-by-step processes involved in obtaining certification identifies root causes of longstanding problems in quality, productivity, or other areas. Certification can be achieved in less than one year (Gasko, 1992). Time and cost to obtain certification are usually directly related.

Benchmarking. Estimates are that three quarters of the Fortune 500 companies are engaged in benchmarking (Mittelstaedt, 1992). This number could be as high as 90%. This section presents history and perspectives; definitions; examples; steps in the process; and advantages.

History and Perspective. Benchmarking was a term originally used in surveying. Benchmark referred to a permanently marked point of known or assumed elevation from which other elevations could be established.

Xerox first used benchmarking as a management tool in 1979. In 1988 it became a requirement for the Baldrige Award. As a partner of TQM, it is used in other measurement and assessment efforts, and has become very popular in the U.S.

The language and processes of benchmarking are qualitative and quantitative. Separately, each method provides vital, yet very different information. Combining quantitative and qualitative information produces synergy. The result becomes greater than the sum of the separate parts. Comparing qualitative and quantitative information helps ensure reliability and validity of results.

Benchmarking is a continuous process, and follows Deming's rational problem-solving process of Plan-Do-Check-Act cycle (Pulat, 1994). Deming attributed this cycle to his mentor, Walter Shewhart. The concept ''learn'' is sometimes substituted for ''check.''

Methods of benchmarking resemble problem solving techniques. Like any change effort, the driving forces behind benchmarking are: (1) top management commitment; (2) desire for better customer service; (3) improved

financial performance; (4) enhanced product development cycle; and (5) shorter delivery time.

Definitions. Of the three types of benchmarking, most definitions are of competitive benchmarking. Benchmarking is often described as a continuous, systematic process for evaluating products, services, and work processes of organizations recognized as industry or world leaders. Operational definitions form the core of benchmarking.

O'Dell (1994), director of the International Benchmarking Clearinghouse, a service of the American Productivity & Quality Center in Houston, defines benchmarking as '' . . . the process of identifying, understanding, and adapting outstanding practices and processes from organizations anywhere in the world to help your organization improve its performance.''

Competitive benchmarking is defined as '' . . . the practice of being humble enough to admit that someone else is better at something and wise enough to try and learn how to match and even surpass them at it'' (O'Dell 1994)

Pulat (1994) proposed the following definitions of benchmarking.

1. Ford Motor Company—a structured approach for learning from others and applying that knowledge.
2. 3M—a tool to search for enablers that allow a company to perform at a best-in-class level in a business process.
3. AT&T Benchmarking Group—the continuous process of measuring current business operations and comparing them to best-in-class companies.

Definitions of benchmarking and of ''best practices'' are essentially moving targets. Some of the following premises underlying benchmarking appear in the definitions.

Types of Benchmarking. The following three types of benchmarking are the most common:

1. Internal benchmarking is the most common type. This is an in-depth comparison and analysis of the internal functional operations of one's company. Specific functions or processes known to be performed well that are also critical to success are examined in detail. It is a form of collaborative benchmarking.
2. Competitive benchmarking is a continuous, systematic process for evaluating the products, services, and work processes of organizations recognized as industry or world leaders. For instance, comparing operations of one's company with L. L. Bean's billing system and Federal Expresses tracking system.
3. Strategic or collaborative benchmarking strategies identify critical success factors and business strategies

in any industry, regardless of the nature of the services or products, or where they are located.

Examples of Benchmarking.

Examples of Benchmarking. Examples are from Xerox, AT&T, and Eastman Kodak.

Example 1: At Xerox, benchmarking is part of a quality process to determine what the customer needs. Other steps are to modify or reengineer the process to fit the customer's need and then measure the process to see if customers' needs were met.

Robert C. Camp of Xerox Corporation pioneered benchmarking in the 1970s. In 1979, Xerox redefined benchmarking as a continuous process used to measure their products, services, and practices against companies recognizes as world leaders, or against competitors.

The 1980 benchmarking study done at Xerox produced sweeping changes in corporate culture through the Leadership Through Quality program. Changes were: (1) top down conversion to the new culture; (2) mutual goal setting and peer level cooperation; and (3) fostering of interpersonal skills and participation of all employees in improvement (Wilson, 1993).

Example 2: At AT&T, continuous internal benchmarking creates a maximum support organization encouraging people to do what they do best. Benchmarking plays a prime role in strategic planning by enabling alliances and partnerships to share information.

The AT&T Benchmarking Group has been in the forefront of the benchmarking movement since 1987. AT&T Network Systems Group, Transmission Systems Unit and AT&T Universal Card Services were 1992 Baldrige Award winners. The AT&T Consumer Communications Services (CCS), the largest of 20 AT&T business units, won the 1994 Baldrige Award for service. The CCS, located in Basking Ridge, New Jersey, provides domestic and international long-distance communications primarily to residential customers. Its 44,000 employees serve more than 80 million customers.

Example 3: The success of Ford Motor Company's Taurus and Sable cars introduced in 1985 is due to benchmarking. In 1980, Ford engineers trucked in and totally dismantled 50 midsize autos from competitors around the world. Of the 400 "best-in-class" features, 80% of these features were designed into the Taurus and Sable models.

Uses of Benchmarking. The driving forces behind benchmarking are: (1) desire for better customer service; (2) enhanced product development cycle; (3) shorter delivery time; (4) improved financial performance; and, most importantly, (5) top management commitment.

Benchmarking can be viewed as a popular measurement tool used: (1) to identify a prospective benchmarking partner; (2) to gauge and improve management culture and styles; and (3) as a main part of TQM.

Benchmarking provides an inelastic yardstick for measurement. When benchmarking methods are standardized within a given unit, department, company, or industry, one-on-one comparisons can be made. For example, the quality of products in manufacturing plants thousands of miles apart could be compared.

Benchmarking is a prime technique for assessing and comparing most organizational processes and products. It forms the core of most quality programs, like (TQM). Benchmarking plays a pivotal role in evaluating and documenting the entire range of organizational processes similar to those evaluated by the Malcolm Baldrige award (United States Department of Commerce, 1994).

Specifically, the benchmarking process:

1. Targets key areas within a company, department, or organization that can be improved.
2. Identifies and studies the best practices others use in these same areas.
3. Implements new processes and systems to enhance productivity and quality.

Few concepts can be benchmarked in any meaningful way unless everyone involved in the process knows exactly what the various terms really mean, or more specifically, what the concepts mean relative to their jobs, and how benchmarking will affect them. Benchmarking is useful only when the knowledge gained provides an foundation for building operational plans to meet and surpass industry best practices (Pluat, 1994).

Steps in the Benchmarking Process. Processes to be benchmarked must first be clearly defined in operational terms before any type of comparisons can be made. Benchmarking requires a level playing field. People up and down the line need to define and understand exactly what is to be benchmarked. Only then is it possible to identify and study the "best practices," and ultimately implement new processes and systems to bring about improvement.

Standard steps in most benchmarking process:

1. Prepare to benchmark by deciding what to benchmark. Form your team. Understand and define the processes and purposes involved.
2. Conduct research, such as collect information, determine who is best, and what to ask.
3. Selecting who to benchmark will require establishing relationships with the benchmark "partner."

4. Collect and share information obtained from surveys, site visits, including third parties.
5. Analyze, adapt and improve processes and products based on comparisons. Make plans to equal or surpass the benchmarked "partner."
6. Implement and monitor plans based on continuous feedback on all facets of the process.

Benchmarking processes used by AT&T and by Xerox are example methods (Mittelstaedt, 1992). The steps AT&T used are described in detail. Steps used by Xerox are grouped into areas similar to those of AT&T.

The benchmarking process at AT&T has nine steps.

1. Project Conception. Create or establish a commitment to benchmarking. Study in order to accurately define the mission. Select a team leader, obtain sponsors (often middle management), and allocate necessary resources.
2. Planning. Determine the specific function/process or product/service to be benchmarked. Establish objectives and develop a detailed benchmarking plan.
3. Preliminary Data Collection. (a) Identify performance variables and metrics based on current operations and customer requirements, including quantitative and qualitative factors that affect performance, like environmental, internal, etc.; (b) collect secondary research on relevant industries and similar operations and on your own processes and internal operations; (c) baseline the effectiveness of current processes; (d) identify problem areas; and (e) develop a set of preliminary questions that the benchmarking effort needs to answer.
4. Best-in-Class Selection. Develop a list of target companies. Collect secondary and primary data on target firms and then identify companies with best-in-class processes to be benchmarked. Select companies to contact and/or visit and develop a customized set of questions for each.
5. Best-in-Class Data Collection. Choose appropriate methods to collect data, such as scheduled visits, use telephone surveys, or questionnaires. Select visiting teams, visit the firms, debrief the visiting teams and prepare reports based on what was learned.
6. Assessment. Compare the process/product benchmarked and determine relevant performance metrics. Identify gaps between best-in-class performance and performance at your own firm and determine why the gaps occurred. Develop recommendations, obtain feedback from others in your firm, and communicate new goals, performance targets, and strategies to improve processes/products benchmarked.
7. Implementation Planning. Develop an operational plan and an overall change strategy. Organize an imple-

mentation team(s) at all levels and ensure they understand the results of benchmarking, and the need to approve and communicate this information throughout the organization.
8. Implementation. Monitor performance and progress against milestones and interim objectives. Prepare progress reports and discuss them with the unit/manager sponsoring benchmarking efforts. Formalize and fine-tune all changes introduced.
9. Recalibration. Because benchmarking is a continuous process, periodically assess processes/products that have been improved and consider future benchmarks. Continue to monitor industry trends and identify internal and external environmental forces that might trigger future benchmarking. Integrate benchmarking into existing quality program(s) and into strategic planning, perhaps even into individual and collective mission and goals statements.

The 10-step Xerox benchmarking process is grouped into four major areas and summarized. Methods of AT&T and Xerox are similar.

1. Planning efforts:
   - Identify the subject of benchmarking.
   - Identify benchmarking partners.
   - Determine data collection methods and collect data.
2. Analysis:
   - Determine current competitive gaps.
   - Project future performance.
3. Integration:
   - Communicate findings and gain acceptance.
   - Establish functional goals.
4. Action:
   - Develop action plans.
   - Implement plans and monitor progress.
   - Recalibrate benchmark.

Benchmarking processes like those of AT&T and Xerox are well planned and require a high level of self-knowledge, clear objectives, and customer awareness. No benchmarking efforts will succeed unless there are appropriate mechanisms to measure performance and implement change anywhere in the company (Mittelstaedt, 1992).

Advantages of Benchmarking. Overall benefits of benchmarking are (Middlestaedt, 1992):

1. Objective evaluation
2. Use of working examples
3. Proactive search of new paradigms and technology
4. Solve real problems
5. Understand inputs and outputs.

Overall, benchmarking should become a company wide process, an ethic, or a way of managing. Quality and innovation go hand in hand.

If benchmarking is done outside your industry, the advantages proposed by O'Dell (1994) may be valuable:

1. Avoid reinventing an existing solution. This saves time, and lets you improve on or even modify a proven practice or established method.
2. Attain breakthrough improvement and speed up change. Rate of change may be from a few percent a year to over 500%.
3. Set "stretch" goals based on credible external evidence. Such goals provide a working model and also encourage people to extend themselves beyond the usual 4–5%.
4. Drive and direct business process reengineering.
5. Overcome the "not invented here" belief. When people see what others are doing, they begin to believe they can do it, too. Resistance to change is reduced, and people begin to believe that new and lasting changes can be made.
6. Stay up with, or even get ahead of the competition. Benchmarking is "state of the art." When additional perspectives, methods, and innovations are added to an existing "good" quality product or service, competitors may be left behind.
7. Eccles (1991) believes benchmarking gives managers a methodology that can be tied to any financial or non-financial measure. Benchmarking has a transforming effect on managerial mind-sets and perspectives.

Although benchmarking seems like a structured process, it is more of an art than a science. People having vested interests will need to be ochestrated carefully. Effort is required to obtain reliable, valid information. Updating and revising findings takes management skill and dedication.

Most benchmarking ultimately enhances quality and productivity down the road. Benchmarking processes provides the key and the building blocks for measurement associated with change efforts in general, and quality improvement in particular.

In general, the quality of products and services can be evaluated along multiple dimensions. Some organizations emphasize one facet of quality over another. Some people are willing to pay for the skilled workmanship in a Cross pen, Rolex watch, or Steinway piano. The major issue is to introduce a dimension of quality that is important to customers. To illustrate, after deregulation, AT&T assumed that residential customers equated quality with a wide range of expensive features. The opposite occurred, as durable, reliable, and easy-to-operate telephones sold much better than the fancy, expensive telephones.

Overview of quality benchmarks:

1. Quality is a company wide process.
2. Quality is what the customers says it is.
3. Quality and cost are a sum, not a difference.
4. Quality requires the dedication and efforts of individuals and groups.
5. Quality is a way of managing.
6. Quality and innovation are mutually dependent.
7. Quality is an ethic.
8. Quality requires continuous improvement.
9. Quality is the most cost effective, least capital intensive route to productivity.
10. Quality is implemented within a total system connected with customers and suppliers.

---

3. If you are involved in benchmarking, indicating the methods and processes being used. Do you feel your efforts are well planned and will provide the results you need?

_____

_____

4. List areas that have or will be benchmarked in your group or organization. Define standards for measurement in precise terms.

_____

_____

5. Will ISO 9000, the Baldrige Award, and other "quality yardsticks" still be used in the 21st century?

_____

_____

With global competition, the need to know where you stand in the race toward productivity and quality is more important now than ever before. Benchmarking tools help establish how you compare with others, but do not tell you how to be become and remain successful. Tools are no substitutes for knowledge and insightful leadership. New mind-sets developed through change efforts in general, not just quality, reflect shared understandings of interrelationships and patterns within and outside the organization. This new way of thinking will gradually replace short-term, linear thinking (Senge, 1990).

QUALITY IN PRODUCT-BASED AND SERVICE-BASED INDUSTRIES

More than 70% of the gross national product of the United States is in the service area. However, many efforts to develop or assess services and relationships with customers are based on the product industry, not on the service industry.

Services should be reevaluated from management and quality control standpoints, as their overall contribution to the nation's economic health are immense. Insurance, financing, transportation, communication, and health care have a dramatic influence on the cost of producing goods domestically.

Product-Based Industries

A product is a transformation of energy and matter into a presumably desirable form, at desirable locations, and at an appropriate time (Schwartz, 1992). Products or goods are often considered outputs, as in manufacturing or materials processing. Products are easy to see and have attributes and deficiencies that can be measured and recorded. Much effort goes into various forms of monitoring and quality control.

Service-Based Industries

Services are all those economic activities in which the primary goal is neither a product nor a construction (Quinn and Gagnon, 1986). Typical service-based industries are health, legal, accounting, travel, education, insurance, automotive, banking, and maintenance. These industries often deal with less tangible aspects like customer satisfaction, goodwill, and value in the marketplace. Concerns relate to the service itself and to the provision of services to discerning customers. To illustrate, airlines strive for

---

6. Refer back to Chapter 12, Question 1. Select one product-based and one-service based area. Indicate the approximate percent of time or effort spent with either internal or external customers and typical problem areas. Specify ways to examine or measure quality.

Product-Based Area	% Customer Contact	Typical Problem Areas	Ways to Examine and Measure Quality

Service-Based Area	% Customer Contact	Typical Problem Areas	Ways to Examine and Measure Quality

7. How do product-based and service-based responses differ?

_____

_____

_____

8. List tasks or jobs you personally perform. How many does you work group perform? Is there high, medium, or low customer contact? Describe the level of quality outcomes in terms of customer satisfaction and meeting personal or company standards.

Tasks	Performed Self	Group	Amount of Customer Contact	Level of Quality Outcomes
_____	_____	_____	_____	_____
_____	_____	_____	_____	_____
_____	_____	_____	_____	_____
_____	_____	_____	_____	_____

on-time flight departures and courteous service by the in-flight crew.

Service businesses are "people-based" and "equipment-based." Peoples' ability levels range from unskilled to professional. Types of services range from heavily automated car washes with low labor content, to service businesses with high professional labor content, like management consulting firms. The health care industry is both people-centered and product-based. Price, delivery, and quality considerations are weighed against pressures to provide better health service for less cost.

Amount of direct customer contact varies. It is high in the fast food area and low in a mail order business. Providing excellent customer service is a major concern in both areas.

Service industries differ from product industries in the following ways:

1. They usually have a higher labor cost relative to total value of output than product-based businesses.
2. Output is basically intangible, which makes measurement difficult. In the health care industry, convenience, savings of time, or the quality of patient care are interpreted in various ways, depending on customers' specific needs. In product-based industries, output is nearly always tangible.
3. Do not have the capacity to store their services, for example, a vacant seat in an airliner that has just taken off. This empty seat is really a perishable commodity. It cannot be saved or reused. Empty seats in airplanes are financial losses just like empty hotel rooms. On the other hand, products can readily be inventoried and stored until needed.
4. The site is much more dependent on location of customers. Restaurants are built in prime locations, or in "restaurant row," to meet the demands of customers and be highly visible. Manufacturing plants and mail order houses can be established nearly anywhere.
5. People serving customers become a major part of the entire service operation. People involved in manufacturing rarely see their customers.

Table 14-1 compares typical product-based and service-based organizations along the dimensions of: (1) type of output; (2) design, development, and delivery; (3) customer orientation; (4) logistics; and (5) measurement.

Table 14-1
Comparison of Typical Product-Based and Service-Based Organizations

Products- and Production-Centered Service Operations	Customer-Centered Services Operations
Type of Products/Activities and Production/Creations	
• Finished goods are tangible and may be an investment • Produced at specific location • Output tangible and unique to manufacturer • Production is independent of consumption • Product design is centered on the customer; process design is centered on the employee	• Services are perishable and consumed when produced, like an airline ticket • Site selection depends on where customers are • Output intangible, as in coordinating activities • Production is often simultaneous with consumption • Both product design and process design are centered on the customer
Design/Development/Delivery	
• Developers seldom have contact with users • Technical skills dominate operations	• Direct contact with partner and end users • Interpersonal skills dominate operations
Customer Orientation	
• Customer loyalty builds over time • May have contact with end user • Customer is involved in very few production processes • Employee-customer relationships are seldom complex, as employees may seldom see customers • End users are gradually forming partnerships with suppliers	• Very dependent on advertising and promotion • Has direct contact with end user • Customer is involved in many production processes • Employee-customer relationships are often very complex, such as terms and conditions of a sale • Often based on customers' perceptions
Logistics	
• Capacity depends on inventory • Work in progress	• Provided on customer demand • Queue(s), or waiting line(s)
Measurement	
• Easy to use standards, measurements, inspection, and control of quality • Output depends on individuals working cooperatively, as in assembly lines • Product or output is homogeneous, as in mass production • Quality is determined by output alone • Quality measurements built into contracts and agreements	• Use flexible standards or guidelines often developed jointly with customers and providers • Output often depends on groups working together synergistically, often at point of delivery • Heterogeneous, due to customer-provider interaction • Often judged by speed, courtesy, completeness of services provided • Quality is judged during service delivery

9. Define quality in product-based and service-based industries. Include a customer orientation.

Definitions of quality in product-based industries:
1.
2.
3.

Definitions of quality in service-based industries:
1.
2.
3.

Products and services can be closely related, as when both are provided by the same supplier or manufacturer. Many computer companies provide software. Services may help sell the product, and conversely.

The gap between what customers expect and what they receive may be getting smaller. Turner (1994) suggests that the service organization should be redesigned, primarily to reflect customer feedback and to empower those delivering services. Myers and Buckman (1992) provide methods to assess the quality of service provided to internal and external customers.

DIRECT AND INDIRECT INDICATORS OF QUALITY

Measures, or indicators of quality, are direct and indirect, or a combination of both. This statement supports the section on qualitative, or soft data, and quantitative, or hard data. As with hard and soft data, direct and indirect indicators of quality can supplement each other.

Direct and indirect indicators listed affect many factors in the organization, not just quality. Examples highlight quality.

Direct

These indicators focus on areas that are well known and easily identified in service-based and product-based areas. Most direct indicators usually represent output, or end-result variables. Data are frequently numeric, and often reported in terms of cost.

1. Customers. Number of repeat, satisfied customers; measures of response time; demands for related services; complaints; number customers reached in a specific time period.
2. Suppliers. Failures like supplier-created losses; substandard goods; warranty, repair, and liability.
3. Publicity. Reactions to publicity range from positive to negative. Litigation or legal problems regarding implied or executed contracts for delivery, and associated contracts, or written, or implied agreements can generate positive or negative publicity.
4. Desirability of services. Needed, timely, flexible, streamlined, etc.
5. Internal failures. Extra scrap, rework, re-inspections, downgrading, maintenance, process control, etc., could be reduced by inspection.

Proactive measures may be training in quality; adhering to procedures and policy manuals; vendor surveys, design and development of reliable equipment; and employing qualified personnel. The number of quality-related prob-

lems can be reduced through careful planning and preventive measures.

Indirect

These indicators cover areas often neglected or ignored. For instance, a leading manufacturer of appliances estimates that one in three dissatisfied customers will complain to the company, but each dissatisfied customer will advertise that complaint to at least 15 friends or acquaintenances (Bain, 1982).

1. Goodwill or reputation. The down sides are penalties against the customers, like non-reimbursed repair costs; equipment downtime causing delays, inflexible refund policy; no substitutions, among others.
2. Unanticipated or unrealistic sanctions, like regulations, or interventions.

When direct and indirect factors affecting quality are known, more effort can be devoted to anticipating and preventing people-related and equipment-based problems.

Internal-External

This is a standard way to evaluate variables within and outside the organization. *Internal variables* are the "inner works" or "knowns" of the organization, like systems, strategy, culture, or infrastructure. Management, current work force, type of products or services provided, and physical plant all play major roles.

External variables outside the organization resemble environmental variables discussed in Chapter 2. These variables can literally make or break a business:

1. Customer expectations for products and services.
2. Continued customer demand in the marketplace.
3. "Customer" quality standards that may exceed the organization's capacity to provide products or services at a profit.
4. Unanticipated or unrealistic sanctions, regulations, or interventions.
5. Litigation or legal problems associated with implied or executed contracts for delivery.
6. Fluctuating or unstable economic climate.
7. Competition from within and outside the United States.

Failure to plan adequately or to respond to certain negative internal and external variables may reduce quality standards. For instance, when "seconds," or lower quality products are produced, markets can be found for discounted merchandise. Customers do not choose "second-class" service.

Examples of ways to evaluate the efficiency and effectiveness of services range from simple questionnaires and interviews to detailed surveys with complex scoring criteria. A specific illustration is the American Customer Satisfaction Index (Brecka, 1994). Service providers' evaluations and clients' perceptions of quality of service should be analyzed and compared over varying periods of time. Main concerns are reliability and validity (Long-Becker and Landauer, 1987).

Most companies rely heavily on outside suppliers for goods and services, as in subcontracting. Technological advances and intense competition place a premium on vendor quality control. Those using vendors and the vendors themselves must meet numerous standards and price ranges. Cost-saving methods require vendors to balance reduced costs against maintenance of quality standards. Standards, such as ISO 9000, help minimize variation and increase quality. Manufacturers' charters are to deliver products at a quality level acceptable to the customer at minimum cost (Grove, 1983).

Quality and Productivity

There are two generally-accepted, completely opposing beliefs about the relationship of productivity and quality. Supporters of "quick-fixes" believe there is little or no relationship.

A positive belief is, "When low cost is the goal, quality often gets lost. But when quality is the goal, lower costs usually follow" (Skinner, 1986). Many cost-reduction programs of cutting corners have short-term targets, and essentially do harm. Cost-cutting greatly reduces flexibility and ability to move quickly to introduce or develop new products or services.

Managers who establish a positive relationship between quality and cost begin by making the long-term investment in people and equipment necessary to improve product quality and reduce costs (Leonard and Sasser, 1982). Such commitments to fundamentals begin with training programs in quality control and related areas. Changes and improvements are easier to make when there is direct, frequent contact with those involved in the design process.

Whether workers are paid on total output or on defect-free output makes a difference. If they are paid on output only, they will not necessarily care about quality. The relationship between quality and productivity is complex. Longstanding experts in the field are Deming and Juran. (See Suggested Readings Section).

Quality improvement, which follows in the same footsteps as productivity improvement, is the most fruitful path to higher productivity and competitive success (Leonard and Sasser, 1982). In any change program, top management support is critical to the success of quality improvement efforts.

Quality and Cost

Major direct indicators of the costs of quality include:

- Prevention—quality training, procedures and manuals, vendor surveys, design and development of equipment.
- Appraisal—inspections in general: vendor, receiving, in-process, finished-goods, process control, quality reports, among others.
- Internal failure—scrap, rework, failure analysis, supplier-caused losses, reinspection, downgrading, etc. Such failures could be reduced by various forms of inspection, maintenance, and process control.
- External failure—complaints, returned goods, repair, warranty and product liability with associated litigation.

Indirect Indicators of the Cost of Quality

Indirect indicators often pertain to interactions with people. As such, they can be observed in some form, and described, but are hard to document and measure. The outcomes, or what happens *after* the sale, are often of great concern, e.g., customer complaints, and possibly legal action.

Major indicators of indirect costs of quality include:

- Customer penalty—warranty, non-reimbursed repair costs, returned goods, reputation, and transportation costs.
- Customer dissatisfaction—the greater the dissatisfaction the higher the associated costs or the greater the probability that future business will be taken elsewhere.
- Loss of goodwill or reputation—lost business and the possibility that customers will complain to others. When customers are consistently treated well, they not only become repeat customers, they spread a "good word" about the company.

Cost that is assessed in the numeric language of accounting is not addressed in this text. However, some direct and indirect "intangible" qualitative issues are covered. When direct and indirect costs of quality are known, more effort can be devoted to anticipating and preventing people-related and equipment-based problems (Bain, 1982).

Costs of quality do not respect organizational boundaries. Every department can add to or reduce the cost of

10. Is quality or productivity more important in your organization? In your job?

_____

_____

_____

quality, namely customer service, accounting, manufacturing, engineering, R&D, and many more.

Quality has a price. The cost of quality permeates all quality change and improvement efforts. Quality built into services or products is the most meaningful and cost-effective in the long run (Suzawa, 1985). Quality can also be inspected in, but only "after-the-fact." Inspection is the only alternative when products are already completed.

The relationship between cost and quality is demonstrated by, "The cost of not doing things right the first time in a quality manner is 20% of sales" (Kearns, 1985).

Good quality yields a higher return on investment (ROI) for any given market share. As quality goes down, so does ROI. Improving product quality is a profitable activity (Garvin, 1983). Most winners of the Malcolm Baldrige award have increased their profits.

FACTORS AFFECTING QUALITY

The following five well-documented categories influencing quality are reviewed (Bain, 1982). Although performance is last in Bain's list, the point is that people are the most valuable resource any organization has. The human element and the importance of motivation, attitude, loyalty, and factors too numerous to list, cannot be underestimated. People and their leaders literally make or break a company.

1. _Design._ The quality of output depends on product design and on the design of the system producing those outputs. This includes the whole spectrum of design and manufacturing processes, e.g., quality control and associated human factors. Type of market (luxury versus economy) and competition are prime factors affecting the design and quality of consumer goods and services.

2. _Equipment._ The ability of equipment, tools, and machinery to produce the desired outputs. Conformance to standards and reliability are important. Decreased cost of repairs, and lowered maintenance budgets are evidence that equipment is functioning properly and has been adequately maintained.

3. _Materials._ Specifications or requirements must be met. A skilled work force is required to operate equipment,

and maximize use of materials to produce an economically competitive product. Quality control, and minimizing scrap and waste are critical issues.

4. _Scheduling._ Poor timing can adversely affect the delivery time of all outputs. If deliveries are late, or if processing time is reduced, and pressure is applied to meet schedules, substandard products may result.

5. _Performance._ Skills and motivation affect performance. Positive attitudes, a results-oriented environment, and supportive management demonstrating genuine concern for employees and customers will maximize performance.

Perspectives on the Dimensions of Quality

Garvin's (1987) eight critical dimensions or categories of quality are a framework for strategic analysis. These include: performance standards, features, reliability, conformance, durability, serviceability, aesthetics, and perceived quality. Some of these areas overlap, as few dimensions stand completely alone. Some products or services may be high in one or more areas, and low in others.

1. _Performance standards_ are based on primary operating characteristics, like an automobile's performance—cruising speed, comfort, or handling. These attributes can be measured and compared with competitors' products. Some performance standards are based on subjective preferences, which can be stronger than the real standard. Some personal preferences like shape, color, and quietness of ride are unrelated to the quality of a car.

2. _Features_ are often the "bells and whistles" or products and services that go beyond the basic functions. Special features are expensive. "Free" drinks on an airplane and automatic tuners on television sets are but two examples. It is difficult to separate primary or major performance characteristics from secondary features or "bells and whistles.' Flexible manufacturing technology allowing customers to personalize more of their purchases, yet decrease cost, is a possible solution.

3. *Reliability* is the probability that a product will malfunction or fail within a specific time period. Reliability is measured by time to first failure, mean time between failures, or the failure rate per unit of time. Reliability also impacts downtime and maintenance, as with computers and copying machines.

4. *Conformance* is the degree to which a product's design and operating characteristics meet established standards. Every product and service has some form of specifications or dimensions for parts or purity standards for materials. Deviation from standards is accepted within certain limits. Statistical parameter are often represented by number of defective parts per thousand or million.

   The problem is that a product may conform to standards, but still have defects. A better, newer way to look at quality is conformance to specifications.

   In product-based or materials processing industries, often two or more parts are fit together. The size of their tolerances, or closeness of fit, often determines how well they will match. One part may be well within the tolerance, but the other part may be outside the accepted limit. In reality, both parts fail, as they will not fit tightly together. One link will wear more than the other link, for some reason. However, a product may conform to standards, yet still have defects.

   Genichi Taguchi, a prize-winning Japanese statistician, indicates that ''loss of function'' is a measure of losses from the time a product is shipped. Losses include warranty costs, non-repeating customers, and other factors directly attributed to quality. Common failures in conformance are defect rates in the factory, and the number of service calls made after a product reaches a customer. In the service areas, deviations from standards include an array of factors like accuracy and timeliness, including processing efforts, unanticipated delays, and other frequent mistakes.

5. *Durability,* one measure of product life, is the amount of use one gets from a product before it deteriorates, such as the number of hours of illumination from a light bulb filament before it burns out. How long a product can be used before it breaks down and is either easier or cheaper to replace than repair is another measure of durability. Durability and reliability are closely related. Some products have lifetime guarantees, like 3M videocassettes. An increase in product life may not be due to technical improvements or to the use of longer-lived materials, but to changes in the economic environment, namely cost to produce a product.

6. *Serviceability* is described in terms of speed, courtesy, competence, and ease of repair. The concern is about product breakdown, *and* with the time needed to restore service. Serviceability also refers to timeliness with which service appointments are kept, and how service personnel respond, for example. Customers' expectations differ widely, depending on the seriousness of the situation and on the direct and indirect cost of downtime. Toll-free telephone hotlines to the customer relations departments are one proactive way to minimize or preempt consumer dissatisfaction. General Electric, Johnson & Johnson, Whirlpool and others do this.

7. *Aesthetics* or how a product looks, feels, sounds, tastes, or smells is frequently a matter of personal judgment reflecting individual differences and preferences. Although aesthetic dimensions are difficult to define, people definitely know what they like and don't like, particularly when it comes to food, clothes, art, and music.

8. *Perceived quality,* an indirect, somewhat inexact measure of quality, often hinges on reputation of ''yesterday's'' products. A somewhat overused example is the high quality and reliability of Maytag clothes washers and dryers. Perceived quality is greatly influenced by customers' expectations and buying history.

---

11. Indicate ways you could build quality into your job. Think of how quality is built into the product or process. If you are familiar with the planning and design processes basic to the success of the Ford Taurus automobile, use these steps as your guide. Otherwise, just think proactively.

_____

_____

_____

Garvin cautions that companies rarely pursue all eight dimensions at the same time. Also, technological limitations due to cost may constrain efforts. Time and cost of retraining employees can slow down or redirect quality efforts. The appropriate balance between providing products that meet as many of the dimensions of quality as possible and also meet customers' needs must be figured out. Market research is one way to determine customers' needs. Garvin states, "Quality is not simply a problem to be solved; it is a competitive opportunity."

Views of the Quality Dilemma

The broad perspectives in the quality arena cover: (1) the technical aspects; (2) various functions or areas of concentration, as on internal and external customers; (3) competitive aspects, like market share; and (4) forward momentum gained from developing and selling innovative products and services.

The following views of the quality dilemma come from 13 American Management Association Councils (Executive Insights, 1991).

- Manager's inability to define quality in clear terms hinders quality efforts.
- Quality starts at the top. Senior management must openly support quality efforts and have the vision to keep it going.
- The lack of measurable results, particularly in white collar and indirect labor areas, frustrates the quality movement.
- It is expensive to maintain quality efforts. However, one of the major goals of quality effort is seen as cost savings.

Major areas of concern in the quality area include:

- Closed-loop thinking, or taking assumptions for granted. Focusing on the short-term accomplishments, like working faster, not smarter, does little to bring about significant, long-term changes. Structured thinking minimizes creativity processes leading to breakthrough thinking.
- Overemphasis on team to the detriment of personal needs for recognition and accomplishment. Successful organizations have high performing individuals and groups.
- Concentration on tools, processes, and procedures without closely examining purpose. Restructuring to accommodate quality improvement may disrupt the concentration on the real goals of quality improvement.

Quality efforts should include all vital roles and functions of the organization. Successful quality movements must foster improvements in products and processes, encourage breakthrough thinking, and stress mutual accountability of individuals and teams (McLagan, 1991).

CUSTOMER FOCUS

The concept of quality, like that for any other concept, can be in the eye of the beholder, namely customers, consumers, clients, partners, and all types of end users and stakeholders. Perception can and does overshadow reality. People judge others according to their own personal perceptions of quality, as when team members and their leaders use different criteria. Clear definitions, as we have discovered, reduce confusion. Agreement can be achieved only when the provider and receiver of "quality" define quality in the same, or very similar terms using operational definitions, established benchmarks, examples, or samples.

According to Ernst & Young, customer-focused quality is " . . . continually increasing customer satisfaction with products and services through attention to performance and conformance issues."

Customer satisfaction can be defined as " . . . the degree of happiness a customer experiences with a company's product or service and which results from the interaction and interrelationships of all people within that company" (Desatnick, 1992).

Customers are increasingly concerned with quality and value. Quality is beginning to be known as a team effort—the product of participation, TQM, even peer review (Kanter, 1992).

Customers want service, consistency, accuracy of orders, flexibility, proper lead time, competitive costs, and quality.

Example 1: L. L. Bean, the Maine-based mail order company, was founded in 1912. Their motto is, "Bean is about people and respect for people."

The TQM initiative at L. L. Bean empowers people to change processes to "do it right the first time." Its salaried employees receive three days of total quality training and all hourly workers receive one day of training.

Their current barometer of success shows a large increase in sales; major decrease in returns due to poor quality; a significant decrease in lost-time injuries; and dramatic improvement of work-in-progress cycle time. Its excellent reputation for customer service now includes internal customers (Anfuso, 1994).

Example 2: TQM principles at Kellogg: (1) the success of the enterprise is closely linked to serving the client; (2) the greatest productivity gains are obtained from transforming adversarial relationships in the work place into cooperative ones; and (3) if it isn't measured, it doesn't matter (Greenbaum, 1993).

Example 3: At Lockheed, customer satisfaction equals the difference between the customer's expectation for product or service quality and the customer's perception of actual quality received, i.e., customer satisfaction = customer perception − customer expectations.

Example 4: IBM recognizes the value of the customer interface that involves customers and non-customers. Their user groups encourage customers and business partners to try out software being developed. IBM believes customers' expectations play major roles in the company's strategic planning efforts.

Example 5: At Xerox Business Products, quality is a customer obsession strategy supported by tools, processes, teams, and people. Customer satisfaction is "corporate objective number one."

Example 6: The four major objectives of American Express are quality, quality, quality, quality.

Example 7: 3M is a leader in the quality field. In 1902, 3M manufactured only sandpaper. Today, it markets more than 50,000 products worldwide. The essentials of 3M's quality philosophy: (1) consistently meet customers's expectations; (2) use indicators of customer satisfaction to measure quality; (3) consistently meet expectations 100% of the time; (4) attain quality through prevention-oriented improvement projects; and (5) ensure that management commitment leads the quality process.

Key elements in 3M's growth and expansion to new markets relate to paying attention to customers. They are dedicated to product and service quality. 3M fosters creativity and innovation. More than 2,000 of 3M's quality improvement teams are actively solving work-related problems (Anderson, 1991).

Example 8: A service audit is one way of outlining and documenting the steps of a customer's service experiences. Services are examined from the customer's view, beginning with initial contact, and ending with incorporating customer feedback to improve service.

Amount of customer satisfaction:

$$\frac{\text{Sales lost in a given period}}{\text{Number of customer complaints in the same period}}$$

Information on customer satisfaction can be accumulated over a period of weeks, months, or years, and data compared. Data can be examined for trends, like number of customer complaints for various periods. At Corning, for example, customers are asked whether requirements are being met on time, the first time, and 100% of the time (Wagel, 1987).

The American Customer Satisfaction Index aims to quantify quality and customer satisfaction and relate them to the firms' financial performance. The Index includes consumer perceptions of the quality of goods and services from companies and governments representing about 50% of the gross domestic product of U.S. Foreign companies having major U.S. market shares are also included (Brecka, 1994).

Every customer, if asked, can provide a wealth of information on nearly every phase of the design, development, testing, implementation, monitoring, and improve-

---

12. Developing an external customer orientation is challenging. Nearly everyone has internal customers. List the type of internal or external customer contact you have on a regular basis and the purpose of the contact. Estimate the percentage of time you use customer input. List the type of quality improvement efforts you are now using. Estimate the percent of improvement in customer relationships resulting from quality programs.

Describe Type Input Used	Purpose of Contact	% Time Customer Input Used	Type of Quality Improvement Program	Percent Improvement of Customer Relationships
_____	_____	_____	_____	_____
_____	_____	_____	_____	_____
_____	_____	_____	_____	_____
_____	_____	_____	_____	_____

ment of products and services. We need to make it easy for them to provide the information required. We can ask questions. After while, we will learn to ask the right questions. Customers really are a vital link in the continuous chain of defining and improving quality, and the unending search for new, cost-effective products and services. Quality function deployment is an aid (Farrell, 1994).

Products and services must be innovative *and* they must be reviewed, verified, produced, and controlled to meet customer requirements. The same may be true of suppliers who sell materials to producers who in turn transform materials into commodities for customers.

Many employees, for instance engineers, in product design, or management information specialists, do not necessarily deal directly with external customers, or even internal customers, for that matter. External customers, end-users, partners or suppliers play major roles in deciding exactly what quality means. These same people, if consulted, can lead the way in not only defining quality, but in suggesting, perhaps even developing, and testing out new services and products. Organizations having an enthusiastic, cooperative relationship with their "customers," whoever they are and wherever they may be, have a definite advantage. "Customers call the shots."

Impact of ISO 9000 and other quality standards, winning the "Baldrige" or other quality rewards have a dual purpose. They favor the customer, yet serve the supplier through public recognition and numerous honors. Orsini (1994) compares Category 7 of the Baldrige Award with ISO 9004. The specific ISO requirements relate to planning and implementation guidance in producing products and service. Category 7, Customer Focus Satisfaction, has 300 points, or 30% of the total.

Within the organization, "in-company" customers require goods and services from each other and from other departments. Company customers may require various forms of information, equipment, sharing of computers, or exchanging ideas. We are all alternately customers and suppliers.

Babich's (1992) customer satisfaction model assumes a closed system of three suppliers providing products of comparable price and performance to a growing customer base. Procedures or algorithms are used to determine how dissatisfied customers choose their next supplier.

Value added is a highly desirable commodity. More effort should be directed to determining exactly what adds value to customer services, processes, and products (Smith, 1995). Customers may be able to operationalize value added. Perhaps it is time to let them try. The market-driven economy is gradually evolving into a customer-driven marketplace. Areas where value could be added include customer service in general, but notably where service has been substandard or questionable.

Quality of service can be improved if employees think of themselves as *the* company. Employees are the customer's first and possibly only contact. Many customers make their decisions to purchase based on how they are treated by front-line people.

The concept of quality is gradually moving from the industrial model that puts people who deliver service to customers last to the service model that puts customers first and designs systems and products for them. This paradigm shift is definitely toward customers (Kanter, 1992).

Total quality focuses on benchmarking customers' needs and customer satisfaction. Once total quality is well under way, it becomes a major competitive advantage. The existence of total quality does not mean companies will become and remain successful. However, companies need winning strategies that come from the minds of leaders. Senior leadership cannot be delegated.

Two important things about customers. First, customers do not willingly choose "second-class" services. Second, reportedly, it costs six times more to get a new customer than to keep an old one.

DESIGNING QUALITY ASSESSMENT AND IMPROVEMENT PROGRAMS

Organizations and people grow and change. The same is true of all types of improvement efforts. Quality is an improvement or change effort. Organizations, like the people in them, differ in age, and grow and mature at different rates. Each has a growing or "start up" period, and alternating periods of growth and stability before reaching maturity. Organizations that grow and change with the times, like Shell companies, IBM, and Johnson & Johnson, each draw on over 100 years of experience.

The following "laundry list" of quality improvement and personal and organizational change efforts are listed alphabetically, not chronologically.

Autonomous work teams
Awareness
Continuous (process) improvement
Cross-functional teams
Employee involvement
Empowerment
Focus groups
Job enrichment
Labor-management groups
Management by objectives
Organizational redesign
Quality circles
Quality control
Quality culture
Quality function deployment

Quality improvement
Quality involvement
Quality management
Quality organization
Quality teams
Quality of work life
Participation in general
Problem solving sessions
Statistical process control
Survey feedback
T-groups
Task forces
Team based initiatives
Total employee involvement
Total quality control
Total quality management

Organizations adopt, use, and discontinue these improvement efforts in different orders. Each organization has its own archaeological history of quality where unsuccessful, even incomplete, quality programs accumulate.

Quality is definitely a part of productivity improvement. Quality must be built into mission and goals statements, and into the strategic plans of the organization. The process of improving quality permeates the organization and becomes the major goal. Planning and prevention are the real keys to increasing and maintaining quality.

Gault (1994) of IBM Corporation summarizes the basic factors that should be considered in any change or improvement effort. These are: strategy; structure; system; style; staffing; skills; and shared values.

Quality Change and Improvement Program

The following steps are important in designing and implementing a quality improvement program.

1. Compare and analyze the major dimensions affecting quality. Relevant dimensions, such as key results areas, should be further examined. It may be important to focus on one important dimension and make an impact on it before starting on another area.
2. Study the framework and function of the organization—structure, shape, strategy, size, systems, control, culture, division of work, as discussed in Chapter 2. Organizations are unique. So are people. The organization's history, leadership style, philosophy, and attitude have a major impact on any type of change effort. Communication channels connect these structures and subsystems together to form a complete, dynamic whole.
3. Determine where the organization is in its life cycle—start-up phase, running fast, running down. Organizations, like every living being, have a life cycle. Systems theory reveals that static organizations do not survive for long.

   Generally, the younger dynamic organizations accept change more readily than older, mature, established organizations. The same is true with people.
4. Understand the type of business the organization is in. Most quality initiatives were originally designed for manufacturing industries, not service industries. What works for products does not necessarily work for customer-related services. The gradual transition from product-based to service-based is far from complete. Old tools and methods from the product world are being changed, often force-fit, to work in the service world. The types of organizations range, in general, from high tech to low tech, from people intensive to machine intensive.
5. Acknowledge and work with people. Despite the impetus behind quality improvement efforts, ideas or mandates, most programs concentrate on teams, leadership, and payout. Some programs are based on the premise the entire organization is static. Other programs are poured over current programs. Few efforts recognize existing pockets of excellence, so the wheel is reinvented again. Although the goal is fast payout, effort is long term. Gaps between goals and expectations are often wide.
6. Build a quality team, department, or organization. This takes leadership, dedication, and compromise. Time and cost are frequently underestimated. Managers, in particular, get anxious for payout on results.
7. Maximize the probability that programs will succeed by ensuring the following:
   - The CEO and upper management understand and visibly support the whole quality process.
   - Organizational structure and infrastructure, style, goals, mission, even vision, are flexible enough to change as goals and accomplishments change.
   - Know, and document, if possible, areas of competence or highly quality. Effort can be redirected to areas of greater need. Programs should be designed for those using it. One program will not fit all needs.
   - Be willing to invest time, effort, and money. Quality improvement cannot be accomplished quickly. Recognize and appropriately reinforce small gains or improvements in quality. Small gains gradually add up and become substantial.
   - Do not superimpose quality programs over other change efforts. It is difficult to work on two fronts at the same time. Companies, like 3M, build quality into their framework.

Example 1. Texas Instruments' commitment to quality and productivity improvement dates back to the 1950s. In 1992, Texas Instruments Defense Systems & Electronics Group became the first defense contractor to win the Baldrige Award (Junkins, 1994).

Example 2. Eastman Kodak in Rochester, New York, achieves quality through the Baldrige Award. A Corporate Quality Breakthrough Council drives breakthrough quality initiatives throughout the company. The senior cross-functional quality leadership team identified key result areas and result measures. They gauge themselves against the Baldrige Leadership Category to find out how many people, including their CEO, have really embedded quality and improvement into their business plans (Helton, 1992).

- Realize that no simple quality effort will work throughout the organization. Like the cafeteria plan for compensation and health benefits, the best parts of several overall quality initiatives can be determined and implemented. Adhering rigidly to one program (because you had the training and the manual) is not always best. The people doing the job usually know it better than anyone else and also what to do to achieve and improve quality. But, you must ask them.

Three common-sense steps that can be used to move toward total quality:

1. Ask everyone in your sphere of influence to make commitments to innovative approaches to quality.
2. Encourage everyone in your company to get directly involved in listening to customers, suppliers, and/or regulators. Practice strategic listening.
3. Insist on impossible goals (like Motorola's 99.997% defect-free manufacturing) and Federal Express' ob-

sessive push toward a 100% quality goal. Let employees determine how to achieve their goals.

Harari (1993) cautions that these three steps will take forever and will never be achieved. The continuous journey was mentioned at the beginning of this chapter.

When people use their own definitions of quality for their own job, they satisfy only their own requirements and go no further. Definitions should go beyond an individual's scope and include peers' and/or supervisors' input, and possible input from customers. In this way, definitions will become better indicators or standards for quality.

Most operational definitions pave the road to measurement, frequently when linked with benchmarking. Definitions of quality standards, such as 99.99% level of customer satisfaction, can be the same for products and services. Descriptive or qualitative operational definitions of quality, like ''total customer satisfaction'' and ''rarely makes a mistake,'' are also very meaningful.

Common Elements of Quality Improvement Efforts

Efforts to improve quality in service and manufacturing areas share common characteristics. Organizations beginning quality improvement efforts may wish to concentrate efforts in one area before starting on another. Many begin with measurement or benchmarking. Areas include:

1. Supportive organizational culture, like patterns of behavior, basic underlying assumptions, and subculture.
2. Customer orientation that recognizes internal and external customers as partners.
3. Teams that function within and outside their own disciplines. Cross-functional teams have power.
4. Continuous problem solving which becomes a way of life.

---

13. Outline the quality program you use personally, or one that is used in your department or organization. How would you improve it? If it can be improved, are you empowered to make the changes?

_____

_____

_____

_____

5. Continuous improvement, which is at the heart of the successful organization, is the driving force behind identifying and solving customers' problems.
6. Measurement that is used to monitor direction and trends, and helps determine the effect of improvement efforts (Westbrook, 1993).

The bottom line for quality is as simple as 1-2-3. One, customers and their unique views, perceptions, and definitions of quality determine the true nature of quality in the marketplace. Two, goals for quality can never be less than 100%. Three, quality and productivity are inseparable.

If overall quality is to be improved, it is important to develop a quality culture and communicate quality per se and quality standards within and beyond the organization. Quality can be achieved by (1) training, (2) changing company culture, (3) variable compensation programs or alternate reward systems that tie remuneration directly to team results based on a specific quality improvement, and (4) recognition programs to promote employment loyalty and improve internal quality management. Some organizations are tying the pay of their CEO and "team at the top" to tangible evidence of quality improvement.

Achieving and maintaining quality should always begin at the top of the organization, and be strongly supported by upper management, particularly the chief executive officer. Quality planning, quality control, and quality improvement are major issues. "It is no longer enough to manage *for* quality; business must manage *by* quality" (Benson, 1991).

Despite the fact many would disagree about the cost effectiveness of quality, over time, quality is the least capital intensive route to quality, productivity, and perhaps even competitive position.

The story of quality will have a happy ending if people approach the ultimate goal of achieving quality standards by first being satisfied with slow, progressive upward steps, and never lose sight of the overall accomplishments.

Developing and supporting quality improvement programs is everyone's responsibility.

Existing objective measures of quality can be used to assess and compare current levels of quality with various standards. Recommendations for quality improvement programs can based on information obtained from daily activities, not necessarily on complex surveys or expensive change programs.

Quality is a major driving force. It is the master switch that turns on the whole system. "The cost of not doing things right the first time in a quality manner is 20% of sales" (Kearns, 1985).

QUALITY ISSUES IN PERSPECTIVE

Most information on quality comes from tangible, "hard" data, like numeric definitions and ratios from production or quality standards, like 6 Sigma, 5 Sigma, etc. Ironically, it is the "soft" or qualitative approaches, like maximizing human resources by recognizing individual differences, and encouraging creativity and innovation, that have the most impact on improving quality and productivity.

Quality occurs when people doing the job have a clear understanding of how the job is to be done, namely do the job right the first time. They also use human and material resources to meet customers' needs in a timely, cost-effective manner.

Corporate cultures and strategies emphasizing quality are excellent ways for a company to respond to competition. Productivity and quality are closely related. Quality should be the major weapon in the battle to restore America's position in the world. Competitive advantage boils down to service (with a smile), quality, and courtesy. "Better" products obviously compete more successfully.

Studies of nearly every company that has won the Baldrige award revealed that the most successful financial

14. If quality was not originally designed into the product or service, how can quality be achieved?

_____

_____

15. If you were to introduce a quality improvement program in your work group . . . company, list the steps you would take.

_____

_____

performers were also the ones demonstrating the most successful continuous improvement (Axland, 1993).

The service industries in the United States offer more opportunity for growth and mismanagement than do product-based industries. It may be a good idea to reevaluate services from the management and quality control standpoints, as their overall contribution to the nation's economic health are immense. By way of illustration, insurance, financing, health care, transportation, and communication have a dramatic influence on the cost of producing goods domestically.

Successful quality control efforts begin with specific strategic plans to prevent failures or increase quality. These practical, step-by-step efforts are used daily. Employees who internalize these plans or standards, and supervisors who wholeheartedly support quality improvement efforts, will dramatically reduce failure rate as much as ten fold.

Major issues are to develop a quality culture and communicate quality standards within and beyond the organization. Quality can be improved by training, changing company culture, and implementing variable compensation programs. However, the key elements are to ensure that people: (1) understand their own jobs and know how quality standards affect their jobs; (2) have control over their jobs so they can improve quality; and (3) know what quality means to internal and external customers and communicate in an open, honest manner.

Quality improvement can be maintained by using alternate reward systems that tie remuneration directly to team results based on a specific quality improvement. Recognition programs also promote employment loyalty and improve internal quality management.

Quality of service can be improved when people think of themselves as the company. Employees are the first and possibly only contact many customers have. Putting customers first is an important, but necessary, paradigm shift. Companies that survived turbulent times will be ones that stand out in their customers' minds—in product superiority or in exceptional service.

Failure to adopt new, flexible technologies will reduce the impact of quality improvement efforts. Cost-cutting efficiencies that can be quantified are common, but many customers' requests for needed services often go unheeded. Improvements will occur when all areas of conflict inhibiting the smooth flow of products from the vendor to the customer are removed or reduced.

The need for better quality services and products is well known and accepted. Doing something about poor quality is the real issue, as often heroic efforts are directed to further improve something that is already functioning well, or has high customer approval and use. It makes good sense to emphasize the areas of greatest need.

Focusing on critical business processes is essential to the organization's long-term ability to achieve its goals. In the past, the obvious, traditional or classically-defined manufacturing processes, and resulting, tangible products, like machine parts, were emphasized. The spotlight was seldom on intangible areas associated with employee and customer satisfaction, as in building loyalty and trust.

Analyzing variables affecting product quality and quantity-related decisions, and identifying the quality levers for products and services provided are everyone's responsibility. No improvement in quality or productivity will occur unless acceptable, standardized methods to measure quality are developed and used consistently, like the Malcolm Baldrige criteria. More and more companies are benchmarking themselves against the Baldrige criteria than ever before, although they may not apply for the award. These methods of comparison provide meaningful feedback on possible ways to change and improve performance. Quality is a prime impetus behind performance improvement.

Benchmarking

Properly planned and executed benchmarking can be the overall organizational effort that literally "turns a company around." Benchmarking can be a process of organizational discovery, even one of "self discovery." The logic and precision of benchmarking and the use of operational definitions can "rub off" on those who are seriously engaged and committed to the process of learning.

Throughout the benchmarking process, look for spin-off ideas for designing new services or products. The processes of doing business throughout the world are similar, although products and outcomes may differ. Standard procedures in one industry may work well in another, perhaps even unrelated industry.

Determine whether the efforts to achieve higher quality through benchmarking are the best alternatives. Quality improvement efforts, although costly in terms of time, effort, and money, are often worthwhile. It is always very important to balance the standards of precision with practicality of the real world.

REFERENCES

1. Anderson, Douglas N. "Quality, A Positive Business Strategy," St. Paul, Minnesota, Special Report, 1991.
2. Anfuso, Dawn. "L. L. Bean's TQM Efforts Put People Before Processes," *Personnel Journal,* July 1994, pp. 72-73, 75-76, 78, 80–83.
3. Axland, Suzanne. "Forecasting the Future of Quality," *Quality Progress,* February 1993, pp. 21–25.

4. Babich, Pete. "Customer Satisfaction: How Good is Good Enough?" *Quality Progress,* December 1992, pp. 65–67.

5. Bain, David. *The Productivity Prescription,* New York: McGraw-Hill Book Company, 1982.

6. Beardsley, Jeff. "Here We Go Again," *Journal for Quality and Participation,* September 1994, pp. 78–80.

7. Bemowski, Karen. "The International Quality Study, *Quality Progress,* November 1991, pp. 33–37.

8. Bemowski, Karen. "The Quality Glossary," *Quality Progress,* February 1992, pp. 18–29.

9. Benson, Tracey E. "Challenging Global Myths," The Industry Management Magazine, October 7, 1991, p. 8

10. Brecka, Jon. "The American Customer Satisfaction Index," *Quality Progress,* October 1994, pp. 41–44.

11. Corrigan, James P. "Is ISO 9000 the Path to TQM?" *Quality Progress,* May 1994, pp. 33–36.

12. Crosby, Philip B. *Quality Is Free,* New York: New American Library, 1979.

13. Crosby, Philip B. *Quality Without Tears,* New York: New American Library-Dutton, 1985.

14. Crosby, Philip B. Running Things, New York: McGraw-Hill Book Publishing Company, 1986.

15. Crosby, Philip B. *The Eternally Successful Organizations,* New York: McGraw-Hill Book Publishing Company, 1988.

16. Crosby, Philip B. *Let's Talk Quality,* New York: McGraw-Hill Book Publishing Company, 1989.

17. DeCarlo, Neil J. and Sterret, W. Kent, "History of the Malcolm Baldrige National Quality Award," *Quality Progress,* March 1990, pp. 21–27.

18. Deming, W. Edwards. *Quality, Productivity and Competitive Position,* Boston, Massachusetts: MIT Press, 1982.

19. Deming, W. Edwards. *Out of Crisis,* Cambridge, Massachusetts: Massachusetts Institute of Technology, 1986.

20. Desatnick, Robert L. "Inside the Baldrige Award Guidelines: Category 7: Customer Focus and Satisfaction," *Quality Progress,* December 1992, pp. 69–74.

21. Desatnick, Robert L. "Managing Customer Service for the 21st Century," *Journal for Quality and Participation,* June 1994, pp. 30–35.

22. Eccles, Robert G. "The Performance Manifesto," *Harvard Business Review,* January–February 1991, pp. 131–137.

23. Ernst & Young. "International Quality Study," Cleveland, Ohio: American Quality Foundation, 1991.

24. Ernst & Young. "Best Practices Report," Cleveland, Ohio: American Quality Foundation, 1992.

25. Executive Insights. "The Quality Dilemma," *Management Review,* November 1991, pp. 30–34.

26. Face to Face. "William Glavin Brings Business Style to Campus," *Management Review,* September 1992, pp. 21–23.

27. Farahmand, Kambiz, Becerra, Rual, and Greene, Juan Ramon. "ISO 9000 Certification: Johnson Control's Inside Story," *Industrial Engineering,* September 1994, pp. 22–23.

28. Farrell, Robert, Jr. "Quality Function Deployment: Helping Business Identify and Integrate the Voice of the Customer," *Industrial Engineering,* October 1994, pp. 44–45.

29. Feigenbaum, Armand V. *Total Quality Control: Engineering and Management,* New York: McGraw-Hill, 1961.

30. Feigenbaum, Armand V. "Quality Education and America's Competitiveness," *Quality Progress,* September 1994, pp. 83–84.

31. Gable, Natalie. "Is 99.9% Good Enough?" *Quality,* March 1991, pp. 40-41.

32. Garvin, David A. "Quality on the Line," *Harvard Business Review,* September–October 1983, pp. 64–75.

33. Garvin, David A. "Competing on the Eight Dimensions of Quality," *Harvard Business Review,* November–December, 1987, pp. 101–109.

34. Garvin, David A. "How the Baldrige Award Really Works," *Harvard Business Review,* November–December 1991, pp. 80–93.

35. Gasko, Helen M. "You Can Earn ISO 9002 Approval in Less Than a Year," *Journal for Quality and Participation,* March 1992, pp. 14–19.

36. Gault, Robert F. "Large Companies, Are You Listening?" *Management Review,* September 1994, pp. 42–44.

37. Greenbaum, Stewart I. "TQM at Kellogg," *Journal of Quality and Participation,* January/February, 1993, pp. 88–92.

38. Grove, Andrew S. *High Output Management,* New York: Random House, 1983.

39. Harari, Oren. "Three Very Difficult Steps to Total Quality," *Management Review,* April 1993, pp. 39–41, 43.

40. *Harvard Business Review* (Debate). "Does the Baldrige Award Really Work?" January–February 1992, pp. 126–129, 132, 134, 136–141, 146–147.

41. Helton, B. Ray. "Getting Started with High-Quality Leadership," *The Quality Observer,* October 1992, pp. 11–12.

42. Johnson, Richard S. *TQM: Leadership for the Quality Transformation.* Milwaukee, Wisconsin: Quality Press, American Society for Quality Control, 1993.

43. Junkins, Jerry R. "Insights of a Baldrige Award Winner," *Quality Progress,* March 1994, pp. 57–58.

44. Juran, Joseph M. "Juran on Quality," *Management Review,* January 1994, pp. 10–13.

45. Juran, Joseph M. *Quality by Design,* New York: Free Press, 1992.

46. Juran, Joseph M. and Gryna, Frank M. *Quality Planning and Analysis,* third edition. New York: McGraw-Hill Book Company, 1993.

47. Kanter, Rosabeth Moss. "Think Like the Customer: The Global Business Logic," *Harvard Business Review,* July–August 1992, pp. 9–10.

48. Kearns, James F. *Conoco85,* 16, No. 3, p. 7.

49. Leonard, Frank and Sasser, W. Earl. "The Incline of Quality," *Harvard Business Review,* September–October, 1982, pp. 163–171.

50. Long-Becker, Linda C. and Landauer, Edwin G. "Service Assessment Matrix: A Measurement Technique for Service Group Evaluation," *Industrial Management,* September–October 1987, pp. 10–16.

51. McFadden, Fred R. "Six-Sigma Quality Programs," *Quality Progress,* June 1993, pp. 37–42.

52. McLagan, Patricia. "The Darker Side of Quality," *Training,* November 1991, pp. 31–33.

53. Marquardt, Donald W. "ISO 9000: A Universal Standard of Quality," *Management Review,* January 1992, pp. 50–52.

54. Mittelstaedt, Robert E., Jr. "Benchmarking: How to Learn from Best-In-Class Practices," *National Productivity Review,* Summer 1992, pp. 301–315.

55. Myers, Ken and Buckman, Jim. "Beyond the Smile: Improving Service Quality at the Grass Roots," *Quality Progress,* December 1992, pp. 55–59.

56. Nakhai, Behnam and Neves, Joao S. "The Deming, Baldrige, and European Quality Awards," *Quality Progress,* April 1994, pp. 33–37.

57. Neves, Joao S. and Nakhai, Behnam. "The Evolution of the Baldrige Award," *Quality Progress,* June 1994, pp. 65–70.

58. O'Dell, Carla. "Out-of-the-Box Benchmarking," *Management Review,* January 1994, p. 63.

59. Orsini, Joseph L. "Make Marketing Part of the Quality Effort," *Quality Progress,* April 1994, pp. 43–46.

60. Peters, Thomas J. and Waterman, Robert H., Jr., *In Search of Excellence,* New York: Warner Books, 1983.

61. Potocki, Kenneth, Brocato, Richard and Popick, Paul R. "How TQM Works in a University Classroom," *Journal for Quality and Participation,* January–February 1994, pp. 68–74.

62. Pulat, B. Mustafa. "Benchmarking Is More Than Organized Tourism," *Industrial Engineering,* March 1994, pp. 22–23.

63. Quinn, James Brian, and Gagnon, Christopher E. "Will Services Follow Manufacturing into Decline?" *Harvard Business Review,* November–December 1986, pp. 95–103.

64. Sashkin, Marshall and Kiser, Kenneth J. *Putting Total Quality Management to Work,* San Francisco: Berrett-Koehler, Publishers, 1993.

65. Schwartz, M. H. "What Do the Words 'Product' and 'Service' Really Mean for Management?" *Quality Progress,* June 1992, pp. 35–39.

66. Senge, Peter M. *The Fifth Discipline,* New York: Doubleday/Currency, 1990.

67. Skinner, Wickham. "The Productivity Paradox," *Harvard Business Review,* July–August 1986, pp. 55–59.

68. Smith, A. Keith. "Total Quality Management in the Public Sector," Part 1, *Quality Progress,* June 1993a, pp. 45–48.

69. Smith, A. Keith. "Total Quality Management in the Public Sector," Part 2, *Quality Progress,* July 1993b, pp. 57–62.

70. Smith, Elizabeth A. "Value Added: Expectations Vs. Perception Vs. Reality," *The Quality Observer,* (in press for July 1995).

71. Spitzer, Richard D. "TQM: The Only Source of Sustainable Competitive Advantage," *Quality Progress,* June 1993a, pp. 59–64.

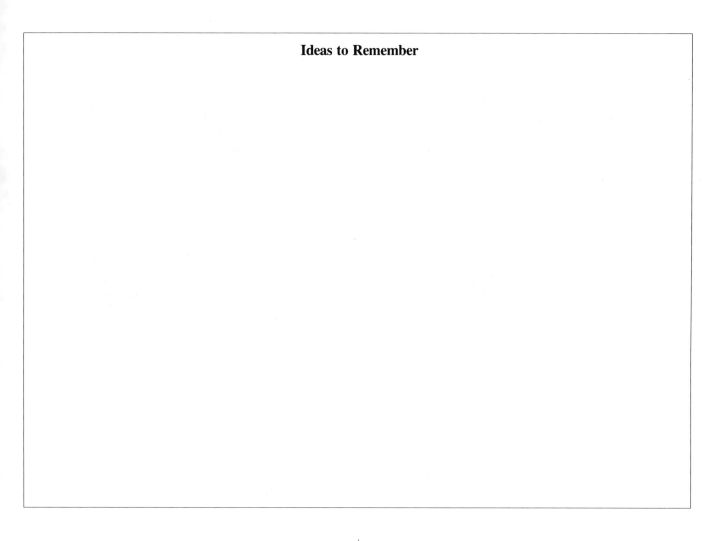

Ideas to Remember

72. Spitzer, Richard D. "Valuing TQM Through Rigorous Financial Analysis," *Quality Progress*, July 1993b, pp. 49–54.

73. Suzawa, Shoichi. "How the Japanese Achieve Excellence," *Training and Development Journal*, May 1985, pp. 110–112, 114–117.

74. Tadikamalla, Pandu R. "The Confusion Over Six-Sigma Quality," *Quality Progress*, November 1994, pp. 83–85.

75. Thomas, Philip R., Gallace, Larry H. and Martin, Kenneth R. *Quality Alone Is Not Enough*, New York: American Management Association, 1992.

76. Townsend, Patrick L. and Gebhardt, Joan E. "Do ISO 9000 Instead of Applying Baldrige Criteria . . . Not," *Journal for Quality and Participation*, January/February, 1994, pp. 94–95.

77. Turner, Dan. "Redesigning the Service Organization," *Journal for Quality and Participation*, July–August 1994, pp. 28–33.

78. United States Department of Commerce. *1994 Award Criteria, The Malcolm Baldrige National Quality Award*, Gaithersburg, Maryland.

79. Walton, Mary. *The Deming Management Method*, New York: The Putnam Publishing Group, 1986.

80. Wagel, William H. "Corning Zeros in on Total Quality," *Personnel*, July 1987, pp. 4–9.

81. Westbrook, Jerry D. "Taking a Multivariate Approach to Total Quality Management," *Industrial Management*, March-April 1993, pp. 2–3.

82. Wilson, Liz. "The Quality Measure is Customer Opinion," *Journal for Quality and Participation*, October–November 1993, pp. 12–14.

83. Zuckerman, Amy. "ISO 9000: Free Trade Boon, Barrier or Boondoggle?" *Journal for Quality and Participation*, January/February 1994, pp. 88–92.

Chapter 14—Answers and Insights

1. Your listing and plans to solve the issues or problems are your guide to action. Discuss your plans and achievements with other members of your work group. By using their expertise and capitalizing on their interest, you will foster ownership and commitment. The probability that you can accomplish what you set out to do is greatly improved when dedicated people work together.

2. Your definition will reflect your background, experience, and your beliefs about quality. Most of all, it will relate specifically to your job. If your organization is involved in a quality improvement effort, the overall definition for quality may be the same throughout the organization.

3. There are many resources on benchmarking. Methods and focus will differ between and within organizations. Studying what someone did is always a good start. Key results areas are prime benchmarking targets. People involved in benchmarking should be trained. Purpose should never be confused with tools. By starting with simple things that can be readily understood and measured, chances of success are increased. Once workable procedures are developed, more ambitious projects can be started.

4. Common areas are quality assurance; quality control; product development; purchasing and sub-contracting; process control-receiving; inspecting and testing; finished product testing; warehousing; shipping; and delivery. Your definitions should stand alone and be detailed enough that other people could use them.

   Measurements should be numeric, as in percent customer satisfaction, errors or defects per thousand, or descriptive terms that accurately convey exactly what was meant and measured. Benchmarking works best when applied with a healthy measure of balance and judgment.

5. Every quality yardstick has a useful lifespan and positive spin-off. The activities or processes involved in evaluating and setting up standards for quality are often more meaningful than the actual documentation of results, or hard data, which may/may not be valid and reliable. The qualitative or ''softer'' information can be more valuable than hard data based on only output. The processes of getting to know customers better, building partnerships with suppliers, and understanding your internal customers may be solutions to problems associated with quality, or any number of other concerns. Quality is one of many issues, although some believe it is the *only* issue.

6. Product-based areas are easier to understand. The form of input and output is usually tangible, like food, chemicals, textiles, road equipment, and buildings. The focus is on the flow of raw materials and production processes leading to output. The step-by-step transformation into finished products is closely monitored, as in scheduling, checking maintenance schedules, and monitoring inventory. Rework, cycle time, cost, and employee motivation are also focal points.

   In service areas, customers want to feel valued. Customers often dictate the level of quality service they want. Unfortunately, many service-based organizations appear to have been originally designed without customers in mind. Progressive organizations favor the customer.

   Internal customers in product-based areas can be the design, marketing, or sales department. People who exchange information back and forth are each others' customers.

   Examining quality in service industries should begin with listening to customers' comments, suggestions, complaints, and using results of surveys and information from benchmarking ''best in class'' companies, like L. L. Bean's superior customer service. Other sources are current technical literature and professional specialty groups. Quality in product-based industries is often controlled and measured using specific manufacturing standards including statistical process control and ISO 9000 standards.

7. Product-based and service-based organizations can differ widely, as indicated in Table 14-1. Generally, products are easy to see and describe. Services are intangible, perishable, and hard to describe and depend on the interactions with ''customers.'' Table 14-1 may help clarify your concept of your own job, the jobs of peers, the role of your customers. Both product-based and service-based jobs have customers, common concerns, market share, cost to produce, cycle time, etc.

In service industries, customers often dictate the type of service they want. Unfortunately, many service-based organizations do not spend enough time finding out what customers really want. Jobs performed will vary from direct, daily, face-to-face contact with customers to developing new services for your "best" customers in another part of the world.

A good example of a customer orientation comes from IBM. Their customer service departments are built around the delivery and support of their own products. IBM employees can describe their work efforts in terms of what the customer wants and needs, but most of all, in terms of satisfaction.

Customers can become partners in designing and testing out new service and products. In many instances, services are developed to fit around the products that were originally produced. Forming partnership with suppliers and a wide array of end-users to help develop new products and services is becoming increasingly common.

8. In service areas having high customer contact, tasks are communicating, coordinating, monitoring, or supervising customer or end user services. Training to improve customer services may be emphasized. Teaching in a university is a high customer-contact area. Customers are students, other faculty members, committee members, deans, and associates in other universities with whom information is shared.

In medium customer-contact service areas, attention to customers, supervising staff, and training and development areas will be balanced.

Low customer-contact services areas are research, use of automated machines.

In product-based activities, major contact is with internal customers who also help create and design products. In car manufacturing, the external customer is the buyer who may live far from the assembly line. Close customer contact occurs when the product is manufactured or repaired on site, as in replacing worn out industrial equipment in a plant.

Table 14-1 compares major activities people perform in products-centered and production-based operations and customer-centered service operations.

The line separating products and services is disappearing slowly. When some products, like computers, are purchased, software and services also come in the package. Previously, all three were obtained from different vendors.

9. Output of product-based industries, manufacturers, laboratories, etc., will be measured with specific, established quality standards, like ISO 9000. Quality of units produced, assembled, or designed depends on humans, and on various automated procedures, which may include robots. The emphasis is on quality control over raw materials, like monitoring and inspection, and work in progress. It is possible to agree on standards with suppliers, partners, and others who provide raw materials or equipment used to make products. Control of processes and quality, and monitoring costs may be major parts of the job. Definitions will be tangible, and concepts and variables used in the definitions relatively easy to describe and measure.

Descriptions or definitions of quality in service-based organizations could come directly from customers; or, a) quality of input, like ideas, and creativity, b) throughput, like coordination, facilitation, and empathy, and c) output, such as innovative or cost-effective services for customers. Definitions are hard to develop, as they will be based on concepts like effective communication, sharing ideas, working together, or producing innovative products. Work processes in many organizations are similar, although the end results (products vs. services) are different.

When excellent organizations are being benchmarked, "best" practices for a given industry, profession, product, or process are determined. Benchmarking also provides baselines on quality so comparisons and standards can be developed and shared locally or throughout the world. If you are involved in benchmarking, you will already have some good definitions and measures of quality-improvement efforts. Quality can be viewed in terms of wholes, or units that can be divided into smaller units or tasks. Then, these smaller units can be examined and measured.

The best definitions in service areas could come from customers' responses to surveys, questionnaires, or face-to-face contact. However, most survey information uses numeric rating scales, which lack the value-added element of the customer's own words. Unless each point in the rating scale is operationally defined by the developer of the scale and the customer, agreement on exactly what a rating of "5" on a 7-point scale really means may be open to question. Customers' own definitions of excellent service are vital to improvement efforts. A customer's definition of quality service could be, "Provide the service when and where I want it at a cost I can afford."

Educational institutions have been involved in various forms of quality programs for some time. The entire September 1994 issue of *Quality Progress* was devoted to quality and education.

10. It depends on how people are paid. In products-based jobs if people are paid on total output, they will probably not care about quality. If they are paid on defect-free output, quality will be very important. Those in service-based jobs will have a difficult time determining whether they performed up to "quality standards." This is where training, role playing, even quality manuals come in handy. Feedback from peers, customers, and others will help improve quality. Quality improvement is one of the most fruitful paths to higher productivity and competitive success. It is important to have standards that people understand. Equally important is providing accurate, timely feedback on performance so people know how they compared with others performing similar jobs. Nearly everyone is hungry for feedback.

11. Customer input is vital. Open, two-way communication with customers using your products or processes is a start. They will know how to improve on everything you do. They may even become partners, or help you design newer, better products and processes. Planning ahead, or having a vision, and then taking the small, gradual steps to get you there is a beginning. Caution—be flexible, and be able to incorporate feedback for improvement.

12. Type of customers and purpose of contact may range from one-of-a-kind encounters to routine. In some customer-driven industries, customers provide ideas for new services and products. This "leading edge" input provides valuable ideas for innovative products and services. You don't have to guess how to improve customer service and relationships. Just ask your customers. Listen. Thank them. Act. Check. Then start the cycle all over again.

Insurance companies, for instance, deal with third-party agents. Insurance policy holders are customers and insurance policies are products that can be improved through better design for more demanding, and cost-conscious customers. In the sequence-based activity of processing insurance claims, people at the beginning of the checking and auditing process may have little information about the number of hands through which the policy will eventually pass. When people at the beginning of the sequence make errors, everyone down the line is affected. If errors are major, the insurance company may end up paying out large claims.

Internal customers are harder to identify, but they surround you at work. The management information system, central records, library, personnel, etc., have customers throughout the organization, including you. In turn, you provide information and valuable services for those in your work team, project group, your supervisors and subordinates. Your internal customers can provide many cost-effective suggestions that can make their jobs or even your job easier.

13. No one quality program will work throughout the organization. Even the most simple, straightforward program must be adapted to fit specific groups, departments, professions, even industries. Selecting the best parts of the quality programs you have read about, even implemented, is often the logical answer. Learning is really all about selecting the "best" methods and applying them in a logical manner that meets your purposes. There is no substitute for knowing the basics, talking with peers and managers, trying something out on a provisional basis, and then making improvements. Achieving a specific level of quality takes time. Worthwhile goals are not achieved

overnight. Neither is quality. Many companies that have achieved the desired or acceptable level of quality have also seen positive results in other, perhaps unexpected areas, like morale, motivation, creativity and innovation, and profits. An increasing number of companies are benchmarking themselves against the Baldrige award for information purposes. Not all who do the benchmarking end up applying for the award. Benchmarking is a learning process.

14. Quality in products can not be inspected in, or achieved after-the-fact. It will be necessary to redesign the product, or redesign or reengineer processes used to manufacture it. One way is to take it apart, and examine it thoroughly, as in reverse engineering. In service areas, work backwards step-by-step from the end-point, as in reverse scenario building. You will know what you have, and how you should have started. User or customer input at every step will be useful. Use creative talents to develop innovative solutions. Team efforts are very important.

15.

1. Determine whether a program is needed. Ask people around you what they think. There is no need (at this point) for a company-wide survey.

2. Compare existing quality standards with company or industry averages for services through customer surveys, or standardized inspection methods for products.

3. Contrast day-to-day accomplishments against vision, mission, and goals statements. Expected milestones for goals should be matched against progress. Failure to achieve at the planned level may indicate other problems, not just problems in the quality area.

4. Design and implement an appraisal program. In products-based industries, major features include: methods; written job instructions; criteria for maintenance; reporting formulas; special requirements; sampling; and other sequential documentation.

In service-based areas, number of customer complaints, comments, suggestions for improvement; waiting time; satisfaction indexes; perceptions; expectations; and other critical areas are important.

5. If a quality training program is to be developed to control and improve the quality of output, consider valuable employee characteristics: (a) unique accomplishments; (b) quality attitude showing a genuine belief in and support of quality output and concern for customers' needs and expectations; (c) quality knowledge, or awareness and understanding of quality requirements and how requirements can be met; and (d) quality skills, or the necessary mental and physical skills needed to meet or exceed job requirements (Bain, 1982).

6. To implement the quality improvement program: (a) create an awareness of the need for the program that results in a standard message about quality; (b) encourage open discussions about how to achieve the specified goals; (c) use with practical, real problems, not theoretical problems or symptoms; (d) demonstrate the relationship of theory and action, being sure to clearly define and achieve agreement on relevant concepts and process; (e) help participants develop their own ideas about the quality improvement and implementation programs, as this process increases commitment; (f) have participants set realistic, achievable goals and have them develop ways to measure steps taken toward the goals; (g) encourage participants to make their programs flexible so alternative paths lead in the same direction; (h) provide a supportive environment that rewards and reinforces all small step in the desired direction; (i) do not let people get discouraged by the slow progress; (j) document achievements, perhaps in a report, but ideally in a manual, including liaison or support and supervisory activities; and (k) introduce recognition programs to promote quality using individual and group-based non-monetary and monetary rewards.

15

Complex Productivity Measures

PURPOSE

- Examine the role of partial-, multiple-, and total-factor productivity measures.
- Determine the usefulness of partial-, multiple-, and total-factor productivity measures.

INTRODUCTION

Different types of ratios meet unique needs and specifications of individuals, groups, and organizations. Ratios having many factors may not necessarily be better than ratios based on a few, well documented, reliable, valid indicators. When input and output from partial factors are combined into a total-factor or multiple-output productivity measure, the overall picture may be blurred.

Measures that appear to best represent data may be ones with the largest number of variables expressed in ratio form. Technical sophistication and precision may need to be sacrificed for simplicity and ease of understanding. Balancing increased accuracy and/or complexity against additional cost and time to develop and test out measures is a delicate job. Time is money.

Those using the various types of ratios need to understand how and why they were developed. Ratios need to meet certain criteria, such as quality standards, and represent reliable, valid data.

SETTING THE STAGE

The major variables of energy, labor, materials, and capital are often used in measurements of partial- and total-factor productivity. All methods and cautions for measurement presented previously apply to partial-, multiple-input and output factors, and total-factor productivity measures.

Even the best measurement system is a tool, not an end in itself (Belcher, 1987). Complex ratios can be very meaningful. But, complexity in itself may occasionally give a false impression of accuracy, particularly when either the detail or the volume of data is excessive.

Additional cost and effort associated with gathering "total" information and developing partial-, total-factor, and multiple-output measures may require extra planning and effort. You should ask the following questions when considering the type of productivity measures to use. Questions 1–9 are general and 10–14 are specific.

1. What is the purpose of measurement?
2. Do input and output come from the same process?
3. What role does throughput play?
4. Are measures designed to fit the uses for which they were intended, i.e., workers, managers, or staff specialists in statistics, accounting, or economics?
5. Are measures based on historical performance data?

176

6. Is what is being measured something that people doing the job can do something about?
7. How costly is measurement in terms of time, effort, and money?
8. Can appropriate statistical procedures be used to present and analyze data, and make sound interpretations and predictions?
9. Can level of productivity be separated from rate of change of productivity? Level can be a "one time" measure.
10. Are partial-, complex-, or total-factor measures an improvement over current measurement systems?
11. If they are an improvement, how much of an improvement are they?
12. If partial-, complex-, or total-factor measures are used, is the available data meaningful and current?
13. Are measures reliable and valid?
14. Are results consistent with established productivity levels or standards for various business units or economic forecasts?

The ultimate test is that appropriate methods are used to obtain meaningful results.

Partial-, multiple-input, multiple-output, and total-factor productivity measures are different ways to present and analyze information. All use various combinations of input and output from specific sources. Sources can be as broad as the whole economy, or as specific as one person's performance on a single, simple task.

The ideal measurement system provides a way to track the productivity of every major organizational component and significant input. But, it is impractical and expensive to track more components than are needed. A compromise is to develop an index identifying the contributions of each major factor or indicator of production. Then, factors can be tracked and combined (Chew, 1988).

Partial-, multiple-, and total-factor productivity measures are described very briefly in the following paragraphs. However, detailed descriptions and examples of each are presented in separate sections.

Simply stated, partial-factor measures represent ratios of total output divided by a single unit of input.

Multiple-factor ratios, also known as multifactor measures, can be based on various types and amounts of input or output. There are multiple-factor input measures, and multiple-factor output measures. They often summarize partial factors, or smaller, independent units of input and output data.

Total-factor measures use all forms of major input and major output from a wide range of sources. They often represent wholes—all facets of a person's performance . . . all variables related to U.S. production.

PARTIAL-FACTOR PRODUCTIVITY

Some partial productivity ratios are obtained by dividing the total output of the organization by a single input. Labor, capital, materials, and energy are used in measures of organizational productivity. Example of organization-wide, or industry-wide partial productivity ratios are (Belcher, 1987):

$$\frac{Output}{Labor} \quad \frac{Output}{Capital} \quad \frac{Output}{Materials} \quad \frac{Output}{Energy}$$

In the four examples that follow, "total" in the numerator represents total output from a large unit. Example 1 uses a "hard-to-measure" job in a high tech area. Partial factors are innovative products developed, technical papers written, and research funds attracted. Example 2 presents typical service-based jobs. Total productivity ratios are computed from sales, hours worked, and satisfied customers. Example 3 illustrates accomplishment that has a specific standard, and Example 4 may be used when it is difficult to document separate inputs and outputs.

Example 1— Output/input ratios are based on innovative products developed by a research and development (R & D) firm within a specific time period:

(Total number of innovative products developed)/(Number of innovative products developed by a specific unit)

One way to look at R & D productivity could be number of publications and research funds attracted in a certain time interval:

(Total number of technical articles published by an organization)/(Number of technical articles submitted for publication by a unit)

In non-profit organizations, budgets often depend on funds raised for the year:

(Total funds raised by organization)/(Funds raised by each fund raising unit in the organization)

Example 2— Output/input ratios from service-based jobs: sales, hours worked, and satisfied customers.

$$\frac{Total\ company\ sales\ for\ year}{Yearly\ sales\ in\ one\ department}$$

$$\frac{Total\ hours\ worked\ per\ week}{Total\ daily\ hours\ worked\ per\ person}$$

$$\frac{\text{Total satisfied customers for one month period}}{\text{Total satisfied customers for one week period}}$$

Example 3—The following ratio is from assembly line jobs having specific standards.

$$\frac{\text{\# of units assembled based on department standards}}{\text{\# of units assembled/hour by Employee A)}}$$

With, for example, ten people in the department, the number of units each employee assembled is totaled and compared for specific time periods. A base rate or index for the department is determined. The number of units each employee completes each hour of the day is computed. Although performance varies within certain limits, any erratic output could be due to poor scheduling, or other problems.

When the volume of data grows, it becomes increasingly difficult to work with. In this example, regression analysis would be one way to examine trends, and determine areas affecting individual and group performance (Crocker, 1983).

Example 4—Time ratio/timeliness, or measure of output, represents a deadline for completing a project. Time can be a relative measure, depending on how it is seen. It can be charged for as in computer time, or donated by volunteers, as in non-profit organizations.

(Total number of projects to be completed within schedule and budget)/(Number of projects completed by unit within schedule and budget)

Output is determined by counting completed projects. Whether these projects are needed, or are worthwhile, is another matter. The time estimated to complete projects varies. Also, the need to meet certain deadlines also varies. Distinguishing between the number of projects scheduled, or ideal, and number of projects completed is often necessary.

Uses of Partial Productivity Ratios

These ratios are used to:

- Determine how each partial factor, such as type of product, quality, seasonal demands, or output of a particular person or department, etc., affects a more comprehensive or total measure of productivity.
- Compare how separate partial factors, namely, specific indexes of quality—durability, precision, strength—relate to each other. How each factor contributes to overall productivity can be determined.
- Make comparisons of separate product lines, or units of production between and within plants. Separate partial ratios for the same product line produced in different plants can be compared for quality, customer appeal, output, or "labor dollars per product." Efficiencies and manufacturing costs in each plant can be compared.
- Examine productivity change in one factor by replacing it with another. This is a quick way to see what is happening, but also can be a "quick fix." To illustrate, substitute well trained employees with ones who have just completed the training program.

Basically, partial factors can be combined into a broader view. Here, we are looking at the separate parts. In multifactor approaches, we are more concerned with the whole. As will be seen, uses of multifactor methods are a reverse of uses of partial factors—see the whole first, then the separate factors. See box.

---

1. Refer to ratios in Table 12-1. Could they function as partial productivity ratios? If so, list several input variables and the broader, total output measures you would use.

MULTIPLE FACTOR VIEWS OF PRODUCTIVITY

Multiple-input and multiple-output indexes provide a broad view of productivity. These multifactor views can be based on several different single-factor or partial measures, or on regression analysis.

Multifactor methods use various types and sources of input and output. Standard examples are labor input and output, and capital input and output. Putting various factors together, as in a multifactor approach, is meaningful only if each separate factor has some proven, or longstanding value, and makes, or is predicted to make, a worthwhile contribution to the whole.

A typical multiple-input productivity measure, also called value-added productivity, is determined as follows (Christopher, 1982):

$$\text{Value-added productivity} = \frac{(\text{Value added})}{\text{Labor input} + \text{Capital input}}$$

Value-added productivity can be determined for a total company, a plant, or profit center business, for example. Value added can be the difference between costs of materials, supplies, and components used in the company's products, and sales revenue. Labor is based on hours worked by all persons. Capital input, which is in constant dollars unaffected by inflation, includes tangible variables like physical plant, equipment, inventory, and land. Value-added can also apply to the contributions made by people and specific units or departments in an organization.

Other multifactor ratios consist of value added in the numerator, with various combinations of labor, capital, energy, and material in the denominator.

Two examples using multiple factors in gain-sharing plans are presented. Gain-sharing programs enable workers and the organization to share monetarily in productivity gains. Specific job-related factors are selected and the amount each factor contributes is determined (see Chapter 18 for details).

The following two examples from industry use specific job-related factors:

Example 1: The multifactor gain-sharing plan at Coshocton Stainless Division of Cyclops Corporation in Coshocton, Ohio is described (Stewart, Cugliari and Hauck, 1987). The company manufactures stainless and specialty steel strip products for various industries, and employs about 450 people.

A ten-member Incentive Advisory Committee developed and installed the plan. Six hourly-paid members

selected by their peers and four salaried members appointed by the division president formed the committee.

The committee's major objectives for the plan were to:

- Be fair for the company and employees.
- Be simple enough for all to understand.
- Mainly use physical productivity measures, and one economic measure under the control of plan participants.
- Foster teamwork and cooperation among employees.

Table 15-1 lists the five productivity measures used in the multifactor gain-sharing ratio. Inputs are in physical units. Output is "total out weight," or total weight in each completed process step for man-hours, energy, operating supplies, and quality. At first, net public shipments for the month were excluded until they exceeded a break-even level. The total weight of shipments is a different type of productivity measure from the other four output factors, because it is affected by changes in plant capacity. At present, the method of calculating shipments is adjusted quarterly.

Measured units of work are hours for man-hours; British Thermal Units (Btu) for energy; indexed dollars for supplies; and pounds of scrap shipped. All allowances are per 1,000 processed pounds.

The year of 1979 was used as the standard. It best represented conditions existing when the plan was being formulated. Productivity standards based on 1,000 process pounds of production were developed for each of the four factors.

Weightings developed by the committee: man-hours, 50 percent; pounds shipped 20 percent; and energy, operating supplies, and quality, 10 percent each.

In mid-1985, two years after the plan was introduced, major capital expenditures caused the committee to review and revise the plan. "Fine tuning" continues—customer returns were added to scrap shipments as the quality factor, and the addition of on-time shipments as a criterion was considered. Regression analysis was used to more clearly define the fixed and variable portions of energy usage.

Example 2: Volvo's multifactor performance gain-sharing plan at the Kalmar auto assembly plant in Sweden is described (Hauck and Ross, 1988).

Each employee is paid the same amount of money for each hour worked. Factors used to calculate the twice yearly bonus are:

- Quality index (based on a point-scoring system).
- Spoilage and adjustments.
- Consumption of materials and supplies.
- Consumption of added materials.
- Man-hours per car, or index of direct labor.
- Capital costs for total inventories and other costs.

Table 15-1
Factors, Units, Standards, and Factor Weights Used in Coshocton Stainless Gain-sharing Plan

Factor	Measured Units	Standards per 1000 Pounds	Factor Weight
Man-Hours	Hours	1.10	50%
Energy	Btu	0.59	10%
Operating Supplies	Indexed $	4.16	10%
Quality (Scrap)	Processed Pounds	16.2	10%
Shipments	Pounds Shipped	(% of Capacity)	20%

- Hours worked by office workers were not a major variable. It did help develop an awareness among factory workers that office employees were important to the plan's success.

MULTI-CRITERIA PERFORMANCE/PRODUCTIVITY MEASUREMENT TECHNIQUE

This technique is based on the objectives matrix (described previously in Chapter 12) (Felix and Riggs, 1983; Riggs and Felix, 1983; and Belcher, 1987). Rows and columns of the matrix contain information on performance level goals for each separate productivity measure, and include weights, scores, and the resulting productivity index. Weights assigned to each criterion of performance are stored and used to compare previous and present performance. This method can be used at the individual or group level.

Multiple linear regression techniques may be used to compute weights for variables, and determine relationships between variables. Linear regression methods are presented in most intermediate level statistics books, such as Edwards (1985). Statistics packages for hand-held calculators and computer programs are readily available.

MULTIPLE OUTPUT PRODUCTIVITY MEASURES (MOPI)

In professional, administrative, and service units, some outputs can be quantified, others cannot. Diverse output makes the job even more difficult. Christopher's (1984) method, which is similar to that presented earlier in Chapter 12, combines output measures into a single, overall measure, or MOPI, and is applied as follows:

1. Define the purpose of the unit.

2. Test the definition of purpose by comparing it to the organization's objectives and purpose or to what is actually done in the unit. Comparisons can also be made with the next higher level in the unit.

3. Identify outputs that demonstrate whether the purpose has been achieved successfully.

4. Determine how each output can be measured.

5. Use the "going in" period as a base. Calculate the measure for each output for this base period (see Table 11-3 or Bain, 1982).

6. Use a rating scale having ten units, for example. Define performance levels for each output on the scale. (Operational definitions are preferred.) Base period performance should be about the middle to allow performance trends to be measured up and down the scale from the base period.

7. Prepare a rating form listing each output and showing ratings for the current period and the position on the scale.

8. Determine weights for each output and combine several output ratings in a Productivity Index (PI) for the unit. Weights can be assigned in such a way that sums total 1.0, 10, or 100.

9. Identify inputs and measures for them.

10. Monitor performance trends for each output, the combined outputs, inputs, and for output related to input (MOPI).

USES OF MULTIFACTOR RATIOS

Multifactor ratios are often used in gain-sharing programs. Another common use is to track productivity trends at plants producing similar products.

As will be seen, uses of partial factors overlap. A multifactor ratio can be the sum of separate partial ratios. Typical uses are to:

- Track the flow of work through various levels in the organization.

- Monitor people at their various jobs. To illustrate, the performance level (amount and quality of output) of each person in an assembly line is critical to the final outcome.
- Compare individuals and groups on a one-time basis, or follow them for certain time intervals.
- Determine profitability, productivity ratios and indexes, and compare results for critical time intervals, specific products, services, or performance in general.
- Compare organizations producing various comparable products or providing similar services.
- Examine whether change in overall productivity is due to simultaneous shifts in the productivity of separate factors or indexes, as illustrated by labor, capital, or materials in the broad sense. See box on next page.

TOTAL-FACTOR PRODUCTIVITY

This method can be used to measure changes in productivity in most areas of an organization.

All factors of production—labor, capital, materials, and energy—are used in total-factor productivity measures (Thor, 1985). In the broadest sense, total-factor productivity is ''. . . the relationship between national output and the sum of the tangible capital and labor inputs'' (Belcher, 1987).

At the national level, total-factor productivity growth averaged 1.3 percent for 1960–1985. It became lower each five-year period from 1960 on until 1980–1985 when it was 0.9 percent (American Productivity Center, 1988).

In the organization, total-factor productivity includes all factors controlled by management that pertain to input and associated output. These factors affect all organizational goals, and are used to assess productivity of a unit, department, or company.

Most of the following descriptive methods focus on financial variables. Capital input also takes the form of equipment, structures, and inventories (Cocks, 1974). Capital input can also be the ''service value'' of fixed assets, cash, accounts receivable, or inventory (Craig and Harris, 1973).

Economic productivity is an ''early warning'' indicator of bottom-line profitability performance (Christopher, 1982). Economic productivity is expressed in current dollars rather than constant dollars. Economic productivity is one way to measure the cost used to create value. Output is value added, as described earlier. Economic productivity can be improved by controlling costs, implementing successful marketing plans, developing new or innovative products and service, or improving productivity.

Separate partial-factor productivity measures expressed in index form, or with a base period of 1.0, can be combined into a total-factor productivity index. A method of computing indexes was presented in Chapter 11.

A total-factor productivity approach can measure the amount and direction of change, and, one hopes, improvement. For instance, economists are particularly concerned with evaluating the changes in the efficiency of production of the economy because costs of all input factors—capital, labor, equipment, and materials—are reflected (Felix, 1983). Total-factor productivity measures or indicators need to be interpreted in a way people understand, which is often in financial terms.

Example 1: The following considers all resources under management control. A total-factor productivity measure of financial indicators as shown by rate of return on assets is (Jamali, 1984):

$$\frac{\text{Total output}}{\text{Labor+Materials+Energy+Capital+Miscellaneous Input}}$$

Primary monitoring variables for gross corporate product could include interest expense, dividends, retained profits, income taxes, depreciation and amortization, and wages, salaries, and benefits.

When several inputs and outputs are combined, as in the previous examples, the probability is high they will lose their identity. Knowing what inputs and outputs to use is the real issue. Ratios are only as good as the data used to develop them.

In the early stages of product or service development, ''planners,'' marketing, and sales evaluate the organization's resource input and determine an overhead ratio. This total factor productivity measurement serves as a cost containment and a control mechanism. Data from the cost/profit analysis is compared against ''marketability,'' or what the product or service will bring on the open market, and a profit ratio is calculated.

Uses of Total-Factor Productivity Measures

Because total-factor productivity ratios can include partial factors, some uses will be the same or similar. Total-factor productivity ratios are used:

- As a national economic indicator of productivity growth. This is a common way to show the overall economic growth of the nation.
- To show the results of many partial productivity gains or losses.
- To analyze individual product lines or separate services provided within or outside the organization.

2. Apply the 10-step method presented above to a manufacturing process where the product is a specific, complete standard unit, for instance, computer chips or light bulbs. Write out answers for each of the 10 questions.

3. Use the same 10-step method to examine a business where ideas are valued output—advertising, sales promotion, or in the early stages of product development.

4. Have you used any multifactor measurement techniques? If so, was linear regression used to analyze data? Do you have faith in the method or model? Did you develop it yourself or was it a "canned" program?

5. Develop a very simple total-factor productivity measure for your work group. Indicate what your work group does. List major outputs of your company. Provide a standard for each major job, and then develop a ratio. Ratings and weights can be used, but they are beyond the scope of this question. The emphasis is on application, not calculation.

Estimate the probability that each ratio will be used, and estimate rank of acceptance by peers and your immediate supervisor. Then, develop a total productivity measure.

My work group does _____

The major output of my company is _____

Standard	Ratio	Probability of Use	Rank (1 . . .7) Acceptance by Peers	Super.
_____	_____	_____	_____	_____
_____	_____	_____	_____	_____
_____	_____	_____	_____	_____
_____	_____	_____	_____	_____

$$\text{Total-factor productivity measure} = \frac{\text{Total output}}{\text{Separate input}}$$

Total output _____

Separate inputs _____

Quality and type of specific products from suppliers, or from subcontractors can be represented.

- To provide insight into net results of pricing activities taken to control resource costs and expand revenues.

The impact of partial factors, such as product mix, seasonal demands, or fluctuations on overall profitability can be assessed. When different products or services are provided on a rotating, or unpredictable basis, partial factors based on established standards can be compared. To illustrate, contrast productivity of separate departments producing different products.

The various types of productivity ratios described serve the same purposes as productivity measures discussed previously. They can be used to compare costs, profits, sales, etc., of similar businesses; serve as a source of information about long-term operating trends; detect rates of change; and determine specific technical and economic parameters. All measures must pass the test of practicality. See box above.

REFERENCES

1. American Productivity Center. "Productivity Perspectives," Houston, Texas, American Productivity and Quality Center, 1988.

2. Bain, David. *The Productivity Prescription*, New York: McGraw-Hill Book Company, 1982.

3. Belcher, John G., Jr. *Productivity Plus+*, Houston, Texas: Gulf Publishing Company, 1987.

4. Chew, W. Bruce. "No-Nonsense Guide to Measuring Productivity," *Harvard Business Review*, January–February, 1988, pp. 110–111, 114–116, 118.

5. Christopher, William F. "How to Develop Productivity Measures that Can Improve Productivity Performance," Special Report. Stamford, Connecticut: Productivity Inc., 1982.

6. _____ . "How to Measure and Improve Productivity in Professional, Administrative, and Service Organizations," in *Issues in White Collar Productiv-*

Ideas to Remember

---

ity, Norcross, Georgia: Industrial and Management Press, 1984, pp. 29–37.

7. Cocks, D. L. "The Measurement of Total Factor Productivity for a Large U.S. Manufacturing Corporation," *Business Economics*, September, 1974, pp. 7–20.

8. Craig, C. E. and Harris, R. C. "Total Productivity Measurement at the Firm Level," *Sloan Management Review*, Spring 1973, pp. 13–29.

9. Crocker, Douglas C. "Multiple Linear Regression Analysis," in Robert N. Lehrer (ed.) *White Collar Productivity*, New York: McGraw-Hill Book Company, 1983, pp. 159–180.

10. Edwards, Allen L. *Multiple Regression and the Analysis of Variance and Covariance,* 2nd Ed., New York: W.H. Freeman and Company, 1985.

11. Felix, Glenn H. *Productivity Measurement with the Objective Matrix*, Oregon Productivity Center, Corvallis, Oregon, 1983.

12. Felix, Glenn H. and Riggs, James L. "Productivity Measurement by Objectives," *National Productivity Review*, Autumn, 1983, pp. 386–393.

13. Hauck, Warren C. and Ross, Timothy L. "Expanded Teamwork At Volvo Through Performance Gainsharing," *Industrial Management*, July–August, 1988, pp. 17–20.

14. Jamali, Shafique. "Putting A Productivity Improvement Program Into Action: A Six-Step Plan," in *Issues in White Collar Productivity,* Norcross, Georgia: Industrial Engineering and Management Press, 1984, pp. 64–74.

15. Moore, Brian F. and Ross, Timothy L. *The Scanlon Way to Improved Productivity,* New York: John Wiley & Sons, 1978.

16. Riggs, James L. and Felix, Glenn H. *Productivity by Objectives*, Englewood Cliffs, New Jersey: Prentice-Hall, 1983.

17. Robertson, R. N. and Osuorah, Chuma I. "Gainsharing in Action at Control Data," *Journal for Quality and Participation,* December 1991, pp. 28–31.

18. Schuster, Michael H. and Schuster, Judith M. "Excellence in Gainsharing: From the Start to Renewal," *Journal for Quality and Participation,* June 1994, pp. 18–25.

19. Stewart, David W., Jr., Cugliari, Frank D. and Hauck, Warren C. "Incorporating Technological Change into a Multi-Factor Gain-sharing Plan," in *Proceedings of the World Forum and the 1987 International Industrial Engineering Conference*, Washington, D.C., May 1987, pp. 605–608.

20. Thor, Carl G. "Productivity Measures: Tailored for Effectiveness," American Productivity Center. *Manager's Notebook*, Vol. 2, No. 3, 1985, pp. 1–4.

Chapter 15—Answers and Insights

1. Answers depend on the job, the person, and the organization. Partial-factor productivity ratios may stand alone, or make up a more comprehensive, total-factor productivity measure. Partial measures of individual productivity can come from tasks performed most often, for instance "core" tasks (Chapter 7).

   Information from Table 11-1, such as skill level, level of difficulty, how often the task is performed, and other variables provide information for determining weights. Weights can be subjective estimates of persons performing the job (and their supervisors). If weights represent beliefs of "workers" and supervisors, jobs with the largest weights will be most meaningful, i.e., contribute the most to productivity measures. There will be differences between and within departments, and organizations.

   Information from the "family of measures," showing ratios from typical activities could be used. Quality, quantity, customer satisfaction, time or timeliness, cost, profit, sales, etc., may make up the ratios.

2. Answers to 10-step method:

   1. Purpose of unit: assemble components and produce computer chips.
   2. Organization makes computer components. Chips are a high-profit item.
   3. Completed chips are boxed ready for shipment. However, variables important to output are waste, scrap, cost to redo, and downtime.
   4. Five people work in the unit. Measurements: waste–cost, scrap–weight, cost to redo–wages, and downtime–lost production in units.
   5. A base rate could be calculated for output, error rate, rejects, etc., for each person in the 5-person unit, or for each unit. When the same, or very similar units exist in the organization, the median or "middlemost" score could serve as a base or standard. Or, averages, or means, and standard deviations based on the same factors used to determine base rates for individuals: output, error rate, rejects, etc., could be used. Also, linear regression methods could reveal additional meaningful information, namely weights.

6. Definitions of rating scale units are: 1=very low; 2=medium low; 3=low; 4=below average; 5=average; 6=above average; 7=medium high; 8=high; 9=very high.

7. I prefer a 9-point rating scale, with 5 the "middle rating." With a 10-point scale, 5 and 6 are both "middle" ratings.

   Each point on the 9-point rating scale should be assigned a specific numeric value, i.e., "9" for highest . . . "1" for lowest. Once numeric values are assigned, output can be rated.

8. Weights can be determined using some multiple of 1.0 (like automatic tellers). Usually, 1.0, 10, and 100 are used. Weights can total to any number. Table 15-2 is an example of how to present data. It uses the concept of "key result areas" from Chapter 6.

9. Example input variables and measures: cost of materials; quality of materials; cost of equipment and equipment repair and maintenance; and labor.

10. Monitoring performance means that either all data, or representative sample data, are obtained and recorded. Data are meaningless until shared with workers. Those performing the job will be the best judges of ways to present and illustrate data: graphs, tables, charts . . . equations. But, records should be simple, easily understood, and highly visible.

    Improving input can be one answer to current problems. Has the nature of input changed in any way? As workers streamline efforts, either through training or experience, performance improves. Often, there is a gradual transition from one form of effort to another. This transition may be invisible on a day-to-day basis, but appears when work is sampled at intervals of weeks or months. Keeping good records and examining "old" data can be meaningful.

3. Steps to produce a new software package are presented in the shortened format in the following section. Answers to the ten questions will provide information for the productivity index.

Table 15-2
Quality/Productivity Measurement

Plant: _____ Department: _____ Month: _____ Year: _____

Key Result Areas	Measurement	This Period's Results	Performance Results Scale										Earned Rating	Relative = Weight	Earned Points
			1	2	3	4	5	6	7	8	9	10			

(Christopher, 1984; and personal communication)

$$\text{Productivity Index:} \quad \frac{\text{Total Earned Points}}{1,000} \times 100 = \frac{\text{Total Earned Points:} \quad \underline{\quad\quad}}{\text{Max Points:} \quad 1,000}$$

Developing a Productivity Index

1. Define the purpose of the unit.
2. Compare the purpose of the unit to the organization's objectives and purpose.
3. List outputs demonstrating successful performance.
4. List ways to measure output.
5. Develop base measures for each output.
6. Define all rating scale units.
7. List each output and show ratings for current period and positions on the scale.
8. Determine weights for each output. Combine several output ratings in a productivity index (PI) for the unit.
9. Identify input variables to be measured and show how they can be measured.
10. Show how performance can be monitored.

Developing a Productivity Index—Answers

1. **Define purpose of unit**—Develop new software package using resources of: R&D; programmers; word processing; supervisors, etc.

2. **Compare purpose of the unit to the organization's objectives and purpose**—Current project is one of 15 similar projects

3. **List outputs demonstrating successful performance**—Completed series of goals from work-flow chart: successful field testing; market demonstrated to exist; pricing shown to be competitive

4. **List ways to measure output**—Number of sales; user complaints; packages returned; customer demand (personal contact with sales representatives, telephone or other inquiries); and time to run program (efficiency of programming)

5. **Develop base measures for each output**—Daily . . . monthly averages for each area in #4, above; obtain data from competitors; match with projections

6. **Define all rating scale units**—"1"=very low . . . "9"=very high

7. **List each output and show ratings for current period and positions on the scale.**

8. **Determine weights for each output.**

Output	Rating	Weight	Rating × Weight
Sales	8	30	240
Packages returned	5	15	75
User complaints	7	20	140
Customer demand	6	10	60
Time to run package	4	25	100
		100	615

Combine several output ratings in a productivity index (PI) for the unit.

$$PI = \frac{\text{Total earned points}}{1,000} \times 100$$

$$PI = \frac{615}{1,000} \times 100 = 61.5$$

For comparison purposes, a low PI would be one with all five ratings 1's, and all weights equal to 20, or $5 \times 1 \times 20 = 100$ for "Total earned points." Using the formula above:

$$PI = \frac{100}{1,000} \times 100 = 10$$

Similarly, a high PI would be one with all five ratings 9's, and all weights equal to 20, or $5 \times 9 \times 20 = 900$. Using the formula above:

$$PI = \frac{900}{1,000} \times 100 = 90$$

PI has no meaning until compared with data from the same or very similar units. When comparisons are made, the five output variables measured must remain the same. Ratings and weights will change as the product moves through the various stages of development. To illustrate, initially, complaints may be the most valuable in product changes and improvement. Later, sales and customer demand may be equally important.

9. **Identify input variables to be measured and show how they can be measured.**

 R&D: Time each person spent on project; number of times specific major deadlines met; rankings of coordination, communication; use of library resources, etc.

 Word Processing: Turnaround time; mistakes; redoing units; and rankings of interfacing with project members.

 Programming: Number of usable lines written in specific time period; actual computer time to run program; errors; number of "trial runs."

 Supervision: Rankings of facilitation, co-operation; open communication; trust; understanding; leadership.

 Revision: Amount of time compared with hours in total project; rank of value of revisions (essential or not); number of people involved; ratings of how initial focus of project may have been affected.

 Some output measures have also been included.

10. **Show how performance can be monitored**—Usual method of keeping track on a convenient, logical basis (hourly . . . monthly, or on a random basis) of critical accomplishments or goals. A table or flowchart showing when scheduled activities were met. This could serve as a base for future similar endeavors, particularly in product development and sales.

4. Multifactor measurement techniques, including linear regression, are useful decision support systems. Regression is one way to examine the value (weights) of separate variables, not necessarily productivity. Note: in regression analysis, weights are not meant to total 1.0. Each weight has meaning for the variables from which it was computed.

"Canned" programs are very helpful, and save time. However, they may not fit your individual needs.

5. The total-factor productivity measure combines individual and group efforts relating to major goals. Measures should be developed by the work groups using them. When similar work groups throughout the organization develop their own total-factor productivity measures, comparisons between groups can be made. This is one way to improve the quality of ratios. However, as the nature and focus of work changes, and new employees join the work group, ratios need to be updated.

No specific answers are provided, although one frame of reference could be from home improvement wallpapering:

$$\frac{\text{Goods} + \text{Services}}{\text{Labor} + \text{Capital} + \text{Energy} + \text{Materials}}$$

where   Goods = wallpaper
         Services = put up in kitchen
         Labor = total hours worked
         Capital = cost of wallpaper
         Energy = efficiency of effort
         Materials = paste or water and assorted tools

Examples of multiple factor ratios are those used in gain-sharing and profit-sharing plans. These plans have a long history, beginning with the Scanlon gain-sharing plan developed in 1935. The Rucker Plan, developed in the late 1930s, is similar to the Scanlon Plan (Moore and Ross, 1978). Improshare® is discussed in Chapter 18.

Purposes of these plans were to increase organizational quality and productivity. If the company makes money, employees share profits based on their own evaluations and on their team leaders' evaluations of their contributions. Employees should be involved in all steps of gain-sharing process. Developing, introducing, modifying, and implementing gain-sharing ranges from two to five years.

Gain-sharing plans are often based on specific, numerically-computed weighted factors related to overall productivity or output of people working in a wide range of jobs. A predetermined formula forms the basis of sharing the gains resulting from improved performance among employees and the company.

Schuster and Schuster (1994) summarize basic gain-sharing concepts and present a simple gain-sharing model. The five gain-sharing cases presented have self-directed work forces and a significant level of employee involvement, namely empowerment. A six-step gain-sharing plan and a gain-sharing implementation process model are discussed. The importance of top management commitment, support, and training, and use of a wide range of vehicles for communication, is stressed.

Unless workers have little influence over the product, their interest may plateau. Robertson and Osuorah (1991) outline the steps used by the Business Management Services Division at Control Data.

Profit-sharing plans pay out on the bottom-line and create a feeling of shared (annual) economic fate between companies and employees. These plans are more closely associated with payout than are gain-sharing plans.

Alternatives to the monetary rewards of profit-sharing and gain-sharing are earned free time and long service leave. Flexible bonus systems (cafeteria plans) and combinations of flexible and bonus-based pay are also possibilities.

The number of gain-sharing plans is increasing due to ups and downs of the business environment. Efforts are being made to design compensation systems that better support achievement of key organizational objectives.

16

Counterproductivity

PURPOSE

- Understand the major causes of counterproductivity.
- Develop methods to deal effectively with counterproductivity.

INTRODUCTION

Anything detracting from goal achievement could be considered counterproductive. Reducing the negative effects of counterproductivity is an obvious step toward improving productivity. But, this is easier said than done.

Counterproductivity and productivity are not necessarily the opposite. Both require effort, and both exist in the same work settings. Counterproductive behavior is a negative reaction to someone or something in the person's work environment. Causes of negative reactions could be the job, people in general, even the environment. Or, causes may be unknown.

Counterproductivity is obvious when employees simply do not come to work. It may also be subtle. The negative impact of slowing down work efforts, or withholding needed information reduces overall effectiveness.

One underperformer can have a negative impact on subordinates and peers by affecting the quality of work relationships. Outside the organization, customer satisfaction and goodwill may be jeopardized, particularly if quality is at stake.

PERSONAL AND JOB-RELATED COUNTERPRODUCTIVITY

Counterproductivity is often a symptom or sign that something is wrong. There are many sources of counterproductivity. Managers or supervisors play major roles in counterproductivity because they can cause it, reduce it, or ignore it.

Most sources of counterproductivity relate to the person doing the job and to the job itself. Only the person and the job will be discussed.

Organizational structures that limit the flow of communication and poorly coordinated work efforts are also problem areas.

Personal Counterproductivity

Issues central to self-concept and self-esteem tend to be resisted. People having high ego involvement in the job may resist suggestions for changes or improvement. Change, or the unknown aspects of change, tend to be resisted. Supervisors who know their employees' concerns and priorities are better prepared to resolve problems, or help employees direct their efforts in more constructive ways.

Lack of training and poor job skills are obvious problems. However, motivation, attitude, and many of the individual difference variables presented in Chapter

6, affect performance. Sometimes, employees do not understand where they fit into the scheme of things. Some employees never ask. Others have supervisors who never tell them.

Job-Related Counterproductivity

Some forms of counterproductivity are hard to avoid. For instance, how work is set up may cause problems ''up the line,'' or anywhere in the organization. Or, the physical arrangement of work or office space may be inefficient.

Examples of standard operating procedures contributing to counterproductivity are ''bottlenecks'' in any process involving a flow of work, or sequence of jobs. Other examples are waiting to use certain equipment; getting approvals from hard-to-find, busy supervisors; or slowdowns caused by lack of information to complete the job.

Poor quality control of raw materials used in materials processing, or product construction can reduce the amount of output and quality. Quantity will be lowered because of increased scrap or waste.

Activities that maximize human efforts and streamline the job reduce counterproductivity. Being productive is essentially everyone's responsibility.

WHAT CAN MANAGERS AND EMPLOYEES DO?

The major issue is to determine the real causes of counterproductive behavior, and estimate the total impact of such activities. Often this is hard to do. Various forms of subversion and work slowdowns, for instance, may be widespread and hard to trace. There are no easy solutions.

Managers who recognize and understand their employees' unique needs and talents can reduce counterproductivity. The following suggestions apply to all levels of employees.

1. More closely match employees' unique talents and needs with job demands.

2. Depending on the type of job and management style, use various participative or high-involvement approaches enabling low performers to have input regarding the best way to perform their jobs.
3. Reinforce productive behavior with positive feedback. This should reduce counterproductive activities.
4. Put low performers in contact with competent, nonthreatening peers having the same or similar jobs. The underperformer can learn to improve or change performance by observing and copying what competent people do.
5. Managers can serve as good role models. Few managers are aware the impact their behavior has on subordinates.
6. Managers can spend time coaching or counseling, stressing positive aspects. This can be done anytime, not just at performance appraisal time.

Serious counterproductivity is a great concern. Causes can be identified using a standard problem-solving approach. Steps are:

1. Identify all possible problem areas.
2. Determine and rank disruption of counterproductive activities.
3. Select the major problem area.
4. Develop a plan of action considering time, effort, and cost involved.
5. Implement the plan.
6. Evaluate outcomes.

Ideally, in participative settings, managers and their ''low producers'' can develop this plan together. See box below and on next page.

REFERENCE

1. Morgan, John S. *Improving Your Creativity on the Job.* New York: American Management Association, 1968.

1. List what are believed to be counterproductive activities of persons whom you supervise. Indicate when, and how often these activities occur. State the direct consequences or results of these activities, and actual or proposed actions taken.

Counterproductive Activities	Occurrence		Results	Action Taken
	When	How Often		
___	___	___	___	___
___	___	___	___	___
___	___	___	___	___
___	___	___	___	___

2. Examine the counterproductive activities listed above. Are they symptoms or the real problem? If they are symptoms, how can you find out the real problems?

3. List five major causes of counterproductivity within your organization. Rank the most disruptive cause 1 . . . and the least disruptive cause 7.

Causes of Counterproductivity   **Rank**

_____   _____
_____   _____
_____   _____
_____   _____
_____   _____

4. List steps required to deal effectively with one of the major causes of counterproductivity given in #3. Estimate the time, effort, and cost to solve or reduce the severity of the problem.

| | Solve Problem | | |
Steps to Be Taken	**Time**	**Effort**	**Cost**
_____	_____	_____	_____
_____	_____	_____	_____
_____	_____	_____	_____
_____	_____	_____	_____
_____	_____	_____	_____

Ideas to Remember

Chapter 16—Answers and Insights

1. Counterproductivity may be a negative reaction to the job, to supervisors, peers, or to the organization as whole. Stress behavior and frustration, for instance, are symptoms that something is wrong.

   Conscious counterproductive reactions can be discussed with employees, and frequency reduced by changing job demands, routine, or work assignments. Some pattern of behavior will emerge when non-productive activities are observed over a period of time. Causes may be seasonal work load fluctuations, or any number of job-related or personal problems. Reducing how often counterproductivity occurs may be a first step in attempting to solve the problem.

2. It is not always realistic or possible to determine causes of counterproductivity on your own. Chapter 4 presents information on dealing with symptoms. Your peers and subordinates and the low performer are the best sources of information. Sometimes peers and managers are part of the problem.

   The low performer's confidence and trust can be gained through open, honest communication. Once rapport is established, it is possible to discuss problems openly, and realistic solutions will likely emerge spontaneously.

3. Causes: Most relate to people as opposed to systems, and may include poor job skills and/or training; poor communication regarding goals and requirements of job; real or imagined personal (not racial) discrimination; or unrealistic demands. Start with the most disruptive, frequently occurring cause with the highest priority.

4. Begin with methods to reduce resistance. It may be possible to work backwards from the solution by starting with the desired productive behavior. (This procedure is reverse scenario building.) Steps should be small and sequential, and fit the underperformer's frame of reference and ability to handle intervention. Outside intervention (professional psychological counseling, or a medical exam to eliminate any possible physical cause) may be necessary.

   The cost of counterproductivity is very high. Seeking out answers and developing realistic, cost-effective solutions is well worth the effort. If counterproductivity and productivity are found to be opposites, one answer may solve two problems.

   Creativity in the form of new ideas, novel solutions, and frontier-breaking processes and products is an antidote to counterproductivity. Conducive environments tolerating risk (even failure) have leaders who foster, encourage, and appropriately recognize and reward creative efforts.

   Assumptions are that managers and leaders basically assume that most people are capable of considerable initiative, self-direction, and self-control and are eager to use their creative talents to achieve worthwhile objectives.

   A "creative" manager or team leader: (1) has respect for and understanding of human factors; (2) has knowledge of the creative process and inhibiting factors; (3) is a good communicator; (4) is willing to give credit and praise; (5) understands and tolerates risk taking; (6) leads by suggestion, not by command; (7) criticizes tactfully; and (8) inspires, encourages, and develops self-confidence in others.

   Creativity and innovation are our greatest untapped potential. Morgan (1968) stated that the average person and the average business likely function at less than 15% of creative potential. This figure could be optimistic.

   Creative potential that is mobilized and directed toward solving important problems and creating new, highly desirable products and processes, can join the long list of competitive advantages.

17

Trends

PURPOSE

- Examine major trends affecting productivity.
- Consider the impact of various trends on the whole productivity awareness/productivity improvement process.

INTRODUCTION

Trends affect the whole productivity process, beginning with awareness and ending with improvement. Knowing the nature and possible impact of major trends makes them easier to interpret and anticipate. Impact is seldom considered at the entry point. However, looking back from a ''fast forward'' leap into the future can provide meaningful information. Proper planning allows certain trends to be used to advantage to eliminate or minimize undesirable side effects.

Trends alter people's personal plans, goals, achievement, and expectations. In the organization, efficiency, effectiveness, profit, and smoothly running operations are focal points.

Technological trends affect the overall organizations and their output—goods, processes, and services provided. Customers, suppliers, and vendors can be involved in endless cycles of costly and time-consuming reactions to change. See box on next page.

MAJOR TRENDS

Major trends outlined and discussed here cover the person, the organization, and technology. These trends are woven throughout the productivity literature and are frequent topics of conversation. Trends tend to overlap, as many are influenced by a common cause, for instance, technology. Trends affecting those who manage were listed in Chapter 12.

Personal Trends

Managers Are Challenged. Challenges come from all directions. The new breed of employees often expects more from their jobs and managers than they get. Other challenges are less formal organizational structure; unpredictable organizational environments; lack of clear authority or rigid controls; and rapidly expanding technology. Employees are learning to accept temporary work relations, and dynamic interactions with peers and supervisors.

In less formal or structured organizations, an open, flexible management style, such as ''ad-hockery,'' is a possibility. Under ''ad-hockery'' a new corporate structure results when the organization is dismantled and restructured. The new structure should be able to better

1. List and describe current or new trends having a major impact on your own productivity. Indicate whether the effect is positive or negative. Rank (1 is low … 7 is high) the influence trends have on your productivity.

Name of Trend	How Influence Occurs	Influence + or −	Rank

accommodate the unpredictable environment (Toffler, 1985).

Managers of adaptation will need to think beyond the "thinkable." They will "rethink" products, procedures, programs, and purposes, and react before crises make drastic changes inescapable. They will need to know how to motivate and appropriately reward employees who rank an interesting, challenging job with security higher than money.

Managers who are productive themselves may be better judges of personal and organizational productivity. They will be able to determine which employees are highly self- motivated, and bring out their best characteristics. Ideally, they will understand the whole productivity effort.

Participative management, discussed in Chapter 18, is also a possibility. However, there is some debate regarding the real role of participative management, currently known as participative involvement, or simply participation. Participation does need to be managed.

Entrepreneurship Is Growing. Major sources of entrepreneurialism are the rapid evolution of knowledge and technology; demographic trends favoring development of service industries; and the emergence of two-earner families. Entrepreneurial managers move swiftly, invent, and make smart mistakes (Toffler, 1985). Domino's Pizza is a good example of entrepreneurship (Stevenson and Gumpert, 1985).

Entrepreneurship is alive and well in the "Third Sector." Examples of Third Sector businesses are health care institutions—some founded by hospitals, and non-profit, nongovernmental private schools (Drucker, 1984).

The "Fourth Sector" is also expanding and exhibiting entrepreneurship in the area of public-private partner-

ships. For instance, government units, namely municipalities, contract fire protection, garbage collection, and bus transportation from private companies (Drucker, 1984).

Small and new businesses are the main driving force in the nation's economic growth in high-tech industries, and in the service sector. These businesses provided most of the 20-odd million new jobs generated from 1970–1980 (Drucker, 1984).

Health and Wellness Are Here to Stay. Nearly 10 percent of the gross national product is spent on health care (Snider, 1989). Health care often focuses on symptoms, such as stress behavior, drug abuse, and smoking. Often, real problems, including poor supervision, burnout, or lack of challenge, are downplayed or dismissed.

For instance, approximately $14 billion per year is spent on diagnoses, operations, rehabilitation, and lost work benefits resulting from bad backs (*Houston Business Journal*, 1984).

Chrysler adds more than $500 to the price of each vehicle manufactured to pay for health care costs (*The Washington Post*, 1984).

The growing trend is to focus on the positive side of health, or wellness. But, few insurers offer coverage of preventive medical procedures (Gelb, 1985).

The Need for Training and Development Programs Is Growing. According to the Bureau of National Affairs, 195 U.S. companies revealed that training and development programs were believed to be the strongest approach to improving quality (World of Work Report, 1985).

A 1985 Carnegie Foundation study reported that corporations spent more than $60 billion on education and training. This amount equals the total yearly budget of all U.S. four-year and graduate-level colleges and universities (Magnus, 1986). Programs focus on a return to basics, such as reading, writing, and mathematics skills and on results-oriented programs on business strategies and achieving corporate objectives.

Drucker (1984) states that the next 15 years will contain the most profound changes in how we teach and learn since the printed book was introduced 500 years ago. Although he makes no predictions, the extent of changes will be major, and sweeping in extent.

One new, cost-effective trend is to use an "educational broker." This creative use of in-house resources lowers the cost of certain types of training. An employee told his "educational broker" that in six months he was being transferred to the company's Brazil plant. He wanted to learn some Portuguese before leaving. The broker keyed a code into the computer, and obtained a printout of the names of 40 people in the company who knew Portuguese. The broker called a person the inquirer happened to know, and arranged for the two to get together several hours a week to work on Portuguese.

IBM has over 22,000 employees in classrooms around the world at a cost of over $1.1 billion annually; Motorola estimates it has spent more than $100 million upgrading its work force (Kolberg, 1991).

Level of Education of the Work Force Is Increasing. This poses problems for management and prospective employees. The educational background of the work force completing four or more years of college grew from 14.7 percent in 1970 to 24.2 percent in 1983 (Best, 1985). Between now and the year 2000, most new jobs will require post-secondary education (Goddard, 1989).

Steadily rising levels of knowledge and the number of people overqualified for their jobs produced two major problems. One, keeping "overtrained" employees motivated and challenged. Two, their need to continue to grow on the job will strain current human and organizational development efforts and budgets.

Training can permeate the organization, beginning with suppliers or vendors, and moving up the organization to the CEO. Essentially, training and continuing education can become a way of life.

Alternative Work Schedules Are More and More Popular. Flexible schedules emphasize personal responsibility and allow freedom from the traditional work day. The usual accepted block time or core time when everyone works is 9:30 a.m. to 12:00 noon, and 2:00 p.m. to 4:00 p.m. The average work day is 7.5 hours, and the maximum is 40 hours per week.

Positive results are reduced absenteeism, lowered turnover, and higher morale, all of which contribute to higher productivity (*World of Work Report*, 1985). Recruiting efforts are more positive because more people want to work for companies having alternative work schedules. A major advantage is that employees can build or earn credit hours to be used at their discretion. Compensatory time off may be offered instead of overtime pay.

Reportedly, 25 percent of all federal workers use alternative schedules. John Hancock Mutual Life employees have been using alternate work schedules for years.

Other arrangements of work schedules include flextime, part-time, and permanent part-time jobs, working out of one's home are examples. Each is discussed.

Under flextime, individual workers or teams establish their own starting and ending times within limits set by the company. They work eight hours each day. In certain instances, workers are also able to bid for jobs they want to perform.

Part-time and permanent part-time jobs have increased from 293,000 in 1977 to 940,000 in 1987. Temporaries represent all professions, including the technical-professional segment, physicians, attorneys, and corporate managers. Estimates of the number of temporaries range from 11 percent (Benedict, 1988) to 20 percent (Goddard, 1989). The payroll for temporaries was $1.4 billion in 1977 and $8.4 billion in 1987 (Benedict, 1988).

Temporaries may not want or need the same benefits or incentives full-time employees receive. For instance, a person whose full-time job provides adequate benefits will not expect or need the same benefits in a temporary job as a person who has only a temporary job. Motivating part-timers and assessing productivity could require flexible approaches specifically designed for each employee. Involving part-time workers in organizational activities is one of many ways to increase job commitment and dedication.

Approximately 4.9 million people have regular, formal arrangements with their employers for working at home. According to Thomas E. Miller, director of research for the Telework Group of Link Resources in New York City, more than half of those working at home consider themselves more productive at home than at the office (Wagel et al., 1988).

The "Greying of the Work Force" Cannot be Ignored. The average age of the work force was 34.8 years in 1982. It is predicted to rise to 39 years by 2000 (Goddard, 1989). As the current generation reaches and passes middle age, advancement opportunities will decrease dramatically. Reduced job satisfaction and lower productivity may result. The number of workers competing for each managerial position will greatly increase in the foreseeable future.

Organizations

The developing and marketing of new products and services are critical to the success of most organizations. New products are always needed to replace those that are no longer competitive. For example, in the typical U.S. company, 35 to 40 percent of present sales and/or profits come from products developed within the last five years. Successful new products are one of the keys to improving America's global competitive position (Hise and Mc-Daniel, 1989).

Innovation and Creativity Are Necessary for Survival. Everyone has a certain level of creativity. Social and educational institutions, and even the work place, enforce conformity. Creative talents are eroded by squelching curiosity and creating fear of failure (Howard, 1985). In general, personality, life style, and a supportive environment play major roles in the development and implementation of novel ideas.

There is a wide gap between ideas and usable products and services. What is missing? "Facilitators" are. Facilitators linking creative idea people to "implementers" are hard to find. Creativity and innovation require a special unstructured, supportive climate that provides people the freedom to think in non-conventional ways, and be given the opportunity to take risks (Howard, 1985). Managing innovation is everyone's job (Berk, 1989).

There are bright spots. One is that creativity is now being taught in some schools of business. Another is that companies are beginning to foster "intrapreneuring." Hewlett-Packard, for instance, provides research and development funding for "intrapreneuring" programs outside the corporate mainstream (Howard, 1985). Other companies noted for intrapreneuring are Kodak and Goodyear.

Methods of Streamlining Inventory and Supply Are Increasingly Cost Effective. One well-known method, "Just-In-Time" (JIT), minimizes cost and effort through production scheduling and inventory control. JIT was developed by Toyota Motor Company, and first introduced in Japan. Profits are increased by reducing waste and costs, associated with production and excess inventory. Required materials are readily available. Also, quality is likely to be high because defective, or out-of-date inventory is not retained.

Productivity savings result from balancing the effort and cost of maintaining an adequate inventory against expenses and logistics associated with on-time-delivery. Motorola and Black and Decker Manufacturing are but two companies that have implemented Just-In-Time in the U.S.

As with any technique to increase efficiency and reduce cost, JIT must represent the best among many alternatives, or it should not be used.

Company Culture Is Very Important. Each organization has a unique culture. Culture, which builds up slowly, represents a collection of shared beliefs and behaviors. Over time, cultures change, even though they represent the experience of generations of employees, or generations of family ownership, for instance, Proctor & Gamble.

The major problem in disseminating concepts or values underlying corporate culture is that people must accept and be committed to the corporation's values. They cannot merely behave and think as they want to believe and think (Lippitt and Hoopes, 1978 and Deal and Kennedy, 1982).

In many companies, the process of systematically translating cultural values at the organizational level into behavior at the individual level is missing (Albert and Silverman, 1984). Companies with strong cultures can respond to the environment and adapt to diverse and changing circumstances. In a turbulent economic environment, or in times of uncertainty, companies can reach deeply into their shared values and beliefs for the truth and courage to see them through. When new challenges arise, adjustments can be made (Deal and Kennedy, 1982).

Strong culture companies are Disney, AT&T, and Pepsi. The primary culture value at Disney is customer service, at AT&T it is marketing, and at Pepsi it is being aggressive in winning.

A Climate for Productivity Is Essential. High productivity efforts are impossible to sustain without support from employees, upper management, and the organization. Three major indicators of such support are (1) existence of high standards, or an atmosphere of excellence; (2) a clearly stated, well-understood set of organizational objectives and performance goals that are often incorporated into the organization's culture; and (3) a cohesive organizational climate fostering creativity and innovation (previously discussed).

Long-range views of the economy, technology, and the changing needs of employees give a better picture of productivity. Corporate vision can be narrowed by preoccupation with getting things done in the present. This "band-aid" approach is characterized by postponing problems in the service of today's opportunity.

The Product Mix Is Growing and Changing. In the last 15 years, new technology has spawned an unprecedented number of products aimed at diverse, new sectors, and market niches. Computer-aided technology and design allow companies to customize almost any product, from designer jeans to designer genes. Examples of this customization are seen in the 300 different types of cars and light trucks, and 400 brands of beer that are available. Researching customers' tastes, interpreting results, and developing and marketing new products and services can be endless (McKenna, 1988).

The Shape of Organizations Is Gradually Changing. Organizations are becoming flatter and leaner in structure. There are fewer managers, particularly at the middle management level. At least 600,000 middle managers were reported to have lost their jobs between 1984–1986 (Goddard, 1989). An increasing number of smaller units are under the direct control of line operations.

New organizational forms and cultures may need to be created to deal effectively with the changing external environment. The current movement is toward hybrid matrix structures of task teams. Short and long-term planning should reflect factors in the external environment that require internal change responses (Davis, 1988).

Technology

The Emphasis on Technology Is Spreading. New technologies related to communication, information processing, microelectronics, and genetics engineering, or biotechnology dominate the work environment (Coleman, 1981). Technological innovations must be proven "manufacturable." Quality needs to be high, and manufacturing costs as low as possible. Value is also a consideration.

There are two opposite ways to look at technology: (1) externally as a catalyst to productivity output, or (2) internally, as an entity requiring software, hardware, skilled work forces, and large budgets for training existing employees. To come "up to speed" has required more effort, time, and expense than many bargained for (Bleecker, 1988). The technology tide is strong. The costs of swimming with or against the tide are both high.

Organizational size, age, culture, growth rate, and human resources affect how technology is assimilated. Well trained first-line supervisors who participate in the design and implementation processes (Crandall, 1988) and supportive management teams (Szakonyi, 1989) greatly contribute to the successful implementation of technology.

According to Brooking's Institution, 44 percent of U.S. productivity improvement is attributable to technological innovation (Slade and Mohindra, 1985).

The Information Age Is Here. Everyone depends on a supply of information (Korda, 1975). Information, a dominant resource, is expandable, compressible, substitutable, highly transportable, diffusible, and sharable (Cleveland, 1984). More information is not necessarily better, but information that is screened, summarized, or condensed provides a valuable service.

The office of today is organized like a factor in which the product is paper (Bleecker, 1986). Exchanging, buying, analyzing, protecting, storing, retrieving, and disseminating information approaches a nation-wide (pre)occupation.

In offices organized around information flow, the office worker enriches the data while it flows through the organization. Essentially, each office worker is a type of value-added reseller of information. After information is taken in, it may be massaged and passed along (Bleecker, 1986), often electronically. Information networks are growing.

Information is powerful, as when people speak from facts, or withhold information. Unfortunately, the more important the information, the further down in the organization it is necessary to go to collect it (Korda, 1975). Time and cost of collecting needed information is seldom considered since time is not usually "purchased."

The current number of information workers may be as high as 50 percent, with the number increasing dramatically by the year 2000 (Goddard, 1989). See box.

---

2. Refer to #1, and review the trends listed there. Under "other" at the end of each of the following sections, list any trends not included in #1. Rank trends (1 is low . . . 7 is high) influencing your own and your work group's productivity. Describe any firm plans to incorporate these trends into existing or future productivity improvement plans. Estimate the approximate time required to implement plans.

(Continued on next page)

Trends	Rank (1 . . .7) Effect on		Type of Plan for Productivity Improvement	Time Needed
	Self	Group		
Person				
1. Managers' challenge	_____	_____	_____	_____
2. Entrepreneurship	_____	_____	_____	_____
3. Health and wellness	_____	_____	_____	_____
4. Training and development	_____	_____	_____	_____
5. Level of education	_____	_____	_____	_____
6. Flexible schedules	_____	_____	_____	_____
7. Greying work force	_____	_____	_____	_____
8. Other:				
_____	_____	_____	_____	_____
_____	_____	_____	_____	_____
Organization				
1. Innovation	_____	_____	_____	_____
2. Inventory control	_____	_____	_____	_____
3. Company culture	_____	_____	_____	_____
4. Productivity climate	_____	_____	_____	_____
5. Product mix	_____	_____	_____	_____
6. Organization shape	_____	_____	_____	_____
7. Other:				
_____	_____	_____	_____	_____
_____	_____	_____	_____	_____
Technology				
1. Growth and cost	_____	_____	_____	_____
2. Information Age	_____	_____	_____	_____
3. Other:				
_____	_____	_____	_____	_____
_____	_____	_____	_____	_____

Ideas to Remember

REFERENCES

1. Albert, Michael and Silverman, Murray. "Thawing Out Your Management Culture," *Training and Development Journal*, February 1984, pp. 22–25.

2. Benedict, Daniel. "Use of Temporary Workers Surging in U.S. Work Place," *Houston Chronicle*, March 6, 1988, Sec. 5, pp. 1 & 17.

3. Berk, Sherrill. "Managing Technology for a Competitive Edge: An AMA Survey," *Management Review*, February 1989, pp. 49–51.

4. Best, Fred. "The Nature of Work in a Changing Society," *Personnel Journal*, January 1985, pp. 36–42.

5. Bleecker, Samuel. "Taking the Factory Out of the Office," *Computerworld*, June 16, 1986, pp. 95–101, 103–104.

6. _____ . Personal communication, May 17, 1988.

7. Cleveland, Harland. "Information as a Resource," *The Futurist*, December 1984, pp. 34–39.

8. Coleman, E. R. *Information and Society*, Basking Ridge, New Jersey: AT&T Emerging Issues Group, July. 1981.

9. Crandall, Richard E. "First-Line Supervisors: Tomorrow's Professionals," *Personnel*, November 1988, pp. 24–31.

10. Davis, Arthur G. "Competitiveness: Survival Strategies for the 1990s," *Industrial Management*, July/August, 1988, pp. 1 and 32.

11. Deal, Terrance E. and Kennedy, Allen A. *Corporate Cultures: The Rites and Ritual of Corporate Life*, Reading, Massachusetts, Addison-Wesley, 1982.

12. Drucker, Peter F. *Our Entrepreneurial Economy. Harvard Business Review*, January–February 1984, pp. 59–64.

13. Gelb, Betsy D. "Preventive Medicine and Employee Productivity," *Harvard Business Review*, March–April, 1985, pp. 12 and 16.

14. Goddard, Robert W. "Work Force 2000," *Personnel Journal*, February 1989, pp. 64–71.

15. Handy, Charles. *The Age of Unreason*, Boston, Massachusetts, Harvard Business Review Press, 1989.

16. Hise, Richard T. and McDaniel, Stephen W. "What Is the CEO's Role in New Product Efforts?" *Management Review*, February 1989, pp. 44–48.

17. *Houston Business Journal*, June 11, 1984.

18. Howard, N. A. "Creativity: A Special Report," *Success*, February 1985, pp. 54–61.

19. Kolberg, William H. "Letter to the Editor," *Harvard Business Review*, May–June, 1991, p. 209–210.

20. Korda, Michael. *Power in the Office*, New York: Random House, 1975.

21. Lippitt, G. and Hoopes, D. *Helping Across Cultures*, Bethesda, Maryland: International Consultants Foundation, 1978.

22. Magnus, Margaret. "Training Futures," *Personnel Journal*, May 1986, pp. 60-63, 66-71.

23. McKenna, Regis. "Marketing in an Age of Diversity," *Harvard Business Review*, September-October 1988, pp. 88-95.

24. Offerman, Lynn R. and Gowing, Marilyn K. "Organizations of the Future," *American Psychologist*, February 1990, pp. 95-108.

25. Slade, Bernard N. and Mohindra, Raj. *Winning the Productivity Race*, Massachusetts: Lexington Books, 1985.

26. Snider, Eliot. "Letters to the Editor," *Harvard Business Review*, July-August 1989, p. 156.

27. Stevenson, Howard H. and Gumpert, David E. "The Heart of Entrepreneurship," *Harvard Business Review*, March-April 1985, pp. 85-94.

28. Szakonyi, Robert. "Top Management, Technology, and a Company's Growth," *Management Review*, February 1989, pp. 52-55.

29. Toffler, Alvin. *The Adaptive Corporation*, New York: McGraw-Hill Book Company, 1985.

30. *The Washington Post*. "Health Care Monster Blamed for Firms' Costs," April 12, 1984.

31. Wagel, William H., Feldman, Diane, Fritz, Norma R., and Bocklyn, Paul L. "Quality—The Bottom Line," *Personnel*, July 1988, pp. 28-34, 36-38, 40-43.

32. *World of Work Report*. "Stacking Up the Strengths of Productivity Programs," Vol. 10, No. 1, 1985.

Chapter 17—Answers and Insights

1. Trends may relate to personal activities or to any level in the organization. Trends can be like a running stream of water—the undercurrents need watching. Going upstream is always difficult, so working with trends reduces effort.

   Organizations that survive will become much less bureaucratic and focus more on human resources. They may even have to reinvent themselves. Managers will gradually change to leaders. Customer input will steadily increase.

   New trends include growing competition at home and abroad; "offshore" manufacturing (Taiwan, Malaysia, Hong Kong, and Mexico); diversification-specialization cycles; and reduced layers of management to make a flatter, more functional organization. (Offerman and Gowing, 1990 and Handy, 1989).

   Employee leasing is growing. Organizations having cyclic needs can reduce the cost of employees' salaries and benefits by leasing. Some people prefer flexible schedules that leasing allows. However, "leased" employees who want job security may never be employed full-time.

2. Today's trends can become history, or they can help you make history. How much the various trends affect overall productivity is a prime concern. Deciding whether to follow trends is a major factor.

   Choices are to acknowledge diverse trends, or accept certain positive ones, and discard others. Following a well reasoned, stable course through time is easier said than done.

   There will always be new trends. The ones you listed in "other" will soon be replaced by new trends.

18

Major Keys To Improving Productivity

PURPOSE

- Compare your knowledge of major keys to productivity improvement with what currently exists or is proposed.
- Consider the contribution of group processes to productivity improvement.
- Examine the feasibility of applying productivity improvement methods.
- Develop plans to increase productivity.

INTRODUCTION

Productivity improvement, like measurement, occurs where the work is done. Measurement comes before improvement. Employees' suggestions for improvement often come from problem areas, or from feedback of results and interpretations of measurement. Selecting the "best" paths for improvement means making the "best" decision(s) based on available information, and following through on it.

Productivity enhancement is a strategically planned, continuous change effort requiring participation and cooperation of the entire work force. Productivity growth and improvement do not just happen. Successful techniques are built within the boundaries of what exists. Don't reinvent the wheel!

People always want to know reasons for change. They are much more likely to accept proposed changes if they have some control over their jobs, and feel changes benefit them. The nature and size of change efforts people are willing or encouraged to undergo make or break productivity measurement and improvement efforts.

CORNERSTONES OF IMPROVEMENT

There are four concepts that are especially important in improvement efforts. Trends discussed in Chapter 16 also have a way of redirecting personal and organizational efforts.

Quality as a "Way of Life." Quality is a major factor in the productivity race. It is a frequent topic in many current journals and magazines. Quality was the focus of the American Management Association's 59th Annual Human Resources Conference and Exposition held in Chicago in April 1988 (Wagel et al., 1988).

Quality is driven by competition, the marketplace, but especially by the customer. Quality begins with people, regardless of where they work, what they do, or what they need.

Time Is a Competitive Weapon. Time, a strategic weapon, is the equivalent of money, productivity, quality, even innovation (Stalck, 1988). We can work more efficiently and complete projects ahead of schedule, for instance. The most successful competitors know how to keep moving, and always stay on the cutting edge. ''Today, time is the cutting edge.''

Human Resources Are the Most Valuable Asset Any Organization Possesses. This has been a continual theme in this book. The human performance side of productivity improvement is affected by how workers view themselves, the type of job they perform, and the environment in which the work is performed (McClelland, 1986).

The Entire Work Force Needs to Be Involved in All Phases of Change Efforts. Concerted efforts to include people in change efforts have positive spinoffs, such as increased commitment, higher productivity, and willing involvement in future change efforts. Briefly, a more informed, dedicated work force results. See box below and on next page.

The following section provides some guidelines on logical beginning points for productivity improvement efforts. Examples are presented.

SOURCES OF PRODUCTIVITY IMPROVEMENT

The ''ideal'' or ultimate system often serves as a reference point. As difficult as attaining the ''ideal'' is, it is often kept in sight, for example, the highest raise given in your department or unit, or excellence in a professional or personal endeavor.

Documenting steps toward this ideal is one way to show progress. Accomplishment can be predictable, or follow an erratic course. But, an optimistic approach supported by genuine enthusiasm, or a ''can do'' attitude raises the likelihood of success.

The following provide the best opportunities for improving productivity:

Area of Most Promise. This could be a unit or department with a cooperative supervisor, where production is down, absenteeism in up, or where quality is a current concern.

Major Areas Where It Is Important to Excel. Critical areas could be ones with the highest visibility, most profitable, or ''showpieces.'' The area could be well known, like a company slogan of ''Think Productivity.'' Most employees know what these areas are.

Routine Activities that Can Be Simplified. Some productivity improvement efforts, like those at Intel, begin with work simplification. Routine activities, such as filing, or basic accounting procedures, are easier to break down into separate jobs or tasks than are more complex activities.

Intel is the inventor and leading manufacturer of microprocessors, which make modern computers possible. Like many organizations' administrative costs, Intel's were the fastest-growing part of its activities. Intel's efforts to increase administrative productivity began with work simplification, or ''getting rid of the smoke.''

Questions #1 through #5 sample accumulated knowledge and experience. Sources of counterproductivity (Chapter 16) may be helpful. Individual summaries and practical applications (Chapter 19) contains ''Ideas to Remember'' from previous chapters. These ''tid bits'' can be used to create meaningful action plans.

1. List the major keys to improving overall productivity. Rank (1 is low . . . 7 is high) importance to your supervisor(s) and subordinates.

Keys to Productivity Improvement	Rank Order of Importance to	
	Supervisors	Subordinates
_____	_____	_____
_____	_____	_____
_____	_____	_____
_____	_____	_____
_____	_____	_____

2. Examine each of the above "keys." Select two that could increase the productivity of your subordinates and two keys that could increase the productivity of the organization. Consider the time to implement each, approximate cost, and probability of each being successful. Propose methods having a realistic chance of being implemented.

Keys to Productivity Improvement	Implemen-tation Time	Estimated Cost	Prob. of Success
Subordinates			
_____	_____	_____	_____
_____	_____	_____	_____
Organization			
_____	_____	_____	_____
_____	_____	_____	_____

Put one asterisk by the keys to productivity improvement to which supervisors will be receptive and two asterisks by those to which subordinates will be receptive.

3. Can the largest productivity gains be made by beginning with the overall organizational picture, or with individual employees? List areas in which the highest time and cost savings have occurred or could occur. Please explain.

Areas of Productivity Gain	Savings	
	Time	Cost
_____	_____	_____
_____	_____	_____
_____	_____	_____
_____	_____	_____
_____	_____	_____

4. List major measurement techniques that can show productivity improvement. Rank (1 is low . . . 7 is high) techniques for effectiveness and quality.

Techniques	Rank of	
	Effectiveness	Quality
_____	_____	_____
_____	_____	_____
_____	_____	_____
_____	_____	_____

5. Minimum productivity change occurs without feedback on performance. If employees receive individualized feedback, indicate the most effective type of feedback.

Intel's first step was to use a participative approach to involve people whose office was under scrutiny. Included in this group were the chief of the office being examined, two or three other managers, two or three clerks, and the head of "job simplification," or his assistant.

Every intricate detail of each administrative procedure was examined, and unnecessary procedures stripped off. Then, each procedure was reassembled in a simpler, more rational form. In some instances, files were discarded, unnecessary units removed, or photocopying eliminated.

The first departments targeted were those having routine activities that were relatively easy to streamline, such as personnel records, and accounts payable. No employee whose job was eliminated was let go (Main, 1984).

Areas Where Some Improvement Has Already Occurred. Ongoing improvement efforts have their own momentum. For instance, a two-year quality improvement program in manufacturing that has successfully reduced defects and errors and increased profits has momentum. This program will likely be continued and the same or similar quality improvement methods applied to other manufacturing processes.

Where Talents or Expertise Can Be Used. Each person has unique talents and areas of expertise that can be used to advantage. Starting out "cold" without any background means you learn as you go, and face daily challenges. On the one hand, "trial-and-error" learning can be beneficial; on the other hand, even expertise can be outdated.

Areas in which Chances Are Better Than 50/50. "Playing the odds" helps ensure some level of success. By doing your "homework," possible places to begin change efforts will emerge. Don't try to be a hero by starting in the most difficult or challenging area just to prove your point, or prove someone else wrong.

Productivity "leverage" points are more effective means to accomplish some purpose. Examples of leverage are automation and work simplification. Typical high leverage activities for managers are time management, coordination and centralization of information, and creating an environment in which motivated people can flourish. Low leverage activities are managerial meddling and delaying decision making (Grove, 1983).

Where a Mechanism Already Exists. It may be possible to build on whatever foundations already exist, like a management information system having printouts of primitive productivity indicators that are not recognized as such (Siegel, 1980). Established review boards, productivity improvement teams, or written records of planned or actual improvement activities are starting points. Documentation from some type of monitoring procedure should be available. Any available standards or performance indicators can be consulted.

Examples of What to Do, or "What Has Worked for Others"

Materials presented, beginning with increasing awareness, and ending with measurement, set the stage for a very important activity—improvement. So far, this book has been a series of rehearsals for your most important act—improving productivity. Productivity improvement is not an "off again, on again" short-term process. Once you begin, your are in it for the long haul.

Ways to improve productivity can be found everywhere. However, one tool is to sharpen your focus to improve vision of what is around you. "Leverage," as previously discussed, can be applied in any area.

The following section reviews basic definitions of productivity, and refocuses on a systems approach. Example methods that follow are not presented in any specific order of importance:

Understand What Measuring and Improving Productivity Mean in Terms of Your Own, Peers', and Subordinates' Jobs. Two common ways to view improved productivity are (1) the *same* number of people produce *more* output; or (2) *more* output is produced in the *same* amount of time.

A systems view begins with input. To repeat, enhancing the quality of input is one approach that is often ignored, but is a major key to improving productivity. Typical ways to increase the amount or quality of input are to streamline operations, or "work smarter." However, many interrelated factors are involved in what appears to be simple efforts.

Emphasize Quality as the Major Driving Force in All Quality Improvement Efforts. In most cases, raising quality almost always results in higher productivity. Quality applies across the board—quality objectives; quality products and services; quality management, quality personnel, and appropriate pay for quality output.

Five industry examples are presented:

- The four major objectives of American Express are quality, quality, quality, quality (Skrzycki, 1987).
- "Think global and act local." This is the essence of Baxter's Quality Leadership Process, a corporate-wide quality improvement effort spanning 33 countries and more than 200 individual sites (McKee, 1988). Baxter is a $6.2 billion multinational corpo-

ration that researches, designs, manufactures, and distributes over 120,000 medical products from surgical gloves to dialysis equipment.

- The "Total Quality Management System" introduced at Corning Glass Works in 1984 has long-range perspectives. Its 5-10-year intensive educational program has reached most of its 25,000 employees in 58 locations worldwide. The program stresses understanding and meeting customers' requirements 100 percent of the time. In summary, ". . . quality is becoming a way of life at Corning" (Wagel, 1987).

- According to a Gallup survey on quality, 615 executives from Fortune 1,000 and smaller companies viewed the task of improving service and product quality as the most critical challenge facing U.S. business in the next three years (Skrzycki, 1987).

- An established concept of quality functional deployment, which originated in 1972 at Mitsubishi's Kobe shipyard site, has emerged as a "house of quality." This concept is founded on the belief that products should be designed to reflect customers' desires and tastes. Marketing people, design engineers, and manufacturing staff work closely together throughout the idea-to-implementation process. "The house of quality is a kind of conceptual map that provides the means for interfunctional planning and communications" (Hauser and Clausing, 1988).

Quality does not necessarily originate in the quality control department. Nor does it apply only to reducing errors or scrap. Quality originates anywhere and everywhere from housekeeping to the front desk and back to manufacturing. To illustrate, people perform to the standards of their leaders. If management thinks people don't care, then people won't care (Crosby, 1979).

Quality managers are broadening their roles to include technical and administrative areas. Competence in two areas increases the flexibility and value of managers. Unfortunately, the mechanism for this "dual role" is only beginning to be recognized.

Quality improvement is the most fruitful path to higher productivity and competitive success (Leonard and Sasser, 1982).

Principles Underlying "Strategic" Planning and Goal Setting Can Be Applied to Other Areas. For instance, when productivity measurement and improvement are incorporated into a company's strategic plans from square one, improvement has a better chance of success.

Individualize Reward Systems that Meet the Varied Needs of the Work Force. Satisfied needs do not motivate. Awards, raises, incentive programs, including employee stock ownership programs, may be useful, but not necessarily universally effective. Most people respond favorably to reward systems that enhance their self image and increase personal decision-making power, for example.

Cafeteria-type health benefits plans appeal to many. Cafeteria-like incentive programs could be one substitute for pay-for-performance, which is not working as well as it should (Rollins, 1987).

Example incentives include use of health facilities; financial planning service; discounts at "company store"; cash bonuses; and profit sharing. Longstanding perks and status symbols people take for granted, such as company cars and cellular phones, may be obstacles to good management (Ninomiya, 1988). Perks lose their meaning when they are no longer considered a privilege. Many forms of compensation are based on competition—someone "wins" and someone "loses." Historically, competition means conflict, not cooperation. The major issue in any compensation plan is to establish a strong link between pay and performance. This concept must be conveyed to employees in a way they understand.

Use the Actual Processes or Efforts Involved in Planning and Setting Up Productivity Measurement and Improvement Systems to Increase Awareness. Processes encouraging cooperation and commitment are particularly valuable. The goal of improving productivity is met when people see their jobs as worthwhile endeavors, and help the change efforts along. Individual or group feedback on positive behavior change further reinforces efforts.

Use Time as a Competitive Weapon. This is one of the four "cornerstones" mentioned previously. "As a strategic weapon, time is the equivalent of money, productivity, quality, even innovation." (Stalck, 1988). The most successful competitors know how to keep moving. They always stay on the competitive cutting edge. "Today, time is on the cutting edge."

Since 1945, the Japanese shifted their strategic focus at least four times: (1) They achieved a competitive advantage through low labor costs; (2) They competed with the West in areas having high labor content—steel, textiles, and shipbuilding; (3) They dramatically increased productivity by building the most capital-intensive facilities technologically feasible; and (4) They managed time to enable top Japanese companies to reduce costs, offer broad product lines, cover more market segments, and upgrade the technological sophistication of their products (Stalk, 1988).

Know Exactly Who the Customer Is. There is growing recognition of internal (customers within the organization) and external customers (those who purchase goods or services). Quality can be customer driven.

Monitor and Record Progress Toward Goals and Objectives on a Predictable Basis—Weekly, Monthly, or Quarterly. As always, feedback on individual and group performance is critical, as in performance appraisals. Benchmarks of group effectiveness can be created by employees themselves. Making results available in a format that can be readily understood is not only important, it helps establish and maintain the need for ongoing feedback.

Balance the Need for Organizational Change with the Ability of the Work Force and the Organization to Cope with Change. A few people welcome change; some ignore it; many fear it. While there is no good time to introduce productivity improvement efforts, stability of the organization and the external environment, management commitment, and other concepts considered in Chapter 17, (Trends) should be major considerations.

PARTICIPATIVE MANAGEMENT

Are we ready for participative management? Has it been oversold and underused? Do employees really want more participation in decision making? Do most employees need some direction? How much follow-up is needed? Answers to these questions differ, depending on the organization's size and maturity, and on employees' self-discipline to take the initiative to set goals, objectives, and priorities (Muczky and Reimann, 1987).

This open management style is based on the premise that everyone has the necessary leadership ability, capacity, and desire to work together to develop and achieve common goals and objectives. Employees throughout the organization are given the right mix of knowledge, information, power, and rewards to enable them to influence and be rewarded for organizational performance. Decision making is delegated downward to the lowest possible level in the organization. People at this level know the territory better than any other person (Townsend, 1984). Those doing the job are the best qualified to improve the job. Specific job-related information is often obtained through suggestion systems.

Under participative, or high involvement management, people have some form of control over the way they do their job. Participative concepts support the belief that employees want to be involved in important organizational activities. People support what they help create, or develop a sense of accomplishment or ''ownership.''

Resulting benefits are increased satisfaction and commitment, and reduced resistance to change. Participative

methods are reported to have varying success rates and must be managed (Boyle, 1984).

The greatest productivity gains have been made without investing a single dollar in new equipment or technology, but by letting employees participate in the business with their ideas and enthusiasm. Intelligence and commitment can improve productivity. Greatest productivity gains have come when the hearts and minds of our associates on the factory floor have been enlisted, e.g., gain sharing, ownership status, quality circles, open communication, and cross-organizational task forces involving both management and nonmanagement (Minnick, 1986).

General forms of employee participation include management by objectives; open door policy; and worker representation on various levels of councils and boards. The main, current forms of employee participation closely related to productivity improvement are quality circles (beyond the scope of this chapter), and quality of work life (introduced in Chapter 1). The following are examples of participative methods.

Example 1: Employee involvement at Olin Corporation represents a ''hands on'' learning experience. Measures and monitoring programs incorporate many factors influencing productivity. Feedback from experiences gained is used to gradually change and improve the system over time. Specific, broad-based objectives are to set goals and provide feedback on achievement; motivate performance improvement; and sustain productivity efforts (Christopher, 1983).

Example 2: Of the 859,039 suggestions Toyota received for improvement, 94 percent were implemented. Toyota's auditors verified savings in excess of $30 million from these suggestions (Suzawa, 1985).

Example 3: Boyle's (1984) information and well-documented experiences implementing participative management at Honeywell revealed that goal setting, defining accountabilities, and using strategic planning approaches are necessary.

The results of participation, or high involvement, are mixed. This is partly because of the various, somewhat unpredictable and uncontrollable influences of the workforce, leaders' own natural or preferred styles, and variables unique to the organization. Bleecker (1988) believes very little participative management is practiced in American offices. However, the practice of participative management may increase when ''conferral systems,'' Bleecker's term for networks used by people to share information and ideas, become more central to office work.

In manufacturing and materials processing industries, assembly-line workers, for instance, interact with materials as they come down the line. These workers know the corrective actions that can be taken to increase efficiency or cost effectiveness. However, their supervisors may not have good insights into corrective actions, or allow workers to make corrections or changes on their own.

Suggestion Systems

The primary purpose of a suggestion system is to elicit employees' ideas on reducing costs, increasing quality, and improving safety. The overall purpose is to generally involve employees in company matters, namely, improving performance, communication, and morale.

Well-administered suggestion systems can become useful incentive plans. Suggestion systems tap the ideas of educated, creative, well-motivated employees, regardless of the job performed, or the work environment. However, not all employees contribute equally.

Participation is not confined to employees. Participation by customers, colleagues, clients, and shareholders ultimately affects services and product design. Sharing of information and opinions, whether through surveys, suggestion systems, or other means, results in new or innovative products and services.

The hundreds of companies participating in the National Association of Suggestion Systems have received suggestions that have saved hundreds of millions of dollars each year (Glueck, 1978).

GROUP PROCESSES FOR IMPROVING PRODUCTIVITY

Group processes encourage commitment and involvement in work efforts. Sharing information, goals, and feelings of accomplishment has a positive effect on productivity. Group processes, as ways to maximize efficiency and effectiveness of work efforts, are growing in number.

Some better known cooperative efforts include team building, job enrichment, employee survey feedback, and problem solving activities. Many focus on the person's skills and knowledge, and resulting unique contributions to group and organizational activities.

There are many good sources of information on participative or group approaches (see Suggested Readings). Only a few group processes have been selected for discussion.

Group Processes

Processes discussed cover a broad range of group activities. Included are self-managing teams; problem-solving teams or groups; work sharing; team building; executive development groups; and gain sharing.

Self-Managing Teams. These groups, also known as autonomous work groups or "teams," were developed to increase productivity, reduce overhead, and minimize

conflict (Sims and Dean, 1985). Use of teams places a remarkably high degree of decision-making responsibility and behavior control in the hands of the work group itself.

A self-managed team usually elects an internal leader. Management often appoints a coordinator, facilitator, or consultant, not a "foreman" or "supervisor."

Typical jobs include solve technical problems; train fellow team members; set team goals; make assignments within groups; record quality control statistics; be responsible for timekeeping and aspects related to decision making, and monitoring.

Teams have an estimated productivity edge of 20 to 40 percent over traditional systems (Sims and Dean, 1985). Employees may not work harder, but savings occur because less surveillance is required, time is used more efficiently, and the number of poor quality products is significantly reduced.

Teams are designed with well-defined physical and task boundaries, matching technical systems, and norms or standards governing interaction. Sophisticated, or computerized information systems may be used to measure input and output across team boundaries. Extensive rapid feedback on quality and quantity of performance is provided.

Advantages are:

- Members develop a variety of skills and are encouraged to learn more about numerous jobs performed by other team members.
- Teams are highly adaptable and flexible.
- Responses to changing conditions and new startups are uniform because of training.
- Adapting to new processes and equipment is relatively trouble-free, and is exemplified by a "can do" attitude.

Disadvantages are:

- Startup costs can be significant.
- Patience is required before the rewards of successful implementation can be repeated, typical waits are as long as 18 months.
- Middle managers in particular feel highly threatened. Their unfounded fear is that "teams" will reduce their power and influence. Even though direct control based on authority is reduced, indirect power derived from influence and achievement is enhanced.

Approximately 200 plants in the U.S. have begun using the self-managing team concept (Sims and Dean, 1985).

Problem-Solving Teams or Groups. These groups help meet workers' needs by building a team-oriented work environment. Involvement in making work-related decisions creates a sense of ownership. Personal growth needs are challenged. A total team management system includes structured team problem solving from the level of the chief executive down to, and including, hourly employees. Team members are lead by their manager. Every team follows a consistent process of data review, objective setting, problem solving, and reinforcement of performance improvement.

Managers need to acknowledge and adjust to changes in relationships, expectations, needs, and values of employees because of employees' expectations for:

- Increased participation and say in things that concern them.
- Being able to contribute valuable ideas to make jobs better.
- Higher levels of performance attributed to an environment that encourages group work and collaborative relationships.
- Improved relationships between managers, their staff, unions, and employees in working toward common goals.

Many of the major gains in productivity and quality in U.S. corporations have come from successful efforts to create team problem-solving and decision-making groups (Tarkenton and Company, 1980). Dramatic improvements in measurable performance are being achieved where the team system has been implemented. Employee involvement is maximized when teams are structured, leaders trained, and meetings held on a regular basis. To achieve good teamwork, teams function on a regular basis, strive to improve productivity and quality, and solve problems before they become crises.

Work Sharing. There are three basic approaches to work sharing (French, 1978): (1) reduce the number of hours worked; (2) divide the work equally among employees as in piecework jobs; and (3) rotate employees and rotate any short layoff periods equally among all employees. People wanting flexible hours may share the same job, for example. Occasionally, work-sharing programs are counterproductive because they dilute the job, or spread the same job among several employees.

Team Building. This method focuses on one team at a time. Training usually lasts two to three days, and often occurs away from the work setting. The curriculum balances cognitive learning (lecture and written material), and experiential learning (discussions, role playing, and various group exercises including problem solving). Team building promotes an increased sense of unity, or team identity and cohesiveness, enabling team members to function together more effectively and smoothly (Schermerhorn, 1986).

The ultimate goal is for a team to gather pertinent data about itself, and deal more effectively with conflicts, choices, and decisions.

Executive Development Groups. These groups are not necessarily confined to presidents, or owners of large businesses, but include other levels in the organization or in private enterprise. Main purposes are self development, share knowledge and information, and achieve the overall goal of increased personal and organizational productivity.

Gain Sharing. This group incentive program is also called productivity incentives, profit sharing, and performance sharing incentives. Gain sharing is based on pay for performance. It enables employees to share in the financial benefits resulting from improved performance, increased efficiency or other indicators of organizational performance.

Gain sharing incorporates the general concepts of identity, participation, and equity. Employees identify with the company, and are actively involved, as they have a say in what happens and in the gain-sharing plan. Equity is based on the measurement standards and methods used to assess performance and determine base periods to compute amount earned (Hauck and Ross, 1988).

Further information on components, considerations, implementation, and possible reasons for failure is available in most management texts. One easy-to-read source is that of Thomas and Olson (1988).

Specific advantages of gain sharing are:

- Break down barriers to communication.
- Boost cooperation.
- Build a stronger sense of company identity and greater employee involvement.
- Enable employees to have a bigger impact on, and share in, the organization's success. For example, gain-sharing programs in general have caused union and management leaders to realize that both sides can gain more through cooperation than through strife or competition.

Most gain-sharing programs have employee task forces, action teams, or committees actively involved in discussing the potential influence of particular bonus formulas (Hatcher and Ross, 1985). Task forces are also instrumental in developing methods designed to ultimately increase morale, decrease labor costs, minimize pay cuts, and reduce layoffs. Examples of such activities are as follows:

Example 1: At Northern Telecom, some division managers and workers jointly designed indexes for their own departments. For instance, one department identified current performance, and long-term and interim goals for each ratio. By revising successive ratios, teams eventually progressed toward agreed on goals that everyone could understand (Chew, 1988).

One set of indexes proposed by a design engineering team addressed reworked drawings and overdue drawings as a percentage of total drawings, and overtime hours as a percentage of total hours. Managers assign weights to the ratios based on their relative importance. Weights total 100. The index provides a single productivity "score," or a weighted average of the ratios. Although weightings were subjective, meaningful ratios resulted.

Example 2: "Improved Productivity Through Sharing," or Improshare®, was created by Mitchell Fein, an industrial engineer. It uses physical measures of productivity and is based on direct labor standards, such as hours worked in a specific job. Gains are shared equally by the organization employees. Bonuses, which are usually calculated and paid weekly, cannot exceed 30 percent of wages. This plan has been successfully implemented by more than one hundred major corporations.

Bullock and Lawler's (1984) survey of 33 plants showed the following positive results of gain sharing:

- Success rate on gain sharing—67 percent.
- Performance improvement—80 percent.
- Cost-savings ideas—89 percent.
- Quality of work life improvement—72 percent.
- Labor-management cooperation—67 percent.

Most of the gain-sharing programs are in manufacturing, but increasing interest is being demonstrated by banks, hospitals, and engineering companies. There were more gain-sharing programs in the last five years than in the previous 50 years (Bullock and Lawler, 1984).

Statistics from a total of 36 plants that had implemented some form of gain sharing are (Hatcher and Ross, 1985):

- Firms with average annual sales of less than $100 million averaged annual work-force savings of 17.3 percent.
- Firms with average annual sales of $100 million or more averaged annual work-force savings of 16.4 percent.
- 80.6 percent reported improved labor-management relations.
- 47.2 percent had fewer grievances.
- 36.1 percent had less absenteeism.
- 36.1 percent reported reduced turnover.

Refer to Chapter 15 for details about the productivity gain-sharing program used at the Kalmar (Volvo) auto assembly plant in Sweden (Hauck and Ross, 1988).

Positive outcomes of group improvement efforts in general are that those who work well in groups or teams understand group processes. It is hoped they will be good group leaders and managers. Increasing emphasis on group achievement, and "group" productivity measurement reduces unfavorable feelings of those who normally resist or fail to accept individual assessments of productivity.

SPINOFF FROM GROUP EFFORTS

Networking and group technology are only two of many group efforts that enhance cooperation and communication throughout the organization. They are also major vehicles to reduce cost and improve amount and quality of output.

Networking

This term is used for the old phenomenon of using personal connections or networks to exchange information. Communication in horizontal, lateral, diagonal, and bottom-up communication network links is based on informality and equality. Network members treat one another as peers, because information, the great equalizer, is what is important (Grove, 1983). Two networking examples follow:

Example 1: Intel uses a network management style allowing employees to participate in discussions as equals. Quality control and purchasing functions become the responsibility of a committee, or council, and do not involve a hierarchical staff reporting to an individual leader.

Example 2: A specialized peer executive network, or "executive committee," meets monthly to discuss cutting-edge input and engage in mutual problem solving. Networks provide mechanisms to exchange information, share creative ideas, and learn in general. No realistic price tag can be placed on the value of "inside information," "scientific breakthroughs," "tips," or personal contacts. Networks provide a mechanism for making the best possible use of human and organizational resources.

The advantages of networking are that it (Lippitt, Lippitt, and Lafferty, 1984):

- Reduces the lag between discovery and implementation of new knowledge and information.
- Establishes resource banks of new knowledge.
- Maximizes the efficiency and speed of communication across distances.
- Is an inexpensive way to keep informed.
- Increases awareness of what each person has to offer personally and professionally.

If networks are to be successful, changes in employee attitudes and learning must occur (Lippitt, Lippitt, and Lafferty, 1984). There will be a general need for training in the techniques and risks of communicating in networks. Power and influence come from the accumulation of knowledge. Overall efforts must be exerted to support inter-organizational communication.

Group Technology (GT)

This approach to manufacturing maximizes production efficiencies and productivity in general by grouping similar or recurring tasks together. For example, books in a library catalog are classified and coded in a way that enables users to find all books written by a certain author, covering a specific topic, or having the same title (Heyer and Wemmerlöv, 1984).

Like the indexes used in libraries, GT serves as an index to common characteristics of activities in specific areas like manufacturing, engineering, purchasing, resource planning or accounting. For example, managers from these different areas determine which of their jobs, processes, and equipment overlap. A GT data base including this information is constructed and used to speed up retrieval of information design processes, planning, operations, and communication between functional areas. As a result, managers from design and manufacturing are able to pool resources and expertise to develop standards, streamline processes, save time, avoid duplication, and reduce overhead. GT is particularly useful in simplifying operations and providing tools for understanding computer-assisted design (CAD), and computer-assisted manufacturing (CAM) areas.

There are numerous advantages to GT (Hyer and Wemmerlöv, 1984):

- Manufacturing companies report impressive benefits, particularly in reduced tooling and fixture expenses, and decreased costs of handling materials.
- Lowered costs in production planning and control efforts.
- Reduced lead times and work-in-process inventories.
- Lower and more accurate cost estimates.
- Increased worker satisfaction.
- Reduced effort associated with the development and retrieval of designs.

Companies that began using GT in the 1970s are John Deere, General Electric, and Black and Decker.

Despite the usual resistance to organizational change, need to coordinate efforts of workers, parts, and equipment, and long implementation periods (as long as three years), GT has positive aspects (Baker and Huang, 1986).

Briefly, any form of participative or involvement system that makes good use of employees' abilities and knowledge creates a sense of involvement in, and commitment to achieving organizational goals. As stated in Chapter 1, productivity can be defined in terms of organizational effectiveness. See box below and on next two pages.

In conclusion, productivity improvement is an individual and team effort and responsibility. The gradual building of winning teams, as demonstrated by self-managed teams, team building, and executive development groups, motivates employees to further improve performance. How well people work together is one indicator of productivity. Group members need to understand what productivity means in terms of their jobs, and jobs of other group members.

Growing emphasis on group achievement, and on "group" productivity measurement reduces unfavorable feelings of those who normally resist or fail to accept individual assessments of productivity.

Teams work together to achieve common goals. Good teamwork is satisfying, stimulating, and enjoyable. It also enhances cooperation, trust, creativity, and communication. Satisfied, motivated team members are productive.

---

6. Comment on the statement, "If managers needed better support to improve their own performance, couldn't the same be said for the persons they supervise?" (from Schermerhorn, 1986).

7. Is the output of your supervisor the output of the organizational units being supervised or managed? What implication does this have for group efforts?

8. List group-based work activities in your organization. Indicate the percentage of time you have been involved in these activities. Rank effectiveness and efficiency of work group efforts to organizational productivity.

Activities	Percent Time Used	(Rank 1 . . .7) Effectiveness	Efficiency
_____	_____	_____	_____
_____	_____	_____	_____
_____	_____	_____	_____
_____	_____	_____	_____

9. How could you use networking and group technology?

10. Develop and list methods for improvement. Estimate the percent of time each is used. Write down the measurement method (either numeric or descriptive), and indicate whether they were developed by yourself or your group.

Improvement Method	Percent Time Used	Measurement Method	Developed by Self Group
_____	_____	_____	___ ___
_____	_____	_____	___ ___
_____	_____	_____	___ ___
_____	_____	_____	___ ___
_____	_____	_____	___ ___

11. Examine the group productivity improvement techniques listed in #10. Group-based methods presented in this chapter are listed. Indicate the ones you use and how often you use them. Rank (1 is low . . . 7 is high) the contribution of each method to productivity improvement. List other group-based techniques used.

Method	Percent Time Used	Rank Contribution to Productivity Improvement
Participative management	_____	_____
Self-managing teams	_____	_____
Problem-solving groups	_____	_____
Team building	_____	_____
Work sharing	_____	_____
Executive development groups	_____	_____
Gain sharing	_____	_____
Other:		
_____	_____	_____
_____	_____	_____
_____	_____	_____

12. What family of measures could be used to measure group productivity? Indicate the weights computed or assigned. Can a specific monetary value be placed group activities? If so, explain.

Ideas to Remember

REFERENCES

1. Baker, William and Huang, Phillip. "Group Technology and the Cost-Accounting System," *Industrial Management*, May–June, 1986, pp. 24–26.

2. Bleecker, Sam. Personal communication, March 15, 1988.

3. Boyle, Richard J. "Wrestling with Jellyfish," *Harvard Business Review*, January–February, 1984, pp. 74–83.

4. Bullock, Robert J., Lawler, E. E., III. *World of Work Report*, Vol. 9, No. 8, 1984.

5. Chew, W. Bruce. "No-Nonsense Guide to Measuring Productivity," *Harvard Business Review*, January–February 1988, pp. 110–111, 114–116, 118.

6. Christopher, William F. "How to Measure and Improve Productivity in Professional, Administrative, and Service Organizations," *Productivity Yardstick*, Vol. 3, 4, 1983, pp. 3–10.

7. Crosby, Philip B. *Quality Is Free*, New York: New American Library, 1979.

8. French, Wendell L. *The Personnel Management Process*, 4th ed. Boston, Massachusetts, Houghton-Mifflin Company, 1978.

9. Glueck, William F. *Personnel: A Diagnostic Approach*, (rev. ed.) Dallas, Texas, Business Publications, Inc., 1978.

10. Grove, Andrew S. *High Output Management,* New York: Random House, 1983.

11. Hatcher, Larry L. and Ross, Timothy L. "Organizational Development Through Productivity Gain Sharing," *Personnel*, October 1985, 42, pp. 44–50.

12. Hauck, Warren and Ross, Timothy L. "Expanded Teamwork at Volvo Through Performance Gain Shar-

ing,'' *Industrial Management,* July–August 1988, pp. 17–20.

13. Hauser, John R. and Clausing, Don. ''The House of Quality,'' *Harvard Business Review,* May–June 1988, pp. 63–73.

14. Heyer, Nancy L. and Wemmerlöv, Urban. ''Group Technology and Productivity,'' *Harvard Business Review,* July–August 1984, pp. 140–149.

15. Leonard, Frank S. and Sasser, W. Earl. ''The Incline of Quality,'' *Harvard Business Review,* September–October 1982, pp. 163–171.

16. Lippitt, Gordon, Lippitt, Ronald and Lafferty, Clayton. ''Cutting Edge Trends in Organizational Development,'' *Training and Development Journal,* July 1984, pp. 59–62.

17. McClelland, Sam. ''The Human Performance Side of Productivity Improvement,'' *Industrial Management,* September–October 1986, pp. 14–17.

18. McKee, Deirdre L. ''Baxter: Total Quality Improvement Effort Crosses Geographic, Cultural Boundaries,'' Case Study 63, March 1988. Houston, Texas: American Productivity Center.

19. Main, Jeremy. ''How to Battle Your Own Bureaucracy,'' *Fortune,* June 29, 1981, pp 54–58.

20. Minnick, Walter C. ''Letters to the Editor,'' *Harvard Business Review,* November–December 1986, p. 131.

21. Mucyzk, Jan P. and Riemann, Bernard C. ''Has Participative Management Been Oversold?'' *Personnel,* May 1987, pp. 52–56.

22. Ninomiya, J. S. ''Wagon Masters and Lesser Managers,'' *Harvard Business Review,* March–April 1988, pp. 84–90.

23. Rollins, Thomas. ''Pay for Performance: The Pros and Cons,'' *Personnel Journal,* June 1987, pp. 104, 106, and 111.

24. Schermerhorn, John R., Jr. ''Team Development for High Performance Management,'' *Training and Development Journal,* November 1986, pp. 38–41.

25. Siegel, Irving H. *Company Productivity: Measurement for Improvement.* Kalamazoo, Michigan: W. E. Upjohn Institute for Employment Research, 1980.

26. Sims, Henry P. and Dean, James W., Jr. ''Beyond Quality Circles: Self-Managing Teams,'' *Personnel,* January 1985, pp. 25–32.

27. Skryzcki, Cindy. ''New Quality Gospel Starting to Pay Dividends in U.S,'' *Houston Chronicle,* November 8, 1987, Sec. 6, p. 5.

28. Stalk, George, Jr. ''Time—The Next Source of Competitive Advantage,'' *Harvard Business Review,* July–August 1988, pp. 41–51.

29. Stayer, Ralph. ''How I Learned to Let My Workers Lead,'' *Harvard Business Review,* November–December 1990, pp. 66–69, 72, 74, 76, 82–83.

30. Suzawa, Soichi. ''How the Japanese Achieve Excellence,'' *Training and Development Journal,* May 1985, pp. 110–112, 114–117.

31. Tarkenton & Company. ''The Team Performance System,'' Atlanta, Georgia: Tarkenton & Company, 1980, 12 pages.

32. Thomas, Barry W. and Olson, Madeline Hess. ''Gain Sharing: The Design Guarantees Success,'' *Personnel Journal,* May 1988, pp. 73–79.

33. Townsend, Robert. *Further Up the Organization,* New York: Alfred Knopf, 1984.

34. Wagel, William H. ''Corning Zeros in On Total Quality,'' *Personnel,* July 1987, pp. 4–9.

35. Wagel, William H., Feldman, Diane, Fritz, Norma R., and Blocklyn, Paul L. ''Quality—The Bottom Line,'' *Personnel,* July 1988, pp. 28–34, 36–38, 40–43.

Chapter 18—Answers and Insights

1. Major keys cover many areas, as needs and circumstances differ. Keys can parallel trends (Chapter 17). Most originate with those doing the work. Keys range from detailed plans to improve various work procedures to an alternative way to do a simple, repetitive task.

   Low supervisor-subordinate agreement can mean differences in how productivity is viewed, or the way improvement is to take place. Agreement can be increased by defining priorities in terms of "must do," "need to do," "important," or "not urgent," for example.

2. Because of the cost of organizational and personal commitment, priorities for productivity improvement need to be established early in the game, and momentum built up. When work force and organization goals are the same or similar, change efforts are easier. When supervisors and subordinates agree on "keys," the first small steps toward improvement can be taken.

3. Where you start is up to you. Begin at the bottom, middle, or top of the organization, or take a diagonal slice of all three. The support of someone who has "clout"—the CEO, or a department or unit manager—is valuable. Your own personal reputation for getting things done is important.

   Some coordinated efforts begin as overall organizational goals, but later single out specific parts of the organization, or certain levels of workers. Pilot projects eliminate some of the "bugs" in the system.

   However, productivity improvement efforts can start anywhere, beginning with you. A starting point could be efficiency—save time, or reduce cost in one process. Other valuable, long-term, but less obvious criteria could be to gradually revise procedures, change suppliers, or steadily reduce problems, defects, overtime, etc.

   If you start with the obvious, are you working with symptoms or problems? Be sure before you begin. Typical areas of time and cost savings: high counterproductivity, low quality, poor service. Areas change as goals and achievements of the organization change. Also, new areas continue to emerge.

4. Ratios and descriptive statements developed in previous sections are helpful. Definitions of productivity, indicators, or indexes could be used to rank measurement techniques. Once time and cost considerations are known (#3), effectiveness and quality can be evaluated.

   At Beechcraft, one measure was " ... equivalent pounds of airframe manufactured ready for delivery per payroll dollar (Siegel, 1980).

   Other general measures are zero defects, ratio of sales to pay (including fringe benefits), overstaffing, underperformance, total labor cost to market value of net sales, and physical output per man year.

   Remember, improvement cannot be documented without good measurement systems, or a reliable, valid "yardstick." Resulting measures are then used to make comparisons.

5. Feedback on performance is essential to improvement. Car mileage, for instance, cannot be increased unless miles per gallon are monitored over a specific time period and something done to improve it.

   When performance is monitored and achievement documented on a relatively frequent basis, standards of comparison, measurement methods, and ratios provide meaningful data for comparison. Feedback lacking base-line data or standards cannot be compared with anything, so it would be impossible to tell if any change (improvement) occurred.

   Most employees currently receive "hit-or-miss" feedback from performance appraisals. But, much of the day could be spent working in groups. People usually want to know how they compare with others. Feedback on individual and group performance enables people to compete with themselves, or others, and have "proof" of improvement.

6. Lack of support is a major cause of poor managerial performance (Schermerhorn, 1986). Peer group and managerial support are mutually reinforcing.

   Performance = Ability × Support × Effort

7. If output is the major standard to determine supervisor productivity, the positive motivational effects of recognizing and suitably rewarding accomplishment of each group member will be lost. Similarly, the positive role throughput variables play in cooperation, open communication, and cohesion will be minimized.

An unfair situation exists if supervisors' activities reduce group accomplishment.

Groups and their supervisors can decide on the most effective rewards. Treating each group member alike may/may not cause problems.

8. The type of work accomplished or activities performed by groups will differ. Some can be done by individuals, although they may take longer. Others, such as the completion of detailed projects, require the expertise and cooperation of many different people.

Compatibility of group members is a consideration. However, those with diverse talents and interests can complement each other. Experience in working together increases efficiency of effort. Activities such as team training can smooth out otherwise rough edges.

9. Networking and group technology involve communication. Sharing important job-related information is a plus. Answers will reflect needs to improve design procedures, increase communication between engineering or design and production, reduce unnecessary duplicate procedures, etc.

10. Concentrate on activities where the need is greatest, or performance the lowest. "Whys" and "hows" of measurement could be reviewed. Effectiveness measures will indicate if you are "doing the right things;" efficiency measures whether you are "doing things right," or in a timely manner.

Techniques are examples only: quality of work life efforts, special gain-sharing plans, joint goal setting, better supervision, improved communication, etc. Use may depend on tradition, special needs, organizational significance, even fads. How group activities contribute to productivity improvement can be determined by monitoring and measuring performance over time and comparing results. What works in one department may not work in

other nearly identical areas. Individual differences (Chapter 6) could also be major contributing factors.

11. Group productivity improvement methods can be helpful motivational and communication tools. Methods may change over time. How much each contributes to productivity depends on the extent of involvement of team members and their supervisors. Some may feel that participating in groups may be a sign of weakness or that they do not possess enough ability or skills to work alone. Others may fear criticism from peers. Obviously, each method takes time to introduce. Coming up to speed may take considerable effort.

"Other" methods reflect what is most relevant to you right now. Although methods will gradually change, most will relate to productivity, quality, and reflect internal and external customers' needs and level of satisfaction.

12. A family of measures for group productivity could include partial factors and total factors. Partial factors: cooperation; sharing of information; communication; contribution of fair share, etc. Total factors: combined group output in each of 5 or 6 major areas divided by individual input in the same area.

Weights could be determined through group discussion and/or consensus, or with techniques presented in Chapter 14. Managers and a resource person could also be involved.

Monetary values in terms of worth and equitable pay are hard to compute. Productive teams are highly valued. Poor performing teams may even have a negative value. Often synergy produced by teams exceeds the sum of the individual contributions. Rewarding employees by sharing financial gains from improved performance is one way to place a value on group activities.

Stepping out of the way and letting workers lead could be one of the best ways to improve productivity (Stayer, 1990).

19

Individualized Summaries and Practical Applications

INTRODUCTION

The real value of any learning experience comes from incorporating it into your frame of reference, using it to make better decisions and applying it on the job. What is learned, and how well it is learned often depends on interest and motivation. An attitude of readiness, or a willingness to accept and participate in the numerous and varied change efforts associated with the ultimate goal of enhancing productivity is essential. Implementing and monitoring change is the essence of the entire process, which begins with creating awareness and ends with improvement.

Questions 1–5 sample major productivity issues. No answers are provided. Your answers reflect ideas and information gathered from the book. You are the best judge of whether answers are reasonable and complete. The practical test of anything is how reliable it is when used, how valid it is, or how well it meets end users' needs.

The core of your answers may reflect the broad concepts of quality, value, efficiency, personal effectiveness, organizational effectiveness, innovation, profitability, and quality of work life. Each concept reflects a slightly different facet of productivity. How you developed standards or methods to measure productivity is influenced by your unique background and skills, and on

your specific immediate and expected needs. See box on next page.

Three different ways to evaluate the contents of this book are presented. The first parallels the order of Chapters 1 through 18. The second is an eclectic list, or "laundry list" of ideas evolving from contents. The third takes a systems approach.

SUMMARY OF IMPORTANT CONCEPTS

- Take a broader look at productivity and what it means in terms of the person, the job, and organization. Many constant factors (regulation, taxes, budget) and variable factors (motivation, competition, experience level) affect productivity. Seeing productivity in different ways increases understanding and encourages creative approaches to productivity problems (Chapter 1).
- Set realistic goals and monitor progress toward these goals. Comparing individual, group, and organizational goal achievement on a regular basis is one of the best ways to assess and monitor productivity. Start with the most basic, short-term accomplishments and end with long-range, overall organizational goals. In some areas, namely, quality, most goals overlap (Chapter 2).

  Typical areas of focus are:

1. Should your original definition of productivity from Chapter 5, Question 5 be modified to include new information? List any changes below.

2. Reread Questions 6, 7, and 8 (goals of my organization, work group, and self, respectively) of Chapter 2. Determine if information in this manual influenced your goals. Then, look at the priorities assigned to these goals, and reevaluate them in terms of your newly acquired information.

3. How do you plan to become better informed about your subordinates' abilities, skills, knowledge, and productivity?

4. How will you help your subordinates and peers become more productive? How can you create the circumstances and build an environment to foster and maintain productivity improvement? List what you plan to do, and when and how you plan to do it.

5. Review your responses to the various questions and "Ideas to Remember" sections at the end of each chapter. What type of information and methods are you most likely to use in your job and in your organization?

Immediate—quality control; turnaround time, production costs; gain-sharing programs; cost-effectiveness of units, etc.

Short-term—stabilize processes; introduce new product lines or services; compare major variables of production.

Long-term—payout of R&D; compare various plants or factories; interpret trends; change systems to parallel major trends; introduce innovative products and services.

• Look at results people have achieved, or are trying to achieve. Go backwards step by step to determine and document possible ways to achieve the desired results. Each step can be critiqued. This is reverse scenario building—construct a mental picture, document it on paper, and then work backwards through the pros and cons of each step. Peers, subordinates, and supervisors can make excellent contributions (Chapter 6).

• Determine the factors that have the most impact on personal productivity. Positive factors can be encouraged. Human potential can be used in unique, meaningful ways to increase performance. Plan for temporary changes in personal productivity level. Fluctuations can be due to interest, age, speed of learning, reassignment, motivation, competition, career plateaus, etc. (Chapter 6).

• Define job related accomplishments in precise, operational terms. This process clarifies meanings of words and concepts commonly used on the job. The mental thought and learning processes needed to produce precise definitions improve awareness and understanding. When activities associated with goal setting and measurement are operationally defined, all steps in the measurement process are easier to take (Chapter 8).

- Develop a feel for what makes up a reliable, valid "yardstick" for measurement. You cannot measure something until you define it. A dependable measurement system that people understand underlies any productivity enhancement process (Chapters 9–15).
- Take a solutions-oriented view. The brilliant Italian painter, sculptor, architect, and poet Michelangelo (1475–1564) reportedly said he had only to carve until he found the statue within the block of marble. Similarly, you can find answers within yourself and within your immediate work environment. Solutions include reducing counterproductivity (Chapter 16), moving with and anticipating trends (Chapter 17), and applying what you know, or have just learned (Chapter 18).

"LAUNDRY LIST"

Lists are helpful reminders and incentives. The following contains logical, common sense ideas.

- See what needs to be done. Determine what can be done well within the various constraints, provided the level of awareness is high enough to begin a program of "change."
- Create a task force or core group and develop various alternative, but overlapping methods in the area of concern. If one tact fails, you can introduce a similar one almost immediately. Start where there is the least resistance and/or most need.
- Consider ways to maximize group achievement, for example, work sharing, team building, and self-monitoring teams. Many people work in groups, and are even more likely to work in groups in the future. Over time, groups mature and grow together. Common work procedures, for example, help save time and enable groups to become more productive. As a result, they also require less obvious management.
- Examine existing records and documents to see what does exist, has been used, or will be used. It is expensive to obtain, store, access, and retrieve information.
- Conscientiously apply what is already known. We know so much more than we use. Use a systematic, logical method.
- Use a positive, solutions-oriented technique. Being positive can be contagious. Positive thoughts bring out the best in people. To illustrate, cooperation is higher in non-threatening, positive atmospheres than under coercive conditions.

- Set a slow, steady pace. Every small success, even in the remotest areas, adds up. Just as pennies turn into dollars over time, small gains when viewed months or years later, appear relatively large. Most progress is slow. Often, results are expected too soon. Patience is required.
- View things from users' or customers' eyes. Seeing things as others see them often provides unexpected, valuable information.
- Focus on quality improvement in general. Doing just one thing better, for instance, can bring about surprising productivity increases.
- Information is a source of power, underlying all organizational processes and affecting every person and every job. Having and doing without information is costly because it takes time and money to obtain or purchase; collect; verify; maintain; store; access; duplicate; replace if lost or destroyed; present in required format; and access alternate sources when primary source is unavailable.
- Be creative. Using creative talents in previously unexplored ways could be the greatest challenge of all, but yield the most meaningful results.

A SYSTEMS APPROACH

The systems approach logically begins with input. Productivity increases are predicted to come from improving significant input variables, like a better trained work force. Improvement in input will have corresponding effects on throughput and output.

- Systems techniques can be used with people—self, peers, managers. Products and processes can be examined in a similar vein. All have many common areas and can be compared for quality, or efficiency, for instance. To illustrate, a high defect rate may be a direct result of poor operator training. The person and the product must both be considered—a cause and effect relationship.
- Systems are affected by the organization's environment. Forces under various levels of control include trends, (de)regulation, inflation, politics, and energy sources. Unpredictable external environments, like increased foreign competition, can drive up the cost of doing business and reduce profits.
- A systems orientation studies input, throughput, output, and their interrelationships. Information from the various feedback processes that is incorporated into input, throughput, and output, helps streamline and improve the system. Feedback in areas of concern, or in high priority areas is often motivational.

List your own practical applications.

Chapter 19—Answers and Insights

1. The "Ideas to Remember" section at the end of each chapter contains pertinent information on methods that can be applied in the organization. Major "ideas" can be copied in the Plan to Do section below. What you do is affected by cost, managerial support, and the vision, mission, and goals of your organization.

2. Essentials include quality, efficiency, effectiveness, profit, (the growing role of internal and external customers, suppliers . . . partners) and some standards unique to your organization.

3. Being better informed means creating awareness and asking questions. Most employees know how to improve their productivity, but they will need encouragement and support.

4. Many people thrive on one-to-one contact, like coaching, counseling, and mentoring. An environment built on trust encourages honest, open, two-way communication. (a) Wholeheartedly support risk taking, as this fosters creativity and innovation leading to new ideas. (b) Recognize that people doing the job usually know it better than anyone else. (c) Ensure that those around you understand and support the vision, mission, and goals of the organization. Jointly develop achievable milestones for goals. (d) Avoid cost-reducing fads, quick-fixes, and cost-cutting efforts adversely affecting the organization's most valuable resource—people.

5. Your beliefs should fit the current organizational structure, systems, culture, goals, and leadership style. Select methods having at least a 50/50 chance of success. New ideas introduced as "trial runs" can become permanent if they work out. A systems approach with real or hypothetical feedback allows new methods to be tested step-by-step.

Plan to Do

Suggested Reading

Chapter 1—Productivity: Viewpoints and Definitions

1. Campbell, John P. and Campbell, Richard J. and Associates. *Productivity in Organizations,* San Francisco: Jossey-Bass, Inc., 1988.
2. Crosby, Philip B. *Let's Talk Quality,* New York: McGraw-Hill, 1989.
3. Eccles, Robert G. "The Performance Manifesto," *Harvard Business Review,* January–February 1991, 131–137.
4. Neuman, John L. "Overhead Value Analysis: A Tool for the Times," in *Handbook of Business Planning and Budgeting,* New York: Van Nostrand Reinhold, 1983, pp. 444–485.
5. Norman, R. G. and Bahiri, S. *Productivity Measurement and Incentives,* London, England: Butterworth and Company, Ltd., 1982.
6. Rice, Robert W., Peirce, Robert S., Moyer, Reed P., and McFarlin, Dean B. "Using Discrepancies to Predict the Perceived Quality of Work Life," *Journal of Business and Psychology,* Vol. 6, No. 1, 1991, pp. 39–55.
7. Skinner, Wickham. "The Productivity Paradox," *Harvard Business Review,* July–August 1986, pp. 55–59.

Chapter 2—Organizational, Group, and Personal Goals

1. Barnard, Chester I. *The Functions of the Executive.* Cambridge, Massachusetts: Harvard University Press, 1938.

2. Bell, R. and Burnham, J. *Managing Change and Productivity,* Cincinnati: South-Western Publishing Company, 1991.
3. Bryson, John M. *Strategic Planning for Public and Nonprofit Organizations,* San Francisco: Jossey-Bass, Inc., 1988.
4. Desatnick, Robert L. "Management Climate Surveys: A Way to Uncover an Organization's Culture," *Personnel,* May 1986, pp. 49–54.
5. Drucker, Peter F. *Innovation and Entrepreneurship,* New York: Harper and Row, 1985.
6. Forehand, Garlie A. and Gilmer, B. Von Heller. "Environmental Variation and Studies of Organizational Behavior," *Psychological Bulletin,* Vol. 62, no. 6, December 1984, pp. 361–382.
7. Goodman, Paul S., Sproull, Lee S., and Associates. *Technology and Organizations,* San Francisco: Jossey-Bass Publishers, Inc., 1990.
8. Gross, Warren and Shichman, Shula. "How to Grow an Organizational Culture," *Personnel,* September 1987, pp. 52–56.
9. Heath, Robert L. and Associates. *Strategic Issues in Management,* San Francisco: Jossey-Bass Inc., 1988.
10. Locke, E. A. and Latham, G. P. *A Theory of Goal Setting and Task Performance,* New Jersey: Englewood Cliffs, Prentice Hall, 1990.
11. London, Manual. *Change Agents.* San Francisco: Jossey-Bass Publishers, Inc., 1988.

12. Miller, Ernest C. "Strategic Planning Pays Off," *Personnel Journal,* April 1989, pp. 127, 129, 130, 132.
13. Odiorne, George S. "The Art of Crafting Strategic Plans," *Training,* October 1987, pp. 94–97.
14. Ohmae, Kenichi. "Getting Back to Strategy,"*Harvard Business Review,* November–December, 1988, pp. 149–156.
15. Robbins, Stephen P. *Organizational Theory: The Structure and Design of Organizations,* New York: Prentice-Hall, Inc., 1983.
16. Schein, Edgar H. *Organizational Culture and Leadership,* San Francisco: Jossey-Bass, Inc., 1985.
17. Weisbord, Marvin R. *Productive Workplaces,* San Francisco: Jossey-Bass Publishers, Inc., 1987.
18. Wheatley, Margaret J. *Leadership and the New Science,* San Francisco: Berrett-Koehler Publishers, 1992.
19. Zaleznik, Abraham. "Real Work,"*Harvard Business Review*, January–February 1989, pp. 57–64.

Chapter 3—Analyzing Input, Throughput, and Output Variables: A Systems Approach

1. Argyris, Chris. "Teaching Smart People How to Learn," *Harvard Business Review,* May–June 1991, pp. 99–109.
2. Dessler, Gary. *Organization and Management: A Contingency Approach.* Englewood Cliffs, New Jersey: Prentice-Hall, Inc., 1976.
3. Likert, Rensis. *The Human Organization: Its Management and Value,* New York: McGraw-Hill, 1967.
4. Strassman, Paul A. *Information Payoff: The Transformation of Work in the Electronic Age,* New York: Free Press/Macmillan, 1985.

Chapter 4—Analyzing Productivity Problems: Real Problems vs. Symptoms

1. Miner, John B. *People Problems: The Executive Answer Book,* New York: Random House, 1985.
2. Mintzberg, Henry. *The Nature of Managerial Work,* New York: Harper & Row Publishers, 1973.

Chapter 6—Major Sources of Personal Productivity Information

1. American Management Association.*Performance Appraisal,* Henry M. Frechette, Jr. and Edward G. Wertheim (eds.), New York: American Management Association, 1985.
2. Berk, Ronald A. (ed.). *Performance Assessment: Methods & Applications,* Baltimore, MD: Johns Hopkins University Press, 1987.
3. Cataldo, Michael F. and Coates, Thomas J. (eds.). *Health and Industry: A Behavioral Medicine Perspective,* New York: John Wiley & Sons, Inc., 1986.
4. Fitz-enz, Jac. *Human Value Management,* San Francisco: Jossey-Bass Publishers, Inc., 1990.
5. Levy, Martin. "Assessment: Almost-Perfect Performance Appraisals," *Personnel Journal,* April 1989, pp. 76, 78, 80 & 83.
6. Neal, James E. *Effective Phrases for Performance Appraisal,* Neal Publications, P. O. Box 451, Perrysburgh, Ohio 43551.
7. Reynolds, Cecil R. and Willson, Victor L. (eds.). *Methodological and Statistical Advances in the Study of Individual Differences: Perspectives on Individual Differences,* New York: Plenum Press, 1985.
8. Schippman, Jeffrey S., Hughes, Garry L. and Prien, Erich P. "Raise Assessment Standards," *Personnel Journal,* July 1988, pp. 68–79.
9. Schutz, Will. *The Human Element.* San Francisco: Jossey-Bass Publishers, Inc., 1994.
10. Single, J. L. "Productivity and the Self-Fulfilling Prophecy," *Management World,* November 1980, pp. 19–20.
11. Sink, D. Scott. *Productivity Management: Planning, Measurement and Evaluation, Control and Improvement,* Somerset, New Jersey: John Wiley & Sons, Inc., 1985.

Chapter 7—Job Analysis and Job Description

1. DeLapa, Judith A. "Job Descriptions That Work," *Personnel Journal,* June 1989, pp. 156–158, 160.
2. Gael, S. *Job Analysis: A Guide to Assessing Work Activities,* San Francisco: Jossey-Bass, Inc., 1983.
3. Plachy, Roger J. *Building a Fair Play Program: A Step by Step Guide,* New York: AMACOM, 1986.
4. Schippmann, Jeffery S., Hughes, Garry L., and Prien, Erich P. "Raise Assessment Standards," *Personnel Journal,* July 1988, p. 68–79.
5. Schippmann, Jeffery S., Prien, Erich P., and Hughes, Garry L., "The Content of Management Work: Formation of Task and Job Skill Composite Classifications," *Journal of Business and Psychology,* Spring 1991, pp. 325–354.
6. Schmidt, F. L., Hunter, J. E. and Pearlman, K. "Assessing the Economic Impact of Personnel Programs on Workforce Productivity," *Personnel Psychology,* 35, pp. 333–347, 1982.

Chapter 8—Basics of Measurement

1. Brinberg, David, and McGrath, Joseph E. *Validity and the Research Process,* Beverly Hills, California: Sage, 1985.
2. Copacino, William C. and Robeson, James F. (eds). *The Logistics Handbook,* New York: The Free Press, 1994.
3. Long-Becker, Linda C. and Landauer, Edwin G. "Service Assessment Matrix: A Measurement Technique for Service Group Evaluation," *Industrial Management,* September–October 1987, pp. 10–16.
4. Ott, Lyman and Hildebrand, David K. *Statistical Thinking for Managers,* Boston, Massachusetts: Duxbury Press, 1983.

Chapter 9—Measurement Standards and Guidelines

1. Phillips, Jack J. *Handbook of Training Evaluation and Measurement,* Houston: Gulf Publishing Company, 1983, pp. 159–180.
2. Skinner, Wickham. "The Productivity Paradox," Harvard Business Review, July–August 1986, p. 55–59.

Chapter 10—Qualitative Assessment

1. Glass, G. V., McGaw, B., and Smith, M. L. *Meta-analysis in Social Research,* Beverly Hills, California, Sage: 1981.
2. Hunter, J. E., Schmidt, F. L., and Jackson, C. B. *Meta-analysis: Cumulating Research Findings Across Studies,* Beverly Hills, California: Sage, 1982.
3. Seashore, Stanley E., Lawler, Edward E., III, Mirvis, Philip H., and Cortland, Cammann (eds.). *Assessing Organizational Change: A Guide to Methods, Measures, and Practices,* New York: John Wiley & Sons, Inc., 1983.

Chapter 11—Quantitative Measurement

1. Christensen, Larry B. and Stoup, Charles M. *Introduction to Statistics for the Social and Behavioral Sciences,* Monterey, California: Brooks/Cole, 1986.
2. Collyer, Charles E. and Enns, James T. *Analysis of Variance: The Basic Designs,* Chicago: Nelson-Hall, 1986.
3. Cronbach, Lee J. "Beyond the Two Disciplines of Scientific Psychology," *American Psychologist,* 1975, 30, pp. 116–127.

4. Deci, Edward L. and Ryan, Richard M. *Intrinsic Motivation and Self-Determination in Human Behavior,* New York: Plenum Press, 1985.
5. Edwards, Allen L. (2nd ed.) *Multiple Regression and the Analysis of Variance and Covariance,* New York: W. H. Freeman and Company, 1985.
6. Gunter, Bert. "Bootstrapping: How to Make Something From Almost Nothing and Get Statistically Valid Answers, Part I," *Quality Progress,* December 1991, pp. 97–103.
7. _____. Part II, *Quality Progress,* February 1992, pp. 83–86.
8. Norton, Sue M. "Peer Assessments of Performance and Ability: An Exploratory Meta-Analysis of Statistical Artifacts and Contextual Moderators," Journal of Business and Psychology, Spring 1992, pp. 387–399.
9. Porter, Joseph, and Hamm, Robert J. *Statistics: Applications for the Behavioral Sciences,* Monterey, California: Brooks/Cole, 1985.
10. Riggs, James L. "Monitoring With a Matrix That Motivates As It Measures," *Industrial Engineering,* January 1986, pp. 34–43.
11. Rosnow, Ralph L. and Rosenthal, Robert. "Statistical Procedures and Justification of Knowledge in Psychological Science," *American Psychologist,* October, 1989, pp. 1276–1284.
12. Sink, D. S. "Much Ado About Productivity: Where Do We Go From Here?" *Industrial Engineering,* October 1983, pp. 36–38, 42–48.
13. Sumanth, D. J. "Productivity Indicators Used by Major U.S. Manufacturing Companies: The Results of a Survey," *Industrial Engineering,* May 1981, pp. 70–73.
14. Tolbert, Charles M. *Introduction to Computing: Applications for the Social Sciences,* Reading, Massachusetts, Addison-Wesley, 1985.
15. Wright, Sonia R. *Quantitative Methods and Statistics,* Beverly Hills, California: Sage, 1979.

Chapter 12—Productivity: Human Resources

1. Baird, Lloyd. *Managing Performance,* New York: John Wiley & Sons, Inc., 1986.
2. Chew, W. Bruce. "No Nonsense Guide to Measuring Productivity." *Harvard Business Review,* January–February 1988, pp. 110–111, 114–116, 118.
3. Christopher, William F. *Management for the 1980s,* New York: AMACOM, 1980.
4. Covey, Stephen R. *The 7 Habits of Highly Effective People,* New York: Simon & Schuster, 1990.

5. Eccles, Robert. "The Performance Manifesto," *Harvard Business Review,* January–February 1991, pp. 131–137.
6. Gregerman, Ira B. *Knowledge Worker Productivity,* New York: AMACOM, 1981.
7. Lea, Dixie and Brostrom, Richard. "Managing the High-Tech Professional," *Personnel,* June 1988, pp. 12, 14, 17, 18, 20, 22.
8. Lehrer, Robert N. (ed.). *White Collar Productivity,* New York: McGraw-Hill, 1983.
9. Mintzberg, Henry. "The Manager's Job: Folklore and Fact," *Harvard Business Review,* July–August 1975, pp. 49–61.
10. Olson, Val. *White Collar Waste: Gain the Productivity Edge,* Englewood Cliffs, New Jersey: Prentice-Hall, 1983.
11. Rosenthall, Robert and Jackson, Lenore. *Pygmalion in the Classroom,* New York: Holt, Reinhart & Winston, Inc., 1968.
12. Smith, Clarence. "Awareness, Analysis and Improvement are Keys to White Collar Productivity," *Issues in White Collar Productivity.* Norcross, Georgia: Industrial Engineering and Management Press, 1984, pp. 5–7.
13. Werther, W., Ruch, W., and McClure, L. *Productivity Through People,* St. Paul, Minnesota: West, 1986.

Chapter 13—Profitability

1. American Productivity Center. "The Other Side of JIT: How Vendors are Meeting the Mandate for Quality," *Productivity Improvement Bulletin,* March 25, 1987, #706, pp. 1–4.
2. Hawkins, David E. "Toward the New Balance Sheet," *Harvard Business Review,* November–December 1984, pp. 156–163.
3. Hayes, Robert H. and Wheelwright, Steven C. *Restoring Our Competitive Edge: Competing Through Manufacturing,* New York: John Wiley & Sons, Inc., 1984.
4. Juran, Joseph M. *Juran on Leadership for Quality: An Executive Handbook,* New York: Free Press, 1989.
5. Maital, Shlomo. *Executive Economics,* New York: The Free Press, 1994.
6. National Association of Accountants. *Professional Publications for the Management Accountant,* P.O. Box 433, Montvale, New Jersey.
7. Ross, Elliot B. "Making Money with Proactive Pricing," *Harvard Business Review,* November–December 1984, pp. 145–155.
8. Schonberger, Richard J. "Frugal Manufacturing," *Harvard Business Review,* September–October 1987, pp. 95–100.

9. Spencer, Lyle. M., Jr. *Calculating Human Resource Costs and Benefits,* New York: John Wiley & Sons, 1986. (Includes numerous worksheets and financial formulas for measuring ROI).
10. Thomas, Philip R. and Martin, Kenneth R. *Getting Competitive: Middle Managers and the Cycle Time Ethic,* New York: McGraw-Hill Book Company, 1991.
11. Thomas, Philip R. Time Warrior, New York: McGraw-Hill Book Company, 1992.

Chapter 14—Quality

1. Barrows, James V. "Does Total Quality Management Equal Organizational Learning?" *Quality Progress,* July 1993, pp. 39–43.
2. Bogan, Christopher E. *Benchmarking for Best Practices,* New York: McGraw Hill, 1994.
3. Bowles, Jerry and Hammond, Joshua. *Beyond Quality: How 50 Winning Companies Use Continuous Improvement,* New York: G. P. Putnam's Sons, 1991.
4. Camp, Robert C. "Benchmarking: The Search for Industry Best Practices That Lead to Superior Performance," Milwaukee, Wisconsin: Quality Press, 1989.
5. Copeland, Ronald and Globerson, Shlomo. "Improving Operational Performance in Service Industries," Industrial Management, July–August 1986, pp. 23–28.
6. Crandall, Richard. "Applying Industrial Engineering Techniques in Service Industries," *Industrial Management,* May-June 1986, pp. 13-16.
7. Duncan, Acheson J. *Quality Control and Industrial Statistics,* Homewood, Illinois: Richard D. Irwin, Inc., 1974.
8. Ettorre, Barbara. "Benchmarking: The Next Generation," *Management Review,* June 1993, pp. 10-16.
9. Garvin, David A. *Managing Quality: The Strategic and Competitive Edge,* New York: The Free Press, 1987.
10. Hodgetts, Richard M. *Blueprints for Continuous Improvement* (Lessons from the Baldrige Winners), New York: American Management Association, 1993.
11. Juran, Joseph M. (ed.). *Quality Control Handbook* (3rd ed.), New York: McGraw-Hill, 1974.
12. Juran, Joseph M. *Juran on Planning for Quality,* New York: Free Press, 1988.
13. Juran, Joseph M. *Juran on Leadership for Quality: An Executive Handbook,* New York: The Free Press, 1989.
14. Juran, Joseph M. *Juran on Quality by Design,* New York: Free Press, 1992.
15. Rabbit, John T. and Berg, Peter A. *The ISO 9000 Book,* White Plains, New York: Quality Resources, 1993.

16. Reichheld, Frederick F. and Sasser, W. Earl, Jr., "Zero Defections: Quality Comes to Services," *Harvard Business Review*, September–October 1991, pp. 105–111.

17. Reimann, Curt W. "The Baldrige Award Criteria Speak for Themselves," *Quality Progress,* May 1991, pp. 41–44.

18. Scheffler, Steve and Powers, Vicki J. "Legal and Ethical Issues in Benchmarking," *Continuous Journey,* December 1992–January 1993, pp. 27–29.

19. Spendolini, Michael J. *The Benchmarking Book.* New York: Amacom, 1993.

20. Steeples, Marion Mills. *The Corporate Guide to the MBNQA,* Homewood: Illinois, Business One Irwin, 1992.

21. Tolchinsky, Paul D. "Preventing TQM Crash Landings," *Journal for Quality and Participation,* July-August 1994, pp. 50–57.

22. Whiteley, Richard C. "Measure, Measure, Measure," *The Customer Driven Company,* Reading, Massachusetts: Addison-Wesley, 1993.

23. Williams, Dale. "Measurement of Work in the Service Sector," *Industrial Engineering News,* Vol. XXVI, No. 2, Spring 1992, pp. 1 & 3.

Chapter 15—Complex Productivity Measures

1. Donovan, Bonnie. "Ethyl Corporation: Diversified Virginia Firm Pursues Total Factor Productivity Improvement," *Issues and Innovation.* Houston, Texas: American Productivity Center, 1987, pp. 88–93.

2. Kendrick, John W. *Improving Company Productivity,* Baltimore, Maryland: The Johns Hopkins University Press, 1984.

3. Lawler, E. E., III. *High-Involvement Management,* San Francisco, California: Jossey-Bass Publishers, 1986.

4. Lawler, E. E., III. "Gain-sharing Theory and Research: Findings and Future Directions," R. W. Woodman and W. A. Pasmore (eds), *Research in Organizational Change and Development,* 1988 (2) pp. 323–344, Greenwich, Connecticut: JAI Press.

5. Schuster, M. H. "Gain-Sharing: Do It Right the First Time," *Sloan Management Review,* 1987, pp. 17–26.

6. Sink, D. Scott. *Productivity Management: Planning, Measurement and Evaluation, Control and Improvement,* Somerset, New Jersey: John Wiley & Sons, Inc., 1985.

7. Smith, Elizabeth A. and Gude, Gerald F. "Reevaluation of The Scanlon Plan as a Motivational Technique," *Personnel Journal,* December 1971, pp. 916–919, 923.

8. White, J. K. "The Scanlon Plan: Causes and Correlates of Success," *Academy of Management Journal,* 1979, Vol. 22, pp. 292–312.

Chapter 16—Counterproductivity

1. Pinchot, Gifford III. *Intrapreneuring.* San Francisco: Harper Collins Inc., 1986.

2. Rickard, Norman E. "The Quest for Quality: A Race Without a Finish," *Industrial Engineering,* January 1991, pp. 25–27.

Chapter 17—Trends

1. Albrecht, Karl. *The Northbound Train,* New York: American Management Association, 1994.

2. Bardwick, Judith M. *Danger in the Comfort Zone,* New York: American Management Association, 1991.

3. Bell, Chip R. *Customers as Partners,* San Francisco, Berrett-Koehler Publishers, Inc., 1994.

4. Bleecker, Samuel E. "Rethinking How We Work," *The Futurist,* July–August 1987, pp. 15–21.

5. Block, Peter. *The Empowered Manager,* San Francisco: Jossey-Bass Publishers, 1987.

6. Davis, Donald D. and Associates. *Managing Technological Innovation,* San Francisco: Jossey-Bass, Inc., 1986.

7. Desatnick, Robert L. "Managing Customer Service for the 21st Century," *Journal for Quality and Participation,* June, 1994, pp. 30–35.

8. Gilbreath, Robert D. *Forward Thinking: A Pragmatist's Guide to Today's Business Trends,* New York: McGraw-Hill, 1987.

9. Goddard, Robert W. "Work Force 2000," *Personnel Journal,* February 1989, pp. 65–71.

10. Hakim, Cliff. *When You Lose Your Job,* San Francisco, Berrett-Koehler Publishers, 1993.

11. _____. *We Are All Self-Employed,* San Francisco, Berrett-Koehler Publishers, 1994.

12. Handy, Charles. *The Age of Paradox.* Boston, Massachusetts: Harvard University Press, 1994.

13. Hrebiniak, Lawrence G. *We Force in Management,* New York: Free Press, 1994.

14. Juran, Joseph M. *Juran on Planning for Quality,* New York: Free Press, 1987.

15. Kanter, Rosabeth Moss. *When Giants Learn to Dance,* New York: Simon and Schuster, 1989.

16. Nadler, Leonard and Nadler, Zeace. *Every Manager's Guide to Human Resource Development,* San Francisco: Jossey-Bass, Inc., Publishers, 1992.

17. Naisbitt, John. *Megatrends.* New York: Warner Books, 1982.

18. Naisbitt, John and Aburdene, Patricia. *Megatrends 2000,* New York: Avon Books, 1991.
19. Odenwald, Sylvia B. *Global Training.* Homewood, Illinois: Richard D. Irwin, 1991.
20. Pinchot, Gifford and Pinchot, Elizabeth. *The End of Bureaucracy & the Rise of the Intelligent Organization,* San Francisco, Berrett-Koehler Publishers, 1994.
21. Renesch, John (ed.) *New Traditions in Business,* San Francisco, Berrett-Koehler Publishers, 1992.
22. Siegel, Irving H. *Company Productivity: Measurement for Improvement,* Kalamazoo, Michigan: W. E. Upjohn Institute for Employment Research, 1980.
23. Stumpf, Stephen A. and DeLuca, Joel R. *Learning to Use What You Already Know,* San Francisco, Berrett-Koehler Publishers, Inc., 1994.
24. Tichy, Noel M. *Managing Strategic Change: Technological, Political and Cultural Dynamics.* New York: John Wiley & Sons, Inc., 1983.
25. Tomasko, Robert M. *Rethinking the Corporation.* New York: American Management Association, 1993.
26. Weisbord, Marvin R. *Productive Workplaces,* San Francisco: Jossey-Bass, Inc., Publishers, 1987.
27. Wiggenhorn, William. "Motorola U: When Training Becomes an Education," *Harvard Business Review,* July–August 1990, pp. 71–83.

Chapter 18—Major Keys to Improving Productivity

1. Asselin, Gerald A. "Promote Productivity: User-Friendly Management," *Personnel Journal,* December 1986, pp. 40–47.
2. Bellman, Geoffrey M. *Getting Things Done When You Are Not in Charge,* San Francisco, Berrett-Koehler Publishers, Inc., 1992.
3. Black, James R. "Work Management as a Means to Increased Productivity," *Industrial Management,* May–June 1986, pp. 8–12.
4. Bower, Joseph L. and Hout, Thomas M. "Fast-Cycle Capability for Competitive Power," *Harvard Business Review,* November–December 1988, pp. 110–118.
5. Brown, J. H. U. and Camola, Jacqueline. *Improving Productivity in Health Care,* Boca Raton, Florida: CRC Press, Inc., 1988.
6. Davis, Arthur G. "Forecast Modelling: A Practical Approach to Productivity Improvement," *Industrial Management,* May–June 1985, pp. 14–17.
7. Deming, W. Edwards. *Quality, Productivity and Competitive Position,* Boston, Massachusetts: MIT Press, 1982.
8. Duncan, Acheson J. *Quality Control and Industrial Statistics* (3rd ed.) New York: Irwin, 1974.

9. Edosomwan, Johnson A. (ed.). *Productivity and Quality Improvement in Electronic Assembly,* New York: McGraw-Hill, 1989.
10. Fox, William M. *Effective Group Problem Solving,* San Francisco: Jossey-Bass, Inc., 1987.
11. Gilbreath, Robert D. *Forward Thinking: A Pragmatist's Guide to Today's Business Trends,* New York: McGraw-Hill, 1987.
12. Goodman, Paul S. and Associates. *Designing Effective Work Groups,* San Francisco: Jossey-Bass, Inc., 1986.
13. Grove, Andrew S. *High Output Management,* New York: Random House, Inc., 1983.
14. Guaspari, John. *I Know It When I See It,* New York: AMACOM, 1985.
15. _____. *Theory Why?* New York: AMACOM, 1986.
16. Harrison, Jared F. *Improving Performance and Productivity: Why Won't They Do What I Want Them To Do?* Reading, Massachusetts: Addison-Wesley, 1978.
17. Hayes, Robert H. and Wheelwright, Steven C. *Restoring Our Competitive Edge: Competing Through Manufacturing,* New York: John Wiley & Sons, Inc., 1984.
18. Helton, B. Ray. "Will the Real Knowledge Worker Please Stand Up?" *Industrial Management,* January–February 1987, pp. 26–29.
19. Herzberg, Frederick. "One More Time: How Do You Motivate Employees?" *Harvard Business Review,* September–October 1987, pp. 109–120.
20. Imai, Masaaki. *Kaizen: The Key to Japan's Competitive Success,* New York: Random House, 1986.
21. Janov, Jill. *The Inventive Organization,* San Francisco: Jossey-Bass Publishers, Inc., 1994.
22. Judson, Arnold S. "The Awkward Truth About Productivity," *Harvard Business Review,* September–October 1982, pp. 93–97.
23. Juran, Joseph M. *Juran on Planning for Quality,* New York: Free Press, 1987.
24. _____. *Juran on Leadership for Quality,* New York: Free Press, 1989.
25. _____. and Gryna, F. M., Jr. *Quality Planning and Analysis,* New York: McGraw-Hill, 1980.
26. Kanter, Rosabeth Moss. "Collaborative Advantage: The Art of Alliances," *Harvard Business Review,* July–August 1994, pp. 96–108.
27. Khaden, Riaz. "One Page Management: A Unified Approach to Productivity," *National Productivity Review,* Winter 1988/89, pp. 45–57.
28. Kilmann, Ralph H. *Beyond the Quick Fix,* San Francisco: Jossey-Bass, Inc., 1984.

29. Kravetz, Dennis J. *The Human Resources Revolution,* San Francisco: Jossey-Bass, Inc., 1988.
30. Lawler, Edward E., III. *High-Involvement Management,* San Francisco: Jossey-Bass, Inc., 1986.
31. _____. and Mohrman, Susan. "High-Involvement Management," *Personnel,* April 1989, pp. 26–31.
32. Layton, William G. and Johnson, Eric J. "Break the Mold: Strategies for Productivity," *Personnel Journal,* May 1987, pp. 74–78.
33. Naisbitt, John and Aburdene, Patricia. *Re-inventing the Corporation: Transforming Your Job and Your Company for the New Information Society,* New York: Warner Books, Inc., 1985.
34. Neuman, John. "MPQ's Productivity Forum: Our Readers Speak Out, *Management Practice Quarterly,* Spring 1986, pp. 13–14.
35. Newman, Betsy. "Expediency as Benefactor: How Team Building Saves Time and Gets the Job Done," *Training & Development Journal,* February 1984, pp. 26–30.
36. Ohmae, Kenichi. "Companyism and Do More Better," *Harvard Business Review,* January–February 1989, pp. 125–132.
37. _____. *Triad Power: The Coming Shape of Global Competition,* New York: Free Press, 1985.
38. Osburn, Jack, et al., *Self-Directed Work Teams: The New American Challenge,* Homewood, Illinois: Irwin Professional Publishing, 1990.
39. Parker, Glenn M. *Cross-Functional Teams,* San Francisco: Jossey-Bass, Publishers, Inc., 1994.
40. Phillips, Jack J. *Recruiting, Training, and Retaining New Employees,* San Francisco: Jossey-Bass, Inc., 1987.
41. Porter, Michael E. and Millar, Victor E. "How Information Gives You Competitive Advantage," *Harvard Business Review,* July–August 1985, pp. 149–160.
42. Quinn, James Brian, and Gagnon, Christopher. "Will Services Follow Manufacturing into Decline?" *Harvard Business Review,* November–December 1986, pp. 95–103.
43. Renesch, John (ed.) *New Traditions in Business,* San Francisco: Berrett-Koehler Publishers, 1992.
44. Ross, Joel E. and Shaw, Eric. "Improving the Productivity of Service Organizations," *Industrial Management,* September–October 1987, pp. 21–24.
45. Sasser, W. Earl and Leonard, Frank S. "The Incline of Quality," *Harvard Business Review,* September–October 1982, pp. 163–171.
46. Schleh, Edward C. *How to Boost Your Return on Management,* New York: McGraw-Hill, 1984.
47. Senge, Peter M. *The Fifth Discipline,* New York: Currency/Doubleday, 1990.
48. Siegel, Irving H. *Company Productivity: Measurement for Improvement,* Kalamazoo, Michigan: W. E. Upjohn Institute for Employment Research, 1980.
49. Shingo, Shigeo. *Zero Quality Control: Source Inspection and the Poka-Yoke System,* Stanford, Connecticut: Productivity Press, 1986.
50. Skinner, Wickham. *Manufacturing: The Formidable Competitive Weapon,* New York: John Wiley & Sons, 1985.
51. Tjosvold, Dean. "Achieving Productive Synergy: Integrating Departments into a Company," *Journal of Business and Psychology,* Fall 1988, pp. 42–53.
52. _____. *Working Together to Get Things Done: Managing for Organizational Productivity,* Boston: Heath, 1986.
53. U.S. Department of Labor, Bureau of Labor-Management Relations and Cooperative Programs, "Participative Approaches to White-Collar Productivity Improvement," BLRM 116, 1987.
54. Vancil, Richard F. and Green, Charles H. "How CEOs Use Top Management Committees," *Harvard Business Review,* January–February 1984, pp. 65–73.
55. Weisbord, Marvin R. *Productive Workplaces,* San Francisco: Jossey-Bass, Inc., 1987.
56. Wellins, Richard S., Byham, William C., and Wilson, J. M. *Empowered Teams,* San Francisco: Jossey-Bass Publishers, 1991.
57. Wellins, Richard S., Byham, William C. and Dixon, George R. *Inside Teams.* Jossey-Bass, Publishers, 1994.
58. Woodcock, Mike. *Team Development Manual,* New York: John Wiley & Sons, Inc., 1979.
59. Zander, Alvin. *Making Groups Effective,* San Francisco: Jossey-Bass, Inc., 1982.

Author Index

Content Index